LIEUT.-COL. J. W. WARDEN, C.B.E., D.S.O.

FROM B. C. TO BAISIEUX

BEING THE NARRATIVE HISTORY
OF THE

102nd Canadian Infantry Battalion

BY

L. McLeod Gould, M.S.M. Croix de Guerre
(B.A. Cantab)
Late Sergeant, Headquarters Staff, 102nd Canadian Infantry Battalion

To the memory of those brave members of the 102nd, Canadian Infantry Battalion who laid down their lives for the Cause of Liberty and Justice this book is reverently dedicated

The Naval & Military Press Ltd

Published by
The Naval & Military Press Ltd
5 Riverside, Brambleside, Bellbrook
Industrial Estate, Uckfield, East Sussex,
TN22 1QQ England

Tel: +44 (0) 1825 749494
Fax: +44 (0) 1825 765701

www.naval-military-press.com
www.nmarchive.com

*In reprinting in facsimile from the original, any imperfections are inevitably reproduced
and the quality may fall short of modern type and cartographic standards.*

THE RUNNERS

By L. McLEOD GOULD.

Inspired by the Runners of the 102nd Canadian Infantry Battalion.
(Reprinted from "Canada in Khaki," 1917.)

When soldiers are ready to drop with fatigue,
And only an Adjutant's brain can intrigue
A vital despatch to his C.O.'s colleague,
Who are the boys who can still stay a league?
                              The Runners.

When wires are broken and pigeons won't fly,
When shrapnel and bullets are raining on high,
When hell's on the earth and earth's in the sky,
Who are the boys who will get through or die?
                              The Runners.

Then here's to all soldiers of every degree,
Be they horsemen, or gunners, or stout infantry,
But specially to those who appeal most to me,
Who tackle their work with a semblance of glee,
                              The Runners.

AUTHOR'S PREFACE

IN THE following pages no attempt has been made to deal with the strategy or tactics involved in the many actions in which the 102nd Battalion took part. I have endeavoured throughout to keep within the limits of my title and to write a Narrative History only, tracing the course of the Battalion from its earliest stages in British Columbia to its last action at Baisieux, and affording, as it were, signposts on the route, marking by-paths of reminiscence down which each man, according to his length of service, can wander at his will.

I have written this book from the point of view of my own rank; in Canada and for seven months in Flanders I was a Private; after that period I attained the dignity of a Sergeant. The opinions freely expressed in the subsequent pages are, in consequence, those of an Other Rank, and, though entirely personal, reflect, I confidently believe, the opinions of the large majority of Other Ranks. I have tried to avoid casting personal reflections, but I have not hesitated to indulge in criticism of the system where such criticism seems well founded. Above all, I have studiously refrained from that fulsome adulation of men in authority which so often detracts from the value of an otherwise admirable publication.

As Regimental Diarist during the whole of the period from August 12th, 1916, to the day of Demobilization, I am in a position to guarantee the accuracy of all dates and places mentioned, and trust that the correctness of the record will compensate my readers for all that they will find lacking in interest and literary style.

I fear that the Nominal Roll at the end of this volume will be found to contain many errors and some omissions, but it represents an honest endeavour to supply a complete Roll containing all the essential information at my disposal. I shall at all times be pleased to furnish any information in my power to those making enquiries of a detailed and personal nature. As I am in possession of duplicates of most of the Battalion Records I am probably better equipped than any other person to answer questions of such a character. I shall also be very glad to receive any corrections with respect to casualties or addresses which may lead to subsequent editions being more perfect.

In conclusion, I wish to acknowledge the courtesy of the Editors of The Vancouver Daily Province and The Vancouver Daily World in according me permission to reproduce in part articles which appeared in their columns during the progress of the war, and to all those members of the Battalion who, by their sympathy and advice, have contributed largely towards the production of this volume, I extend my sincere thanks.

L. McLEOD GOULD.

P.O. Box 721, Victoria, B.C., October 1st, 1919.

The Song of the Spit

(Sung to the tune of "John Brown's Body")

We're Warden's weary warriors, a'drilling on the sand.
And paying out a buck a day to help the bloomin' band.
But what they do with all the cash, we don't quite understand,
    As we go marching on.

The Colonel forms us up in line and hands us lots of bull:
"You are the finest bunch of men that trigger e'er did pull."
On beef and beans and bread and jam we keep our bellies full,
    As we go marching on.

The sand gets in our blankets, and the wind blows chill and drear.
If life was dull at Comox, it's a damned sight duller here,
You have to go a mile or so to get a glass of beer,
    As we go marching on.

Chorus:
    We are Warden's weary warriors,
    We are Warden's weary warriors,
    We are Warden's weary warriors,
        The gallant One-O-Two.

CHAPTER I.

Early Experiences in Canada—The Spit, Comox, B.C.—
The First of Many Moves.

HE official date for the mobilization of the 102nd Canadian Infantry Battalion, whose adventures in Canada, England, France and Belgium during the days of The Great War it is the object of this book to chronicle, is given as November 3rd, 1915, on which date authority was issued to Lieut.-Colonel John Weightman Warden, formerly of St. John's, N.B., but then of Vancouver, B.C., to raise a battalion for service overseas, this battalion to be raised in Northern British Columbia and to be styled the 102nd (Comox-Atlin) Overseas Battalion. A newspaper story, which may or may not have some foundation in fact, states that the inauguration of the unit was the outcome of a wager laid between Mr. H. Clements, M.P. for Comox-Atlin, and one of his colleagues in the Federal House, the latter having jestingly challenged him to produce a unit from his barren constituency. If there be any truth in the yarn it certainly affords an excellent example of the adage that from small beginnings great things do grow.

The officer to whom this commission was entrusted was a veteran of experience. A native of New Brunswick, he had enlisted in the Canadian Contingent at the time of the Great Boer War, exchanging later into the South African Constabulary and serving continuously in South Africa thereafter until March, 1906, when he returned to Canada. On his arrival he felt the call of the West and migrated to Vancouver where he engaged in the business of general broker and real estate dealer, satisfying his military propensities by first enlisting in the 6th (D.C.O.R) Regiment and later, in May, 1911, taking out a commission in the same unit. Lt.-Col. Warden claims to be the first man in British Columbia, if not the first in the Dominion, to volunteer for service in the war just concluded, as he submitted his name to the Volunteer List on the very day on which Austria declared war on Serbia. However that may be, he crossed over with the First Contingent and as a captain in the 7th Battalion was

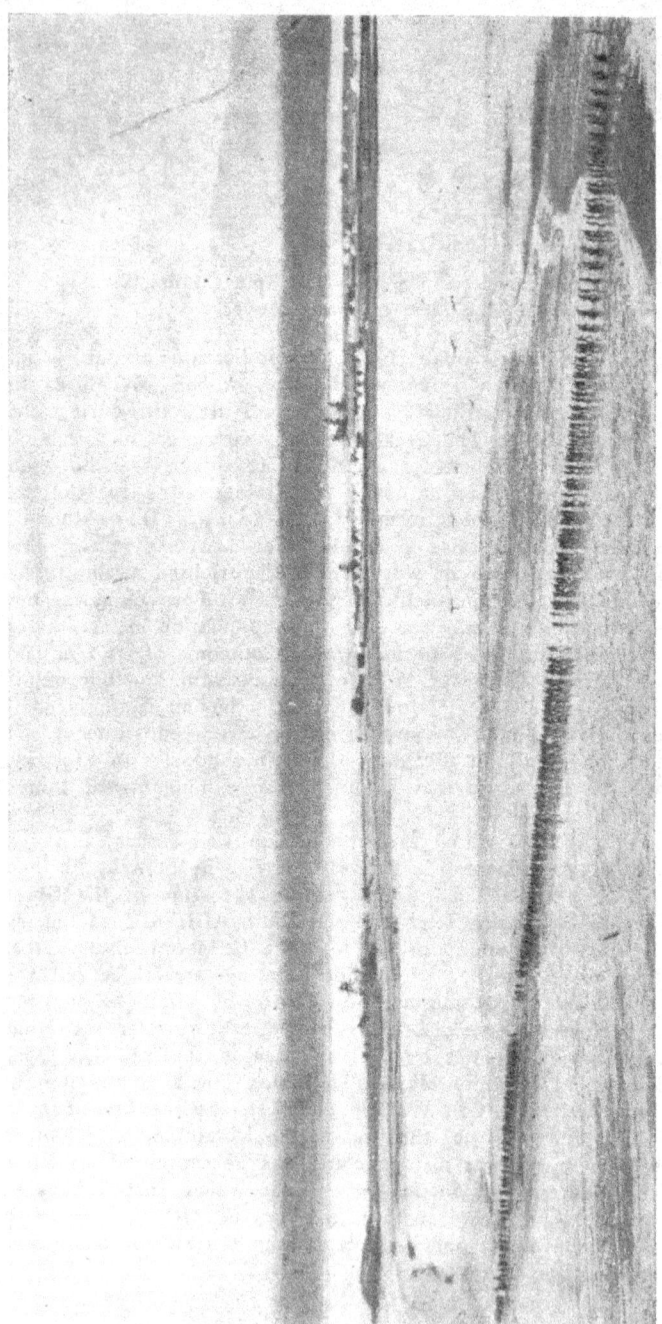

GOOSE SPIT, COMOX, B.C.

seriously wounded at Ypres on April 24th, 1915. He was invalided to England and on his discharge from hospital, during convalescence, came back to Canada on furlough. It was whilst he was in Canada on this furlough that he was granted the commission of Lieutenant-Colonel and given the authority to raise the new battalion.

Having due regard to the type of men from amongst whom the new recruits were to be sought, no better choice of a Commanding Officer could have been made. There was plenty of material available, but it lay underneath the hard exterior of the average British Columbia fisherman, miner and logger. A polished officer of the old school would have made no headway in his recruiting campaigns, but "Honest John" Warden appealed immensely to these men: he had done plenty of "roughing it" himself in his life; he had served as a private; he had been to the front and been wounded, and, above all, there was absolutely no "swank" about him. To the very end of his career with the 102nd Battalion the original members of the battalion always referred to him in terms of genuine affection.

Immediately on receipt of his commission Colonel Warden set out on the first of many recruiting journeys throughout the length and breadth of the Province and opened up recruiting stations at central points. The most important of these was in Vancouver where Lieut. R. G. H. Brydon was placed in charge; Lieut. J. F. Brandt undertook similar duties at Prince Rupert, Lieut. J. C. Halsey at Prince George, Lieut. F. Lister at Cranbrook, Lieut. J. H. Grant at Nelson, and Sergt. A. A. F. Calland at Vernon.

As soon as this preliminary work had been accomplished whereby recruiting could be commenced without loss of time, it became necessary to decide on a suitable location for Battalion Headquarters and for a mobilization camp. In view of the fact that the Battalion to be raised was to be known as the Comox-Atlin Battalion it was felt that mobilization and training should be carried out within the precincts of that constituency, and after much deliberation it was decided to form the camp on Goose Spit, Comox. As this was the first home of the 102nd it is but fitting here to give a somewhat detailed description of this camp.

Comox is a small sea-port lying some 150 miles North from Victoria on the East coast of Vancouver Island. It is a port of considerable importance, lying as it does close to the coal fields of Cumberland and possessing an excellent harbour. It is a regular port of call for steamers plying from Vancouver and Nanaimo; moreover, it is but three miles distant from Courtenay, the northern railhead of the E. & N. Railway. On the east the harbour is protected by a mushroom-shaped tongue of land connected with the coast by a narrow neck of sand; this is Goose Spit. In the days when the Imperial Navy used Esquimalt as a

Pacific base this Spit had been used as a range and traces of such use were still in evidence at the time when the 102nd settled down for training. But much had to be done before this took place, and, as will be seen later, great hardships had to be endured by the first-comers before the camp was in readiness to receive the bulk of the battalion.

Battalion Headquarters were established in Victoria where close connection could be maintained with Headquarters, M. D. No. XI., which were situated at Work Point, and offices were opened on the ground floor of the Union Bank Building, View Street. The officer who had the responsibility of conducting the early work of the battalion at Headquarters was Major L. M. Hagar, an officer of great experience in military routine work, and within two or three days he had enrolled a complete clerical staff headed by Sgt. J. L. Lloyd as Orderly Room Sergeant, under whom were Ptes. J. C. Howden, H. Hudson, L. McL. Gould, J. L. Campbell and F. E. W. Smith. During these early days Major Hagar acted as Colonel Warden's personal representative in Victoria. He was soon joined by Capt. H. B. Scharschmidt whom Colonel Warden had selected as his Adjutant. Capt. Scharschmidt had already seen service in Flanders, having proceeded overseas with the 7th Battalion and taken part in the bloody fray of the 2nd Battle of Ypres, where he was badly gassed. His restoration to health found him keenly eager to go back to France and he welcomed the opportunity afforded him by his old comrade in arms. Prior to the outbreak of the war he had had five years' experience as a commissioned officer of the 6th (D.C.O.R.) Regiment in Vancouver. A third officer to report for duty at Battalion Headquarters was Lieut. R. D. Forrester, whose previous training had been carried out in the C. A. S. C. at Vancouver. Lieut. Forrester undertook the duties of Assistant Adjutant. A few weeks after the opening of these Headquarters Major C. B. Worsnop reported to take over the duties of Second-in-Command, though he was not officially gazetted as such until the unit left for England. Headquarters establishment was further augmented by the appointment of Lieut. T. P. O'Kelly, an experienced ex-transportation official of the Hudson's Bay Co., as Transport Officer, and W. H. Long of the Vancouver Police Force, an ex-Hussar with a long Indian Service record, as Regimental Sergeant-Major.

In the meantime both the Battalion Pay Department and the Quartermaster's Department had been organized and established in Victoria. Capt. J. A. Kirkpatrick, of Prince Rupert, had received the appointment of Paymaster and chosen as his Sergeant W. F. Beak, who hailed from the same city. With Ptes. J. Wilson and W. Paterson the Pay Office was complete and carried on work in the same office as the Battalion Orderly Room. Capt. F. Stead, late of the C. A. S. C. in Vancouver, was Quartermaster and he brought as his Quartermaster-Sergeant G. S. Hutchings who had already seen active service in South Africa and had transferred to the 102nd Bn. from the C. A. S. C. Ptes. O. L. McDougal, G. S. Clarke and W. W. Bechtel completed the Quartermaster's establishment and the stores were opened on Bastion Street.

So much for the organization of Headquarters in Victoria, where routine work was carried on until the second week in March. In addition to the registering of all recruits whose papers were forwarded from the recruiting stations mentioned above, an active recruiting campaign was maintained in Victoria itself and Sgt. G. B. Thompson, who also acted as Provost-Sergeant, did yeoman service in meeting all boats and conducting likely candidates first to Headquarters and then to the office of Capt. A. E. McMicking, who acted as Battalion Medical Officer in the city.

Meanwhile recruiting was going on merrily throughout the Province. In the majority of cases where men were enlisted in the vicinity of any of the interior recruiting stations they took advantage of the clause in the Act and remained billeted in their own homes on a subsistence allowance, reporting daily to their local headquarters for drill and preliminary training. Others were billeted in local quarters; but where this practice did not prevail the men were forwarded direct to the mobilization camp. For those who shared this fate the winter of 1915-16 will always have many bitter memories. Frankly, conditions at Comox and Courtenay were deplorable. The men were told in all good faith to take nothing with them; that clothing, blankets and almost all the luxuries of home would be waiting for them on arrival; the half-hearted suggestion of a moving-picture proprietor that he might open up a show in camp in the future was exaggerated until the recruit believed that he would find the white lights of Broadway twinkling on the Spit. And when the men arrived by ones and twos, or in parties, they found—nothing, not even clothes. There was a "hold-up" somewhere and it was a long and tedious job to pry loose the fingers that were holding so fast to the supplies, and all the time, throughout the bitterest winter that had been known for years on Vancouver Island, the newly recruited men, who had deliberately left behind them warm clothing, were starved with cold. The fact was, so many battalions were recruiting at one and the same time that as fast as supplies reached the centres of population they were seized for the men on the spot, and the poor fellows in isolated Comox had to share the fate of all those who are out of sight. At least, that is the most charitable explanation. No blame attaches to the Quartermaster's Department of the unit; Capt. Stead made frantic efforts to supply deficiencies, but he could not create what was not there and supplies continued to go forward in exasperatingly small quantities.

However, clothing or no clothing, the nucleus of a battalion carried on at Comox and Courtenay. Major G. Rothnie, of

Kamloops, who had served in the Canadian Contingent during the Boer War and had also seen service with the First Contingent in Flanders, whence he had returned wounded in the foot, was in command, and with him was associated Capt. A. T. Johnston, another South African veteran. Sgt. Harold Brown acted as local orderly room sergeant and assisting him were Ptes. F. Field and F. du Jardin. These five comprised what might be called Advanced Headquarters. At first lack of accommodation in Comox made it necessary to divide the men into two companies, one being stationed in Courtenay and the other in Comox, but this arrangement was found to be unsatisfactory and as soon as possible the Spit itself was made habitable and the larger portion of the men were housed under canvas, the balance being quartered in the Hotel Port Augusta, Comox, which was requisitioned as a sort of receiving station.

It is not easy to describe the hardships which these pioneers of the Spit camp had to undergo. A reference has already been made to the severity of the weather; the snowfall was phenomenal and on more than one occasion the men were called out of their beds to clear the roof before the weight of snow brought it down on their heads. Moreover, before the Spit could be used, it was necessary to lay a water pipe from a spring on the mainland across the shallow bay formed by the curve of the peninsula. To do this the men had to work up to their thighs in water, and that in December and January. Buildings had to be erected for mess-halls and recreation rooms; a bath-house had to be constructed, kitchens made and all the other appurtenances of a military camp. The first building erected for a mess-hall collapsed, partly owing to snow but more largely because the small body of Engineers on the spot who were responsible for its design were more competent in theory than in practice. Colonel Warden pleaded that his recruits, who were all practical, out-door men, be allowed to go ahead and make a camp for themselves, but Red Tape ruled that if the Government supplied the material, it should also supply the brains; unfortunately the Government was only in a position to supply heads. In addition to this kind of work the troops at Comox rendered enormous benefits to the people of the district in helping them to clear away the snow which in every locality was proving a very real menace to safety.

And so the winter passed. That it passed without any fatality from disease occurring was no credit to responsible authority; it was merely a striking evidence of the physical fitness and calibre of the men. That it passed without any outward sign of discontent was a tribute to the patriotism of the rank and file and the tact and sympathy of the officers on the spot. That Colonel Warden could frequently visit these men and receive a hearty welcome was in itself sufficient proof that they never blamed him for their straits, but realized that he was doing all he could to overcome the apathy which was reacting with such severity upon the early members of the unit.

With the coming of spring conditions improved. Early in March Headquarters moved up from Victoria and after a brief sojourn in Port Augusta were established in a large marquee on the Spit itself. The men from Vancouver, Nelson and Vernon had already arrived. Soon after, the men from Prince Rupert and Prince George marched in under the leadership of Lieut. J. F. Brandt; so numerous was this party that it was formed into a company by itself and No. 2. Co. later known as "B" Co., was the rallying point for all the hardy men from that district. A notable incident took place on the occasion of the arrival of the Prince Rupert men. Capt. J. S. Matthews happened to be the senior officer on the Spit when they marched in and he welcomed them by calling for cheers in the following words: "North British Columbians, three cheers for the men from Prince Rupert." That was the first occasion on which the battalion had been styled "North British Columbians" and from that date onwards the title has held, being adopted in place of the words "Comox-Atlin." Thereafter the battalion was known as the 102nd (North British Columbians) Overseas Battalion, and the title obtained on the battalion crest. Still a little later and Lieut. F. Lister appeared at the head of his Cranbrook men. A volume could be written on the difficulties with which this officer, destined to be our second Colonel and to lead the battalion home again, had had to contend; suffice it to say that only by an admirable exhibition of tact and firmness had he been enabled to keep for the 102nd Battalion those men whom he had personally enlisted and whom local jealousies had tried to wean from the battalion of their first choice.

Training now began in earnest. With the severity of winter passed, it would have been hard to find a healthier spot for the location of a training camp. Practically surrounded by the sea, swept by the four winds of heaven, with a dry sandy soil, the Spit proved up on all that its advocates had had to say for it. During the whole of our three months' sojourn there as a battalion there was but one fatal casualty, and that was due to a stroke of apoplexy for which the climate could not be blamed. There was an epidemic of measles, but it carried with it no harmful after-effects. With that exception, the Battalion Medical Officer, Capt. N. M. McNeil of Prince Rupert, had nothing more serious to contend with than occasional colds and inevitable cuts and bruises. As the spring wore on to summer first-class bathing was obtainable off the end of the Spit, and there was ample room for all kinds of outdoor games. But life was dull on the Spit: there's no denying it. We had no rifles, except for a dozen or so Ross rifles which were periodically exhibited on wet days by some enthusiastic sergeant with confidence in his vocal chords and his ability in the art of demonstration. The only training we could undergo was drill in one of its four forms, section, platoon, company and battalion—and the greatest of these is platoon—and route marching. There was no recreation except what we could make for ourselves. The people of Comox and Courtenay, though they must have benefited enormously from the presence of a battalion in their midst, failed to take advantage of the opportunities afforded to men of enterprise and offered nothing in the way of evening entertainment. Time hung heavily after the day's work was done, and even the proverbial mischief which Satan is popularly credited with having on tap for idle hands seldom materialized. A walk to Comox after supper, a drink at "The Lorne," another at "The Elk," perhaps more, not likely less, and then home by our own little launch "The Joan," and the evening's amusements were exhausted, save for cards and prayer-meetings, which usually went on simultaneously in the big mess-hall.

Throughout the three months which the battalion as a mobilized whole put in on the Spit Colonel Warden was seldom with us for more than two or three nights at a time. He was indefatigable in his journeyings up and down the Province, addressing meetings, stimulating recruiting and interviewing officials on behalf of the unit, but his frequent visits to Comox were a never-ending source of joy to the men assembled there. No matter where he had been he always returned with a telegram which he had received just before reaching camp. He would have the battalion formed up on parade and after calling it to "Attention" he would invariably start by saying, "I have just received a telegram" and then would follow an optimistic message which tended to prove infallibly that within an incredibly short time we should be in France. These telegrams became the subject of ribald jests, and after parade the regular slogan was "Come on, boys, whip round for another ten cents apiece; it's time we got some more hay for the Colonel's bull." But we loved those cheering messages all the same, no matter whence they materialized, and when all is said and done the Colonel did actually get the battalion over to France within five months from mobilization, which was "some record."

With the end of May it became obvious that a move of some kind in the near future was imperative. The water supply was beginning to fail and the oldest inhabitants warned us that with the advent of an average summer we could no longer depend on our mainland spring. Seeing that on this spring we relied entirely for both drinking and washing water and that there was no other source of supply available in the near neighbourhood preparations were made for a move. The past weeks had been filled with many rumors; it had been freely stated at one time that the 102nd Bn. would go to India; Bermuda had been quoted as a likely harbourage for us; again an almost, but not quite, official notice was received that we should be brigaded at

OFFICERS' GROUP, COMOX, MAY, 1916

From left to Right—Lt. J. M. Whitehead, Lt. G. B. Proctor, Lt. H. E. Whyte, Lt. J. C. Halsey, Lt. K. G. Mackenzie, Lt. R. A. Stalker, Lt. W. J. Sturgeon, Lt. H. Wilson, Lt. R. D. Forrester, Lt. J. H. Grant, Lt. J. F. Brandt, Major G. Rothnie, Capt. N. M. McNeill, Capt. F. Quinn (temporarily attached from Dental Service), Lt.-Col. J. W. Warden, Lt. T. P. Copp, Major L. M. Hagar, Lt. H. E. Homer Dixon, Lt. J. B. Bailey, Capt. A. T. Johnston, Lt. R. G. H. Brydon, Capt. F. Stent, Lt. A. Carss, Capt. T. C. Colwell, Lt. P. Matheson, Capt. J. A. Kirkpatrick, Lt. R. McCuaig, Lt. McI. Gordon.

Vernon. With the failure of our water, however, it was decided that the 102nd, together with the 103rd, and possibly the "Bantams," should be quartered for the summer at Sidney and matters had so far progressed in this direction that an advance party consisting of the Medical Officer and the Second-in-Command had gone ahead to map out a route, mark water supplies and arrange for camps so that the battalion might march to Sidney, when the bolt fell from a blue sky. The D.O.C., Colonel Ogilvy, was coming to inspect us, and on his decision would depend our immediate future. He came, he saw, and we conquered. The fiat went forth that the 102nd Bn. would proceed overseas immediately and in a bustle and rush everything was made ready, last records were compiled and inspectors satisfied and on Saturday, June 10th, 1916, the battalion proceeded in full marching order, which included kit-bags and two blankets per man, across the narrow neck of sand for the last time, and embarked on the S.S. "Princess Charlotte" for Vancouver. The Terminal City was reached at 10 p.m. and a large crowd of relatives had assembled at the station to see the last of their men and to say what was, alas, in many cases the last good-bye. At midnight the train pulled out and the 102nd (North British Columbians) was in good truth an overseas unit.

The following officers proceeded with the unit from Comox: Lieut.-Colonel J. W. Warden; Major C. B. Worsnop; Major L. M. Hagar; Capt. H. B. Scharschmidt, Adjutant; Lieut. J. B. Bailey, Asst. Adjutant; Lieut. J. M. Whitehead, i|c, Machine Gun Section; Lieut. G. B. Proctor, i|c, Signalling Section; Capt. F. Stead, Quartermaster; Capt. J. A. Kirkpatrick, Paymaster; Lieut. T. P. O'Kelly, Transport Officer; Capt. T. C. Colwell, Chaplain; Capt. J. Fall, O.C., No. 1 Co.; Capt. A. T. Johnston, O.C. No. 2 Co.; Capt. J. S. Matthews, O.C. No. 3 Co.; Major G. Rothnie, O.C. No. 4 Co. Capt. J. H. Ross; Capt. J. F. Brandt; Capt. H. E. Homer Dixon; Lieuts. R. G. H. Brydon, R. McCuaig, H. E. Whyte, T. R. Griffith, K. G. Mackenzie, T. P. Copp, R. P. Matheson, A. G. MacDonald, R. D. Forrester, J. H. Wilson, McL. Gordon, W. J. Sturgeon, J. H. Grant, R. Burde, F. Lister, J. C. Halsey and R. A. Stalker; Capt. N. M. McNeill was attached from the C.A.M.C. to the Battalion as Medical Officer.

CHAPTER II.

Across the Continent—Steamer Hardships— Six Weeks in England.

UR journey across the Continent was unmarked by any untoward incident. Accommodation was good on board the train and the messing arrangements were excellent. Two trains sufficed to transport the unit, the first being under the command of Major Worsnop and the second under that of the Colonel. Two stops a day were made of sufficient duration to enable the men to get exercise by parading through the main streets of some town and it was not until we reached Ottawa that any event occurred to break the usual monotony of a long train journey. At the Capital the battalion was reviewed by H.R.H. the Duke of Connaught, then Governor-General of Canada, accompanying whom was General Sir Sam Hughes, then Minister of Militia. On the same day the journey was resumed and on Sunday afternoon, June 18th, we reached Halifax and embarked on the C.P.R. S.S. "Empress of Britain," which pulled out into the fairway on the same evening but did not leave Halifax until the morning of June 20th, when, with H.M.S. "Drake" as escort, she started off upon her submarine-infested course.

Of that voyage the less said the better, but common decency demands that some criticism be offered on the accommodation afforded the troops. In addition to the 102nd Bn. the steamer carried the 65th and 84th Bns., together with some Medical Details and a draft for the Pioneers. It was freely stated that in the Mediterranean the "Empress of Britain" had carried 6,000 troops; if that were so, she must indeed have been a living hell. With only two-thirds that number on board the conditions that prevailed were well-nigh intolerable, and this is written after two and a half years in France and Belgium where the writer had some experience of hardship. The 102nd Bn. was the junior battalion and also the last aboard, but that should not account for the fact that there was literally not sufficient accommodation for all below and that, if the weather had been bad, so that men could not have slept on deck, there would have been no place for them to sleep at all. The food was atrocious. Apart from the fact that we had to eat in the bowels of the ship where the atmosphere was stifling, every article of food cooked was permeated with some disgusting preservative which caused all dishes to taste alike, all being equally objectionable. Fortunately the weather was gloriously fine and the sea as calm as a duck-pond throughout the voyage. Imagination fails at the conditions which would have prevailed had sea-sickness been prevalent instead of non-existent. Just exactly how many submarines were observed when nearing the Irish Coast no historian could compute; probably each man saw three, but as the official records relate that none were in evidence it is unlikely that we were ever in very great danger, in spite of the numerous hair's breadth escapes which were narrated after disembarkation.

On the evening of June 28th Liverpool was reached but the steamer anchored over-night in the Mersey and it was not until the following morning that the troops disembarked and lined up on the wharf. A tedious period of waiting then followed and it was afternoon before we boarded trains which conveyed us over nearly every railway system in England to our destination, Bordon, where we arrived at one o'clock on the morning of the 30th. It was pouring with rain when we fell in on the station platform, but we were lucky in our quarters, which were in the married men's huts in Bordon and were both clean and comfortable.

The first days of our stay in England were anxious ones indeed; right and left of us we saw battalions being broken up; both the 65th and 84th Bns. with whom we had come overseas suffered this fate on the very next day after arrival, and we were the junior battalion in England at the time. What mercy could we expect? Well, we did not get mercy, but we got justice, and when the authorities found that we were the tallest, the heaviest, and the most maturely aged of any unit that had reached England, and when they saw for themselves the physique of the men who composed the 102nd Bn. they just naturally had no choice in the matter and within two or three days we received the glad news that we were no longer under the special care of Broxted House, that wet nurse of newly arrived units, but that we had been brigaded and henceforth were the junior battalion in the 11th Brigade, 4th Canadian Division, commanded respectively by Brig.-General V. W. Odlum, D.S.O., and Major-General D. Watson, C.M.G. Our future was assured.

But there was a tremendous amount of work ahead of us in England, and but little time to do it in. The Fourth Division was expected to proceed to France very shortly and we had to do in six weeks what our sister battalions had taken months to accomplish. Musketry, of course, was our first and most pressing need and as soon as we had been issued with rifles many days were spent at Whitehill in passing the various tests. Then there were long hours to be spent on bayonet fighting and on musketry drill, but before the end of the month our musketry was over and we left for Bramshott to take up our place by the side of the three battalions with whom we were to be associated for so many arduous months abroad, the 54th (Kootenay) Bn.; the 75th (Toronto) Bn., and the 87th (Montreal) Bn. The remaining days at Bramshott were spent mostly in continuous drill, the only leave obtainable being two short week-ends, one of which was cut shorter by the desire of Sir Sam Hughes to inspect the 4th Division before his departure to Canada. We surely did love our Minister of Militia when this news came through.

In connection with this review justice demands that a tragedy be related and if at this late date exposure could cause the lopping off of a few official heads there are many 102nd men now living who would indeed feel that "God's in His heaven; all's right with the world." We were on the eve of departure and orders were issued that all private or Governmental property carried by the men which would not be taken overseas was to be packed in the men's individual kit-bags; these kit-bags were to be clearly marked with name and number and piled at a specified place. It was clearly stated that these kit-bags would be stored under Government care and that when on leave in after months men would be able to reclaim their kit-bags and possessions. In pursuance of these orders kit-bags were packed and piled as directed, and the battalion marched away to parade with the Division at the grand review. During its absence a party of men acting under orders went through the kit-bags and burnt or distributed to pedlars all the contents. Absolutely unworn Stanfield's underwear, boots, spare socks and other wearing apparel were either wantonly burnt or given away; that was a shameful waste of public money and an economic outrage. In addition, the private property of the men was burnt, bibles, keepsakes from relatives and all the variety of personal effects which most men carry round with them, were consigned to the flames; that was a damnable vandalism and an outrage on the feelings of God and man alike. Someone must have blundered; the act was worse than criminal; it was foolish; but the Army is a past-master in the art of "passing the buck" and to this day the responsibility for this wholesale destruction has never been disclosed officially. Nothing could be done then, nor can anything be done now to compensate the men for the sentimental losses they sustained; but it is never too late for the Government to recover the monetary value of good under-clothing wantonly destroyed.

Reference was made above to leave. The 102nd Bn. was unfortunate in its King's leave. Whilst at Comox frequent weekend leave had been granted to Vancouver, Victoria and places near-by, but when our sudden departure was announced there was no opportunity for men to get leave who lived far away. "Never mind," said the Colonel; "my men are all British-born, and their relations are in England. They'll get leave over there." One cannot blame the Colonel; we were all keen to get away, and a demand for leave would have robbed us of the chance. But mark well what happened. We reached England in time to join the 4th Division, if we could make the grade; but this would be impossible if each man was to have his King's leave. "Never mind," said the Colonel; "my men don't want leave in England. They are Canadians and have already said good-bye to their kith and kin." Again, one can't blame the Colonel; we all wanted to get across to France, but he was scarcely logical, to say the least of it.

During the six weeks spent in England considerable change was made in the personnel of the battalion. A rigorous medical inspection resulted in the transfer of every man who was not in the pink of condition to a reserve unit; thus we lost many who were not considered fit for the strenuous work of the front line, though eminently capable of fulfilling essential duties which did not call for physical perfection. The officers left behind when the battalion proceeded to France were Major L. M. Hagar, Capt. J. H. Ross, Capt. J. Fall, Lieut. G. B. Proctor and Capt. T. C. Colwell. At Bramshott also we lost the majority of our Bugle Band, which was for the most part composed of boys under age who were later returned to Canada, only to come out again when Time had made them eligible. Many boys, however, who nobly "got away" with their age, accompanied the unit across the Channel and proved invaluable as Runners. To fill up the deficiencies in our numbers we received the following reinforcements while at Bramshott: Capt. J. G. Spencer and 27 O.R. from the 71st Bn.; Capt. W. J. Loudon, Capt. R. W. Nicholls, Capt. A. C. Trousdale and 112 O.R. from the 74th Bn.; Capt. E. J. Gook; Lieuts. C. C. Tunnard, R. Fitzmaurice, L. J. Bettison, C. T. Rush and T. E. Dent from the 11th C.M.R., and Lieuts. W. S. Barton and W. Bell from the 103rd Bn. Capts. A. T. Johnston, J. S. Matthews and H. E. Homer Dixon received promotion in England and the first named took over No. 1 Co. in place of Capt. Fall, Major Homer Dixon assuming command of No. 2 Co. Lieut. J. H. Grant was appointed Assistant Adjutant in place of Lieut. R. A. Stalker who had succeeded Lieut. J. B. Bailey. Capt. I. J. E. Daniel proceeded with the batalion as Chaplain (R.C.) in place of Capt. Colwell.

The last few days passed quickly, and finally, on a sweltering hot day, August 11th, 1916, the 102nd Bn. marched from Bramshott to Liphook, where it entrained for Southampton. Arrived there we boarded the small cross-channel transport "Connaught" and awoke on the morning of the 12th to find ourselves in the harbour of Le Havre. Just five months from mobilization in Comox and we were standing on the threshold of our ambitions. How those ambitions were fulfilled the succeeding chapters will relate.

CHAPTER III.

By Side-door Pullman to Belgium—Our Baptism of Blood—
Flirtations With Gas—Trench Routine—
The Army Idea of Rest.

ISEMBARKATION at Le Havre took place at 7.00 a.m. on August 12th, and we were immediately marched up a precipitous road to Rest Camp No. 1, where we were to remain during the day. The day was excessively hot and everyone was glad of the opportunity afforded in the afternoon of bathing off the beach. Orders were received for the unit to entrain at midnight and at that hour we were all assembled at the station, where we waited for a considerable time before our train was ready. Then we had our first shock and learned what travel in Flanders means for the enlisted man. It was pitch dark when we boarded the train and nobody was supplied with candles; it is easy, therefore, to imagine the confusion which reigned in a cattle-car packed with 40 men, each carrying full equipment. In later days these cars rarely carried more than 32 men, so we had the advantage of seeing travel at its worst on our first journey; moreover, at that stage in the war no effort was made to clean the cars after they had been used for cattle before they were turned over for the accommodation of troops. The next day and the following night were spent on the train and at 10 a.m. on August 14 we arrived at our destination, a station in Belgium with the imposing name of Godewaersvelde. Here we detrained and marched about five miles to our halting place, a tented camp about half-a-mile N.E. of Abiele. This camp boasts in its vicinity one of the many barn doors which are shown to new-comers as being in each case the identical one on which the Canadian sergeant was found crucified. At this point we were informally visited by the Corps Commander, Lieut.-General Sir Julian Byng, K.C.B., K.C.M.G., M.V.O.

We were now in the neighbourhood of St. Eloi trenches, Ypres Salient, a portion of the line which was used at that time for the training under fire of newly arrived battalions. The routine of trench life had to be learned under actual service conditions and to obtain

the necessary experience units were required to send forward their
companies, one at a time, to undertake a tour in the trenches under
the guidance and tuition of some battalion qualified to "put them
wise" to trench warfare. And how ignorant the new battalion can
be was well exemplified when No. 1 Co., under Major A. T. Johnston
went forward for instruction on the night of August 15th. We had
not been issued with steel helmets; it is to be doubted whether
anyone at Brigade Headquarters had ever given a thought to steel
helmets; such things were not in the early days of the war when
our veteran leaders had seen their previous service. Accordingly
No. 1 Co. went gaily forward in their service caps. Again, in previous
days men had always gone forward in full kit; the style of trench
existing in 1916, which barely permits the passage of a man so
equipped, had not been contemplated by officers of the 11th Bde.
Consequently No. 1 Co. burst upon the astonished vision of the 29th
Bn., whose members were to act as tutors and instructors, jauntily
adorned with service caps, which were anathema in the front line,
and staggering under full kit instead of the then regulation battle
order. To them we must have been as refreshing as a stage hayseed
in a down-town café. To the eternal credit of the 29th be it said
that, though they smiled, they did their job and "put us wise," so
that when the second company went up on the following night and
presented themselves to the 24th Bn., which had relieved the 29th,
the men were safely and sanely equipped. On the 17th and 18th
respectively Nos. 3 and 4 Coys. went forward for instruction,
relieving their predecessors, and it was on the 19th that No. 3 Co.,
which was in the front line, underwent the baptism of blood and
learned what real warfare means. Throughout that day the Hun
kept up a terrific bombardment of the front line system, throwing
over every conceivable form of shell, wrecking the trenches and
taking first toll from the 102nd Bn. in the shape of six men killed
and 12 men wounded. The first man of the 102nd Bn. to give his
life for the Cause was Pte. R. Simmers of Victoria. Throughout
the bombardment the steadiness of the men was so noticeable that
the O. C. 24th Bn. ordered the company to remain an extra 24 hours,
as he feared that an attack in force would follow the artillery
preparation.

It was during our brief stay in the tented camp above referred
to that we had our initiation into the mysteries of gas. A demonstration and an open-air lecture were given and we were sent through
a cloud of poison gas with our P. H. Helmets on and another cloud
of tear gas without them. Thereafter for two or three weeks our
lives were made miserable by frequent gas alarms, all of which
proved to be false. There is no doubt but that we were all "on
edge" with regard to this gas proposition during early days, and
when our subsequent attitude towards this invention of the devil
is compared with that of the first few months "it makes to laugh,"
as our Gallic friends would say. We were a long way from the line

both in the tented camp and in Devonshire Lines to which we marched on August 17th, but distance was not allowed to baulk the activity of our gas sentries, who forced us to sleep with our P. H.'s on our chests at the alert and woke us up time and again to wait patiently, ready masked, for the gas that never came. Later, when gas shells were introduced by the Hun and we were never safe from that class of attack we became callous and would idly ponder as to whether there was enough gas to make it worth while putting on a respirator, and whether it would be a kindness or not to wake up so-and-so to allow him to adjust his.

We remained at Devonshire Lines, a camp close to Reninghelst, till the 24th of the month. We found it in a filthy condition when we entered it and this was an experience which was destined to be repeated with painful regularity throughout two and a half years' campaigning. Some battalions were naturally decent and had healthy views with regard to sanitation and camp cleanliness; other battalions were most distinctly opposite in this respect, and it may be said in passing, that of these the Imperials were the worst. But throughout our period of the war it seemed to be the fate of the 102nd to clean up every time it entered a new camp. It was in Devonshire Lines also that we lost one of our cherished illusions; we had been told, as doubtless every other unit which ever went over to France had been told, that "over there" we should never require any polishing outfit. In the theatre of war glistening brass work would be "tabu," and in our innocence we believed, as many other luckless thousands believed. Well, in Devonshire Lines, we discovered that there was more polishing to be done in France than had ever been dreamed of in our Canadian philosophy.

By August 24th all sections of the Battalion had had some instruction in trench routine and on that day the unit was assigned to regular tours of duty as follows:—One company to Dickiebusch for general fatigues; one company to Voormezeele for garrison duty; one company to Scottish Woods for garrison duty and one company with Headquarters to Micmac Camp to act as reserve. As we remained in this area a month and when out of the trenches were generally disposed in some such formation, it will be well to try and give some description of the neighborhood.

The big town of the district was Reninghelst, lying between Ypres and Poperinghe; this was but a small town, but larger than the ruined hamlets in the neighbourhood; here were situated Divisional Headquarters. Dickiebusch, which was our own more immediate centre, was a small, badly shell-shocked village which boasted one large farm, known as Burgomaster's farm, where 11th Bde. Headquarters were established. Here Brigadier-General V. W. Odlum, D. S. O. Commanding the 11th Brigade, took up his quarters; at that time Capt. Henniker was acting as Brigade-Major and Major Perry as Staff Captain. A feature of the Brigade establishment was the excellently camouflaged Signal Station, which figured prominently as a haystack.

At the back of Dickiebusch was a large lake and bordering this was Scottish Woods, through which a day-trail led past Voormezeele by way of Convent Lane to the trenches of St. Eloi. Under cover of darkness the trenches could be reached by road running up from the Café Belge, and this route was the one followed nightly by the transport when conveying rations. But this was a dangerous piece of road; it was under observation and was constantly swept by machine gun fire. One of the most remarkable features of the 102nd Bn. period of service was the immunity which the Transport and ration parties had from casualties during the whole of the tour of duty in the St. Eloi sector. Micmac Camp was a hutted camp lying between Dickiebusch and Ouderdom and boasted no special features except the presence of a small café where eggs and coffee were procurable. Of the inhabitants of this neighbourhood there is little that is pleasant to say; they were peasants of the least intelligent type, Flemish with pronounced German sympathies; espionage was rampant and more than one suffered the extreme penalty when caught red-handed as a spy or a sniper. There was nothing in the personality of these people to appeal to the sympathetic imagination of troops who had come over fired with the tale of Belgian wrongs.

Amid these surroundings the 102nd Bn. spent the next month, engaged in regular tours of duty either in the front line trenches, or as outlined above. Both in the Front Line trenches and in the Support and Reserve positions the work required was for the most part that of increasing and improving the existing protection. The Hun was unceasingly battering down parapets and parados which had as often to be repaired; there was an insufficiency of shelters, and the unit was responsible for a big improvement in this direction, making a large number of shelters against the winter; above all, the trenches were in a shocking state as soon as wet weather set in; the mud was liquid and the bath-mats were floating on the top. Working-parties were constantly employed draining the trenches and stabilizing the bath-mats. Though no active offensive was undertaken casualties occurred with painful frequency. On the morning of Sept. 1st Sergt. C. C. Higgs, Scout Sergeant, and Pte. W. F. Brewer, one of his section, were killed in No Man's Land, whilst patrolling the front. On the evening of the following day an irreparable loss was sustained in the death of Major A. T. Johnston, O. C. No. 1 Co. He was waiting with his company in Reserve trenches immediately in rear of the Support Line, ready to go forward in relief of No. 2 Co. As the hour approached he came out of his dug-out to make a preliminary observation of the situation over the edge of his parapet just at a point on which the enemy had a machine gun trained, with the result that he was instantaneously killed by a bullet through the brain. His death was an immense blow to the battalion; one of our earliest and most efficient officers he was beloved and respected by all ranks. He was succeeded in command of No. 1 Co. by Capt. Gook. On Sept. 8th No. 2 Co. suffered heavily through the bursting of an enemy high explosive shell in the mouth of a dug-out in Scottish Woods. This one shell was responsible for the killing outright of eight men and for the wounding of nine more, two of whom succumbed on the following day. On Sept. 12th C. S. M. Paton, one of our finest N.C.O.'s, was shot dead. With casualties occurring in this manner from day to day we were glad to receive a draft of men from the 66th and 82nd Bns., numbering nearly a hundred, and hailing for the most part from Calgary, who reported at Micmac Camp on Sept. 8th.

On all the occasions when the battalion was in the line Advanced Headquarters were established in Shelley Lane, a semi-natural trench built up on the banks of a somewhat foul little stream; the whole appearance of the trench was more that of a woodland path, shaded with trees and pitted with caves, and during the summer months it was quite a pretty spot; but it was none the less an easy target for the Hun artillerymen and on several occasions it was necessary for its temporary inhabitants to take shelter in a large tunnel opening out of the extreme end.

We were now rapidly approaching the end of our stay in this sector but before we left we were to have some experience, though not an active share, in a raid. The 54th Bn. on our right was detailed to raid the opposing trenches for the purpose of obtaining indentifications and the hour was set for midnight of Sept. 16th. Our share was merely to "stand to" and be prepared for any eventualities and to learn what we could for our own future use. The raid was entirely successful and resulted in the capture of six prisoners from amongst the Wurtemburgers.

And so we came to the 17th when we were relieved on this front by the 15th Bn., 4th Bde., 4th Div., Australians, and made ourselves ready to go out and understand the real meaning of a Divisional Rest. Now in case this book should ever fall into the hands of a layman, one who has not been to France and therefore imagines that English words as used by the Army have the same meaning as when used by civilians, it may be well to explain that the word "rest" merely means "safety." A battalion at rest is a battalion which is not actually under shell fire and in direct ratio to the importance of the unit adjective prefixed to the word the measure of safety is computed. The higher you go, the fewer—shells; thus Divisional Rest is safer than Brigade Rest. In the same way "bath" must not be confounded with the civilian idea of a bath; sometimes it happens that if bath-house attendants are in a good temper enough water will be supplied from the showers to wash the soap off the lathered body, but it frequently happens that the water supply is stopped before the soap disappears, and then a few handfuls of dirty water have to suffice. Again the use of the word "clean" when applied to underwear which has been treated by the Divisional baths, has little connection with the same word when applied to clothing which has passed through a civilian laundry. The Army word "clean" means that the clothing has been treated according to Army regulations; it has been steamed, which process theoretically kills vermin, and it has had a certain amount of ordinary washing, but it is only clean in comparison with what it was before, and though the vermin may be killed theoretically, they remain very much alive practically, or at any rate, their eggs remain pregnant with life which bursts into joyous being after a few minutes association with the beloved human body. Possibly in the next war a little more serious attention will be paid to the louse question; during the last war, though much was written and more said nothing was done which was really efficient, and none of the advertised powders were of the slightest use in combatting the plague. Creolin, which was not too easily obtainable, was the only effective antidote, and that was not discovered, or at any rate was not made easily available until the closing stages of the struggle.

It was on the occasion of this our first relief that we became cognizant of these details, and the truths then learned were proved time and again during the subsequent years. Reninghelst gave us our first experience of the Army bathing and washing system, and though the bathing gradually improved throughout the war, the washing maintained the same average of gross inefficiency.

Having partially cleaned ourselves (the Regimental Diary says "Made an attempt to get men bathed; succeeded in getting 2 companies through only, as no socks or underclothes were available for balance of battalion") we set out for St. Omer at 6.00 a.m. on Sept. 20th and that evening reached Haazebruck, where we were billeted for the night. This is a fair-sized town and undamaged by shell-fire. The battalion after a preliminary experience of 27 days constant trench work was in poor condition for marching, but the men managed to carry on and on the following night reached Arques, in spite of the fact that on our arrival at Haazebruck we had all our sick men returned to us from hospital; it is difficult to understand why these could not have been sent forward to our final destination. As it was ten of them had to be sent immediately to ambulance for transportation. From Arques we had one more day's march, which brought us to Tournehem, which was to be the scene of the great rest of which we had heard much and of which we had dreamed dreams. Here we were to remain until Oct. 3rd. Tournehem was a delightful little French village, rather larger than most, prettily situated in the midst of a rolling landscape and peopled by a most hospitable community. We were immediately taken in and "made a fuss of" and throughout our stay the inhabitants did all they possibly could to make us comfortable. For many a long month thereafter the memory of Tournehem would rise up and bring back longings which were closely akin to homesickness.

But the rest! Well the rest consisted of the hardest kind of open-air training the battalion had yet put in. The Brigade training ground was about four miles distant and here every day the four battalions, all of whom were nearly equi-distant, assembled for a gruelling day of drill or practice warfare; the weather was hot and the roads dusty, but though the work was hard it brought all the battalions into excellent shape and fitted them well for the real hardships which were about to meet them in the ill-famed Somme area. For that was our next objective and for the successful carrying out of their work in that region the troops certainly needed "some" training.

MT. ST. ELOY
A February Afternoon Impression
as seen from Vimy Ridge.

CHAPTER IV.

En Route for the Somme—Albert, Tara Hill and Chalk Pits—"Over the Top" at Regina—New German Trench—Connecting Desire and Regina—Out of the Mouth of Hell

LEAVING its pleasant summer quarters at Tournehem on the 3rd day of October, the Battalion set out for the Somme. Opinions differ as to the comparative conditions of the Somme and of Passchendaele which we were destined to visit just a year later, but it is generally agreed that, though the enemy artillery work in the latter area was more intense and the protection afforded practically non-existent, and though the Passchendaele landscape was dreary in the extreme and the mud intolerable, yet the Somme left a more indelible impression of sordid misery on the minds of those who saw service on both fronts. For a month and a half the battalion struggled in a sea of mud against an implacable enemy and the majority of those who survived to the end regard the Somme tour as the most exhausting and nerve-racking which the battalion undertook throughout its period of service.

Prior to departure every man exchanged his Ross rifle for a Lee-Enfield and was issued with one of the new small box respirators which had come to take the place of the old P-H helmets, though the latter were carried for use in emergencies for another eighteen months or so. The new respirators were a great improvement, but it may be said in passing that the battalion as a whole was never called on to undertake any operation on a large scale under conditions which made the wearing of respirators necessary; we never had to face cloud gas and though in later days we were constantly harassed by gas shells, these were purely local in their effects and rarely necessitated the wearing of the respirator for any length of time.

An afternoon's march on October 3rd brought the battalion to Arduicq at 5.30 p.m., where train was taken for Doullens, which was reached twelve hours later; Doullens is a fair-sized town with tempting out-door cafés, but we were not destined to gain any enjoyment therefrom, marching direct from the station through the town to Gézaincourt, where were were billeted for the night. Gézaincourt proved to be larger than the majority of villages, boasting an extensive hospital building. Hence we proceeded on Oct. 5th to Val de Maison where the night was spent under canvas. The following day's march brought us to Vadincourt, an apology for a hamlet lying on the hill above Contay where Canadian Corps Headquarters had been established. Vadincourt remains a damp and dismal memory of rain-soaked shelters erected in a dripping wood on soggy soil. Here we stayed for three days during the course of which an attack scheme for later use was assiduously practised. On Oct. 10th we left Vadincourt and marched into Albert towards the end of the afternoon.

For the next six weeks Albert was to be our Base Headquarters; here the Transport Lines, which comprised, in addition to the Transport, the Quartermaster's Stores, the Paymaster's Office and the Base Orderly Room, were situated. It was the first time we had seen ruin on a large scale and from the weird statue of the Virgin and Child suspended at right angles from the topmost pinnacle of the Cathedral to the shattered cellar of a beggar's hovel, everything impressed the beholder with the same dull feeling of stark misery. Albert was not wholly destroyed; many civilians still remained and some continued to run their little businesses, but for the most part the place was deserted. The Hun maintained a desultory bombardment of the town and occasional enemy aeroplanes circled above, but few bombs were dropped; it was not till later that the Transport Lines by night became as dangerous as the front line by day. For some reason or other, which possibly the psychologists can explain, the bombardment of a town reacts more violently on the nerves than a bombardment in the open, and during our stay in this sector the men from the front line could always count on amusing stories of temporary shell-shock being retailed for their benefit when they returned for a brief spell of rest. It would be invidious to recall such stories in a publication of this nature, but some of those who read these lines will be able to supplement them with many an instance of a grimly jesting nature.

On arrival at Albert the troops were billeted for the night, but a small party of officers was detailed to go forward and visit the front line, which at this time was situated between Death Valley and Regina Trench. On the following day the four companies went out some two miles and took up their quarters on Tara Hill, an eminence west of Albert on the Bapaume Road, and camped under bivouacs. From Tara Hill half the Headquarters Details, including the Band, were sent forward another five miles to Bailey Woods, a treeless area in Sausage Valley, where the 11th Brigade Headquarters had been established. This party was to be used as a night-carrying party and did yeoman service throughout the early part of the tour, after which they were relieved. For six days the companies remained at Tara Hill, organizing for the offensive which was to develop on the 21st and practising the attack. During this period Lieuts. J. Mont and G. Ledingham reported for duty.

It was a busy scene on which the men looked down from their camp on the top of Tara Hill. The Albert-Bapaume Road was

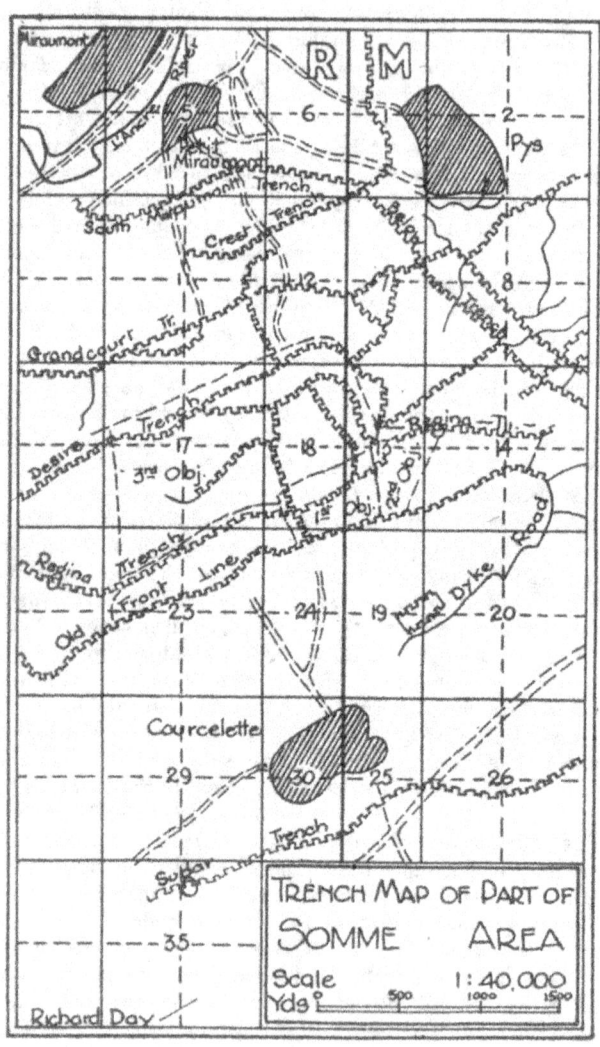

literally alive by day and night with a never-ending stream of vehicles of all kinds travelling east or west; lorries ladened with ammunition going east, or crowded with weary soldiers coming west, ambulances, ration waggons, motor-cycles, all the traffic of an army actively engaged poured ceaselessly back and forth along this main highway which miraculously escaped complete destruction by the enemy's artillery. About four miles east of Albert the road forks into a "Y"; here at the apex once stood the village of La Boisselle, of which one stone did not remain upon another; close by were two enormous craters worthy of notice. The left fork carried on past Pozières, a mere geographical expression of which no trace remained, to the Sunken Road and thence to the German positions astride Bapaume; at the Sunken Road Tenth Street afforded a safe passage-way to the ill-omened but well-named Death Valley, on the eastern side of which lay the then front line. The right fork at La Boisselle ran up to Contelmaison, of which but a few cellar stones remained, and here a track diverged to Sausage Valley past the Chalk Pits which we were to know so well before we left the Somme. From Sausage Valley a trail, followed later by a light railway, ran across the ghastly Plain of Courcelette, reeking with the debris, human and otherwise, of battle. Doré could have found no finer inspiration for his illustrations of the "Inferno" than the scene presented on a wet November evening by the Plain of Courcelette.

At Tara Hill we remained until the 18th, which was to mark the first step in the series of operations which culminated in the capture of Regina Trench, the first great achievement of the 102nd Bn., and it was during this period of waiting that the practice of referring to the companies by numerals was abandoned in favor of alphabetical letters, No. 1 Co. becoming "A" Co. and so on. Regina Trench had already been the object of two determined attacks by the Canadian Corps, the first commencing on Oct. 1st, and the second on Oct. 8th. In both attacks the trench had been reached, but violent counter-attacks had forced a retirement from the position when won, and it was left for the 4th Canadian Division both to capture and to hold this important position. As the three senior Divisions had been withdrawn from the area immediately after the arrival on the scene of the 4th Division, the latter was attached to the 2nd Corps for all its operations on the Somme. The following narrative of the capture is taken from the official report of the operation forwarded by Colonel Warden to 11th Brigade Headquarters, and only concerns that portion of Regina Trench which was allotted to the 102nd Bn. as its objective.

On the evening of Oct. 18th the 102nd Bn. took over from the 87th Bn. the front line trenches on the left sector of the Brigade, situated on a line running from R. 18, c. 4, 0. to M. 13, d, 2, 2., this being a front of 500 yards extending from Courcelette Trench on the left flank to Ross Communication Trench on the right. The night was very dark and it was raining hard, so that the ground was a sea of mud with quagmires on every side, making the trenches almost impassable. As the men were lining up in the Support Trench the enemy delivered a bombing attack on the left flank of the 87th Bn. Word was passed down that the Hun was attacking and that the 102nd was to come up on the double. This was done in absolute silence and as the men passed Headquarters, jumping over trenches and shell-holes, they looked like phantoms in the dark, illumined by the light of German flares and leaping to the crash of bursting shells. Here and there a man was seen to fall, the shelling being very heavy, but the bombers were driven off and the rest of the night spent in preparation for the morrow's work. Rain continued and throughout the night there was constant shelling.

Day broke with rain pouring down in torrents, making the ground absolutely impassable and the Higher Command decided to postpone operations until the 21st inst. "B," "C," and "D" Coys. therefore returned to camp at Tara Hill, leaving "A" Co. to hold the line. Never did the men of the 102nd better deserve their reputation for physique and tenacity of purpose than in their fight against the mud after their exhausting night in the trenches. The mud was hip-high between the trenches and the Bapaume Road and the men had to be literally dug out by their comrades as they sank exhausted in the liquid, glue-like substance. The weather cleared, the ground becoming somewhat more dry and on the evening of the 20th the three companies were again brought into the front line, relieving "A" Co. which went into Support. During the night of Oct. 20-21 the three companies worked hard at digging assembly trenches in which to mass and at forming battalion dumps; the men worked magnificently and at dawn all was ready.

Zero hour was fixed for 12-06 p.m. and at that hour the barrage opened and the men of the 102nd went "over the top"; following the barrage like a wall, lying down until it again lifted and advancing as it moved, all in perfect uniformity. The first two waves consisted of "C" Co. under Maj. J. S. Matthews, on the left and "B" Co. under Maj. H. E. H. Dixon on the right. The remaining two waves were furnished by "D" Co. under Major G. Rothnie. The moment that the barrage lifted over Regina Trench the men were over the parapet; the assault was carried out with such dash, vigour and impetuosity that the Germans were completely demoralized and immediately threw up their hands in surrender. The first wave passed 150 yards beyond the trench, forming a screen; the second rounded up the prisoners and consolidated the positions secured, in which they were assisted by men of the third wave, whilst the fourth wave was occupied in carrying up supplies from the old dumps to the new. For his magnificent services in this work of consolidation under heavy fire Lieut. R. P. Matheson received the Military Cross. The casualties sustained in the assault itself were very light, amounting to about five killed and ten wounded, as the enemy barrage did not come down until about six minutes after ours had started; the Germans, however, had suffered heavily and their trench was piled with dead and wounded.

Our casualties were to occur later, when, within an hour and a half, three separate counter-attacks were launched; these were all successfully opposed, but during the remainder of the day and throughout the ensuing night and day, when "A" Co. under Capt. J. F. Brandt arrived to relieve "D" Co., a constant barrage of shell fire was poured into our positions, with the result that the total casualty list showed six officers and 46 Other Ranks killed with eight and seventy wounded. On the night of the 23rd the battalion was relieved by the 54th and the men marched to the Chalk Pits, half a mile south of Pozières, where they went into dug-outs for rest and reorganization.

There were many individual deeds of heroism, but the following incidents may serve to illustrate the spirit of the battalion. Although seven machine guns were in action only four of the original six which started were among that number; two were hopelessly bogged and these were actually replaced during the operation by guns brought up with the utmost difficulty from reserve, whilst the seventh was "resurrected" from the old line of trenches and put into working order under heavy fire. The Machine Gun Section, which was under the Command of Lieuts. J. M. Whitehead and J. H. Grant, the latter being mortally wounded, sustained 30 casualties out of 70 men engaged; of these Sgt. M. M. Brown, though severely wounded, refused to leave his guns until a proper state of defence had been organized. For his supreme courage and devotion this gallant N.C.O. was awarded the D.C.M. The Report goes on to make special mention of the work done by the Battalion Scouts under Capt. A. C. Trousdale in keeping open communications between Headquarters and the front line, and by the Runners and Signallers; the former were in constant use under very heavy fire, but only sustained one casualty, young Stanley Wolverson, who, after being twice wounded in the leg, accepted the advice of his officer, Lieut. R. D. Forrester, that he go to the Dressing Station for treatment only on condition that he might take a prisoner with him; the latter had a particularly hazardous task, the wires being frequently broken and needing constant repair under heavy fire. The Stretcher-bearers also did magnificent work, many, though wounded, persisting in their task of tending the casualties. It was on such an errand that Lieut. A. Carss, though not a member of the Medical Detail, met with his death; he went to succour a wounded Hun who treacherously hurled a bomb at him causing fatal injuries. In this connection it may be mentioned that all prisoners taken had bombs in their pockets, in their haversacks and slung round their necks. Just two more instances of the unquenchable spirit exhibited by the men on this historic occasion:—Pte. A. E. Bailey of "C" Co. had his foot blown off; he rendered himself first aid and in the early hours of the morning of the 22nd was seen hobbling along on his stump towards the new trench; when drawn up over the parapet he lay down apparently oblivious of his own agony to discuss the events of the previous day. L.-Cpl. W. Miller of the Scouts, when lying mortally wounded, remembered orders and handed his prismatic compass to a comrade saying, "Give this to the captain; I have no further use for it."

Such is the story of the 102nd Bn's share in the capture of Regina Trench. It was a great achievement, and in recognition of his valuable services in this operation Lieut.-Colonel Warden was later in the year awarded the D.S.O. But the success was a costly one and the casualty figures given above witness the price paid and include the following officers:—Killed—Capt. R. W. Nicholls, Lieuts. A. Carss, T. P. Copp, McL. Gordon, J. H. Grant (died of wounds), and C. T. Rush. Missing, believed killed—Major G. Rothnie. Wounded—Majors H. E. H. Dixon, J. S. Matthews; Capts. W. J. Loudon, J. E. Spencer; Lieuts. L. J. Bettison, A. G. MacDonald, J. H. Wilson.

For twelve days the battalion remained in the Chalk Pits, a muddy depression honeycombed with inadequate shelters, lying between Headquarters at Bailey Woods and Pozières. The weather was wet and the chalky soil was quickly reduced to a deep stickiness which made every movement a labour; a battery of "Heavies" had taken up its position in the same area and the resultant din added greatly to the general discomfort. During this period working-parties were requisitioned regularly for the units in the line, or to construct the great sand-bag wall which was to protect the south-western end of Death Valley. This was a tremendous undertaking of great importance. Death Valley had well earned its name. Lying as it did between our base and the front and being under direct observation by the enemy who raked it constantly with shell and machine gun fire, it had proved a veritable death-trap. For the protection of the troops a huge barricade of sand-bags was erected across the valley and it long remained as a monument to the devotion of the 102nd Bn., which was largely responsible for its completion. The work entailed on the carrying parties was exhausting in the extreme; it must be remembered that everything that went forward of the Sunken Road, about two miles east of Pozières, had to be taken in by hand; the light railways which were to prove such a boon in other sectors were practically useless in the Somme, as they were destroyed by shell-fire as soon as laid. Every shell for the Field Guns had to be packed in by mule teams; drinking-water had to be carried through miles of trench system in converted gasoline tins, and every man had to carry in addition to his burden his full fighting equipment. Add to this the handicap which the mud and darkness entailed and the reader will have some faint idea of the exhausting strain placed upon the troops when in Reserve after a front line tour. And then a paragraph like the following is to be found in the Regimental Diary: "Oct. 29th.—Church Parade was ordered for 9.45 a.m., but owing to inclement weather this had to be cancelled." Thank God sometimes for the rain; these Church Parades on active service, especially when called in the Forward Area, were the grimmest and ghastliest of Service jokes, and were provocative of more blasphemy and discontent than any active operation.

It may be well here to make mention of two special features in the modern army for the initiation of which the 102nd Bn. is entitled to a full share of credit. The one was the Tump-line Section for packing supplies up the line. All Western Canadians know what the Tump-line is, but for the benefit of others it may be explained as an old time Indian device for packing an extraordinary amount of material by the scientific distribution of weight; the tump-line passes over the forehead down the back. We had many men, strong huskies from the Interior and Northern Coast regions of British Columbia, who were experts in tumping and long before the system was in general operation throughout the Corps the 102nd contingent of the 11th Brigade Tump-line Section under Cpl. Raymond had become famous as phenomenal packers, who could carry anything, anywhere, in record time. The second feature was the Hot Food Container, which later became standardized as a sort of gigantic Thermos flask adapted for the back, but it had its origin in a much more simple device, credit for which was due to our Quartermaster, Capt. F. Stead. The question of the feasibility of conveying hot food up to the men in the front had been mooted by Brigade and suggestions called for, and it was Capt. Stead who was responsible for the scheme employed. This took the form of gasoline tins packed tightly round with paper and carried in remade biscuit tins; it was found that the paper proved an excellent non-conductor and the contents of the interior tin reached the men fairly hot after six hours.

On Nov. 4th we marched back to Albert where we remained for four days, returning to Chalk Pits for one night, preparatory to our second tour in the line which commenced on Nov. 9th. At 1.00 p.m. on the latter date the battalion fell in under the command of Major C. B. Worsnop and marched to Brigade Headquarters, where the men were issued with gum boots for use in the slime of the front line. It was a glorious day; a bright sun blazing in a cloudless sky showed up in sharp relief the horrors of the devastated plain round Courcelette, pocked-marked with shell-holes, dotted with fragments of discarded equipment, with here and there a mouldering corpse of man or horse, but it was dusk when the battalion finally marched off from Brigade Headquarters and darkness had fallen before the men had relieved the 75th Bn., and taken up their appointed stations, "A" and "C" Cos. in Regina Trench; "B" Co. in the old front line trench, "D" Co. in Sugar Trench. The weather continued to improve and the Higher Command decided that the time was ripe for seizing the hitherto unoccupied portion of Regina Trench which was still in German hands and was separated from our men by an extensive block. The 102nd Bn. was on the spot and, with the 47th co-operating on the right, was ordered to assault the position and also to storm a new trench running north from Regina, recently constructed by the Hun and known as New German Trench.

The ranks of the 102nd Bn. were woefully thin; death, wounds and sickness had claimed many; a large number were in Brigade employ, serving in the Tump-line or Pack-train; including Headquarters Staff, Medical Details, Runners and Signallers, who, though essential, cannot be included in the effective fighting strength of a battalion, only 375 men had marched out and the task set was no light one. To "C" Co., under Lieut. R. P. Matheson, numbering 50 men, to whom were added 20 men from "A" Co., was assigned the offensive on Regina; "D" Co., under Lieut. Mackenzie, numbering 76, was to attack the new trench. The balance of "A" Co. was appointed as a carrying-party and "B" Co. was held in reserve. Midnight of Nov. 10-11 was the hour when the barrage would start, lasting eight minutes and then lifting 150 yards, when the two assaults were to be delivered. During the course of the evening Capt. A. C. Trousdale, commanding our Scouts, who was later severely wounded, reported that the enemy was effecting a strong relief and that New German Trench was being held in strength.

It was a brilliant night; a full moon was shining in a cloudless sky, and everything was as easily visible as in the day-time. This was in favor of the attacking force, who possessed all the psychological advantages offered by a night attack undiminished by the handicaps imposed by darkness. At midnight the barrage started and at 12.30 a.m. a Runner reached Headquarters with the news that "C" Co. had gained their objective, but had had to extend considerably to the right in order to keep in touch with the 47th. In the end it was found that this company was occupying and holding 350 yards more than its allotted portion. At 12.35 the news came in that "D" Co. had been similarly successful and an hour later the first batch of prisoners arrived, to be closely interrogated by the Brigadier who spent the night in Battalion Headquarters. The objectives had been gained, but the enemy was not disposed to part with them without a final struggle. Fierce counter-attacks were launched and Lieuts. Matheson and Sturgeon were badly wounded. At 2.30 a.m. Lieut. Lister was ordered to take up reinforcements from "A" Co. and assume command of operations in Regina Trench, which he did with success. Such alarmist reports, however, continued to come in through the medium of casualties that at 4.15 General Odlum took charge of the operation himself and eased the situation by directing a well-sustained artillery fire against the massing Huns. It was during these counter-attacks that the majority of our casualties were incurred, the Hun maintaining a hail of shells on all our positions. The Regimental Aid Post, or Dressing Station, in the Red Chateau at the north end of Death Valley became the centre of a particularly fierce bombardment and a report reached Headquarters that all the occupants had been buried. A rescue party under Lieut. J. B. Bailey was hastily organized and went out armed with shovels, only to find that the report was luckily false. By morning positions had been consolidated and once more the 102nd Bn. had a fine achievement to its credit, as is shown by the following letter which was read out on parade in Albert on the 13th.

12-11-16.

"Dear Colonel Warden:—

"I want to congratulate you and through you all the officers and men of your battalion who took part in it, on last night's splendid operation. It was one of the best I have seen. The Divisional, Corps and Army Commanders also send their congratulations. Special commendation is due to Major Worsnop, Capt. Trousdale, Lieut. Lister, Lieut. Mackenzie and Lieut. Matheson. The 102nd Bn. has now carried out two successful operations and I am exceedingly proud of it. The battalion has already established a record to live up to.

"Sincerely,

"V. W. ODLUM,
"Commdg. 11th C.I.B."

For conspicuous services in the field, Lieut. Lister was awarded the Military Cross and Sergt. E. W. Holbrook the D.C.M., the latter storming single-handed a machine gun post, accounting for its defenders and capturing the weapon intact. To illustrate the dash and enthusiasm of the men and to emphasize the difficulties under which operations were carried out during that season of the year the following is recorded. As mentioned above, gum boots had been issued for use during the time that the men were in the trenches, but the mud was so deep and so sticky that the men literally had to pull their feet out of their boots and then their boots out of the mud. In the assault at least three men sprang to the charge leaving their boots sticking behind them and covered the ground to the opposing parapet and went over the latter in stockinged feet.

Such was the second successful operation of the 102nd Bn., who returned to Albert on the following evening, once more to reorganize and to await the next call to duty; nor did they have long to wait. On the 17th the battalion once more found itself encamped at Brigade Headquarters supplying working parties, and two days later orders were suddenly received to relieve the 75th Bn. in the front line. Two hours after receipt of the order the battalion with Lieut.-Colonel Warden in command ploughed its way in the gathering dusk through the familiar mud of Courcelette. The night was more than usually dark and the mud worse than ever; in consequence it was not until the early hours of the 20th that final relief was effected. This meant that the men had been struggling through natural difficulties for many hours before their real ordeal commenced. Throughout the coming tour of duty our men found the Germans even more active and aggressive than on previous occasions. Though there was no "going over the top" the tour was a heavy one. The battalion was beginning to feel exhausted before going in, and the long stretch of hard work under particularly galling conditions tried the men severely. Moreover a paralyzing blow had been sustained during the brief spell spent out of the front line; orders had been received from Brigade that for the future the rum issue for all units of the 11th Brigade would be discontinued. What gratuitous hardship this deprivation under conditions obtaining on the Somme entailed on the men no pen can describe; in wet and cold and mud rum is no longer "The Demon Rum; it is "The Life Saver," the one thing which restores the frozen circulation and combats the deadening chill. But the decree went forth and for four months spent in the raw and bitter Somme area and later on the wild and freezing slopes of Vimy Ridge the 11th Brigade struggled to its duties unsustained by the one drop of comfort which is laid down in K., R. & O. as a permissible issue. To add insult to injury hot soup was substituted which always came up the line over salt, increasing the thirst which even before was a recognized torture of a front line where water had to be hauled up on men's backs, and earning for the 11th Brigade the unenviable cognomen of "The Pea-Soup Brigade." May the Moral Reformer and the Teetotal Crank gain comfort to their souls by the reflection that for four months some 4,000 men had their hardships increased by the cruel enforcement of their bigoted doctrines. And these men were all volunteers.

For 96 hours the battalion remained in the trenches, working by night at the construction of a long communication trench running north-west from Regina to a trench known as Desire which had been captured on the 18th by units of the 4th Division, and withstanding by day very heavy shelling and persistent sniping. It was originally intended that this digging was to be but the prelude to another offensive which the 102nd would undertake, but it was found that the total length of the trench would have to be much greater than at first contemplated and that it would be impossible to get the work finished within the scheduled time. So the offensive was abandoned, but the battalion found that the work of digging was to tax its strength severely. For two nights work was maintained under heavy fire by the companies assisted by parties from the 67th Bn. and the Engineers, the men digging towards each other from either end and covered from surprise attacks by a screen of Scouts who on the first night with the co-operation of a carrying-party of the 67th succeeded in enclosing an enemy patrol which had wandered through their outposts and was successfully accounted for. Before dawn on the 22nd the trench was completed and on the evening of the 23rd the last tour on the Somme came to an end, the 102nd being relieved by the 47th Bn. and returning to billets in Albert with another fine piece of work to its credit. Our casualties numbered Major K. G. Mackenzie, O.C. "D" Co., and four O. R. killed; Major A. B. Carey, who had recently joined us from the 67th, and 40 O. R. wounded.

The tour on the Somme was now completed; at length the Division was to move and take up its position with the other three Divisions of the Canadian Corps on the slopes of Vimy and on Nov. 26th the battalion paraded for the last time in Albert and set out on a long six days' march to the new area, completely outfitted with Web equipment which had been issued in Albert to replace the old Oliver equipment which we had brought with us from Canada. The morning

ALBERT CEMETERY

of the 26th broke wet and it was through a dismal rain that we started off over the muddy roads which were crowded with traffic to our first halting place, Léonvillers, which we reached in the late afternoon. It was bitterly cold, and the billets were very poor; to add to our discomfort the Transport was held up by traffic, took a wrong turning and did not arrive with the kitchens until midnight. The following night one officer and nine men left on the first allotment of leave, which had come to us rather earlier than anticipated; but this allotment did not last long and it was late summer before leave opened at all generously. On Nov. 30th we left Léonvillers and marched nine miles to Authieule, leaving early on the next morning on a twelve-mile march to Noeux; here the greatest difficulty was encountered in obtaining sufficient fuel to cook the men's supper; Filleevres was our next objective, quite the pleasantest village we had visited since Tournehem and one capable of catering to the thirsty needs of men fresh from the line; another twelve miles saw us at Monchy on Dec. 3rd; a straggling village where the companies were widely dispersed; here we received a hundred reinforcements and so strengthened we faced the last spell of marching on a glorious frosty morning on Dec. 4th and covered twelve miles to La Comté, where good billets were provided against a prolonged stay. Here we may be said to have closed the chapter on the Somme preparatory to continuing our history on Vimy Ridge.

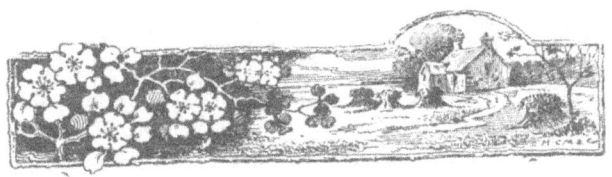

CHAPTER V.

Trench Tours on Vimy Ridge—Capture of Vimy Ridge—Road Building After the Victory—Arrival of the 67th Bn.—Two Tours in "The Triangle"—Concerning Moving Pictures.

FROM the beginning of 1917 throughout the series of operations which culminated in the capture of Vimy Ridge on April 9th the history of the 102nd Bn. is a story of preparation, progress and achievement. When the battalion entered the Vimy Sector the latter had a reputation for quietness and peace unequalled in any other sector; casualties were few; the awful slaughters of 1915 when French blood had flowed like water to gain the Ridge were a memory of the past. The later struggle when the British, to whom the Ridge had been handed over, failed through insufficient artillery to hold it against overwhelming odds backed by guns of every calibre, was almost forgotten. The Germans were now firmly and as they believed impregnably established on the crest of Vimy Ridge, whence they had complete observation of all the country lying to the south, whilst the British were entrenched on the southern slope leading down to Zouave Valley, every approach to which was in full view of the Hun. Supply trains had nightly to run the gauntlet of the enemy's fire and the situation had gradually settled down to the trench life of regular monotony which had featured the years of warfare since the Battle of the Aisne.

The operations of the 102nd Bn. which now entered the area are clearly divided into three distinct sections:—the first, a series of five tours in the trenches with six days' interval between each, lasting from Dec. 21st, 1916, to the end of March, 1917; the second, the ten-day tour which included the Battle of Vimy Ridge; the third, a series of three tours in the area lying between the crest of the Ridge and the suburbs of Lens, comprising the actions known in the battalion as the First and Second Triangle operations. When it is realised that the casualties for the first section only totalled 14 Other Ranks killed, and 1 Officer and 24 O. R. wounded, whilst the second was responsible for 6 Officers and 121 O. R. killed, 9 Officers and 185 O.R. wounded and 27 O. R. then reported missing, and the third for 5

Officers and 46 O. R. killed, 9 Officers and 239 O. R. wounded with 6 O. R. then reported missing, ·the increasing severity of the operations in this sector will be at once obvious.

It was not until Dec. 20th that the battalion entered into any active operations, and for fifteen days we lay at La Comté, thoroughly appreciating the rest and change after the arduous tour on the Somme and the heavy marching which had supervened. At best, however, La Comté was no village to write home about and during our stay the weather was for the most part so atrocious that it was only by comparison that our surroundings could be considered enjoyable. There was no form of recreation available, and the nearest town, Bruay, was too far distant to be of much practical use, besides being out of bounds. On the 9th the battalion went over there to use the miners' baths and the excellence of the accommodation was a revelation to most of us who had no idea that Industrial France was so up to date in this form of sanitation. Generally speaking sanitation is so much at a discount both in French and Belgian country districts that the public bathing facilities in the industrial areas always came as a pleasant surprise. On the occasion of this bathing parade we had experience of one of those curious anomalies which have always been such a feature of the British way of doing things. It was a pouring wet day and the men had to march five miles through the rain and mud to Bruay and ·back the same distance; on the return journey they met a large detachment of German prisoners being driven in motor trucks to take their periodical bath; the Soldiers of the King had to "hoof it"; the ex-soldiers of the Kaiser drove to their ablutions in state! Further comment is unnecessary. On the same night an anniversary dinner in honour of the inauguration of the battalion was held in the Officers' Mess and was attended by the Divisional and Brigade Commanders with their respective Staffs. During the following week we had three important visitations:—measles appeared in our midst, but fortunately there was no serious outbreak and prompt quarantine measures sufficed to hold the epidemic in check; the second event was the arrival of the ballot and those men who had not previously voted in England on "Prohibition" and "Woman's Suffrage" were privileged to register the votes which were never afterwards taken into account. It is a wonderful system which goes to the trouble and expense of registering votes which are later to be thrown out of court, but every country has its own peculiarities as we had ample opportunity of judging. Continental Europe has a penchant for advertising its manure heaps outside its private houses; Canada rather enjoys washing its dirty linen in public; it's merely a distinction without much difference. Thirdly, and this was the most important event, the Corps Commander, Lieut.-General Sir Julian H. C. Byng, K.C.B., K.C.M.G., M.V.O., visited the area and held a Decoration Parade at which some of the medals won on the Somme were presented to members of the 102nd after which the battalion "marched past."

On the 16th December Colonel Warden left the unit for a ten-day course at Boulogne, leaving Major Worsnop in command, and the following day saw the battalion in heavy marching order, enduring first a C. O.'s inspection and then a long Church Service. It is seriously open to doubt whether the cause of religion is furthered by the infliction of unnecessary physical discomforts, and to keep men standing long hours in bad weather heavily burdened with their full equipment savours more of the worship of the Devil than of the Prince of Peace. It certainly drives more men to the former than it leads to the latter.

On Dec. 20th our days of rest were numbered; no one was very sorry to leave La Comté and certainly nobody regretted saying farewell to the ancient chatelaine of the Chateau where Headquarters had been established, a virulent grand-dame with the disposition of a crab-apple and the tongue of a dyspeptic corncake. It was 7.00 a.m. when we fell in and marched off to Cambligneul, a rather large village ten miles away, where the Companies and Headquarters were billeted for the night, the Transport Lines proceeding three miles further to Gouy Servins, a hamlet which was to serve as our base for some weeks to come and in the neighbourhood of which we were to be quartered at intervals for another eighteen months. The following morning saw us on the way to the Forward Area where we were to relieve the 15th Bn. in Support in Cabaret Rouge, Headquarters being established on the Arras-Souchez road in view of Lens. Here we were temporarily attached to the First Division and for two days supplied working-parties. On Christmas Eve we were relieved by the 75th Bn. and marched back to Reserve in an oasis of mud known as Berthonval which we were to know well during the next six months. Our first view of Berthonval was our worst; it was dark when we arrived, rain was falling and the mud was treacnerous and slippery; accommodation was very bad. In course of time Berthonval was made into a good camp; for three months the same Brigade used the area and the battalions had a chance to make things rather more comfortable, but in the beginning it was bad. The whole of this area, Front Line, Support and Reserve, betrayed the grossest neglect by the units using it in the summer and autumn, no effort apparently having been made to put it in good shape for the winter. In this wilderness we spent our first Christmas "over there" and not even the small portion of plum-pudding which was served out at dinner could create any kind of a festive atmosphere. On the 27th we moved up to the Front Line and relieved the 54th Bn. on the northern side of Zouave Valley. The first view of this valley as approached through Wortley Trench was rather wonderful. The Ridge rises up behind it and the whole of the hillside facing the oncomer is honeycombed with dug-outs, the general effect calling to mind the pictures of the Cave-dwellers of Central America. The Ridge itself was a marvel of engineering; it was pierced here and there with tunnels, each having extensive ramifications; a light railway ran down the valley on its southern slope; water was piped to it across miles of open country. It sometimes seemed as though the Hun was so confident that it could never be captured that he was willing to allow any reasonable operations to be carried on without too much interference on his part, just so as to keep his enemies busy and incapable of doing him mischief elsewhere.

To a battalion with previous experience on two other fronts the first tour in a new area was naturally of peculiar interest; but when all is said and done, there was not much to choose in Front Line work. If the mud in the Salient was stickier, the mud on the Somme was deeper, and that at Vimy was remarkably like both varieties, though it had a tendency to dry up quicker. The scenery was certainly better than that on the Somme and the local inhabitants were certainly pleasanter than those we had first met in Flanders, but the Front Line trenches and the work involved by their occupation remained the same; so many days in Support, furnishing working parties, so many in Reserve, furnishing working-parties, and so many more in the Front Line itself, mounting guard, manning posts, sending out patrols, ever in readiness to resist attack, subjected to Fritz' Hymn of Hate, whenever he felt like hating, and, so as not to lose the habit, furnishing working-parties. Then, after the 18-day tour, a tramp back from mud up to the thighs, through mud up to the knees, to mud well over the ankles. The six-day rest was always a gamble; the battalion might be sent to a town where eggs and chips could be bought and where estaminets, as the local "pubs" are called, provided a little refreshment in the shape of beer or stout; or it might be sent to one of the rest camps provided, isolated huts in a sea of mud, with one Y.M.C.A. tent providing the sole form of recreation for two or more battalions.

Our first rest, on Jan. 2nd, took us to Camblain L'Abbé, one of the many villages in the rear of the Allied positions and all very much alike. Divisional Headquarters were established in Camblain L'Abbé and perhaps it was one of the best villages in the area from the point of view of the "egg and chip" fiend, but the Divisional baths there were particularly vile; the Diary for its entry of Jan. 3rd states: "Bathing parade; by far the worst managed and most insanitary baths yet encountered; very little water, very thinly sprinkled; both time and water insufficient for the men to cleanse themselves. Underclothing insufficient and not properly sterilised." Such extracts may appear in the light of a comedy nearly three years after the event, but they more nearly approached the narration of a tragedy when they were originally penned. During this first week the battalion was reinforced by a draft of 195 men who were formed into an "E" Co. and underwent special training under Brigade.

The second tour in Vimy differed little from the first save in the location of the Support area which was changed to a series of trenches known generally by the name of "Music-Hall," the subsidiary trenches being named after well-known London music-halls, most certainly an instance of "lucus a non lucendo," for the only music heard was the humming of aeroplanes and the whistling of shells; this Support position was located on the ridge bounding the south of Zouave Valley. During all tours in this area one company of the battalion in support was sent forward to be attacked as a working-party to the battalion in the front line. The weather grew steadily colder, but this was a welcome change; the days were bright and clear and the frost kept the trenches clear of mud. Our second tour came to an end on Jan. 26 when the battalion marched out before noon to Villers-au-Bois, a ruined village whose only feature of interest was the big cemetery, where wagons were waiting to take the men's kits; our destination was Coupigny, eleven miles from the Front Line, and a hot meal was served at Villers before the men continued on the long tramp to billets. Coupigny deserves a new paragraph to itself, but it is necessary first to make some digression and relate various important changes which were made in the personnel of the Battalion Staff during the early part of 1917.

On Dec. 31st Major C. B. Worsnop, D.S.O., was notified that he had been appointed to the temporary command of the 50th Bn. and on that day he left the 102nd. This officer was later transferred to the command of the 75th Bn. which he commanded on April 9th, subsequently being transferred to England where he eventually took over the command of the 16th Reserve Battalion at Seaford. His place as Second-in-Command was taken by Major A. B. Carey, who had joined us from the 67th during the Somme operations where he had been wounded, and on Feb. 14th the latter succeeded to the Acting Command of the battalion owing to the absence of Colonel Warden, who was struck down by paratyphoid and sent to the South of France for treatment. This position Major Carey held until Colonel Warden's return at the close of the great battle on Easter Monday, his own duties as Second being taken over by Major F. Lister, M.C. The Adjutant throughout practically the whole of the Vimy Ridge tours was Capt. J. B. Bailey, with Lieut. J. L. Lloyd, who had been granted a commission at the end of December as Assistant Adjutant. The four Company Commanders of "A," "B," "C" and "D" Coys. respectively were Major F. Lister, succeeded by Lieut. J. H. Wilson, Major J. F. Brandt, succeeded by Lieut. E. L. Peers, Major R. G. H. Brydon and Major H. B. Scharschmidt, succeeded by Lieut. H. G. Dimsdale. Capt. N. M. McNeill who had come over with the unit as Medical Officer had been invalided sick in the Somme, and his place taken by Capt. L. B. Graham, who, on going sick, made way for Capt. Woodley, who was in his turn relieved by Major W. Bapty, of Victoria, B.C., on March 12th. Major Bapty had already seen active service with the 2nd C.M.R., having joined that unit as a combatant officer and later transferring to the C.A.M.C. Major Bapty remained as M. O. with the 102nd Bn. for eight months, and was twice wounded in that time, being finally invalided to England in consequence of a wound received at Passchendaele. It may be permitted here to remark that in addition to being a first-class M.O. he was a most inveterate souvenir hunter and if only a reasonable percentage of his packages reached their destination he must now have a most wonderful collection of battlefield junk. The duties of Quartermaster were largely undertaken by Lieut. R. Fitzmaurice acting for Capt. Stead who was under medical care during the greater part of this period.

Coupigny, whither we repaired on Jan. 26th, was by far the best place in which we had yet been billeted; it could be dignified by the name of a town; it was really a double-barrelled affair and was more correctly known as Hersin-Coupigny, Hersin being the town at the south-western end, stretching away to the coal mines at Noeux-les-Mines, and Coupigny lying nearer to our own front; the two being connected by a long street. At Coupigny good hut accommodation was provided, though on the occasion of our first visit the cold was so intense and fuel so scarce that it was difficult to keep warm enough to sleep. But for the first time since we had landed in France we had a real town to look at and spend money in and the change was exceedingly welcome. Later on the Transport Lines were to move down from Gouy Servins and take up quarters in Hersin, an inconvenient arrangement from the point of view of transport as there was a very bad hill leading out of Coupigny which entailed a very severe strain on the horses. But Hersin was a far better permanent base than Gouy, concerning which some description will be given later.

The third tour in the line, which started on Feb. 1st, was marked by increasing aerial activity, in which the enemy generally seemed to hold the advantage; one little red machine of his was particularly noticeable and scored victory after victory. The artillery work on both sides increased in volume throughout this tour and four raids, two by the 72nd Bn., one by the 38th, and another by the 10th Brigade were staged. An incident occurred on the night of Feb. 17th, which might have had very serious results for the battalion. A supply of gas was being brought up to Zouave Valley for use in a big gas attack planned for the end of the month; the gas came up as usual in big cylinders transported by the mule team over the light railway; just as the train came into the 102nd area the Hun opened up a fierce bombardment of the valley with whizz-bangs which fell all round the train, causing several casualties and killing two of the mules, but not one of the dangerous cylinders was touched. On the conclusion of the third tour, on Feb. 19th, the unit returned to Coupigny Huts.

The fourth tour did not open until the 1st March though we had all expected to move up as usual after six days. The reason for this delay was the postponement of the gas attack referred to above which was rendered inevitable by the wind conditions. The 54th and 75th Bns. had been scheduled to take part in the raid which was to follow the projection of the gas and these two units had to remain in the line until the wind was favourable; meantime the 102nd was ordered to "stand to" in rest billets ready to move up at a moment's notice. On the last night of the month the attack and raid were delivered and, though successful from a military standpoint, entailed disastrous results to the two battalions of the 11th Bde. concerned. The gas hung low on the area over which it had been projected and when the time came for the raid it had not been sufficiently dispersed; moreover the enemy in anticipation of this "follow-up" swept the gassed area with his fire, with the result that the 54th and 75th suffered heavily in casualties which included Lieut.-Col. Kemball and Lieut.-Col. Beckett, commanding the two units respectively. On the following day the 102nd moved into reserve at Berthonval, the delay slightly altering the usual routine, and remained there till the 7th, when it moved into the Front Line, relieving the 87th and taking over the positions usually embraced by both the 11th and 12th Brigades. The Front Line trenches were in bad shape; the retaliatory bombardment by the enemy had merged Sombart and Snargate trenches into one and a great deal of hard work was needed to put the area into a safe condition. This was our "job" till the 11th, when we moved back to rest in what was perhaps the worst camp outside of Vadincourt that we ever visited, Bouvigny Huts. It was a nine-mile march to this camp, which was situated in a wood on a hill above Gouy Servins; the weather was bad, the mud intense, the accommodation crowded: the 87th shared the camp with us and for eight days we lingered there with no recreation other than that afforded by one Y.M.C.A. hut which was always packed to the doors. It is a positive fact that man after man when out at rest under these conditions would emphatically declare that he was looking forward to going up the line again because life in the trenches was less irksome and monotonous and no more beastly than in places like Bouvigny Huts. This is merely a statement of fact and not a criticism of the organization: in view of the number of troops to be looked after and the limited possibilities of accommodation in the whole of the shell-shocked area round Vimy we were lucky not to be sleeping on the ground; but the statement is made to show that life behind the lines was not lived out upon a bed of roses. On the 19th, we moved forward again for our fifth tour, the principal object of which was the digging of a new front line trench; all the trenches were in bad condition, but few men could be spared for maintenance work, and throughout the tour every effort was concentrated on the successful completion of the task assigned. Two days after our entry into the Forward Area our spirits were cheered and our bodies refreshed by the re-appearance of the rum issue. Reference has already been made to the stopping of this issue in the 11th Brigade, and now at long last the restriction was removed, largely owing, it is believed, to the representations of medical authorities, although it was also realized that discipline was threatened when men of one brigade were thus penalized, though working in juxtaposition with men of other brigades who were permitted to enjoy the issue. On the 25th the new trench was completed, and on the following day the Battalion was relieved by the 54th, "A" and "B" Companies, with Headquarters, moving to St. Lawrence Camp at

Chateau de la Haie, "C" and "D" Companies remaining at Berthonval, under Major Lister, to provide working-parties; these Companies exchanged positions on the 30th.

This was our first experience of the newly-constructed camps in the grounds of the Chateau de la Haie. The latter was a fine stone building standing in beautiful park grounds which had been taken over by the Allies for military purposes. For very many months it was used for Brigade Headquarters by the Divisions operating in the Vimy sector, and in the surrounding grounds there sprang up four camps, known as St. Lawrence, Niagara, Canada, and Vancouver. A good bath-house was constructed at the bottom of the slope leading down from the Chateau, and later in the year a fine theatre was built. During the summer the camps around the Chateau were pleasant enough, but in the early days of their being, when the weather was inclement and the accommodation limited they suffered badly from the mud, which was always well over the boot-tops and frequently engulfed a man to the knees. It was to St. Lawrence Camp that the 102nd Bn. came on the completion of the fifth tour, which also saw the end of the first section of operations on Vimy Ridge. It must not be imagined that because this first section has been dismissed with scant reference to the sterner side of war that the Battalion had been having an easy time during the first three months of 1917. It is true that casualties had been few, but the work throughout the five tours had been hard and unceasing, and the discomforts of trench life had been encountered in their most exaggerated form. The trenches, when not frozen, had been frequently flooded and were always full of mud; vermin were at their worst, and these conditions had produced an epidemic of myalgia, violent and unremitting pains, principally in the legs; except in very severe cases, however, where a high temperature obtained, this malady did not excuse a man from duty. Trench feet, fortunately, were unknown on Vimy Ridge, owing to unremitting attention which ensured nightly rubbing of the feet with whale oil, and a plentiful supply of socks, for which all thanks are due to the women of Canada. It had been a hard, hard winter, but the 102nd had won through and found itself ready at the end of March to carry out the second section of operations which culminated in the glorious victory of Easter Monday.

§ii.

The second section opened with half the Battalion at rest in St. Lawrence Camp and the other half located at Berthonval, whence parties were furnished nightly to the front line to dig an Assembly Trench for the impending major operation. A training course was taped out in the grounds of the Chateau showing the exact positions of the objectives to be taken in the grand assault, and the men rehearsed "going over" wearing the battalion equipment which they would be carrying on the day itself. Nothing was left to chance. By the time that the Battalion was ordered into the trenches, not only the commissioned and non-commissioned officers, but every individual man, knew what he had to do and when he had to do it. This training was carried on under very trying weather conditions, which grew worse each day, ending with a heavy snowstorm on April 2nd, which gradually assumed the proportions of a blizzard on the following day. Through this the Battalion went forward on April 3rd, leaving the camp at 9.30 a.m., "A" and "B" Companies going straight through to Cavalier Tunnel, "D" Company with Headquarters moving as far as Music Hall and "C" Company being posted in Berthonval Wood. The next six days saw an ever-increasing artillery fire from our own batteries, with such feeble response from the Hun that grave fears were entertained lest he were already retiring from the Ridge in his own time. On April 6th our artillery started wire-cutting, but weather conditions were such that the hour for attack, which had been set for 5.30 a.m. on April 8th, was postponed for twenty-four hours. It was not, therefore, until noon on the 8th that the whole Battalion assembled in the long caves and tunnels running from Zouave Valley to the front line on which the men had worked so laboriously for the past three months. Here they rested until 8.30 p.m., when the four Company commanders, Lieut. J. H. Wilson, Lieut. E. J. Peers, Major R. G. H. Brydon and Lieut. H. G. Dimsdale, reported to the Acting C.O. for final instructions; these were given and then the companies left for their appointed positions. In the forthcoming operation the 102nd Bn. was supported by the 54th, which was to pass through the former when the first objectives had been taken, thus pushing the attack further home. On the left flank was the 87th Bn., similarly supported by the 75th. On the right lay the 42nd Bn., a connecting link between the 102nd and the "Princess Pats."

All was now in readiness. It was past midnight, and the dawn of Easter Monday would see "Warden's Warriors" in the thick of the biggest fight in which they had yet been engaged. Outside the weather had grown steadily colder, and when at the stroke of 5.30 a.m. the barrage opened, a driving snow was falling. It was just light enough to see, and within five minutes observers came down to report that the men of the 102nd had gone over as one man in perfect formation. The first report from the front line was brought by a "D" Coy. runner, who brought the news that Lieut. H. G. Dimsdale had been wounded in hand and leg, and in a few minutes that officer appeared en route for the Dressing Station. He stated that the wire had been crossed and that the enemy front line trench had been won. At 6.00 a.m. Lieut. H. M. Bennett, walking wounded and bringing in a prisoner, reported that the second line of trenches had been gained, and forty minutes later Lieut. J. Robbins, also wounded, brought in the news that the Hun had lost his third line of trenches. The 102nd had already captured its three objectives, but it remained for the positions to be consolidated and held against the fierce counter-attacks which were certain to develop. The Scout Officer, Lieut.

E. J. B. Fallis, was accordingly sent up to report on this consolidation, as there were rumours that on the right things were not going well; at this time the left flank appeared to be well protected. Before he could reach the line, however, two Runners from "D" Co. came in with the news that we had by this time established two strong points of our own well forward, and had in addition, by a clever circling movement, captured an enemy strong-point on the left of Broadmarsh Crater. No officers, however, were to be seen anywhere; all had become casualties, and the active command of the Battalion in front had devolved on C. S. M. Russell, of "C" Coy., whilst Sgt. D. S. Georgeson, M.M., was holding the Broadmarsh Crater strong-point with a platoon. It now appeared that the 54th, who in accordance with orders had passed through our ranks, had been compelled to fall back and were holding the new front line in conjunction with our men against the massing Hun. Moreover, the affair was not progressing well on our left; the 87th Bn. had not yet gained its objectives, with the result that our flank was in the air and being exposed to terrible sniping. At 9.00 a.m. the Scout Officer reported that consolidation had been completed, but almost immediately afterwards news was received that he had been killed and that C.S.M. Russell had been seriously wounded. In view of the serious aspect of the case, Major Carey obtained permission from Brigade Headquarters to go up in person and reconnoitre the position for himself. Accompanied by Scout-Sergt. F. B. Vogel, who was killed "en route," and Pte. J. A. Hall, of the Battalion Runners, he left Headquarters at 9.30 a.m., returning after three hours, satisfied that the Battalion was securely dug in. But the sniping was terrific, being mainly directed from Hill 145 on the left, and supplies of bombs and S.A.A. were urgently needed at the front. A carrying-party under Lieut. S. F. Knight, the Battalion Lewis Gun Officer, was accordingly organized, and after four attempts this band contrived to win their way through with the required ammunition. During the balance of the day the situation remained unchanged, the men lying well under cover, and at 6.30 p.m. the 85th Bn. captured Hill 145, whence so much of our danger had come, and thereafter, to a large extent, sniping ceased. At 7:30 p.m. Major Lister arrived at Headquarters from the Transport Lines with the news that Col. Warden had returned and would be up in the morning. Major Lister then went up to the front and remained there all night.

The battle, so far as the 102nd was concerned, was over; the victory won. The Hun had left the Ridge he had held so long and retreated across the flat ground on the other side towards the outskirts of Lens, where he had another line of defence. It but remained to count the spoils and calculate the cost—alas, a heavy one. Our casualties for the day were as follows:—Killed: Major R. G. H. Brydon, Lieuts. R. A. Stalker, E. J. B. Fallis, D. A. Boyes and 113 Other Ranks, with 27 Other Ranks reported missing. Died of wounds: Lieuts. J. H. Wilson, A. Lineham, and 6 Other Ranks. Wounded: Lieuts. J. Robbins, H. G. Dimsdale, H. M. Bennett, R. S. Wright, W. L. Frame, E. L. Peers, A. C. Buchan, H. T. M. Love, E. G. Lester and 180 Other Ranks. The spoils of war consisted of 119 prisoners; 1 Minnenwerfer; 4 Bomb Throwers; 2 Machine Guns.

Dawn broke with snow on the ground; on our own front the day was absolutely uneventful. There was some hope of being relieved that night, but it was finally decided that relief would take place on the morrow. At 10:30 a.m. on April 11th orders were received to move back to St. Lawrence Camp, our place being taken for 24 hours by the 54th Bn. against the arrival of Imperials. The march back to camp was undertaken in the teeth of a heavy snowstorm, which added another hardship to be borne by the already exhausted men, and on arrival we found that accommodation was extremely limited, the whole area being packed with troops. It was the intention that the men should have a thorough rest on the following day. but this was frustrated by sudden orders received to march up to Souchez, in the 10th Brigade area, and support that Brigade. In the then depleted state of the Battalion it was found possible to assemble only 360 effectives, and at 2.00 p.m. that number moved out under the command of Col. Warden. The conditions that prevailed at the Souchez end of the valley were at that time unknown to us, and in consequence the 102nd performed an hitherto unattempted feat in crossing over the duck-walk at Souchez in broad daylight. That no casualties occurred was not the fault of the German gunners, but due to the mud; that treacherous element on this occasion served the Battalion well, as the high-explosive shells buried themselves so deeply in the ooze that the effect of their explosion was neutralized.

Headquarters were established in Souchez Tunnel, a subterranean sewer, but always ankle-deep and more often knee-deep with water instead of sewage. The Battalion Orderly Room was a fair-sized chamber raised above water level, but as it had also to serve the four Battalions of the 10th Brigade our own Headquarters Staff was neither welcome nor needed, seeing that the 102nd was divided up into two Companies, and attached to the 44th and 46th Bns. respectively. These Companies, were, however, largely self-dependent: the 10th Brigade Runners were incapable of leading them in to their positions, and it was only due to the wonderful sagacity of our own Battalion Runners that the men ever found their rightful locations: moreover, the 102nd had to depend on itself to secure rations and munitions; these were at Rugby Dump, a far journey through the mud of a winding trench. It is to the lasting credit of the 102nd Battalion Runners, under Cpl. J. McHugh, M.M., and the limited number of Pioneers present under Cpl. C. B. Kirby, that the men in the trenches had supplies brought to them. The companies were too weak, both physically and numerically, to form ration parties, and it was left to the Runners, mere boys for the most part, reinforced by the three or four Pioneers present, to go backwards and forwards, heavily laden with food and ammunition; and this in addition to the ordinary Runners' duties, always a hard and perilous task in the front line, and rendered doubly so in the present case, as the territory was strange and unsurveyed by them and the enemy artillery and machine-gun fire was particularly vicious. Most welcome orders to move back were received at noon on the following day, the 13th April, and the attenuated Battalion came out of the line by platoons, but the men were so exhausted that they had to be permitted to make their own way back to camp, and from 6.00 p.m. till after midnight they straggled into St. Lawrence Camp, there to find sleeping accommodation wherever there was room in a hut to squeeze in. The Artillery was moving up as fast as possible, and every available inch of covered space in camp was at a premium. It was, however, for only one night that these conditions prevailed, as on the next day we moved out in small parties to excellent billets in Cambligneul, the village where we had stayed one night on our first entry into the Vimy sector.

§iii.

We come now to the third section of operations, viz.: three tours of duty north of the Ridge, and on the outskirts of Lens prior to the street fighting in the latter town, which will form the subject of another chapter. The first essential after the capture of the Ridge was the construction of roads for the passage of heavy artillery, and on April 21st the Battalion moved forward to a newly-formed camp at La Targette to do its share in this important task. It seemed wonderful to be out in the open on ground which had so recently been the home of the Hun, whence he had directed his devastating fire on all the ground south of the Ridge. Where formerly we had crawled in trenches we now gaily marched overland, and we could also see for ourselves what wonderful observation he had enjoyed of all that had taken place in our area during the past months. From April 21st to May 6th the Battalion was engaged in road-making. The 18-pounders had already gone forward, but every available ounce of man-power was needed to pave a way for the "Heavies." Signallers, clerks, batmen and others usually exempt from such "Fatigues" were pressed into the service; the Transport Lines were combed again and again. By such means, and by the addition of the Brigade Machine Gun Co. and the Brigade Tump-line Section, the 102nd was enabled to supply 600 men daily to the Engineers. The work ,though arduous, was fairly safe, and only two casualties, wounded, were reported during this period. On April 24th we moved camp back to a new location just forward of our old Berthonval quarters. The new camp, later christened Comox Camp, lay on a down-like expanse of ground which had not been too badly cut up by shell-fire nor churned into mud during wet weather; water for all purposes had to be hauled a considerable distance and very rigid economy had to be exercised in its distribution, but that was a disadvantage to which we had all been long accustomed. The weather was fine, and during the evenings we were able to enjoy the Battalion Band, whilst in the distance could be seen that famous land-mark, the ruined tower of Mt. St. Eloy About this time the Transport Lines were moved from Hersin to Carency.

On May 2nd the 102nd Bn. was enriched by a large contingent of 30 officers and 260 Other Ranks from the 67th (Pioneer) Battalion, which had been broken up for reason political to make room for the 124th (Pioneer) Battalion, an Eastern aggregation. It was a sad blow to befall a very fine Battalion with nine months' service in France to its credit, but it was pure gain to the 102nd, which received a most welcome number of the finest kind of reinforcements. With this draft came the Pipe Band under Pipe-Major W. J. Wishart. It had long been Col. Warden's dream to have a Pipe Band; whilst at Bordon we had enjoyed (or otherwise, according to our musical disposition) the services of the Pipe Band of the 74th Bn., but we had been unable to retain this; now we had Pipers of our own, though eventually they had to be disbanded owing to establishment restrictions. Numbered amongst these newcomers was Piper James Wallace, of Victoria, a veteran of the Zulu War of 1879, who on a later occasion had the honour of receiving a personal salute from H.R.H. the Duke of Connaught, who singled him out when the massed bands of the Corps played before him at Camblain L'Abbé.

On May 6th we moved back still further to Canada Camp, there remaining until the evening of the 10th, when the Battalion fell in and marched off to relieve the 47th Bn. in support on the Vimy-Angres line, with Headquarters in a commodious concrete dug-out in the railway embankment. One platoon per company was detailed to report to the 50th Bn. in the front-line trenches, which had been hastily constructed and were both shallow and exposed, with the result that casualties were heavy. On the following night we relieved the 50th, a difficult operation, as owing to some misunderstanding we had to find our own positions; in reconnoitring "A" Coy.'s position Lieut. C. G. Huggins ran into a German patrol of six men whom he successfully put to flight; a very brilliant young officer who, alas, fell a casualty during the tour. This tour, which is generally referred to as "The First Triangle," afforded nothing spectacular in the way of operations, but much good work was done in improving the front line, with the result that on handing over to the 78th on the 20th the latter unit found a line of trenches well dug, straightened and secure. The morning of the 18th was marked by a minor operation to be carried out by "D" Coy. in co-operation with the 87th on our right. The 139th Brigade on our left was putting on a raid, and under cover of a feint barrage on our front "D" Coy. was to establish a post 100 yards in advance of our line; the 87th on the right were to do the same and connect with our men. Unfortunately the latter Battalion failed to succeed, and instead of finding them connecting on the right,

"D" Coy. found the Hun attacking from the rear and flank; our men drove back the enemy, but were compelled to abandon the post. On the 20th we were relieved in the front line by the 78th, and in support by the 85th, the Battalion marching back to Vancouver Camp, Chateau de la Haie. The shelling throughout the tour had been heavy, with the result that casualties were numerous, Lieuts. C. G. Huggins, C. de West, J. S. Rodgerson and 21 Other Ranks being killed, and Lieut. J. E. Manning with 92 Other Ranks being wounded.

On the day on which we came out of the line R.S.M. Long, who had filled the position of Regimental Sergeant-Major since the inception of the unit, left the Battalion to take up a position with Division; he was later appointed an Instructor in the Corps School, thereafter being transferred to England to fill an important position at Bexhill. His last act before leaving was to organize a Sergeants' Mess, which up to that time had always been found to be an impracticable institution, owing to the impossibility of obtaining accommodation, and on May 23rd, for the first time since leaving England, a Sergeants' Mess was inaugurated. The retiring R.S.M. was succeeded in his duties by C.S.M. Mirams, who had joined the unit on the 2nd inst. from the 67th and was later confirmed in his new rank. On the 24th Col. Warden took over the duties of Brigadier, owing to the absence of Brig.-General V. W. Odlum on leave, and Major F. Lister and Major H. B. Scharschmidt were appointed temporary C.O. and Second-in-Command respectively, Major A. B. Carey having left the 102nd on the 22nd inst. to take over the command of the 54th. On the 28th the Battalion moved up to Comox Camp.

The fortnight which elapsed between the operations known as those of "The First and Second Triangle" was spent in very severe training for the strenuous fighting which the second operation was to entail. The forthcoming tour was to see the 102nd for the first time at grips with the Hun, swaying back and forth before winning the gage of victory. In previous offensives victory had been "rushed" and some period of time afforded for consolidation before the counter-attack developed; the Second Triangle was to see fierce hand-to-hand fighting before the victory could be counted sure. Careful rehearsals of the proposed operations over a taped-out course were carried out; a miniature out-door map of the enemy's positions was constructed by the Engineers and elaborately explained to all ranks, and it was a well-instructed unit that moved up the line on June 3rd under the command of Col. Warden, who had been relieved of his duties as Acting-Brigadier by the return of General Odlum.

Three important tasks were set the Battalion on this tour; one was to capture and mop up the series of trenches known as "The Triangle"; the second to capture a strong-point consisting of a concrete machine-gun emplacement set in the railway embankment and formidably protected; the third to capture, consolidate and hold a line east of the Generating Station, establishing thereby a new front line.

All these tasks were eventually accomplished, but not without bitter and fierce fighting. On June 5th, "D" Coy., under Major H. B. Scharschmidt, under cover of a rifle grenade and machine-gun barrage, managed to occupy the Generating Station and advance in the direction of the Brewery and the suburb of Leaurette, but this success was offset by the failure of two attempts to capture the strong point referred to; the Battalion also sustained a serious loss in the gassing of Major Scharschmidt, who was so severely affected as to be permanently invalided out of France. A third attempt to capture the strong-point on the 7th failed of its purpose. On the following day two important operations were carried out. No. 6 Platoon of "B" Coy., under Lieut. G. Lowrie, was detailed to attack "The Triangle" and to hand same over to the 5th Leicesters on our left. The attack took place at 8.30 p.m., and at the first assault Lieut. Lowrie was killed, his place being taken by Lieut. J. G. Knight; under a hail of machine-gun bullets and high-explosive shells the men cut through the wire and bombed their way to the enemy positions; the resistance encountered was very stubborn, but "The Triangle" was eventually captured, together with 15 unwounded prisoners, and handed over to the Leicesters, and No. 6 Platoon returned to its starting-point. Throughout this operation visibility had been hampered by smoke, both from the barrage and from a burning coal dump in Fosse 3, but the affair had been brilliantly conceived and as brilliantly carried out, earning the following commendation from the Brigadier addressed to the C.O.: "Please convey to Lieut. Knight my sincere appreciation of the work he did on the night of the 8th inst. The operation in "The Triangle" was as brilliant as anything I have seen in France." The second operation did not commence until 11:45 p.m. This was an attack on the whole Battalion frontage, with the intention of capturing and consolidating enemy positions, establishing a new front line and mopping up all enemy dug-outs between the Generating Station and Souchez River. "A" Coy. and one platoon of "C" Coy., under Maj. R. J. Burde, M.C., were detailed for this task. "C" Coy.'s platoon managed to get round the wire, but "A" Coy. found the wire impassable and, in spite of a second heroic attempt under Sgt. Z. Kirby, who rallied the men in a desperate endeavour to penetrate to the enemy's position, the troops had to be recalled to their jumping-off place and to consolidate there. Two hours later the disheartening news was received that the Leicesters had been forced out of "The Triangle," which was once more in German hands. The main objects of the two operations had not been successful, but the enemy dug-outs had been thoroughly bombed and enormous casualties had been inflicted. The balance of the day, June 9th, was quiet; hardly a shot was fired, but plans were being formulated for another attack on the 10th. Again the attack took a dual form. A platoon of "A" Coy., under Lieut. C. S. Griffin, was ordered to capture, mop up and hold a trench known as "Calico-Candle" to its junction with Canada trench, and to carry out the same operation with Canada trench; the first part of this plan was successfully carried out, but Canada trench was found to be nonexistent, having been completely demolished by shell fire and affording no sort of cover against a tempest of shot; further advance was impossible. The second attack was directed against the concrete gun-emplacement which had already resisted three attempts at capture, and took the form of a stealth raid by a bombing section of "B" Coy., under Sgt. A. Law. Unfortunately whilst proceeding down the embankment on the way to the attack he touched a trap wire which exploded a small mine, arousing the enemy to a sense of his danger; the surprise element had failed and our men had to retire under cover of rifle and rifle-grenade fire and a Stokes gun barrage which caused heavy casualties to the enemy. June 11th was a comparatively quiet day, an inter-company relief taking place, but "D" Coy. contrived to advance its line 75 yards along Candle trench until contact with the enemy was made, when a bombing fight ensued and a new strong-point was established there. In the meantime preparations were made for a final offensive on the 12th, the main object of which was to capture the concrete strong-point, and to effect a union with the Lincolns, who had replaced the Leicesters on the left and were to retake "The Triangle." At 7.00 a.m. an intense barrage was laid down and a platoon of "A" Coy., under Lieut Griffin, assaulted the emplacement and captured it, together with two machine-guns and 16 prisoners, inflicting at the same time very heavy casualties on the defenders. Strong counter-attacks were delivered by the Hun, and Lieut. Griffin's party was reinforced from "B" Coy., with the result that all the enemy's efforts were in vain, the strong-point remained in our possession and connection was established with the Lincolns, who had stormed through "The Triangle" and effected a junction at the point designated. Towards midnight relief was effected by the 85th Bn., and the 102nd moved out to Vancouver Camp.

Such, in brief, is the story of "The Second Triangle" tour, one of the most brilliant, as it was one of the most strenuous, in the history of the 102nd Bn. In nine days the Battalion, or some substantial part of it, had "gone over the top" six times; in the face of desperate resistance it had eventually carried out all the tasks assigned to it, and in addition to immeasurably strengthening the Canadian positions in the area it had inflicted incredible casualties on the enemy. But our own losses were found to be very heavy. Lieuts. E. J. Norwood and G. Lowrie and 25 Other Ranks were killed; Major H. B. Scharschmidt. Major W. Bapty, Lieuts. L. A. Gritten, M. A. M. Marsden, C. S Griffin, S. J. L. Chalifour, F. Richardson and 145 Other Ranks were wounded, whilst six Other Ranks were reported missing, making a total of 185 casualties out of the 563 effectives who went into the line.

For the benefit of many who believe that the moving-pictures taken under the auspices of the Canadian Records Office are "faked" it may here be related that during this tour the official photographer

ON VIMY RIDGE

appeared at Battalion Headquarters one evening an hour before a double offensive was due. He had been sent up in view of the importance of these operations, and requested to be forwarded up the line. The C.O. promptly detailed Major E. J. Ryan to take him up to "D" Coy.'s Headquarters, and he was subsequently posted in "No Man's Land" beside the Power Station, where he established himself with his camera. When the action started the shelling was so terrific on both sides that it was impossible to see ten yards in any direction, dry mud was being blown from two to thre hundred feet in the air, and this, with the smoke, made everything as dark as night. He was therefore unable to take any pictures and returned to Headquarters, merely remarking that there was rather warm work going on up there, about the hottest he had yet been in, and that if the 102nd got through they were heroes every one of them. Fifteen months later we met this same photographer during the offensive of September 2nd, 1918, when the Hindenburg Switch line was in process of being smashed.

This concludes the story of the series of operations conducted by the 102nd Bn. in the Vimy Sector; though we were constantly in the same area, subsequent oerations are referred to under other designations. For over five months and a half we had fought along the Ridge, and now on its crest stand two monuments closely inscribed with names; one is erected to the memory of those brave men who laid down their lives during the long months of preparation or during the three tours which succeeded the great victory of April 9th, 1917: the other to those who fell on the day of the great victory itself. On one or other are inscribed the names of all who made the Supreme Sacrifice from the date of our entry into the Vimy Sector to the conclusion of the battle of the Second Triangle.

CHAPTER VI.

Divisional Rest at Gouy Servins—Street Fighting in Lens—Growth of Carency—South of Avion

CEASELESS round of active duties had been engaging the 102nd Bn. for six months; the unit was now to enjoy six weeks of comparative rest, prior to carrying out a series of operations on the outskirts and in the suburbs of Lens. This rest opened on June 13th in Vancouver Camp, where we remained for six days, moving up to Comox Camp on the 19th, and finally back to the Chateau in Gouy Servins on July 1st. For the most part the weather was good, and the whole countryside was looking its best at that time of the year; the woods and grounds surrounding Chateau de la Haie were a veritable Paradise after the conditions under which we had been living for so long, and the long rest in June and July, followed by a second and shorter one during the middle of September, stand out in welcome relief to the general sordid nature of our surroundings. Of Gouy Servins but little has yet been said, but it had gradually been assuming a position of importance, both as being the nearest village to the camps at the Chateau de la Haie and as being a supply assembly point on the narrow-guage railway which served the Lens front. In the middle of the village is the usual village pond, artificially constructed and filled with the semi-stagnant water which seems to characterize all the village ponds in France. An enormous Chateau is the principal feature of the place, a building large enough to accommodate two battalions with sleeping quarters and boasting grounds which gave every accommodation for parades, messes, theatres, and all the outside buildings which spring up in the vicinity of every camp. During the summer Gouy Servins proved an ideal resting-place. The inhabitants by this time had come to know the members of the 11th Brigade well and regarded us with affection. There were village belles, of whom perhaps the fair Josephine will linger longest in the memory; there were village estaminets and various private establishments where wines and beer could be purchased by those who came armed with a fitting introduction (What sweet memories in these days of Canadian drought cling around the portals of No. 7!) and there were village shops where the odd biscuit or tin of fruit could be bought. There was no great craving when out

of the line for the bright lights of theatre or "movie" palace; it was good enough to wander quietly through the country lanes, or quaff the country wines and just appreciate the joys of peace and quietness when leisure permitted.

There was, however, a good deal of work done during those days. The mornings were devoted to training, especially to the perfecting of the "Tactical Platoon," well known to those who served, and a description of which will not interest those who did not. To start with, training commenced at 5.30 a.m. and went on till noon, the rest of the day being at the men's own disposal; later the hours were altered to 9.00 a.m. to 1.00 p.m. There were Athletic Sports of all kinds arranged for the afternoons, with big Field Days when Brigade vied with Brigade to win the Divisional honours. There were sundry entertainments in one or other of the two buildings provided for such purposes, as when on July 6th we saw for the first time the moving pictures taken of the Battalion in Comox, or when on July 20th the Sergeants entertained the Brigadier and Battalion Officers at a smoking-concert in the fine mess building they had erected. On July 11th H.M. King George passed through from Villers to Camblain L'Abbé and the Brigade units lined the road informally and gave him a welcome which, it is to be hoped, had the unrehearsed effect which had been so assiduously practised. In addition to the regular work, and to add zest to the amusements offered, there were occasional inspections of a peculiarly searching kind, going into details of feet and the interior of packs. It was after one such inspection that the shadow of tragedy hung over the Battalion, when one of our draft men, an alien by birth, "ran amok" and shot the first officer he could see, who happened to be Capt. Carew Martin, of the 11th Brigade Staff, a most popular officer and the very last whom anyone in his senses would have thought of shooting; fortunately the wound, though serious, was not fatal; the miscreant having been lucky enough to escape lynching, was further lucky enough to get off with a life sentence.

On the 13th July we lost the services of our Adjutant, Major J. B. Bailey, who followed Lieut.-Col. A. B. Carey to undertake the duties of Second-in-Command of the 54th. Major Bailey, at one time Acting R.S.M. on the Spit, had come over as a subaltern and had gained well-earned promotion by his unremitting activity in performing the harassing duties of Adjutant during the Vimy operations. After his departure Lieut. J. L. Lloyd became Acting Adjutant until the following October. We had already temporarily lost the services of Major F. Lister, M.C. This officer had greatly distinguished himself during the tours on "The Triangle," for which he was later awarded the D.S.O., and for the first fortnight on coming out of the line had assumed the command of the unit whilst Col. Warden was away on leave. The latter returned on July 3rd, and on the next day Major

Lister left for England to undergo a three months' Commanding Officers' Course at Aldershot.

On July 26th we moved out in the evening to a camp which had been constructed at the Souchez end of Zouave Valley, known as Cobourg Street. Here we found that the 46th had been billeted in the area which should have been reserved for us, and we had to make the best shift we could to the left; this contretemps saved us five casualties on the following day. Plenty of water abounded at this end of the valley and an improvised swimming tank gave great relief, as the weather became abnormally hot. Aug. 1st saw us moving up the line into our new battle area, taking over the front line from the 87th with Headquarters established in a ruined chateau in Liévin. The latter was one of the suburbs of Lens and was exposed to constant bombardments; the road running from Souchez through Liévin up to the Red Mill where the Transport waggons nightly reported was perilous in the extreme, but our Transport had amazing luck and never lost a man. Liévin was a mass of ruins, but the cellar accommodation was good and there was plenty of water available. From the point of view of billets we were probably better off on this front than in any other sector throughout the war. The front line itself consisted of a series of posts established in houses. From the date of our entry into the Lens Sector we began to get accustomed to the continuous use by the Hun of gas shells; they had been encountered by us before, notably in the Second Triangle tour, but from this time on they became a regular nuisance against which every man, whether in the front line or back with Headquarters, had to be on his guard. Our several tours on this front were chiefly marked by a series of raids carried out either by our own companies alone or in conjunction with units on the flanks. The first of these took place on Aug. 5th, when "D" Coy., under the direct supervision of Col. Warden, carried out a daylight raid on a crater at the junction of Bell Street and the Liévin-Lens Road. This operation was completely successful, and the dug-outs found in the crater and the tunnels connecting it with the enemy lines were thoroughly bombed out. A similarly successful enterprise was undertaken on the 9th by "B" Coy., when one party under Sgt. O. Massey stormed an enemy strongpoint, drove out its occupants and established a block further up the trench, whilst a second party under Cpl. C. V. Brewer raided the crater a second time and undid all the repair work the Hun had effected. On this occasion the defenders fled overland and came under the fire of a Lewis Gun Section which had been strategically planted for that very purpose.

On the 10th we moved back into Support, and Headquarters retired from the Chateau a couple of hundred yards down the street to the building which in pre-war days had been the Gendarmerie, a large block of buildings surrounding a big courtyard. Here we remained only four clear days, as on the 15th we were hurriedly ordered into the line to relieve the 87th, which had been badly cut up in an offensive which failed and been driven back 200 yards behind their original front line; this relief we carried out in broad daylight because of the urgency of the call. On Aug. 17th an operation on a more extended scale was carried out, with the 4th Brigade co-operating on the left. The object of this offensive was to reorganize the line, which had been handed over in a badly dented condition, gaps existing between the companies and between our left flank and the adjoining battalion, the 18th. These gaps had been occupied by the enemy, and it was decided by a combined offensive to straighten out the line and establish a safe connection between all the units holding. The barrage opened at 4.32 a.m. "C" Coy., under Maj. R. J. Burde, M.C., was to co-operate with the 18th Bn. on the left and clean up the system of enemy trenches known as Cotton and Amulet and at the same time to co-operate with "B" Coy. under Maj. F. J. Gary, M.C., on the right. The latter Company in addition was to attack and hold the Schoolhouse which the enemy was using as a strong-point. The first part of the operation failed through the failure of the 4th Brigade to co-operate as planned; owing to some misunderstanding they never reached Amulet Trench at all, and finally Major Burde had to recall his men to their original positions. "B" Coy., after overcoming strenuous opposition, managed to secure a footing in the Schoolhouse, but failing to find the left flank secured owing to the non-fulfilment of the first part of the operation, also had to fall back to original positions. The same night we were relieved by the 46th Battalion and returned to Niagara Camp. The total casualties incurred during this first tour in Lens were as follows: Killed: Lieut. E. L. Gleason and 10 Other Ranks. Died of wounds: Three Other Ranks. Missing: Two Other Ranks. Wounded: Lieuts. V. Z. Manning, J. A. Cresswell, C. H. Packman, G. G. Allum, W. W. Dunlop (at duty), and 86 Other Ranks.

It was not until the early hours of the morning that the troops began to arrive at Niagara Camp; there is a wonderful satisfaction in wandering into camp at such an hour and finding the Base Details waiting up with hot food and hand-shakes and then turning in, knowing that for at least six days there will be comparative comfort and rest. The following day was a Sunday, and the conflicting claims of godliness and cleanliness caused a terrible fiasco, owing to the well-meant endeavours of the officiating chaplain to harmonize the two. "If your men have to go to the baths," said he, "well and good; I know that the baths are the first consideration; but let them come into the Church Service on their way back." The chaplain was right, from the point of view of common sense and Christianity, but, sad to relate, it fell out that a party of Brass Hats thought well to attend Divine Service that morning, and anyone who has had experience of Brass Hats and their way of looking at things will readily understand the consternation caused in their breasts when sundry members of the 102nd turned up with no puttees on their legs, but with towels hanging around their necks. It is entirely contrary to K. R. & O. for an enlisted man to worship his Creator unless he is properly dressed, and the Brass Hats did not fail to register their opinions in the quarters where such registration might be expected to do the most good. But what a blessing it is that some of us have been endowed with a sense of humour and with backs akin to those of ducks! It was on the occasion of this interval between tours that elimination contests were held to select marksmen for the Corps Rifle Shoot, which raises a curious question. Why on earth should the best marksmen in an army be kept out of the line to shoot for prizes instead of being sent up the line to kill Huns? The Army goes to all kinds of expense in order to train men to kill the enemy, and then it keeps the best it has to shoot for sport instead of for business. And yet we won the war!

August 20th figures as an important date in the history of the 102nd Bn., as on that day the news was received that we had ceased to be a British Columbia unit, and had been posted to the 2nd Central Ontario Regiment. The news came as somewhat of a shock at first, though general relief was felt that the rumours which had been prevalent of an impending break-up of the Battalion had been proved false. The reasons which led to the 54th and 102nd Bns. being thus transferred to Eastern postings are well known; British Columbia was too weak numerically as a Province to continue to supply reinforcements to all the units she had in the field. Two alternatives were open; to merge some of her Battalions and reorganize the Brigades affected, or to re-post some units. Henceforth all our reinforcements were drawn from the East, but a great hardship was inflicted on those original British Columbia men who, when evacuated sick or wounded to England, were there posted to the British Columbia depot and sent back to France to fight in strange battalions where they had to re-establish their footing. It is hard on a man who has served for over a year in a Battalion and made friends and perhaps put himself in the way of promotion, to find that an unlucky wound has caused him to be transferred to a Battalion where he knows nobody and where he has to start in from the beginning to prove his worth. But the war was full of injustices of this nature. If Canada had in the beginning allowed only that number of Battalions to be raised which could be reinforced, there would have been none of the breaking-up of units which resulted in such anomalies as the Battalion Quartermaster-Sergeant of a unit in England being sent out to serve as a Private with a strange unit in France, or the man whose work in the line had entitled him to promotion having to stand aside to see men of confirmed rank being absorbed from other Battalions and barring his way. If, however, the 102nd was unlucky in losing so many of its original British Columbia men, it was lucky in having them replaced by the fine class of reinforcement which systematically came to it from the 2nd Central Ontario Depot, whose Commanding Officer for many months, Major Fleming, made every effort to inspire the drafts he sent with a proper "esprit de corps" with respect to the unit they were reinforcing.

On Aug. 22nd we moved out to Zouave Valley, occupying there the same camp as on the previous occasion, and two days later moved up to Liévin, relieving the 54th in Support. The 10th Brigade was holding the line and sustained very heavy casualties, with the result that it was relieved by the 11th on the 25th, and the 54th Bn. was brought up into Support, the 102nd moving Headquarters across to a location further to the left, which had previously been used as a Company Headquarters. During this tour Major R. J. Burde, M.C., left for England on a three months' exchange, and Lieut. H. E. A. Pentreath, who had come over as a Private, but had obtained a commission in England, reported for duty. Sept. 1st found us in the front line in relief of the 87th, and Headquarters were established as before in the Chateau. On the 3rd, "D" Company, under Capt. S. H. Okell, under cover of a raid by the 8th Bn. on our left, managed to steal a little territory from the Hun, successfully advancing the front line posts, but the principal honours of this tour went to "A" Coy., under Lieut. I. C. R. Atkin, which carried out a highly successful operation in the early morning of September 6th. in conjunction with the 54th on the right. Under cover of an unusually feeble barrage patrols stole forward and bombed their way to the positions selected for the new advanced posts. It was on this occasion that Lance-Cpl. F. Quinn won his D.C.M. He was in charge of one of these patrols, which successfully gained its objective, but was unable to drive the enemy clear out of the house on the other side; dawn broke, and for twelve hours he maintained his position in his side of the house against vastly superior numbers, sending out a messenger under cover of night to secure the needed relief. At 7.20 p.m. the enemy was observed to be massing for a counter-attack to regain the valuable positions lost; Lieut. Atkin promptly withdrew his outposts to better defensive positions, and called for artillery support which was furnished by the 5th Canadian Divisional Artillery, which made its début on this occasion in the line, with the result that the oncoming Hun was caught in a deluge of fire and left the new positions in our hands for good. The following night we were relieved by the 7th Battalion, and once more returned to Niagara Camp.

From September 8th to the 18th the Battalion remained in Niagara Camp and enjoyed the best rest the men had yet had. The weather was fine throughout; the mornings were devoted to training and the afternoons to sports. On the 9th Col. Warden assumed temporarily the duties of the Brigadier, General Odlum having proceeded to England on duty, and took up his quarters at King's Cross, Souchez. Major E. J. Ryan assumed command of the Battalion, Major Lister being still in England and Major G. L. Dempster being sick. The latter officer had joined us during the Vimy operations and had more recently been in command of "A" Coy. It was a great loss to the Battalion when his health broke down and he was finally invalided out of France. Mention should here be made of the 4th Divisional Concert Party, later known as "The Maple Leaves"; in which Pte. F. E. Petch, who resigned his post as Mail Orderly in order to cater to the amusement of the troops, played a prominent part. From small beginnings, this organization grew to be an important factor in the Division, and for long had its headquarters in the Irving Theatre in the Chateau de la Haie grounds: so called after Col. Irving, of the 4th Divisional Engineers, who was responsible for its construction, but, alas, was killed before it was officially opened. It was really a very perfect little theatre, electrically lighted, with seating capacity for 1,000, and possessing magnificent acoustic properties. Life was becoming quite civilized in the area. The summer had seen a remarkable change in the road between Carency, which was still the home of the Quartermaster's Department, and Zouave Valley. The Transport Lines of all the units were moved nearer the Valley and horse lines constructed between Hospital Corner and the Arras-Souchez road. New and good Divisional baths were constructed in the same area. New camps were in process of construction, of which Alberta Camp, close to King's Cross, was already in occupation. At King's Cross itself a regular settlement was springing up, where Pioneers from all four Battalions, under charge of Cpl. C. B. Kirby, were building huts. A Chinese Labour Battalion was working on road improvement, sewer-work, etc., and the Transports of each Battalion were busy bringing out stacks of salvage from Liévin for use in making comfortable winter quarters. In short, it was evident that strenuous efforts were being made to ensure the comfort of the troops during the coming winter. The irony of it all was that when the winter came we were, for the most part, in another area, and what we had sown another reaped, even to the vegetables in the agricultural allotments which had been laid out in accordance with a settled policy of "Grow your own vegetables."

In the afternoon of September 19th we moved forward again to Support lines south of Avion by way of Clucas Trench, a long communication trench running down the northern slopes of Vimy Ridge, and relieved the 38th Bn. Headquarters were established in Anxious Trench. This tour was marked by the introduction of Battalion Tump-liners as a recognized Headquarters Detail, and they made their début under the command of Sgt. J. King. Their inestimable value was proved later in Passchendaele, and it is hard in the light of later events to see why they had not figured as a Battalion unit in the days of the Somme. In this connection a story may well be told which has the hall-mark of truth upon it. A demonstration of the use of the tump-line was being held at Corps Headquarters and Capt. Archibald, who was responsible for the scheme being brought before the Higher

ABLAIN ST. NAZAIRE

Command, had sent for a squad of 102nd men to act as demonstrators; amongst these was Pte. Frank Campbell, one of our "Originals" from the logging camps, and he came back terribly aggrieved at the ignorance which he claimed existed in the British Royal Family. It appeared that H.R.H. the Prince of Wales was present at the demonstration, and Frank was asked if he could move a piano. "Sure!" said Frank; "I'll move any blamed thing if I can get it on my back." So a piano was produced and Frank slung two tump-lines round it, gave a bit of a hoist and marched away, showing that such a feat was possible. "And how far could you carry that?" queried the Prince. "About a block," replied Frank. "And what's a block?" came back the answer. "Such ignorance!" Frank used to say when retailing the story, "and him a Prince with all the advantages of a Prince's education!" Alas, poor Frank will never move any more pianos; he "went West" the following December. As for the Prince, by the time he has completed the Canadian tour which is in progress whilst these lines are being written, he will probably have a very distinct idea of what a "block" is.

On the 23rd we moved into the front line, relieving the 54th, and Headquarters were moved away over to the right to a set of dug-outs on the Lens-Arras Road. The enemy evidently realized that this relief was in progress, as he put over a considerable barrage and attempted a raid on "B" Coy.'s position; his attacking party, however, did not manage to advance nearer than our Listening Posts. This uneventful tour came to an end on the evening of the 27th, and on relief being effected by the 44th and 47th Bns. we returned to billets in the Chateau, Gouy Servins. As soon as the men had been thoroughly rested intensive training was carried out on a scheme which had been prepared for the immediate capture of Lens. On the extensive grounds of the Chateau de la Haie a taped-out course was laid down, over which the Battalion practised the attack assiduously. At Souchez also a course had been prepared and there the Model Platoon, an aggregation composed of men who did not go up the line but were constantly drilled as a model, through which all reinforcements passed, gave carefully rehearsed exhibitions of the pending operation. Everyone was on the tip-toe of expectation, and then, like a bolt from a blue sky, came word that the offensive was "off" and that we were destined for a tour in Passchendaele. Whether our Intelligence Department had received word that the Hun had obtained information as to the plan for the capture of Lens, or whether the whole thing had been a gigantic "bluff" to deceive his watching aeroplanes the chronicler is in no position to state, but it is at least significant that all this training should have been carried out in broad daylight in full view of the enemy aeroplanes which were constantly hovering overhead. Whatever the answer to that problem, Oct. 4th saw us on our way to Ypres and the blood-stained ridge of Passchendaele.

CHAPTER VII.

First Visit to Divion—Two Tours in Passchendaele—Divion Again—Pre-Christmas Celebrations

N Oct. 4th the whole Battalion, including the Transport and all Base personnel, pulled out of the Gouy area and marched five miles to Gauchin Egal, a hamlet nestling in the valley between two precipitous hills; here a halt was made for one night and early next morning we set out for Divion, marching past the First Army Commander, Sir H. S. Horne, K.C.B., "en route." Divion is a coal-mining village about a mile and a half from Bruay, well peopled with prosperous miners who did not regard the billeted soldiery as their sole means of support and therefore lawful prey, but on the other hand took them to their hearts and homes and treated them all with the utmost hospitality. Tournehem, Divion and, later, Boitsfort will always be remembered by the men of the 102nd with feelings of genuine affection and gratitude. Billets at Divion were good; the place is lighted by electricity, a fact well worthy of note in French and Belgian country districts; it is divided into two distinct sections, the upper portion being known amongst the troops as "Transvaal," where for a long time the Canadian Light Horse were billeted, and the lower town being reserved for transient troops, for whom there was ample accommodation. There was a sufficient number of fair-sized houses to make it an easy matter to arrange both officers' and sergeants' messes for each Company and Headquarters; an open space in the middle of the village afforded plenty of room for a Battalion parade, whilst on the outskirts was a field suitable for Battalion drill. On the occasion of our first visit Headquarters were established in a large brewery. Shortly after our arrival we were rejoined by Major Lister, who returned from his Course in England to take up the duties of Second-in-Command. On the 8th, Major A. Graham, formerly of the 29th Battalion and more recently O.C. 2nd Divisional School, reported for duty and took over the duties of Adjutant. Throughout the week rain was prevalent and an inspection by the Army Commander at Houdain had to be cancelled, to the great joy of the troops. If anybody ever believes that the troops who look so nice and smiling on parade during the course of a big

review or inspection are really as happy as they look, he is greatly mistaken; they may not be dressed in sheep's clothing, but their inner feelings closely approximate to those of ravening wolves.

A move was made on the 11th, when we entrained at Houdain for Thiennes, which was reached at 3.00 p.m. From the station we marched by a most circuitous route to Boeseghem, a distance of five miles, only to find that we had proceeded three parts round a circle and that the station we had left was about a mile and a half from us. Great difficulty was experienced in billeting the men here: Imperials had not moved out, as expected, and the members of the billeting party had a long tramp up and down the roadways of a widely scattered village before they could find accommodation for all. Some of us will long remember a tiny house which looked as though it had walked out of a child's picture-book, which not only housed a dozen burly sergeants in a hay-loft, but managed to feed them on fried potatoes and beer and whose occupants were afterwards polite enough to pretend that they enjoyed the singing. A march of ten miles next day brought us to Ste. Marie Cappel, a village nestling under the shadow of the hill on which Cassel, the home of the 2nd Army Headquarters, was perched. Here we found a tented camp, which afforded good accommodation in spite of heavy rain. A move was expected daily, but did not take place until the 22nd, and during the interim the usual drills and parades took place, special attention being paid to the training of all Specialist branches. The villagers round this neighbourhood have a very fair knowledge of English, which was not to be wondered at, seeing that British troops had been quartered in their neighbourhood since the beginning of the war. The Sisters Susie ("Susie" seeming to be the generic name for the bar-ladies of this district) were really wonderfully proficient, seeing that all their education had come from business relations over the counter with the soldiers. Still, to use a colloquialism, that's "some" relationship.

Our real work in Passchendaele started on Oct. 22nd, when at 6.45 a.m. we entered 'buses and drove to the outskirts of Ypres, marching thence through the historic city to a dismal swamp a mile and a half to the north known as Potijze. The 4th Division was relieving the Australians in this area and the 102nd was now in Support. Headquarters were established in Hussar Farm, and the Companies were dispersed in tents or bivouacs which maintained a precarious anchorage in a sea of mud. In Potijze we remained, furnishing working-parties in large numbers by day and night; these were used for cable burying or supply carrying, and in view of the natural conditions prevailing the labour entailed was exhausting in the extreme, to say nothing of the fact that all work had to be carried on under a desultory artillery fire which caused occasional casualties. On the 27th we moved back into Reserve, rejoining our Transport Lines at Toronto Camp, Brandhoek, seven miles behind the Support position. The main Ypres road recalled memories of the Albert-

Bapaume road of the previous year, being crowded with transport of every kind. Close to Brandhoek was an enormous lorry park, which gave the visitor some faint idea of the vast numbers of lorries which were in use on even a single front. Toronto Camp was a good camp, and a large Y.M.C.A. catered well to the needs of the men, but the baths at Brandhoek were too small for the work, and for some reason there was a "hold-up" in clothing. Though it was now the end of October and the weather was both wet and cold, no sufficient supply of winter clothing could be obtained until November had well set in. It was whilst we were in this area that we first became accustomed to night bombing. Previously we had had experience of the odd bomb or so; from now onwards they became part of our normal life.

A sudden call to support the 12th Brigade took the Battalion up the line again on the 30th. Orders were received at 11.50 a.m., and within 40 minutes the Companies had entrained at Brandhoek Siding and were ready to proceed, a promptness of action which met with its due reward when the Battalion was kept waiting in the cold at Potijze for exact instructions as to its ultimate destination. Eventually orders came in that we were to dig-in on Abraham Heights, a position reached by duck-walks laid over the mud; the latter was deep enough to engulf a man up to his arm-pits. This advance was made under heavy fire which caused 13 casualties, and on arrival the only shelter the men could get was what they could dig for themselves. At 6.00 p.m. on the last night of the month the Battalion moved up to the front line, relieving the 85th Bn. This move was conducted throughout under heavy fire, including many gas shells, from the effects of which barrage we lost the services of Major W. Bapty, our Medical Officer, whose place was taken by Capt. H. Dunlop, C.A.M.C. The Companies only remained in the front line one night and one day, being relieved on the night of November 1st by the 9th Australian Bn., but a heavy barrage prevailed all the time and the front line trenches afforded little if any shelter; consequently casualties were frequent, showing a total of 28 Other Ranks killed for the whole of the first tour in Passchendaele, with Major W. Bapty, Lieuts. D. E. Webster, J. J. Rowland and 74 Other Ranks wounded or gassed. This last tour over the front line was responsible for the only casualties which ever occurred during the war amongst the Other Ranks personnel of the Battalion Orderly Room, Sgt. H. N. Monk being wounded (at duty) by a shell splinter in the arm, and Pte. F. C. Morgan being badly gassed. On relief the men spent the night at Potijze, returning by train to Brandhoek in the morning.

On the afternoon of Nov. 3rd we entrained again at Brandhoek Siding for Caestre, whence we marched a couple of miles to Koorten-Loop. Here we found that the Transport had already arrived, together with a lorry-load of Base personnel and stores, and that billets had already been secured. Headquarters was established in a commodious and spotlessly clean estaminet, not the least charming feature of which was another "Susie" in the person of the daughter of the house, who would have graced the stage of any music-hall in the world. Lying between Caestre and Haazebruck, two important railway centres, Koorten-Loop is surrounded by the farming country typical of that portion of Flanders; the landscape is rolling rather than hilly and traversed in every direction with the cobbled roads known as "pavés," which, though well calculated to withstand the march of time, are uncomfortably adapted for the march of troops. The time was chiefly spent in general reorganization. On the 5th the Corps Commander held a review of the 11th Brigade at Hondeghem, in our immediate neighbourhood, and on the 8th Col. Warden proceeded to England on duty, followed by leave, handing over the command to Major Lister, with Major E. J. Ryan acting as Second. On the next day we once more set our faces towards Passschendaele, and proceeding by train from Caestre detrained at Ypres, leaving the Base details at Brandhoek, where they arrived twenty-four hours before they were expected and had the utmost difficulty in obtaining accommodation. In fact, the whole unit seemed to have taken time by the forelock, as on arrival at Potijze in driving rain and gathering darkness we found a muddy field and a pile of tents which had been begged, borrowed or stolen by our B.Q.M.S. Frank Hallas, when he discovered that no arrangements had been made for our disposal. Owing to some element of misunderstanding conditions were unnecessarily as full of discomfort as possible. A corrugated iron hut, isolated in the darkness of a remote corner of the area, was found for a Headquarters, and even from this meagre shelter we were ejected on the following day, as it was claimed to be the property of another unit. Headquarters was accordingly moved to the scullery of a ruined house, which served well enough until a heavy fall of rain left an inch of water on the floor, which could have been tolerated, but effectually made work impossible by dripping on all the papers, necessitating twenty-four hours building and repair work by the Pioneers. Four working-parties were sent out on the 10th, of which only two were able to complete the tasks set, one of the others having been wrongly directed and the second finding the area assigned congested with men and being heavily shelled. The explanation was that the Engineers had contracted the habit of asking for more men than they needed, as it was so often impossible to fulfil their demands; consequently when a full complement was sent, as in this case, so many men appeared on the scene as both to hamper themselves and to draw the enemy's fire.

Nov. 12th saw us on our way to Support area on Abraham Heights. The intention was that the Battalion would only stay in the Forward area a couple of nights, pending relief by the Imperials, and orders were issued that no shaving kits of any description were to be taken up; this order was gleefully obeyed by nearly everybody. As it turned out, we remained in the line seven full days, and the results were rather comical. On arrival at Boathoek, where Headquarters was to be established, we found that the 87th Bn., whom we were relieving, were not yet ready to proceed up to the front line, as their rations had not come up. We were accordingly kept waiting for two hours standing round in pitch darkness; in the meantime the Hun shelled the ration dump, inflicting serious casualties on the 87th, with the result that after all we had later on to supply carrying parties to take up their rations. In addition, during the next three nights we were kept busy sending up stretcher-bearing parties to bring out their casualties, as they seemed to be utterly unable to cope with these themselves. Finally at about 10.00 p.m. the 87th, to our great relief, moved up and allowed us to settle down. During this tour Lieut.-Col. J. T. O'Donohue, D.S.O., commanding the 87th, was acting as Brigadier in the absence of Brigadier-General Odlum, who was acting as Divisional Commander. For three days we furnished working-parties of all sorts, Support area being subjected all the time to heavy artillery fire, which caused many casualties. Headquarters had its full share of this bombardment, but the pill-box which served as an office was built by the Hun for just such contingencies, and though several direct hits were registered the only damage done was to the officers' breakfast on the morning of the 15th. On the afternoon of the 16th the Battalion moved up by platoons to relieve the 87th in the front line. It is impossible to give any adequate idea of the scenery on the way to the summit of Passchendaele Ridge. There is just a brown landscape, an interminable acreage of mud and shell-holes billowing up in a gradual ascent, with depressions rather than valleys between each billow, until a flat and desolate top is reached, on which no semblance of any human habitation remains; like a map, it represents merely a number of topographical expressions. The ascent is made by means of an elaborate system of bath-mats which spread like threads in every direction, whilst here and there on the hillside is seen a battery, ostrich-like, unable to see the enemy but hoping that a scant shelter of brushwood is shielding it from the eyes of the prying aeroplanes. Enemy planes were very active over Passchendaele and seemed to be having it all their own way.

The move to the front line was carried out without casualties, the Hun being kept busy attending to a minor offensive which was taking place on his right flank, but immediately after relief a fierce barrage came down, and for the next 48 hours a very heavy artillery fire was maintained on the whole of our area, "D" Coy., whose turn it was to have the usually preferable position of local Support, by the irony of fate suffering particularly heavy casualties. On the night of the 17th, a reconnoitring party from the Suffolks reached Headquarters and requested to be sent up the line; hardly had they gone 200 yards from the pill-box when they were caught by the splinters of a shell which burst well away to their left, but claimed seven casualties, two being fatal. The following night our relief by the Suffolks began at 5.00 p.m., and the Battalion proceeded by small parties to Potijze, where a hot meal was in readiness and a halt was made for the night.

It is worthy of mention that the 102nd Bn. was the last Canadian unit to leave the Heights of Passchendaele, but we had gained no particular honour or glory there. Our tours in the line had been short and had involved no offensives; they had entailed much hard work in burying cable, digging trenches and putting the line in better shape, and they had called for the staying quality which enables men to lie down for long hours in ill-protected positions under incessant bombardments. We had just done the little that we had been set to do, but had suffered casualties out of all proportion to our task, and that it is which makes the memory of Passchendaele a nightmare in the minds of all those who had a share in a particularly odious experience. The second tour cost in casualties: Killed, 20 Other Ranks. Wounded, Lieuts. A. R. Turner, W. W. Dunlop (at duty), G. T. Lyall (at duty), and 47 Other Ranks.

In the early afternoon of the 19th the Battalion fell in, marched to Ypres and entrained for Poperinghe, whence we marched to a camping-ground about two miles outside the town. A sorry-looking crew we were as we marched proudly through the streets of Poperinghe, thronged with civilians and spruce-looking soldiers. Our razors had all gone with the Transport when we first left Potijze seven days before, and we were hairy men. The C.O. was a dream, but the Adjutant and R.S.M., with one or two Company officers, had basely betrayed us and smuggled razors up the line, and thought they made a hit as they marched through the streets with baby-smooth chins. The camp where we spent the next two nights was close to the first camp we had struck on arrival in Belgium, and here we met with one of those churls who so often disgraced his country in the eyes of the troops who were fighting as her Allies. After seven days without a wash or a shave it may be imagined that water was the first requirement, but the owner of the neighbouring farm was not going to have his water supply tampered with for a lot of dirty soldiers, not he; so he removed the pump handle. And it was not as though this happened in the middle of a hot summer and his well was likely to run dry; God knows, there was enough rain in the country at that time of year! Would that we had been Huns, to throw him down his well after we had used it, there to perish miserably and to poison the water for the balance of his family. And to add to our grievance, the baths provided in Poperinghe proved to be the worst we had yet encountered. On the 21st we went by 'bus to a point just outside Merville, quite a fine town, where steaks and eggs in large quantities could be purchased in real restaurants, thence on foot to a point between Busnes and Lillers, and so through Lillers and Rambert, until on the 23rd we found ourselves again in Divion. And did Divion look good? It did.

For over three weeks we were to stay in Divion, and throughout our sojourn the weather was good, cold and frosty, but without rain. On the 27th Col. Warden returned from leave and resumed command, and during this period Major R. J. Burde also reported back from England. There is not much to relate about this three weeks; on the 3rd the vote for the Dominion election was taken, Lieut. C. A. Schell acting as Returning Officer; there were sundry parades and inspections, but the most important events were the series of Christmas Dinners which were held in the Hotel Moderne, Bruay, as it was known that for a second time we should be in the trenches on the day itself. It was decided to use a portion of the Canteen funds for this purpose and surely never were funds devoted to a more popular object. On the 12th the C.O. and Officers of the Battalion gave a dinner to the Sergeants, and as we are now nearing the time when Col. Warden was to leave us it may be in order to relate an incident which took place at the dinner, illustrative of his all-time optimism and boundless confidence in the Battalion, and in its power of belief. "I was walking down Piccadilly when on leave," he stated, in his after-dinner speech, "when I was overtaken by a naval officer, an admiral in the British Navy. He had noticed my 102nd badges and rank as I had passed him and had hurried after me to ask whether I was really Col. Warden of the 102nd. I told him that I was, and he said that he wanted to shake me by the hand; that he had never met me, but that he, like everybody else in England, had heard of 'Warden's Warriors,' and that he wanted to congratulate me on commanding the finest Battalion on the Allied front." And then above the roar of applause was heard the reedy voice of the privileged member of the Battalion, piping: "Just ten cents more, boys; divvy up ten cents apiece, please; it's time to buy some more hay for that old bull of the Colonel's." And so with turkey and chicken and beer and other things during the week-end of the second week in December our stay in Divion came to an end, and with it we close the chapter on Passchendaele.

CHAPTER VIII.

From Divion to Mericourt—Col. Warden's Departure—Lievin Once More—Back to Divion—Lens Again—Ecurie and the Oppy Front —Acheville—Mericourt—Out of the Line to Frevillers

MIDST the tearful "au revoirs" of Blanche, Gaby, "Min Laute," and others whose names will be readily recalled by those who know their Divion, we left our billets on October 18th and marched off to Camblain L'Abbé, where we stayed one night. On the following morning we proceeded along the Mt. St. Eloy road, expecting to be reviewed by the Corps Commander, but he did not appear, and about a mile outside the village we boarded flat cars on the Light Railway and rode up the line to Neuville St. Vaast. It was bitterly cold, even marching, and on the cars it was almost intolerable. A well-laid-out camp was ready for us on arrival, but there was practically no fuel, except for cooking purposes, and the weather grew steadily colder. At noon next day, under the command of Major Lister, Col. Warden having been detailed to attend an aerial course, we went up the line to relieve the 22nd (French-Canadian) Bn. in the front line on the Mericourt Sector. It was a terrible march; the ground was covered with ice, and our way took us along narrow trails bordering deep trenches. If it had not been bright daylight under a blue sky and a brilliant sun the progress of Christian through the Valley of the Shadow of Death would have been remarkably well paralleled. We now encountered a unique feature in front line work, a set of Headquarters lighted by electricity and watered by electrical pumps. This marvel of modern warfare was found in the Quarries, an enormous quarry entered by a long tunnel and honeycombed with dug-outs, which afforded us the best and most comfortable headquarters we ever had in the front line. The tour itself was singularly without incident, and by arrangement with the 54th we agreed upon one ten-day tour each in the front line instead of undertaking two five-day tours apiece. Here we spent our second Christmas, and, thanks to Capt. Fisher, of the Y.M.C.A., we had a Christmas present of cigarettes and chocolate sufficient to provide something for every man. The ten days were principally spent in wiring in front of our positions and in improving the trenches, and on the 30th we exchanged

LIEUT.-COLONEL F. LISTER, C.M.G., D.S.O., M.C.

positions with the 54th and fell back into Support, with Headquarters in a railway embankment, which was under close observation by the enemy from one side. New Year's Day was ushered in by two raids, one by the Hun and one by the 75th, who managed to secure valuable information, but the balance of the tour passed as uneventfully as had the first ten days, and on the 9th we were relieved by the 72nd and made our way through a blinding snowstorm to Hill's Camp, Neuville St. Vaast. Here it was that we lost the services of Lieut.-Colonel J. W. Warden, D.S.O., who had raised the Battalion and brought it overseas. On the 11th he left to take up special service in Mesopotamia. Though he had anticipated his early departure his move orders came in so suddenly that he had no time to take a farewell of his men on parade, but left the following message to be issued as a Special Order of the Day:

"To the Officers, N.C.O.'s and Men of the 102nd Cdn. Inf. Bn.:

"On relinquishing command of the Battalion in order to take up a Special Service appointment for which I volunteered, I wish to express my deep appreciation of the spirit of loyalty and service which has pervaded all ranks from the time of mobilization back in Comox to the present day.

"I should have preferred to address you personally before my departure, but the hour for the latter was unexpectedly advanced, and I had to leave at an early hour this morning. I must, therefore, convey to you through the medium of Battalion Orders those feelings of pride and gratitude which overwhelm me when I recall the endurance, perseverance and courage which you have exhibited throughout your period of service in Belgium and France.

"It is with the deepest regret that I sever my connection with the 102nd Battalion, but the conviction that I can perform better service for the Empire in a different sphere of duty has compelled me to take this step.

"To all of you I say, not 'Good-bye' but 'Au revoir,' and may the best of luck attend you all. I leave you in the full confidence that you will extend to my successor the same loyal service that you have always given me, and that you will 'carry on' as you have done, to the honour and glory of the 102nd and the successful consummation of the objects of the Cause for which we are all striving.

"J. W. WARDEN,
"11-1-18." "Lieut.-Colonel."

The departure of the Colonel came as a great surprise to most of the Battalion and was very genuinely regretted, especially by those of the old-timers who were left. But we were fortunate in having as his successor an officer whom we all knew well, also an "original" from the Spit, who had worked up from the position of a subaltern in command of a platoon to that of Second-in-Command, and whose distinguished services had already been recognized by the award of the

Military Cross and the Distinguished Service Order. At the time that Col. Warden left us Major Lister was in England on leave, but he rejoined us on January 19th as Lieut.-Colonel in command of the Battalion. In the meantime Major A. Graham assumed command. The Adjutant's duties had been undertaken at the beginning of the last tour by Capt. S. H. Okell, who carried on in that capacity until wounded nine months later. Lieut. R. Fitzmaurice was Transport Officer, Lieut. T. R. Griffith, M.C., who had succeeded Capt. O'Kelly in the previous autumn, having been promoted captain and given command of "C" Coy. "A," "B" and "D" Coys. were under the command respectively of Lieut. I. C. R. Atkin, M.C., Major J. F. Gary, M.C., and Lieut. V. C. Brimacombe.

Hill's Camp was a good camp, but we had great difficulty with the water, which was continually frozen; a good Y.M.C.A. entertainment of moving-pictures, etc., was nightly staged in a large hut; the baths also were good, and we were sorry when on the 15th we had to move back to Vancouver Camp, for here we found many dilapidations. For three months the camps in the Chateau de la Haie grounds had been in the occupation of Imperials, and they showed it. Whatever the Imperial Army may have been in the good old days before the war, there is no getting away from the fact that the battalions of the Citizen Army called forth during the war had no consideration for the units which might follow them in their several camps. We found that the linings of the Nissen huts had been wantonly torn out to provide fuel, that the water system had gone out of order, and that no effort had been made to keep the camp generally in a good state of repair. Whatever faults may from time to time have been urged against the Canadian Corps, it was at least a matter of pride with its units that they improved every camp they went to and made it more habitable than they found it. Besides, it's a foolish bird as well as an ill one that fouls its own nest, and we knew by experience that it did not pay from the point of view of personal comfort to break up a camp for fuel or to allow the bath-mats to deteriorate. The result was as might have been expected; we were perpetually being used to make good other people's defections, and in this case the 4th Division undertook the good work. On the 17th we attended "en masse" the 4th Divisional Concert Party's wonderful pantomime, called "A Lad in France," a really clever piece of work, well staged in the Irving Theatre, and well acted, abounding in topical allusions and evoking whole-hearted enthusiasm from all who saw it.

Jan. 19th saw us in the line again, this time once more on the Lens front. Spending a night in Liévin "en route," in some very old disused billets, we relieved the P.P.C.L.I. on the evening of the 20th in the right sub-section. The billets in this area were good, and for Headquarters, at any rate, there was plenty of water in the shape of a lake which lay between us and our old positions in "The Triangle." The front was quiet, but enemy machine-gunners and snipers were very much on the alert, and absolutely no movement overland was permissible; there was also a good deal of artillery action on both sides, the Hun steadily bombarding Liévin in the rear, and paying particular attention to Brigade Headquarters there. On the occasion of this tour we found him using a new form of gas shell of low velocity, exploding with the sound of a High Explosive and emitting a gas which we had not before encountered; it took a little time to get sufficiently accustomed to this new device to be able to recognize it immediately on approach. But, as has been said before, we were, on the whole, very lucky with regard to gas, and though we were never careless we became sufficiently expert in the use of our respirators to be able to continue a quiet game of poker in our masks what time the Hun was under the impression that he was causing us untold anguish, as was instanced by a little party held in our old Headquarters in the Gendarmerie, to which we returned on the 25th when relieved in the front line by the 54th, and where we remained until the 30th, when, on relief by the 85th, we marched back to Vancouver Camp.

We had now had two very uninteresting tours in the line, and were expecting the same routine to prevail for a few months; it was somewhat of a surprise, therefore, to find that what we had supposed would prove to be the regular six-day rest was in reality the preliminary for a long period out of the line. For over a fortnight we remained at Vancouver Camp, and the gods were propitious; we had the time, we had the place, and, "mirabile dictu," some of us had the wherewithal, thanks to the proximity of the Canadian Expeditionary Force Canteen, and there were sundry decorations to be "christened" and more than one birthday to be celebrated. During the early part of February Vancouver Camp was well out of the "dry belt." On the 15th a move was made to Alberta Camp, an aggregation of good Nissen huts situated between Hospital Corner and King's Cross and scientifically laid out in scattered formation as an anti-aircraft precaution, and on the 18th we once more marched back to Gouy "en route" for Divion, which we reached on the 20th. We were now in First Army Reserve, but had orders to be ready to move at twelve hours' notice. We entered Divion under the command of Major Ryan, Col. Lister having proceeded with other Battalion commanders on a tour of inspection of Base Depot organizations. Amongst other points of interest visited by this party was the huge Salvage Depot at Le Havre, and the Colonel returned on the 24th, very enthusiastic over the wonderful system of salvage and repair work which he had seen in operation. On the occasion of this visit to Divion the Battalion Headquarters were moved to the further end of the village, much to the chagrin of the local brewer, whose dignity was pathetically upset by having his magnificent accommodation demeaned by the presence of a mere Company Headquarters. In Divion we remained eleven days, the only outstanding event of which was a grand review of the 11th Brigade by Field Marshal Sir Douglas Haig, K.T., G.C.B.,

NAPOO CORNER, LIEVIN.

G.C.V.O., K.C.I.E., Commander-in-Chief of the British Forces in France, at Houdain, about two miles distant from our billets.

For the last time we said "good-bye" in Divion on March 3rd, marching to Bois des Froissart, a new camp just north of our old stamping-ground of Hersin, where the Battalion was employed in wiring the front line in the St. Emile Sector. The Hun was very active on this front, and on the 4th of the month raided the Allied positions very successfully, penetrating to within 150 yards of the front line Battalion Headquarters. Whilst in this camp a spirited inter-platoon competition was organized to select the platoon which would compete against Brigade units before the Brigadier in a general efficiency contest. The palm of victory went to No. 15 Platoon, "D" Coy., whose immediate reward was a dinner at the Canteen expense in Hersin and the privilege of being left out of the line for the Brigade contest when the rest of us moved up to Liévin in relief of the 29th Bn. on the evening of the 11th March.

Liévin was by now beginning to look like a home from home to us; we were always reasonably sure of good accommodation in this ruined suburb, we knew where all the water supplies were, and we knew that although the Hun would ceaselessly shell Napoo Corner he would never hit anything. On the 12th we moved up and took over the left sub-section of St. Emile Sector, Lens Section (about this time we all became very particular as to the correctly exact naming of our front line positions) from the 27th Bn., "A" and "B" Coys. taking over a three-company frontage. This was just as well, as the Hun was shelling the line systematically, and the fewer the number of men up in front the safer they were. It was often a difficulty during this period of the war to conform with the rigid orders of the Higher Command that every man not absolutely essential to the proper conduct of the Transport lines be sent up to the front and at the same time to avoid overcrowding. Our Headquarters in this area were situated in an old brick-kiln, in the foundations of which a spring of water had broken out, necessitating constant pumping by day and night; this pleasant duty fell to the lot of the Headquarters batmen, who were organized into two-hour reliefs; it was hard work, especially for batmen, who were unanimous in their expressed opinion that it was a perfectly horrid war. On the 17th we were relieved by the 54th, and returned to Liévin, where we were greeted the same evening by a hot gas-shell bombardment which fell all round Headquarters and claimed four casualties. While we were in Support we had our first meeting with the Allied "Frightfulness" gang, officially known as "Special O Squad" of the Engineers; these men made a specialty of beating the Hun at his own game, and one of their favourite devices was gas projection from a new type of cylinder. The gas is projected in a form of bomb which explodes behind the enemy's lines; the noise it makes when fired is truly awe-inspiring, and the spectacular effect is wonderful. On the 21st we witnessed such a projection, but we never heard any details as to the results obtained, as we went up to relieve the 54th again in the front line on the next night. This tour was marked by increased vigilance, if such a thing were possible. The Hun was in the first stages of his successful March offensive, and everyone was "on edge" as to where he would make his next push. All English leave was cancelled and unfortunates who had just left were being returned daily. But though everyone was on the "qui vive," and battle quarters were assigned to the veriest non-combatant of the Headquarters Staff, no offensive materialized on our front, and on the 28th we were relieved in this sector by the 16th Suffolks. But, though we had been fortunate, others had experienced a different fate. Well to our right the Hun had broken through and forced back the line on the right of the 3rd Division, causing a composite unit to be hurriedly formed under command of Brigadier-General V. W. Odlum, this body being known as "Odlum's Composite Brigade," and sent off to support the 168th Bdge. The crisis, however, passed before this body could be brought into action, and it was disbanded into its original units within a couple of days. Meantime, on the 28th, various conflicting orders were received at 102nd Bn. Headquarters as to our destination on relief. This was changed several times, with the result that when relief was completed at 9.15 p.m. a part of the Battalion had already set out for Ecoivres, a village near Mt. St. Eloy, about twelve miles from the line, whilst subsequent orders detailed Ecurie, on the Oppy front, as our camping place. Consequently the Battalion was divided into two, it being then impossible to recall those who had already set out. These men had a hard time of it; after a long night march they had to fall in again at 7.15 a.m. on the 29th and tramp through bitter squalls of sleet and hail another seven miles to rejoin the main body at Ecurie. This place lies south of Neuville St. Vaast, S.S.W. of Lens, between the Lens-Arras and Bethune-Arras roads; a good enough camp, but, like most, dependent on water-carts for all water. Here we remained until April 4th, under orders to be ready to move off at 15 minutes' notice with filled water-bottles. Everything pointed to an immediate action on a large scale, but our time was not yet.

At Ecurie we were in closer contact with the Imperials than at any previous time; there were several Imperial units billeted in the neighbourhood, including a battery of "Heavies" and a section of the R.A.F. A Balloon Section was also in the area, and for miles on every side the big observation balloons hung in the air all day long, except when, as on April 1st, a sporting Hun airman came darting down the line and took toll of four in succession, sending them all down in flames. A couple of miles nearer the line was Roclincourt, where good baths were located, but the Roclincourt road was a target for the enemy artillery, who registered many direct hits on it. Life at Ecurie was not unpleasant, but it was marred by that 15-minute readiness clause in Orders, and it was really a relief when, on April 4th, we moved up and took over the front in the right sub-section, Oppy Sector, with Headquarters in an enormous rambling dug-out with tunnel communications of an extensive nature. This front was well supplied with water, which was piped in all directions and even supplied a small bath-house hollowed out of the protecting bank. There was also a well in the neighbourhood, as one of "A" Coy.'s men found to his cost. He did not break his leg, but he found it uncomfortable as a night's billet.

On April 10th a highly successful raid was carried out by four Officers and 132 Other Ranks from "B" Coy., under the personal charge of Major F. J. Gary, M.C. The raid was timed for 5.00 a.m., and was undertaken for the purpose of obtaining identifications, inflicting casualties and demoralizing the enemy. The Raiding Party assembled in accordance with orders and followed up a two-minute barrage, but on account of the great depth of No Man's Land on this front some difficulty was experienced in locating the openings in the enemy's wire; eventually the right party had to cut its way through under cover of a fierce bomb and rifle barrage which effectually kept down the Hun heads. Finally this party reached the trench, but had to withdraw without prisoners, as their difficulties in the wire had already brought them within their time limit. The left party was more successful, and came back with ten prisoners from the 102nd Saxon Regiment. Our own casualties numbered Lieut. E. McCrea and 11 Other Ranks wounded, whereas the estimated casualties inflicted on the enemy were over 50, of whom 28 are known to have been killed. An individual feature of this road was the "berserk" fighting of Sgt. C. V. Brewer, who strove like a Viking of old until "time" was called, when he managed to bring himself out of the line sorely wounded, but not until he had seen that his officer and other wounded men were safe; his valour on this occasion added the D.C.M. to the M.M. he had won at Lens. The following telegram was received the same morning, to be treasured as another proof of how the 102nd Bn. "made good":

"Divisional and Brigade Commanders congratulate O.C. 102nd and all Officers and Other Ranks of the Battalion who participated either in the preparations for this morning's raid or in the raid itself, upon the success obtained. The Brigade Commander is proud of the fighting spirit shown by the raiding parties and of the heavy casualties inflicted on the enemy.
"V. W. ODLUM, Commanding 11th C.I.B."

That same evening we were relieved by the 78th Bn. and proceeded to Victory and Portsmouth Camps, near Ecurie. Early next morning orders were received that we were to relieve the 1st C.M.R. that night in the Acheville Sector, making our Headquarters in the same area that we had used when we went into Support on the Mericourt front at the New Year. On arrival, however, we found that there had been "dirty work at the cross-roads," and that the Hun had totally demolished our previous billets in the embankment, forcing us to occupy straitened quarters in Grand Trunk Trench; this trench was under constant fire from the enemy gunners, and, in addition, the accommodation was so limited that it was decided to find better quarters if possible; consequently, on the 13th, we moved over to some old Artillery positions close to Victoria Dump, where we contrived to make ourselves very comfortable, abundant water being procurable about 400 yards away at the other end of a secluded valley. It was not long, however, before the Hun realized that the deserted positions were again in occupation, and he marked his appreciation of the fact in the usual manner. During this tour a Brigade Composite unit was formed under Major Moffat, being composed of all men who had hitherto remained at the Transport Lines, but who could not be retained there under the new ruling that the personnel of Transport Lines must be cut down to 68, all ranks. This unit was retained for some time as a special Brigade Reserve for use in case of emergency; fortunately, its services were never required. On the 17th we moved up to our old Headquarters in the Quarries which we had occupied at Christmas. The situation was still critical, and Headquarters Details were now all mustered into separate units under Specialist officers. Battalion wits, seeing the pampered (?) individuals of Headquarters Staff thus mobilized into real fighting units, amused themselves by inventing suitable names of an opprobrious nature for the different sections; thus we had "Okie's 'Opeless Oafs" lining up with "Perry's Priceless Pierrots", and "Packman's Palsied Pippins" vieing with "Manning's Measly Microbes"; but these alliteratively-named squads were never called on to prove their prowess. To facilitate the assembly of Headquarters in their battle stations a new exit from the quarry was completed during this tour, and in honour of our Second-in-Command was christened "Paddy's Passage." Only one incident of interest occurred during the tour, when, on the night of April 21st, a midnight patrol from "D" Coy., under Lieut. J. R. Wilson, ran into an enemy patrol proceeding in force towards a gap in our wire; our men promptly engaged the enemy with rifle fire, but on being threatened by a second party from the rear, had to bomb through the latter and take cover in a shell-hole, where they were actively attacked by the Huns, reinforced by a third party. Our patrol successfully repulsed all attacks, and the enemy finally withdrew, after sustaining heavy casualties; this action on the part of Lieut. Wilson's patrol undoubtedly checked a raid on our positions.

On the night of the 23rd we were relieved by the 75th Bn., and made our way to Cellar Camp, Neuville St. Vaast. Mention has already been made of the good work which the Canadian Corps always did in the matter of improving and preserving billets, and the following letter, addressed by the C.O. 75th Bn. to the Brigadier, will show that the 102nd was not backward in this respect:

"Dear General Odlum,—I have never taken over front line trenches from any Battalion which were as clean and in as good shape as those the 102nd Bn. handed over today. We shall maintain and improve where possible. C.C. Harbottle. 23-4-18." This was forwarded with a covering letter from the Brigadier reading:—"My dear Lister,—Herewith a note from Harbottle, which has pleased me very much. I want to thank you and all concerned for the effort you must have made. The 102nd is pleasing me very much. V. W. Odlum."

Amenities such as the above do a lot of good, and when they occurred were very generally appreciated. Our new camp was a good one, with a big Y.M.C.A. hut in the neighbourhood, where the 4th Divisional Concert Party put on a good original entertainment entitled "Camouflage." After six days' rest we moved up for our last tour in the line before the long summer training which was to keep us in the back area for over two months, and on April 29th we relieved the 54th in the left sub-section, Mericourt Sector, with Headquarters in one of the old Company Headquarters dug-outs, and remained in the line until the 7th May, when we were relieved by the Argyle and Sutherland Bn., which had just arrived from Palestine, where it had been quartered for three years without home leave; the men had all been under the impression that they would be going to England when they were landed at Marseilles, and it was a sadly disappointed unit which took our place. These men had never had any experience at all of trench warfare, and the Hun gave them a very warm welcome, developing the only activity he had shown in a week just after they had come into the line. As for us, we marched down to a point on the Neuville St. Vaast road where 'buses and motor lorries picked us up and carried us many miles to the rear, depositing us at 6.30 a.m. on April 8th in the village of Frévillers.

The last three months and a half had been singularly without incident, but they had entailed a great deal of nervous strain. It is a great deal more trying to keep on waiting for an enemy's offensive which does not develop than to take part in one planned and developed by one's own side. During the past month, especially, the Battalion had been kept on the tip-toe of expectation; it had been switched from front to front in constant suspense, and though, with the exception of the one raid already mentioned, it had seen no real fighting, it was quite ready to enjoy a rest from front line work, even though that rest was to be filled with the hardest kind of intensive training in preparation for the strenuous days of open warfare which were to come towards the close of the summer.

Let the chapter close with an anecdote illustrating the literary endowments of our Water Detail. On one of the recent tours Lieut. D. Macbeth came down in the early morning to interview the Medical Officer; as was customary, he was wearing a private's tunic, and one of the Water Detail on duty, not recognizing him, gruffly demanded his business. "I want to see the M.O.," said the officer. "Well, you can't see him yet," replied the man on duty; "he ain't up yet; wait till the proper time." "Do you know whom you are talking to?" answered the other, "my name's Macbeth." "And I don't care if it's bloody Hamlet," came back the answer; "the M.O.'s been up all night, and unless you're wounded he's going to get some sleep before he prescribes your No. 9's."

DAWN

Reprinted from the Battalion Christmas Card, 1918.

(These lines were written during the interval between the 2nd Battle of Arras and the 2nd Battle of Cambrai.)

Dawn! And the sky grows brighter,
  The darkness and mist disappear;
Passed are the shadows of evening,
  The things that we fought for grow clear;
And the doubts that have troubled the nations
  Are stilled, as our triumph draws near.

Dawn! And the night shrinks cowering,
  The Powers of Darkness decrease.
Soon o'er the ruins of Europe
  Will hover the Angel of Peace;
And the lives that the struggle has parted
  Will meet, when all warfare shall cease.

Dawn! And this Christmas morning
  Brings hope to a suffering world.
E'en now from their tottering strongholds
  The Forces of Evil are hurled;
And the nations are banded together
  'Neath the banner of Freedom unfurled.

—L. McLEOD GOULD.

CHAPTER IX.

Frevillers—Training for Open Warfare—Huclier, Conteville and Bethonval—Intensive Training Intensified—Life in Rural France—On the Oppy Front Again—The Eve of Open Warfare

ATIENCE was needed for that drive to Frévillers, since we had been kept waiting on the road so that the whole Battalion could proceed together; consequently it was a cramped and tired crowd that "debussed" at Frévillers. Of all the weird and horrible words that ever crept into the War Vocabulary the two worst were "embuss" and "debuss"; to take the last syllable of a Latin trisyllable, graft on a prefix and, as compensation, to double the final consonant in order to force the accent on the last syllable, constituted an outrage on all the "ologies," but it afforded a cheap and effective method of describing the desired act, and was found in all Orders emanating from Higher Up. We "debussed," then, in the early hours of a beautiful spring morning, to find the country looking its best, and breakfast looking and tasting just three hours old—which it was, as our arrival had been expected earlier; and so, to bed.

It was soon made abundantly clear that our period out of the line was to be spent in hard intensive training to fit the Battalion for the open warfare which it was expected that we should be called upon to carry out later in the year, and an exceedingly comprehensive scheme of training was immediately drawn up by Brigade, the principal features of which were the time to be spent on Musketry and the arrangements made for regular field operations to be carried out under the conditions which we should meet in the real thing. In addition, it was desired to harden the Battalion physically as much as possible; exercise and open air were to be enjoyed to the full, and the time not actually spent in military training was to be devoted to open-air sports of every kind. It was absolutely necessary that by the time the call came the Battalion as a whole should be able to stand the fatigue of long and continuous marches. That this system of training was successfully carried out was proved up to the hilt during the following August, when a series of gruelling night marches was immediately capped by a brilliant offensive and the quick following up of a retreating enemy.

It is unnecessary to deal in detail with the events of the next two weeks; on days when there were no manoeuvres the mornings were devoted to drill or musketry practice and the afternoons to athletics. In this connection the following paragraph from the Regimental Diary may prove of interest: "A great deal more zest and keenness in the matter of athletics was observable amongst the men than had been the case in 1917. This may have been due to the greater interest shown by the officers throughout the Battalion; moreover, we now had a sportsman as Chaplain, in the person of Capt. C. A. Fallon, who entered keenly into the men's pleasures." It is certainly true that if we had had more chaplains in the Corps of the type of Capt. C. A. Fallon the Cause of Religion would have benefited; he was not merely a chaplain and a good fellow out of the line; he figured that a chaplain had his uses when fighting was going on, and during the succeeding campaign he did invaluable work in the way of locating the wounded in open country and ministering to them under fire, and no award of the Military Cross was more popular throughout the unit than the one which bestowed that decoration on Capt. Fallon for his services rendered in the 2nd Battle of Cambrai.

Another entry in the Diary dated May 21st may be quoted: written as it was on the spot, it illustrates well the general feeling obtaining throughout the unit amid our then surroundings, and reads as follows: "Seldom have we felt so cut off from the war when in Corps Reserve as we have done in this village. On the eve of the Third Great Hun offensive, within earshot of our guns, which most nights can be heard muttering their barrages, close enough to St. Pol to hear the German bombs crashing therein at night, we seem to live in a world apart from the war itself. Never has our training been more severe; every day makes it clearer that when we move it will be to enter the bloodiest fight in which we have yet taken part, but our hours of rest seem to belie all this. This is probably due to the season and also to the phenomenal weather. We were in the Forward Area during the first beginnings of spring, and came out to find ourselves plunged suddenly into summer in an unravished part of the country where summer is at its best. A large number of men desert their billets at night and sleep under the trees in the open. This rest has put new life into the Battalion."

The weather was perfect; so hot that all training was carried out without tunics. Fortunately we were, for once, able to indulge in good bathing. Frévillers was situated close to La Comté, the village where we billeted before entering the Vimy Sector, and just beyond La Comté was an enormous quarry which had been flooded by springs with water. This formed a magnificent bathing pool; it was more than a pool; it was more like a lake, 450 yards by 150, and nightly it was crowded with enthusiastic swimmers.

On the 25th of the month we left Frévillers with its flowering cactus and charming denizens, some of whom we had known in Hersin, whence they had fled to a more secure refuge when the March offensive began, and moved off to the Diéval area; here we were quartered in three villages, all about a mile apart, Headquarters, with "A" and "B" Coys., being billeted in Conteville, "C" Coy. and the Transport Lines in Béthonval, and "D" Coy. in Huclier. Brigade Headquarters were situated at Diéval, about nine miles away; the 54th Bn. was at La Comté and Ourton, the 75th at Camblain Chatelain, and the 87th at Valhoun. The last-named was nearest to Brigade, and even the 87th was a good five miles away; never had the Brigade been so scattered. The training-ground selected for the use of the 11th Brigade was near Magnicourt, about nine miles from Conteville, and about six miles from the nearest Battalion, the 87th. Here the four units used to assemble twice a week between eight and nine o'clock in the morning; this meant rising at 2:30 a.m. in order to have time to get breakfast over and cover the distance in comfortable time to rest before the strenuous part of the day's work began; when the latter was over there was the long march home to billets. It may be imagined that after a few of these manoeuvres, carried out in hot weather over a dust-laden country, the units began to feel physically fit. On days when there were no manoeuvres there was perpetual drill or inspection in the mornings and good hard physical exercise at games or athletic sports in the afternoons and evenings. On Sundays a Church Parade would be frequently held over at Brigade Headquarters in Diéval, necessitating a long day's march. In short, nothing was neglected which might serve to harden the troops and fit them for long marching under the severest conditions. Incidentally, about two miles from Conteville was a creek which served admirably as a swimming-bath. On June 15th, Divisional Sports were held at Pernes, where Capt. T. R. Griffith, M.C., and Sergt. R. L. Algie, both of the 102nd, won the 100 yards' and 200 yards' events respectively. We had a first-class Lacrosse team at this time, which won its way through to the Finals, but failed to beat the 47th Bn. Our Baseball team, which had previously held a good record, fell to pieces during the early part of the season and rallied too late to redeem the ground lost. At a later date Battalion Headquarters Massed Football team covered themselves with glory by winning the Brigade Championship. On Dominion Day, when a Corps Sports Meet was held at Tinques, Sgt. Algie, our only representative, ran second in the 100 yards' final.

No amount of physical perfection, however, sufficed to save the Battalion from an epidemic of "Spanish Influenza," which, during June, made rapid strides throughout the Allied Armies in France. We were fortunate in having within our area a disused aerodrome on which the hangars had been left, and we obtained permission to fit two of these up as temporary hospitals. Consequently we were able to attend to almost all cases, who numbered something like 75 per cent of the unit, on the ground, without having to send them out to Field Ambulance. Very few cases were serious enough to need further

OFFICERS' GROUP, CONTEVILLE, July, 1918.—From left to Right: Top Row—Lt. P. R. Pae, Lt. C. H. Parkman, Lt. A. M. Morrison, Lt. G. Vancorlar, M.C., Lt. R. V. Lewer, Lt. H. D. McBrennan, Lt. J. A. Mann, Lt. J. R. Wilson, Lt. J. K. Dawson, Lt. V. Z. Manning, Lt. S. G. Moore, D.C.M., Lt. M. R. K. Devine, Lt. E. S. Channon. Second Row—Lt. H. J. Goodyear, Lt. A. T. Livingstone, Lt. F. J. Waite, Lt. C. T. Peers, Lt. C. W. McDermid, Lt. W. H. C. Stanley, Lt. C. E. Henderson, Lt. F. L. Mitchell, Lt. A. D. Duncan, Lt. H. E. A. Feetreath, Lt. C. A. Sabell, Lt. E. R. Nibbett, Lt. J. L. Lloyd, Lt. H. J. Frooch. Bottom Row—Lt. T. W. Peers, Lt. W. W. Dudop, M.C., Capt. E. Stead, Capt. W. Mck. Walwyn, Capt. W. G. Brimacombe, Major F. J. Gay, M.C., Major E. J. Ryan, Capt. S. H. Obell, M.C., Cmdt. I. C. R. Atkie, M.C., Capt. J. O. Knight, M.C., Capt. C. A. Fallon, Capt. H. Dunlop, Capt. R. Fitzmaurice, Lt. J. S. Lamrock.

attention than the Battalion Medical Detail was qualified to bestow, and long before we were moved into the line the epidemic had subsided.

Seeing that we remained in Conteville for nearly six weeks it may not be out of place to try and give some description of the surrounding country and of life in general in French farming villages as seen by visiting troops. Conteville is a typical village, consisting of one main street and a couple of side issues, and was inhabited solely by a farming community. As is usual in France and Belgium, the farmers live in the village as a community and go out to their fields by day; it is rare indeed to find an outlying farmhouse. This system tends to wasting a certain amount of time in the coming and going; but it gives the farmer the advantage of living amongst his own kind instead of being isolated in the midst of his acres. The principal industry in the agricultural districts would seem to be the manufacture of manure, which is the pride and delight of every prosperous farmer; the more successful the agriculturist and the higher his standing in the community, the bigger and richer his manure heap. Every farmhouse is built round a large court-yard which is constructed after the fashion of a big swimming-bath, being graded from the level of the ground at the street end to a depth of about four feet at the other. In this excavation, which measures approximately 100 feet by 30, is heaped the valued treasure: here it festers in the rains of winter and the hot sunshine of summer, and it advertises the wealth and social standing of its owner by the richness of its effluvia. How it is that the natives do not die of typhoid is one of the mysteries which confronts the visiting Canadian. As may be imagined, in farms where the manure pile reaches up to within three feet of the front door and the dining-room windows no special sanitary precautions are taken to ensure the cleanliness of the cows and to prevent the infection of their milk. And yet the children thrive! Verily it raises a doubt as to whether our elaborate precautions on this continent are really justified. Whether or not the microbe is indigenous to the American Continent, it is very certain that his presence does not in the least annoy the inhabitants of rural France. Every village is dependent for its water supply on wells which are sunk to an incredible depth; sometimes the rope on which the bucket hangs is broken and the villagers are content to use another well until a beneficent Providence sends along an Engineer unit to billet in the place, or some other military formation which will take steps to supply a new rope. Another thing which amazes the Canadian is that though the interior of the houses and all their fittings are kept scrupulously clean, and though the people themselves on Sundays and holidays appear in snowy linen and with well-washed faces, no house is ever found to be equipped with anything in the shape of a bath: a tin tub big enough to wash clothes in, but by no means big enough to sit in, apparently suffices for any ablutions which might seem to demand more accommodation than a hand basin can supply. These observations apply to every village in the agricultural district we visited. during our period of service in France and Belgium.

Conteville itself has quite a standing in the neighbourhood, owing to the presence in its midst of a patron saint in effigy, St. Benoit by name. This was a very devout person who lived in mediaeval times and made a pilgrimage to Rome, and his fame seems to have rested principally on some wonderful letters which he wrote home to his parish priest. A wax model of the good gentleman now lies in a shrine adjoining the church, very badly dressed in a shabby gown and a really disgraceful pair of socks, though the latter may possibly have been substituted for a good pair when the villagers heard that the Canadians were coming to live amongst them. The scenery round Conteville is beautiful in the extreme; the country is wide and rolling, well treed and apparently very fertile, though during our stay we saw no farming being done except by the wonderful French women, who from early womanhood to crabbed old age seem imbued with an absolutely tireless energy, and by a few old men and children. About three miles away over the fields lies St. Pol, quite a good-sized town, which showed many evidences of the proximity of the Hun artillery; moreover, his airmen made frequent visits in their big bombing machines, but the material damage they did was very slight. At Martin l'Eglise, which lay close to our village of Béthonval, a Tank Corps was established, and it was here that we first became at all well acquainted with these strange monsters. Béthonval during our sojourn enjoyed quite a local reputation, though for a very different reason from that which gave Conteville its place in the sun; at Béthonval dwelt Juliette, and Juliette was a very fair damsel and exceedingly good to look upon, and what was far more important, Juliette managed to get, by means unknown, a regular supply of excellent liqueurs, which made life very pleasant for "C" Coy. and the personnel of the Transport Lines, who usually contrived to finish up each stock on arrival before the outlying companies had a chance to participate.

At length, on July 10, our time at Conteville came to a close, and we received orders to move forward. Lieut.-Col. Lister had left for England on leave eight days before, and when our move orders came Major Ryan was in command of the Battalion. There were some other changes to be chronicled; Lieut. J. L. Lloyd, who had just completed a six-weeks course, was promoted from the position of Assistant-Adjutant, which he had held, when he was not acting as Adjutant, almost continuously from the beginning of 1917, to the position of Second-in-Command of "D" Coy., and Lieut. W. W. Dunlop, M.C., was transferred to Headquarters to fill the vacant position. Lieut. C. W. McDermid was created Scout Officer in place of Lieut. R. Adams, transferred to the R.A.F. Lieut. W. H. C. Stanley undertook the duties of Bombing Officer during the absence of Lieut. R. Perry, sick, and Capt. W. McL. Walwyn was appointed Second-in-Command of "C" Coy.

It was 8.00 p.m. when we pulled out of Conteville on July 10th. Strange to say, we had few regrets at leaving; though we had been there much longer than in any other settlement we had never succeeded in establishing really friendly relations with the villagers; on our arrival they had stood aloof, and they maintained the same attitude throughout our stay. They were the only people with whom we came into close contact throughout our 33 months in France or Belgium who did not shed a few tears on our departure or with whom some correspondence was not later maintained. An hour before midnight we arrived at Diéval, where we entrained for Mt. S. Eloy, which we reached at 5.00 a.m. on the following morning, marching off immediately to Brant and Cliff Camps at Ecoivres, close at hand; here we found breakfast, after which we turned in for a few hours' sleep, proceeding at 3.45 p.m. through pouring rain to a camp at Maison Blanche, the Transport going ahead to Ecurie Corner for the night, but returning next day, owing to excessive shelling, to a position next Headquarters. On the same day "B" and "D" Coys. went forward to Blanche Post, in the Reserve Line, where they were joined on the 13th by Headquarters, "A" and "C" Coys. being billeted in Roclincourt. The general lay-out of the ground round Blanche Post was slightly reminiscent of Zouave Valley in the days before the capture of the Ridge, but there was one added feature which was immensely popular, viz., four cold water showers with heaps of water laid on. On the 17th we moved up to the Front Line in relief of the 87th. We were now back on the Oppy front, just to the right of the positions we had occupied in April, so close, in fact, that our Medical Detail used the same quarters for their Regimental Aid Post.

The feature of this tour was a successful raid carried out on the night of June 23-24 by "D" Coy. Two days were spent in preparation, during which some very valuable work was done by the Battalion Scouts, under Lieut. R. L. Gale, Intelligence Officer, in the course of a daylight reconnaissance of the trenches leading N.E. from our Front Line in the vicinity of the intended raid. When close to the block in the trench which marked the dividing line between the Hun and ourselves the Scouts noticed first a trap bomb and later a trap alarm; these they carefully avoided, and Pte. E. W. Fenton, carefully and quietly climbing the parapet, was enabled to observe the enemy's dispositions on the other side of the block in great detail. Had it not been that a raid was in course of preparation it would have been easy to kill or capture the Hun outpost, but this would have entailed increased vigilance on his part and would have imperilled the success of the larger operation. The raid itself followed the barrage at midnight, and was carried out by three parties, one under Lieut. J. H. French, a second under Lieut. T. W. Peers, with a third party in support, under Lieut. A. M. Morrison. The first party found more wire than had been anticipated, as the high grass had hidden it from view, and some difficulty was encountered in negotiating it; finally they cut their way through and entered the enemy trench, where they captured six prisoners and inflicted many casualties. The second party unfortunately lost time owing to the intense darkness, entering the trench on our own side of the block; by the time this mistake had been rectified the Hun had had time to escape, and only three prisoners were captured, though heavy casualties were inflicted. On our side we lost one Other Rank killed and 12 wounded, but the result of the raid was net gain, including, as it did, nine prisoners, the certainty of from 15 to 20 Huns killed, and the knowledge that many more had been wounded. Half the object of these raids was to weaken the enemy's morale, and now more than at any other time it was necessary to carry on this good work; on that account alone the raid would have been deemed successful; in addition, we brought back prisoners who afforded identifications and useful information. Illustrative of the spirit of our men after their nine weeks out of the line the Diary has the following:—"Pte. Wren lost his rifle in the wire, but he leaped into the trench and tackled the enemy with his bare hands; he seized two Huns by the throat, and dashed their heads together till they surrendered. Pte. Twell saw a comrade fall mortally wounded; he dragged him to a shell-hole and with his rifle fought off all efforts of the enemy to surround him; eventually he obtained assistance and brought the man in."

The Higher Command was more than well pleased with the work of the 102nd Bn. in this raid, as is shown by the following messages received: "My dear Lister,—Hearty congratulations to all concerned on your good work. The nine prisoners and the dead Germans leave a fine record. I am very much pleased. Your raid was as neat a one as has been pulled off. Special credit is due Ryan and Gale. Please congratulate all concerned for me. Congratulations have also come in for you from the Divisional Commander and from the G.O.C. 10th and 12th Brigades. Very sincerely, V. W. Odlum." Later the Brigadier forwarded this second message: "11th C.I.B. 28|7|18. My dear Colonel Lister,—I have just received a letter from Sir David Watson from which I quote: 'I have much pleasure in enclosing you herewith copy of a letter which I have received from Lieut.-General Sir A. W. Currie, Commanding Canadian Corps, in connection with the recent raid of the 102nd Bn. In speaking with me on this matter General Currie expressed himself as greatly delighted with the splendid work carried out by this Battalion, as well as with the effort of the 54th on the same night. Would you be good enough to transmit these messages to the respective Battalions.' The letter from Sir Arthur Currrie to which the Divisional Commander refers is as follows: 'Dear Watson,—Please convey my congratulations to the G.O.C. 11th Brigade and to the 102nd Bn. for the splendid raid carried out by them a few nights ago. I consider the operation a splendid success, showing in all concerned fighting qualities of a high order. Yours ever, A. W. Currie.' It gives me a great deal of pleasure to be able to add this message to the other congratulations I have already forwarded you. Victor W. Odlum, Commanding 11th Canadian Inf. Brigade."

On the evening of the 23rd we moved out to Support, taking the place of the 87th. Our quarters here were distinctly poor and needed much improvement, some of which they received; incidentally the Hun made them more uncomfortable by throwing over a lot of gas shells every night. Whilst we were in this area we began to see signs of the times in the movement of tanks and cavalry. "The Day" for us was now approaching fast, but it was not to find us in the area where we expected to be, and when we were relieved by the 7th Bn. Royal Scots on July 31st and moved out to Ecoivres, we did not realize that we were taking the first step in a series of operations which were still further to enhance the fame of the Canadian Corps.

CHAPTER X.

From Ecoivres to Berneville—Night Marching to the South—The Dawn of "The Day"—Battle of Amiens—Rosieres—A Record Train Journey—Ready for the Hindenburg Switch

NOT until the small hours of the morning did the tail end of the Battalion reach Village Camp, Ecoivres, as the relieving Battalion, being ignorant of conditions in the Oppy sector, required considerable instruction before taking over the new positions; moreover, the Hun airmen were unwontedly active and successful with the bombing machines, harassing the outgoing troops considerably and inflicting seven casualties in "A" Coy. But by 10.00 a.m. on Aug. 1st everyone had returned and rested and was in a position to appreciate the baths and clean underwear which had been arranged for the Battalion, with the prophetic warning attached that it might be some time before another such opportunity occurred. In the afternoon we fell in and marched ten miles to Berneville; it was strange to see how the brief respite of barely three weeks which had elapsed since the severe training at Conteville, coupled with the days of enforced inactivity which trench warfare entails, reacted on the men; three weeks before they could tackle an eighteen-mile march with field manoeuvres thrown in; now a little ten-mile march in heavy order was an effort, and swollen feet and blisters accounted for a large number of stragglers. But this was merely a temporary reaction, and a couple of days of open life served to put everybody literally "on their feet" again Berneville was quite a serviceable little place and the camp was good, though recent rain had made it very muddy; an open-air swimming tank was in evidence, but at the time of our arrival the weather was unpropitious for bathing, and we left after a two-night stay.

The departure was marked by a degree of secrecy hitherto unknown in the Corps. This was the occasion when representatives of Canadian units were deliberately sent north with the express intention of hoodwinking the Hun; every effort was being made to instil a belief amongst the country people that the Canadian Corps was going to Belgium again, and it is well known that this information was transmitted through various sources to the enemy, who was in consequence the more astounded when we appeared in his midst five days later near Amiens.

The orders laid down for march discipline to be observed during the forthcoming series of marches were exceedingly strict; absolutely no straggling was to be countenanced, and each unit was to have a rear-guard marching at the pace of its weakest member to bring up all who fell out from the main body.. Every effort was to be made by day to keep the troops under cover, and every precaution was to be taken which might ensure the movement of the Corps being kept as secret as possible. On the evening of the 3rd we marched a mile or so down the road where 'buses were drawn up to convey us to our unknown destination, for we were proceeding under sealed orders; for nine hours we drove through an unknown country, the general direction being south, though it was evident that the route had been chosen with the deliberate intention of confusing any spies, as it kept on' diverging to different points of the compass. On the way we passed several units from the American Expeditionary Force, who gave us a rousing welcome and showered cigarettes on us as we drove through their lines. At 5.30 a.m. on the 4th our 'buses stopped and we descended to find ourselves in the middle of Nowhere, just a cross-roads with not a house in sight. Though August, it was bitterly cold at that hour of the morning, and we had been sitting cramped and chilled throughout a long night's drive; we stood about and cursed the war whilst the sealed orders were opened and maps consulted, with the result that we took the cross-road to the right and marched five miles to the hamlet of Fresnes-Tilloluy, where we had breakfast and turned in out of sight, remaining under cover all day. In this village we left all packs and officers' bed-rolls, little dreaming that it would be three weeks before we saw them again, and then at 9:30 p.m. we fell in for the first of the series of night marches which were destined to bring us to the Amiens front.

It was extraordinarily dark for the time of year; there was no moon, and a great part of our way lay along roads heavily shrouded with trees which allowed not a glimmer of starlight to penetrate. Our route led us back over the ground covered the same morning, and over a small part of the ground which we had traversed in the 'buses, a fact which aroused much resentment amongst the "foot-sloggers." Soldiers, as a class, detest marching, and anything which can possibly be construed as unnecessary distance always excites their bitterest criticism, but in the present case some Battalion had to be selected for the extra miles, as all the Brigade units could not be billeted together, and the 102nd, as was usually the case, being the junior Battalion, was chosen as the "goat." At 2.00 a.m. we reached Metigny, where it rained most of the day; a good thing, as it kept the men hidden and laid the dust; besides, we were quite willing to sleep, anyway. At 9.00 p.m. we fell in again ready to move off, but for some reason unknown were kept standing around for an hour before we actually set out on what was officially stated to be a 21-mile march; 25 miles was more probably the distance covered, and covered as it was in battle order with empty haversacks and yawning stomachs it seemed like 30. It is not easy to understand why some provision was not made for a bite to eat on these long night marches. When battalions marched by day a stop was always made for lunch, and sandwiches or their equivalent were invariably carried in the haversack; why the darkness should have been presumed to counteract hunger is a mystery. As the dawn broke we found that we were traversing a very beautiful part of the country, more open and billowy than that around Conteville, which was softer in its aspect, and very different in character from that to which we had for so long been accustomed in Flanders and the northern portion of France. The villages were more widely scattered, but larger and more prosperous in their appearance. The term "La Belle France" had long been a joke amongst those of the Canadians who had never seen anything of it save for the shell-shocked areas of the Somme and Vimy; now the expression took on a new meaning, and the men were loud in their admiration of the country through which they were marching. Our destination on this occasion was Creuse, which proved to be a fair-sized settlement almost worthy of being called a town, and which we reached at 9.00 a.m. on the 6th. The Battalion had shown up well on this extra long march; there were some sore feet, but nothing which a few hours' rest would not mend. A more serious trouble, however, stared us in the face; we were confronted with a shortage in tobacco and matches, a shortage which lasted without much alleviation throughout the whole month.

At Creuse we rested until 8.45 p.m., when once more we set out, this time for Boves Wood, an extensive wood on a hill which served as a concentration point for 50,000 men and 25,000 horses immediately before the great push of August 8th. Owing to the incompetency of our guides we took a wrong turn in the dark, and the subsequent retracing of our steps took us through deep mud and darkened woods, which not only added mileage but considerable discomfort to our labours. The main roads we found to be crowded with French troops, mostly Transport and Artillery. To our way of thinking the Transport waggons of the French Army are grossly overloaded and disgracefully shabby in appearance; they remind the spectator irresistibly of the average third-rate travelling circus; the horses also look in wretched condition and excite ridicule at first sight. But they do most certainly "deliver the goods," and the way in which they cover the ground and get through with the job they have on hand ends by exciting a very genuine admiration. It was not until 4:30 a.m. on the 7th that we eventually reached the Chateau in Boves Wood which was our halting-place; there were no billets, but the ground was soft, if wet, and there was abundance of undergrowth with which to make comfortable bedding; our orders were to lie well hidden, and we were well content to do so. The undergrowth was so dense and the overhead cover so luxuriant that it was easy to understand that the wood sheltered the numbers above mentioned. What would not the Hun have given to know that well within his artillery range so formidable a force was already massed to give him the first of those deadly blows which were to result in three months in the signing of the Armistice! During the course of the day a meeting of all Officers and N.C.O.'s in charge of Sections was held and every detail of the next day's offensive was elaborately explained and every position in our own area of operations carefully pointed out on the map. By 10.00 p.m., when the Battalion fell in for the last time before the battle began, every man had a clear and distinct idea of what his own particular job would be and of what part we were playing in the general scheme of operations. And so, under the command of Lieut.-Col. Lister, we marched off in the gathering dusk through Boves town and across the Luce River to take up our position in the First Assembly Point behind Gentelles Wood.

This wood, standing on the top of an eminence, acted as an excellent screen, and here all the Brigade units assembled by midnight and settled down to take what rest was possible before the barrage started at 4.20 a.m. on the 8th. It was a cold night and the ground was wet with dew, consequently the issue of rum which was served out at dawn was doubly welcome. It may here be stated that during the whole of our stay with the Fourth Army under General Rawlinson, to which the Corps was attached for this offensive, our creature comforts were better looked after than in any other Army, and during our service in France we had experience of all save the Fifth. At 4.20 a.m. to the dot a terrific barrage opened, eclipsing anything we had yet heard; this same expression will be found in accounts of the succeeding battles up to the time of the Armistice, as the Allies increased the ferocity of their opening barrages with each successive push. Ahead of us was the 7th Brigade of the 3rd Canadian Division, through whom we were to pass at a later stage, and with the opening of the barrage they moved forward to the attack. There was a white mist hanging low which was greatly in favour of the attacking forces, but as the sun came up this quickly disappeared. An hour later it was our turn to move forward in closer support. Our way led through fields of ripening corn, past innumerable batteries of every calibre, across the swamps of the Luce, through orchards and then along the side of the Amiens-Roye Road, where we saw the firstfruits of the battle in the shape of large bodies of Hun prisoners being marched to the rear, and a number of our own walking wounded. The latter seemed to be intoxicated with success; the Hun had been caught entirely by surprise; if he had thought of the Canadians at all he had thought of them as preparing an offensive up north. He certainly had the surprise of his life on August 8th. Our second Assembly Point was reached at 9.30 a.m., and here we received orders to halt until 12.10 p.m., when we moved forward again in Artillery formation in lines of platoons to our Jumping-off place, where our own share in the attack was to commence. Up to this point we sustained no casualties.

    Connecting on the right with the 54th and on the left with the 78th, we now passed through the 7th Brigade and plunged forward. Our first objective was a sunken road, which was taken by "B" and "D" Coys. without serious difficulty by 3.00 p.m. The second was a more serious matter, being the forward edge of Beaucourt Wood in our front. "A" and "C" Coys. now passed through the other two and pressed on, but encountered very severe opposition, consisting of heavy machine gun fire from the wood on our immediate front, machine gun fire from a wood on our left flank, which was exposed owing to the 78th having fallen behind our advance, and long-distance machine gun and trench mortar fire from the right flank of Beaucourt Wood; this flank was to have been protected by two tanks attached for that purpose, but they had been unable to keep up with our rapid advance, and it was not until two tanks attached to the 54th had come round to our assistance that "A" Coy., on the right, was able to make further progress, which it did by section rushes and then, when within fifty yards of the woods, charging and capturing the place by storm. In this operation we were greatly helped by the 54th on the right, who outflanked the wood and diverted much of the enemy's fire. After gaining the edge of the wood there was still hard work ahead of "A" Coy., as the ends of the wood were very strongly held; "D" Coy. was consequently brought up as reinforcement and the wood was eventually cleared, but on reaching the forward edge our men again came under very heavy machine gun fire, this time from a trench lying in the open on the brow of the opposite hill and from another sunken road. At this juncture two whippet tanks gave us great assistance, enabling us to engage the enemy hand-to-hand, when we inflicted further heavy casualties and captured from 50 to 60 prisoners, though being subjected all the time to machine gun and trench mortar fire from still another wood. In the meantime "C" Coy. on the left had been encountering very strong opposition from a system of trenches held by the enemy in force; the 78th was still behind the line of advance, its nearest unit to us being one platoon which had lost its Battalion and was following us up about 400 yards distant; consequently "C" Coy. had to overcome this opposition without assistance, which was not as originally laid down in the programme. The feat was done, however, with several resultant prisoners. and thereafter the opposition manifestly weakened, the enemy retiring in some disorder to other trenches in the open, from which he was successively ejected, the only serious opposition coming from three or four determined machine gun crews, all of whom were eventually either killed or captured. "C" Coy. reached its final objective at 4.35 p.m. The Battalion was now ensconced in the position it had set out to capture, and protective posts were immediately put out, but these could not go very far forward owing to the heavy fire which the enemy was maintaining on our positions from the high ground in front, and our left flank was still exposed; consequently the latter was withdrawn a little as a protective flank until the arrival of the 78th shortly afterwards.

During the course of this operation we captured 159 prisoners, 4 light trench mortars, 2 granatenwerfers, 5 heavy machine guns. 5 light machine guns. The trophies were all carefully tagged and left in accordance with instructions for shipment to Ordnance, but, as usually happened in the case of spoils of war, half of them were stolen by succeeding battalions. Captured trophies gave more trouble and were worth less than anything else; they were provocative of much dishonesty, every battalion naturally desiring to furnish ocular proof of its prowess, and they were the cause of much disappointment to home towns, where the authorities would be warned of the pending arrival of trophies which never reached their destination. Our own casualties on August 8th were as follows: Lieuts. J. L. Lloyd, J. K. Dawson, C. T. Peers, and 20 Other Ranks killed or died of wounds; Lieuts. E. R. Niblett, E. S. Chagnon and 88 Other Ranks wounded. The Company Commanders on this day were Capt. I. C. R. Atkin, M.C., Capt. J. A. Mann, Major W. McL. Walwyn, and Lieut. V. C. Brimacombe, commanding "A,""B," "C" and "D" Coys. respectively.

After the capture of the final objective Headquarters was established in this wood, where a well-appointed German camp was found; all sorts of supplies were in evidence, beer, food, including good cake, and a German Field Ambulance full of their wounded and well stocked with hospital supplies. Some enemy bombardment was sustained throughout the night, but no damage was done. Meantime the 75th had passed through us, and the 87th had their Headquarters with ours; on the morning of the 9th they continued the attack and captured their objectives, leaving us in Brigade Reserve. That night we moved Headquarters further up towards the front to another wood, proceeding still farther forward on the 10th to the last of a series of woods bordering on a wide open expanse traversed by good roads all leading eastwards towards the enemy positions. These roads were continuously crowded with transport of all kinds, interspersed with which were numerous batteries and large bodies of cavalry, all going forward in pursuit of the Hun. On the 13th we took over the Front Line from the 85th and 38th Bns., remaining one night, when we returned to the last mentioned wood on relief by the 22nd Bn. Plans for another offensive were on foot, but these were subsequently cancelled, and we were glad of the opportunity to reorganize and absorb drafts of reinforcements which arrived during this period. On the 17th, Brigade Reserve was established at Rosières, whither we moved. Here we had a good chance to see something of the German method behind his own lines. Ten days before Rosières had been well within his Reserve area and had been used as an internment camp and a base of supplies. Here also was an enormous salvage dump, piled high in a well organized system, with captured munitions and looted plunder. A standard gauge railway ran through the camp, and when we arrived German engines were already busy hauling out for our own use salvaged cars. On the 20th we moved up to the Front Line again, relieving the 87th, and it was during this tour that Lieut. H. J. Goodyear met with his death whilst in charge of a night patrol sent out to connect with the Australians on our left. This was our last tour of duty on the Amiens front, as we were relieved on the night of the 24th by the 1st Bn. 88th R.I. (French). This was the first occasion on which the Battalion had handed over direct to a French unit, and the differences between their organization and ours were very obvious. The relieving Battalion was formed of a magnificent body of men, who once again dispelled the utterly erroneous but always preconceived notion that the French infantryman is a man of small stature. We returned to our Base camp in the early morning of the 25th, rested all day, and at 6.00 p.m. marched off to Bois de Blangny, making a small detour to get baths on the way. This bath was a nightmare; it was situated in a wood, and the men had to undress in the open, line up naked with their dirty clothes in their arms, exchange their clothing, line up again, and then find cold water only. Incidentally there were not enough clothes to go round, and a thunderstorm broke out in the middle of the operation. It was a pitch-dark night and a broken road to follow, full of shell-holes, as the Adjutant's horse found, and very muddy, but we eventually reached Bois-de Blangny at 3.30 a.m. on the 26th and remained there one night, lying out under the trees. Here we found our packs, which had been left three weeks before at Fresnes-Tilloluy. On the following day we marched off to Longeau, about three miles distant, where we entrained for an unknown destination.

The journey on which we were now embarked is well worthy of mention. It was made on scheduled time. Punctually to the minute the train pulled out at 2.18 a.m. on the morning of the 28th. Twelve hours later we detrained at Acq, in the old Vimy area; here we were told that 'buses would be found ready and waiting for us up the road; and the 'buses were actually there and ready to take us, as soon as we had boarded them, to our old camp at Berneville, which we had occupied before starting out on the historic round trip to Amiens and back. In the words of the Diary: "The move from Longeau to Berneville was planned, detailed and executed admirably; there was no waiting and no confusion; a marked contrast to most."

CHAPTER XI.

Neuville Vitasse—Second Battle of Arras—A Fortnight in Reserve—Second Battle of Cambrai.

E ONLY remained one night in Berneville, and on August 29th the Battalion, including the Transport Lines, which had been brigaded, moved up to a trench system on the outskirts of the ruined village of Neuville Vitasse. The day was very warm, and the unaccustomed packs weighed heavy on the nine-mile march, which took us over the same old shell-shocked style of country with which we had been so well acquainted, but which we had failed to see down south. Our new camp was situated in the middle of a trench system which had been at one time part of the Hun Front Line, but it had been disused for a long time and was in an appalling state of neglect and dirt. After settling down we were informed that we should take part in big operations which were planned for the immediate future, the object of which would be the breaking of the famous Hindenburg Switch Line, also known as the Drocourt-Quéant Line and the Wotan Line, an immensely strong series of defensive positions lying west of the Canal du Nord and straddling the main Arras-Cambrai road. At this point Lieut.-Colonel Lister left us to go into hospital, sick, and the command of the Battalion fell to Major E. J. Ryan, who conducted the Battalion's operations in what is generally known as the Second Battle of Arras. Major F. J. Gary, M.C., who had just returned from a Senior Officers' Course in England, acted as Second-in-Command, Capt. S. H. Okell, M.C., was still our Adjutant, and the four Company Commanders were Capt. J. A. Mann, Capt. J. G. Knight, M.C., Capt. T. R. Griffith, M.C., and Lieut. J. R. Wilson, commanding "A," "B," "C" and "D" Coys. respectively.

At 8.30 p.m. on the evening of Sept. 1st the Battalion fell in and marched off to the First Assembly Point in Vis-en-Artois. It was a bright starlight night, and the roads were packed with traffic of all kinds. Enemy planes were very active, and on the way we were held up by a blazing ammunition lorry which had been fired by a bomb and was shooting off the contents of its dangerous load in every

direction. The approach to our Assembly Point was difficult in the extreme, lying on the other side of a rolling expanse which was thickly fenced with our own barbed wire; in the starlight it was difficult to keep to the winding trails which led through the barriers, and the whole surface of the ground was deeply furrowed with disused trenches. By 1.00 o'clock the following morning, however, we reached our destination, an extensive sand-pit which afforded excellent cover from the shells which began to drop around us immediately on our arrival. Here we slept until gas shells falling in our midst at 4.45 a.m. compelled our unwilling arousal and the furtive fingering of the ever-objectionable gas mask. It was a chilly dawn, and we were heartily thankful for the tot of rum which was served out just as the barrage broke out at 5.00 a.m., the signal for the First Canadian Division to "go over." Directly in front of the 11th Brigade was the 12th, to whom had been allotted the task of actually breaking through the main line of defence; behind the 12th Brigade, on our own immediate front, was the 87th Bn., who were to pass through the former east of the Drocourt-Quéant Line, and through whom we were to leap-frog after they had captured Ecourt St. Quentin, our own objective being first laid down as Oisy-le-Verger, on the east bank of the Canal du Nord, though this programme was subsequently modified.

The barrage was extraordinarily intense, and one hour after its commencement we moved forward, maintaining a distance of 1,000 yards from the 87th Bn. Within half-an-hour we passed into a zone of continuous barrage fire put over by the Hun to catch the supporting units. The terrain in this district is undulating, and the descending slopes were pitilessly swept by a hail of shell and machine gun fire, causing comparatively heavy casualties. It was at this point that Major J. F. Gary, M.C., fell mortally wounded by a shell; another claimed six of the Headquarters batmen and cooks, killing one outright, fatally wounding a second and seriously wounding the remaining four. It was a long tramp under such conditions to Drocourt Trench, which had been the jumping-off place for the 87th, and where we were due to remain until such time as we were to go forward to take our share in the active work ahead, the Companies taking shelter in Dury Road. Shortly after noon "C" Coy. moved forward, keeping in touch with the 87th, but on reaching the crest of the opposite hill Lieut. C. W. McDermid, the Scout Officer, and the four Battalion Scouts who were maintaining connection with the 87th, were wounded and were unable to report progress; at the same time Capt. T. R. Griffith, the Company Commander, became a casualty, and before Major Walwyn, upon whom the command then devolved, was aware either that his leader was wounded or that the connecting link with the forward Battalion had been broken, "C" Coy. found itself up in the Front Line, fighting side by side with the 87th, who had been held up by a very vigorous opposition, resistance being concentrated chiefly in the vicinity of the Dury Windmill, which stands out as a landmark in the neighbourhood. When the Higher Command learned that the forward battalions were engaged in heavy fighting, orders were sent to Major Walwyn to withdraw "C" Coy. into Support, where it rightly belonged, and the other three companies, which were cautiously moving forward, were ordered to take up defensive positions in the Drocourt-Quéant Line, after which "C" Coy. was brought back into Brigade Reserve. At 3.30 a.m. on Sept. 3rd we were sent forward to relieve the 72nd Bn. astride the Arras-Cambrai Road, a very difficult operation, as the night was intensely dark and the guides which were to have been detailed to meet our Companies were not forthcoming; but the relief was successfully effected, and at 7:30 a.m. we were ordered forward to locate the enemy, who was reported to be withdrawing. Our route now lay due east, parallel with the Arras-Cambrai Road, along which were dotted the frequent bodies of men, mules and horses, whilst in the middle of the road lay the wreckage of more than one armoured car, testifying to the destructive fire which the enemy had maintained on this main artery of communication. The Companies moved forward in the order ,"A," "B" and "D," the three leap-frogging each other, the last named to pass through up to the banks of the Canal. Very little opposition was encountered during the early stages of this advance, but after "D" had leap-frogged, the men were subjected to very heavy fire. "B" Coy. took up defensive positions and dug-in against the storm of machine-gun bullets, but "D" pushed on to the bank of the Canal. During this advance we were continually in touch with the 54th Bn. on our left and the 8th, 10th and 31st Bns. on our right. By nightfall the position was as follows: "D" Coy. was holding the Front Line on the right; "B" Coy. had moved up on the left and was holding the line on that flank in direct communication with the 54th, "C" Coy. was in Support and "A" in Reserve. Headquarters was established in a system of dug-outs adjoining the Arras-Cambrai Road.

At dusk battle patrols were sent forward to ascertain the state of the bridges across the Canal and to report on the feasibility of forcing a passage. This was a very hazardous and difficult task, as the ground west of the Canal was continuously swept with machine-gun fire; but the patrols managed to scout along the whole of the bank and sent back a report that all the bridges were down; later the enemy was definitely located as holding Lock Wood, a copse west of the Canal and just north of the Arras-Cambrai Road; this was in "D" Coy's area, and to this company was allotted the duty of clearing the wood. The attack was carried out in the face of very heavy machine-gun fire and the difficulties of the assault were increased by the nature of the ground, which was marshy and little better than a swamp; the men had to cross over this unfavourable surface in the open and sustained a hot fire, not only from the wood which was their immediate objective, but from the high ground east of the Canal. The assault was, however, successfully delivered, and the enemy was driven from the wood, but "D" Coy. suffered heavily in casualties. After the loss of the wood the enemy retaliated by a fierce barrage along the whole Battalion frontage, and in addition mercilessly pounded our Support area. It was now obvious that a passage of the Canal was impracticable without the active co-operation of heavy artillery, which was still too far in the rear, owing to the rapid nature of our advance, to be available. "D" Coy., numbering but a remnant of its fighting strength, was relieved by the 27th Bn. on the night of the 4th, and "B" Coy., which had not suffered so severely, side-slipped further to the left and pushed closer to the Canal, sending out battle patrols and scouts once more to confirm the report that all bridges were down and that passage was impossible, as the enemy was holding the eastern bank in strength. On the morning of the 5th patrols were again sent out, this time to ascertain whether there was any truth in the report that the enemy was retiring from his side of the bank; considerable sniping and machine-gun firing proved conclusively that the answer was in the negative. During the remainder of the day the Battalion lay dug-in, and though considerable shelling and sniping was indulged in by the enemy no serious casualties were incurred. The same night we were relieved by the 49th Bn. and returned by road to Neuville Vitasse; this necessitated a long 8-mile march along a route which was continually peppered with bombs and shells, and imposed an enormous strain on troops who had been carrying on the hardest kind of fighting for four days. Our casualties for the 2nd Battle of Arras were as follows: Killed or Died of Wounds—Major F. J. Gary, M.C., and 42 Other Ranks; Wounded—Capt. S. H. Okell (at duty), Capt. T. R. Griffith, M.C., Lieuts. C. W. McDermid, H. D. McClenahan, T. W. Peers, J. S. Lamrock, J. Palmer (at duty), A. M. Morrison, A. D. Duncan and 145 Other Ranks. Three Other Ranks who were at the time attached from the Battalion to the 11th Brigade were also killed in action, including Pte. R. S. Ketcheson, a Battalion Runner and one of the finest boys in the most popular section of the unit, a modern incarnation of Juvenal's immortal "ingenui vultus puer ingenuique pudoris."

On our arrival at Neuville Vitasse we stayed quiet all day, making little attempt to improve the general lay-out of the camp or to put the dug-outs in good shape, as we fully expected move orders that night or early the following day, but none came, and it was gradually borne in on us that we had to make our dwelling-place once more in the wilderness. Work was accordingly started on camp improvement, and a terrific thunderstorm which struck us on the 7th and flooded all the dug-outs made this work the more imperative. Forthwith the area became tunnelled with serviceable dug-outs and dotted with iron-sheet huts; a small quantity of bivouacs were also available for use. The Transport Lines at this time were all brigaded about half a mile to our rear. The adaptability of the modern Army, and particularly of the Canadian Corps, was never better illustrated than in the area which we now occupied. To our left lay Corps Headquarters, which presented all the features of a model village with an electric lighting plant installed. Naturally there were no regular baths in the vicinity, but a few kilometres away, at Heninel, lay a couple of small ponds, they might almost have been styled puddles, but the Engineers were called upon to exercise their ingenuity, and by the use of several large tarpaulins they converted these wayside puddles into very serviceable baths, with three sprinklers doing good work and accommodating as many as 150 men in an hour. This improvised bath-house was an infinitely better one than the majority of those erected under more favourable conditions. On the 14th of the month a big Decoration Parade for the 11th Brigade was held in the 54th area, and medals were awarded to their recipients by the Corps Commander, who, in a speech after the parade, told us that we should have at least one more big battle that year. Thereafter, during our stay in Neuville Vitasse, preparations were made for the impending offensive, which was to launch the third smashing blow delivered by the Corps to the Hun, and which is styled the Second Battle of Cambrai.

On the 17th Lieut.-Colonel Lister reported back for duty and resumed command of the Battalion, going forward two days later to reconnoitre the ground over which we should soon be operating, and on the evening of the 25th we fell in and marched to our staging area near Bullecourt. It may here be remarked that nothing changes so quickly as an army vocabulary. A new word appears from no one knows where and is adopted for a season on every possible occasion. During the recent push the word "element" had appeared, and for the whole of that tour it was to be in the fashion to speak of "elements of the Bosche"; now we came across "staging area"; previously we had been content to speak of "assembly points"; a philologist might well be able to date the progress of the war by careful reference to the use of words and expressions. Some words had a long life, such as "odd," introduced by Capt. Okell when he first became Adjutant; food became the "odd bite"; a written message, "the odd chit"; sleep was "the odd wink," and so on; but "elements" died a quick death, though Major Ryan made desperate efforts to rehabilitate it when he returned from leave after the Cambrai affair. Whether or not the change of name had anything to do with it may be open to doubt, but the fact remains that we had the greatest difficulty in locating our proper place near Bullecourt; we were supposed to be taking over lines occupied by the 42nd Bn., but on our arrival we found that the 78th had got in ahead of us, and we had eventually to make what shift we could in the open; it was then midnight and very dark, but the weather, though cold, was fine. Throughout the whole of the next day, the 26th, we lay quiet, and at 10.30 we fell in and moved off towards our next halting-place, Inchy-en-Artois, but we were held back by the presence of troops ahead, and made a detour up into the old Hindenburg Support trenches for a couple of hours' rest; it was not a happy move; the trenches were almost impassable owing to the slippery mud and darkness, and what rest we obtained was more than counterbalanced by the fatigue sustained in reaching the dug-outs. Here we stayed till 2.30 a.m. on Sept. 27th, moving forward then to the trenches in Inchy-en-Artois, where we awaited the barrage, which was timed for 5.20. Once more we were robbed of the privilege of being the first troops to follow the barrage. In a surprise attack of this kind the leading troops have a double advantage; they have the honour and glory of actually storming the line and taking most prisoners, and at the same time they are usually ensconced in the enemy's trenches by the time the answering barrage begins to fall; moreover, this barrage is always largely directed over their heads, being designed to catch the supporting battalions coming up behind; this is what we suffered from so severely on Sept. 2nd. Again, by the time the supporting troops have passed through the original storming parties and are ready to deliver their attack on their own objective the element of surprise has been lost, and the positions against which their assaults are directed are by this time strongly defended. On this occasion the 10th Brigade was in the lead, and it was our duty to pass through them in due course and carry the attack forward to Bourlon Wood, which was our final objective for that portion of the operation. On our left was the 87th Battalion, through whom the 54th were to pass when the main attack on Bourlon Wood was to be delivered. The 4|7th King's Liverpool Regiment was on our right.

At 5.20 a.m. an intense barrage broke out, and at 6.00 a.m. we moved off from Inchy-en-Artois, maintaining close touch with the 10th Brigade in front. As soon as the latter had taken their objectives, "A" and "B" Coys., under Capt. I. C. R. Atkin, M.C., and Lieut. R. V. Leese respectively, went forward on the right and left, and succeeded in capturing their objectives, the enemy positions which lay in front of the main object of attack, Bourlon Wood; this was left for "C" and "D" Coys., under Lieuts. V. Z. Manning and J. R. Wilson, M.C., but when the latter commenced to advance they found that the Imperials on the right were not up, and that their right flank was consequently exposed to a full tempest of heavy artillery and machine-gun fire. In spite of this they pushed their way forward until within about 100 yards of their objective, where they halted for cover in the shelter of a sunken road and of a line of trenches from which they had successfully ousted the Hun. It was at this time that an unparalleled misfortune overtook the Battalion; Headquarters had advanced behind the companies and had been established in a German pill-box on the top of a small eminence, whence a good view of the operations on the opposite slope leading up to Bourlon Wood could be obtained; hardly had the Colonel taken up his quarters there when, at about 9.30 a.m., a shell landed right in the opening of the doorway and severely wounded both Colonel Lister and Capt. Okell, the Adjutant, at the same time killing outright Lieut. S. G. Moore, D.C.M., the

Signalling Officer, who was standing outside, and three Runners from other Battalions who were awaiting replies to their messages. This was a double catastrophe indeed, as there was nobody by this time left in the Battalion to take the Colonel's place; the companies had all suffered heavily in casualties, and not a senior officer was available. In this emergency Lieut. C. H. Packman, the Battalion Lewis Gun Officer, sent off a message to Brigade detailing the disaster which had occurred, and the Brigadier responded by appointing Lieut.-Col. Thompson, D.S.O., of the 124th Bn., who was acting in command of the 75th in our Support, to take over the temporary command of the 102nd. This officer immediately moved up two companies of the 75th into positions round the 102nd Bn. headquarters. As soon as the news of what had happened reached the Transport Lines Lieut. W. W. Dunlop, M.C., who, as Assistant Adjutant, had been left behind, came right up to the Front Line and took over the duties of Adjutant, which he continued to carry out with conspicuous success until the day of demobilization.

In the meantime the Hun was pounding our positions with every kind of missile. To the rear of Headquarters was a large Forward Dressing Station; though its non-combatant profession was conspicuously advertised by a big Red Cross flag the enemy systematically bombarded it, and it was here that we lost poor "Bobby" Duncan, our Medical Sergeant, who was struck by a machine-gun bullet whilst he was ministering to the wounded, and succumbed later to his injuries. The work of the Red Cross men in this exposed position was beyond all praise, and our own Medical Officer, Capt. H. Dunlop, M.C., and Capt. C. A. Fallon, Chaplain, greatly distinguished themselves by their devoted service amongst the wounded.

Every effort was now made to get the Imperials up on the right, and an extensive "shoot" was put over at about 4.00 p.m., but this was unsuccessful in its object; the Imperials were unable to force their way through, and the two leading companies of the 102nd, who had by this time had a certain amount of rest, though under heavy fire all the time, were ordered to push the attack home on Bourlon Wood and then to form a defensive flank facing south to protect the right flank of the rest of the Brigade. After a great effort this was done; the western and southern portion of the wood was captured and measures taken to prevent any counter-attack from the Hun by way of the southern extremity. Later in the evening the 54th were detailed to capture Fontaine-Notre-Dame, a village lying in the wood itself, and "D" Coy. were ordered to co-operate in this operation. On the way this company was met by a fierce counter-attack which the men succeeded in driving back, but they themselves were unable to advance any further. Bourlon Wood was to all intents and purposes captured, but it had not yet been "mopped up"; that is to say, the Hun had not been entirely driven out; consequently orders came in later that night stating that on the morning of the 28th the Third Division would continue the attack, leap-frogging the 11th Brigade, and that when this operation started at daybreak Bourlon Wood was to be wholly cleared of the enemy; to assist in this work the C.O. sent forward a Company of the 75th, and the wood was "mopped up."

At noon on the 28th, orders were received that the Brigade would concentrate about the Quarry near Bourlon Village and that Major J. B. Bailey, Second-in-Command of the 54th, who had been an "original" officer of the 102nd Bn., would take temporary command of the latter unit, leaving Colonel Thompson free to return to the 75th. The Battalion accordingly moved to the new area under Major Bailey's command, the kitchens were brought up and the men made comfortable for the night. The first part of the 2nd Battle of Cambrai was over; fighting was still raging ahead of us, and we were destined to continue our share in the bloody fray before we finally came out of the line, but for the moment we were at liberty to rest and take stock of the casualties. These, alas, were very heavy, as the following list will show: Killed or Died of Wounds—Lieuts. A. M. Brighton, S. G. Moore, W. Henry, T. McClatchey, J. R. Brown, F. R. Harker-Thomas and 55 Other Ranks; Wounded—Lieut.-Col. F. Lister, Capt. S. H. Okell, Capt. I. C. R. Atkin, Lieuts. R. V. Leese, O. Massey, E. H. Murphy, G. W. Archibald, and 151 Other Ranks. Missing, 3 Other Ranks. Our captures included 257 prisoners, 15 pieces of artillery and 18 machine guns. We had successfully taken our objectives and we had inflicted exceedingly heavy casualties on the enemy.

During the night a bombing attack was delivered by enemy planes on the Transport Lines of the whole Brigade, which were greatly crowded in a limited area; this attack resulted in several casualties, though the 102nd Battalion was fortunate in losing only animals and no men. Before dawn orders were received detailing the second phase of the Cambrai operation, and at 7.30 a.m. on the 29th we fell in and moved forward in support of the 12th Brigade, taking up our position round the Farme des Lilles, where we were to await the developments of the attack on our front. On this occasion the whole Corps movement was delayed by the failure of the Imperials on the extreme left of the First Division, who in their turn were on the left of the Fourth, to keep up with our advance. Consequently we were not called upon to advance further that day, but at 4:30 on the morning of the 30th we fell in once more and moved forward to take part in an attack which was to be delivered by the 11th Brigade against the Hun positions south of Sancourt, Blecourt and Bantigny, after which we were to swing to the right towards the bridge-head at Eswars. It was very dark when we moved off, and we suffered casualties "en route" from shell fire before we took up our position as Reserve Battalion west of the Cambrai-Douai Road, moving forward half-an-hour later in support of the 87th, crossing the road in good order but under a heavy barrage. Headquarters were also moved up well to the fore, east of the road, but at this juncture there was a halt, as the attack in front had been held up. After a conference in which the Brigadier, Major Bailey and the O.C. 87th Bn. took part it was decided to pull back the 102nd to the west of the road, where it was to take up a defensive position as Reserve Battalion; this was done and the men dug themselves in, as it was by now evident that the Hun was attacking in strength and that the day's work would not lie in reaching the objectives originally planned, but in staying this attack. All day the enemy spent his forces in vain. After a personal reconnaissance the Brigadier gave orders that the attack would be delivered on the morning of the 1st October, and that this time the 102nd would lead the attack, with the 87th leap-frogging them when the objectives had been taken. Accordingly, at 5.00 on the morning of the 1st, "A" Coy. on the right and "C" Coy. on the left went forward to take the first objective; this was strongly held, but by skilful manoeuvring and heroic fighting the two companies captured their position and sent back a number of prisoners, whereupon "B" Coy. leap-frogged and fought its way through the second objective; this company suffered heavily, but by 10.00 the men had stormed the Hun position and had settled down to withstand the fierce counter-attacks which were already being massed against them and were pouring over from the direction of Bantigny over the ridge to the north; moreover, Blecourt had not yet been cleared of enemy machine gunners who were considerably hampering our movements. At this point our artillery was called upon to concentrate on the enemy reinforcements and upon the machine gun emplacements in Blecourt, and we were also instrumental in giving valuable information to batteries belonging to the First and Second Divisions. But the fortunes of the day were in hazard, and "D" Company was brought up to form a flank facing Blecourt, when the company Lewis gunners did wonderful execution on the enemy massing round that village. Still the position was dangerous; the right flank of the Brigade was in the air, as the units on the right had fallen back; but, if we were nearly exhausted, so was the Hun—while he could yet put up a good defensive fight he had had almost enough, and it was decided to build up a strong defence along the positions which had been won, so that a well-consolidated line could be handed over to the 5th Brigade. This was done, and on the evening of the 1st we were relieved by the 28th Bn. and made our way back to the Transport Lines on the outskirts of Bourlon Village. In this second phase of the battle we captured 443 prisoners, one gun and 32 machine guns. Our casualties were: Killed or Died of Wounds—Lieuts. H. Banks, P. R. Pae and 31 Other Ranks; Wounded—Lieuts. J. S. Lamrock, V. Z. Manning, W. E. Crothers, G. Vancorbac, M.C., J. S. Rankin, D. Davidson (at duty), and 135 Other Ranks; Missing—3 Other Ranks.

It was during the fighting from September 27th to October 1st that Lieut. Graham Thomson Lyall won the only Victoria Cross awarded to the 102nd Battalion for a series of brilliant achievements carried out on September 27th and October 1st, during the course of which he was personally instrumental in the capture of 3 Officers, 182 Other Ranks, 26 Machine Guns and 1 Field Gun.

BATTALION HEADQUARTERS, SEPT. 27TH, 1918

CHAPTER XII.

Queant and Maroeuil—In Pursuit of the Hun—Booby-Traps—Herin and Denain—We Enter Valenciennes—The Last Offensive —From B.C. to Baisieux.

FTER one night spent in the camp at Bourlon, orders were received to move further back to a system of trenches lying in the open near the wholly ruined village of Quéant. On our arrival we were joined by Capt. J. A. Mann, M.C., who had been attached to Brigade as Liaison Officer during the last operation, and who, as Senior Officer present, took command of the Battalion until the return of Major E. J. Ryan, D.S.O., from leave a day or so later; thereafter and until the return of Captain Lister half-way through November, Major Ryan acted as Commanding Officer. Our new camp was a comfortable one; the men either slept in good dug-outs or camped out under bivouacs; in Quéant itself a cinema show had been established, and baths of a kind—very much of a kind—were available, and six days were spent in comparative ease, fulfilling the usual routine consequent on a strenuous and costly tour in the Front Line. On the night of the 7th we were relieved by the 42nd (Black Watch) Bn., and proceeded in 'buses to what were known as the "Y" Huts, in the training area close to the village town of Maroeuil. The whole Brigade was encamped in this area, which lies midway between Maroeuil and Agny-les-Duisans, and for five days the ordinary training routine was carried on, special attention being paid to musketry. About this time the air was full of Peace or Armistice rumours, and we were fully convinced that we had seen the end of all fighting, at any rate for the year. Dame Rumour's reputation, however, suffered a blow on Oct. 14th, when we fell in at 10.30 a.m. and marched to Agny-les-Duisans, where we took train for Marcoing, whence we were to proceed in pursuit of the fast retreating Hun and to take our share in the last offensive of the war.

Owing to the derailment of a train ahead of us we were delayed seven hours on this journey and did not reach Marcoing until an hour before midnight, after which we had to march about three miles to billets in Saudemont. Orders received on arrival necessitated an early start next morning, and at 5:30 a.m. we left for Palluel, where we were to relieve the 7th Middlesex Bn. in Brigade Support. At Saudemont we left sundry baggage; in fact all through the ensuing advance we kept dropping off various stores and other impedimenta with a small guard, and later on, when Armistice had been signed, we had the greatest difficulty in securing transport for picking up all our possessions and regaining our men. Ever since open warfare had started the lot of the Transport Lines personnel had been an unhappy one. It is one thing to belong to the Transport Lines when the unit is more or less settled in a permanent area, and quite another when the whole unit moves, bag and baggage too, day after day and night after night, and when stores and boxes have to be loaded on the waggons again almost as soon as they have been unloaded. The greatest credit is due to all ranks of the Quartermaster's Department and the Transport Section for the way in which they managed to keep up with the Unit in spite of hurried moves, and how Sgt. H. N. Monk, who was in charge of the Battalion Orderly Room, with all its records, correspondence files and official documents, managed to keep up with the Battalion and keep up with his work at the same time will for ever be a mystery. It is a matter of common knowledge that the other Units fell behind with their Orderly Room routine, but "Harry" Monk was always there on time, and not only kept up to date with "Returns," but was even able to keep the Brigade fully informed as to the exact number of socks each man in the Battalion had in his possession, to say nothing of those at the wash, at any given moment. Brigade was perpetually asking for these absurd details during times of stress.

Palluel was rather a delightful little village on the banks of the Canal du Nord and introduced us to a new experience in the way of billets. From now on the towns and villages we visited, whether deserted or not, had houses which were well furnished and possessed good gardens well stocked with vegetables. The interiors of the houses were usually ransacked and the furniture spoiled, but enough was left to provide comfortable accommodation for the troops, and the vegetables were an indescribable boon. At Palluel, for the first and last time, the Forward Battalion Orderly Room was located in an upstairs room, and remarkably unsafe it felt at times as the Hun was subjecting these villages in his rear to an intermittent bombardment. At Palluel were Headquarters, with "A" and "D" Coys. under Lieut. C. E. Henderson and Lieut. H. J. French, M.C. "B" and "C" Coys., under Capt. J. G. Knight, M.C., and Lieut. G. T. Lyall, V.C., were quartered in Hamel, a mile or so away. During the three days that we spent in this area gas shelling was very frequent, and the troops were required to wear their gas masks practically every night.

In the Front Line at this time were the 54th and 87th Bns., who were being held up by the Canal de la Sensée, which offered a formidable barrier to their advance, being strongly defended by the enemy. On the 17th information was received that the latter was retiring from his positions, and the two Front Line units were accordingly ordered to cross the Canal and push forward the advance, the 102nd Bn. following up behind the 87th, and being prepared to leap-frog on the easterly outskirts of the village of Villers-au-Tertre. Accordingly, on the evening of the 17th we moved up to Arleux, on the banks of the Canal de la Sensée, which the 87th vacated on their advance, and on the morning of the 18th the whole Battalion crossed the Canal by means of an improvised swinging bridge and proceeded through Bugnicourt to Villers-au-Tertre, where "A" and "D" Coys. passed through the 87th, and "B" and "C" remained in support. At this point the Battalion was joined by a troop of cavalry and a platoon of cyclists, who reported to the O.C., together with a battery of field guns. Considerable opposition was offered our two forward companies in the neighborhood of Fosse St. Roche and Fosse St. Erchin, and the enemy was greatly aided by the presence of a fog which hampered troops endeavouring to surround and cut off machine-gun nests. By noon, however, these two points were in our possession, and "A" and "D" had pushed forward in face of heavy shelling and machine-gun fire coming from the direction of Auberchicourt to the outskirts of that town. That afternoon "B" and "C" Coys. were sent forward to Fosse St. Roche with orders to pass through the line companies in the morning if the situation warranted.

At 3.30 on the morning of the 19th the situation was much quieter, and a dog was discovered in a house which the enemy was known to have occupied the night before. The animal had evidently been left to give notice of our advance. The two rear companies were accordingly sent forward through the other two, and Headquarters were moved up to Fosse St. Roche, where they remained a few hours, advancing in the afternoon to Auberchicourt, which had been taken by our two leading companies with very little opposition. The retiring Hun had made every effort to destroy the road behind him, but with conspicuously ill success; at the intersection of roads he had blown up mines, but though the corners were impassable a broad trail always led through the middle and afforded safe passage to vehicles. He had not the time necessary to destroy the town, but he had shown his petty spite by wilfully doing all the damage he could to the contents of the houses, and he had left some of the damnable "booby-traps" which were daily adding further disgrace to his foul and dirty reputation. An artilleryman in Auberchicourt was blown to pieces by a bomb hidden in a piano which exploded when the first chord was struck. In this connection there hangs a tale.

Our own Headquarters were located in a large china and glass warehouse, large enough to accommodate the whole of the staff. During the process of settling down an orderly, whom we will designate "X," came up to the Advanced Orderly Room Sergeant and pointed out what looked like a stick-bomb lying behind a passage-door. The sergeant, being discreet and disinclined to meddle with other people's business, promptly brought the Intelligence Officer to the spot and "passed the buck." The Intelligence Officer summoned his batman, and between them they ascertained that the machine was not infernal. But the incident set everyone "on edge," and when taken in connection with the tragedy mentioned above it created an atmosphere of suspicion. Consequently, when "X" again approached his sergeant and told him that he had this time found a real infernal machine the latter hastened to make investigations. Sure enough, in the dim recesses of the back office could be heard the deadly "tick-tick" of clock-work, and the sergeant suddenly espied a clock lying on a chair. Once more his stern sense of duty impelled him to inform the Intelligence Officer, and this time not only that important person, but the O.C. himself and the Adjutant and the Scout Officer all came round to investigate the trouble. One look was enough for the O.C. "That's a job for the Engineers," said he; "somebody go for the man who is attached to the unit for this kind of work. No; wait a minute; I'll go myself." And the O.C. hurried off. But a morbid curiosity impelled the other three officers to remain; and the sergeant, very much against his will, had to remain, as he was backed into a corner and couldn't get out without making his departure rather conspicuous; besides, he had no excuse; the O.C. had already gone for the Engineers. "X" also waited. Those three wretched officers "monkeyed" round with the clock for five minutes, first examining it from every angle; then pointing their fingers at it, next touching it gingerly and then more confidently and finally lifting it up, only to find that it was merely a clock-face with no subtle attachments. They went away puzzled, and the sergeant remarked to "X," "Well, its funny; but somebody must have put it there with a purpose." "Yes," said "X," "I did!" And the two of them reached the Orderly Room in time to hear the O.C. loudly declaiming that there was not a shadow of doubt but that the Hun had intended to leave a time-bomb there, and that our too rapid advance had thwarted his dastardly purpose! The old bull was still eating hay with the Battalion all right.

Meantime "B" and "C" Coys. had over-run their objective, Abscon, and had taken that allotted to the 54th at the railway embankment beyond that town. They were accordingly pulled back and billeted for the night in Abscon. In this place were 3,300 civilians, the first to be liberated from the Hun by any unit in the Division, and the welcome they gave our troops was marked by every evidence of enthusiastic delight. On the morning of the 20th we fell in at 7:30 and marched on through Escaudain; east of this town we expected to leap-frog the 87th, who had passed through us at Abscon, but the forward battalions were held up by an unexpected resistance, and we consequently billeted in Escaudain for two nights. On this occasion our Transport Lines moved up ahead of the main body of the Battalion and billeted about 200 yards in advance. When the time came for us to move, on the 22nd, resistance had died away, and we proceeded without opposition to the village of Herin, where we remained for six days. The billets here were excellent; Herin had been the

Headquarters for a German general, and his billets in the Brewery were just exactly what a German general would be expected to occupy. The gardens were all well stocked with vegetables, which we devoured in large quantities. During our stay we were subjected to a good deal of shell fire, one shell penetrating the corner of the Headquarters' Sergeants' billet, causing the unfortunate "Sam" Sorensen to throw down "four kings," which he was holding against a big "full"; all bets were cancelled in the mad rush for the cellar, and it took hours to divide up to everybody's satisfaction the money found afterwards on the floor. The Signallers also had a narrow escape during this tour, having a shell pass right through their billet and explode on the far side. Brigade Headquarters fared worst of all; they were located at Aubry, where they were badly gassed and shelled and lost all their documents when Headquarters were practically blown sky-high. On the 27th a great religious ceremony was held in Denain, a neighbouring town, to celebrate the liberation of the town from the Hun by the Canadian Corps; this was attended by H.R.H. the Prince of Wales, the Corps, Divisional and Brigade Commanders with their staffs, and by the senior officers of all the Battalions in the vicinity.

It was to this town of Denain that we moved on the night of October 28th, the Brigade being relieved in the Front Line by the 9th Canadian Brigade. Our entry was in the nature of a triumphal procession; it was very dark, but on every doorstep stood men, women and children holding up lighted candles and cheering themselves hoarse. We were billeted in a large block of buildings which had evidently been used as some sort of collegiate institution prior to the war, but which the Hun had used as a prison camp. Denain was the largest town, outside the Coast towns, which we had yet visited, but there is little of interest or beauty in it. The civilians were still trying to realize their freedom and showed their gratitude by entertaining any soldiers who gave them the opportunity. All had the same tale to tell, but it appeared that the individual German soldier, when billeted in a house and left alone by his superior officers, was a harmless guest; there was abundant proof that the hardships endured by the civilians were those provoked by organized authority and, save in a few isolated instances, were not caused by the license or violence of the individual soldier.

On the afternoon of Oct. 31st we left Denain and moved to Thiant, where we were to support the attack which the 10th Brigade was to launch on the morning of the 1st in the effort to penetrate to Valenciennes. This attack was preceded by the most intense barrage which we had yet heard in France, and by 9:30 a.m. prisoners began streaming in, including in their number the Regimental Commander of Valenciennes. An hour later we in our turn moved forward to Maing, where we waited until 4.00 p.m., when we set out to relieve Imperial units northeast of Aulnoy, on the east side of the Rhonnell River. Owing to the congestion of traffic on the roads our progress was slow and difficult, and when we reached Aulnoy we found three battalions of the 164th Brigade more or less mixed up. Just as details for the relief were completed orders came in cancelling same, and the Battalion was billeted in Aulnoy until the following morning, when we were to continue the attack in conjunction with the 54th. Shells fell intermittently throughout the night, the bombardment increasing in violence after dawn, and it was during the course of this shelling that we lost Capt. H. Dunlop, M.C. (C.A.M.C.), our Medical Officer, who had just completed a year's service with the unit. He was aroused from sleep to attend to a sick civilian, and just as he was going out of the doorway of Headquarters he was struck by the fragments of a bursting shell, from the effects of which he died before reaching Field Ambulance and without recovering consciousness. He was immensely popular, as well with the rank and file as with the members of the Officers' Mess, and his death was a sad blow to the Battalion. Aulnoy had been found crowded with civilians who for 48 hours had been living in cellars and dug-outs; there was a tremendous amount of gas about from gas-shells, and it was with a distinct feeling of relief that we left at 11.00 a.m. to take part in the fight for Valenciennes. The general plan was for "B" and "D" Coys., with the other Companies in Support, to push through the 54th at Marly and attack in an easterly direction, with the left flank resting on the Valenciennes-Mons Road and the right flank in touch with the 54th. Headquarters were established opposite those of the 54th in Marly. By 1.30 p.m. the forward companies were well in position and were pushing forward covering the left half of the Brigade, as detailed; considerable enemy machine-gun fire was encountered, but by dusk a line had been established about 400 yards west of a sunken road which ran north and south across the Brigade frontage and was strongly held by the enemy. The night of the 2nd-3rd was spent in readiness to resist an expected counter-attack which did not, however, materialize, and it was found possible to establish an Advanced Headquarters in Valenciennes itself by midnight. The following morning we were relieved by the 12th Brigade on the left and by the 54th Bn. on the right, and went into billets at Valenciennes, which had already been cleared of Huns by the 10th Brigade.

Valenciennes was in a very good state of preservation. The contents of the houses, of course, had been badly treated, but there was little material damage done to the buildings. There were few civilians to be seen on our first appearance, but it did not take long for them to flock back in large numbers. In good weather and at the proper season Valenciennes is doubtless a very beautiful city, but we saw it under poor weather conditions; November is not a good sight-seeing month, and there was too much of the aftermath of the war visible on every hand to allow of a favourable impression being made. There is a very fine block of municipal buildings occupying one side of the principal square, and these buildings still bore the "Kommandatur" sign and other evidences of German occupation. There is a fine theatre in Valenciennes, where later we were to see a Canadian Company giving nightly performances to the élite of the Lace City.

We were only in the city two nights, but before we had time to move out the Mayor, whose house we were using as a Headquarters, returned, and we were served with a notice that we should have to vacate the premises, as His Worship wished to resume residence. Seeing that he had been left homeless for a very long time by the Hun it would have been more graceful on his part to have refrained from serving an eviction notice so quickly on his country's Allies, but it didn't do him much good or us much harm; we stayed the odd night anyway and received orders to advance on the morning of the 5th. At 12:30 p.m. on that day we reached Rombies, which had been the Headquarters of the 87th, who with the 75th, were supposed to be cleaning up the high ground between the Aunnelle and Honnelle Rivers; it was our task to pass through the 87th after they had attained their objectives, and to clean up the country west of the Grande Honnelle River and, if possible, to capture the village of Baisieux east of that stream. Though we did not know it for certain, we were on the eve of our last offensive, and to the 102nd Bn. was to belong the honour of capturing the last position taken by the 4th Division. By midnight the 87th had failed to take their final objective, a road from which we were to jump-off in our turn; in consequence we had to start 700 yards this side of the road and had that much more ground to cover to begin the day's work with. To "C" Coy., on the right, under Lieut. M. K. Devine, was allotted the task of crossing the Grande Honnelle River if possible and establishing themselves in Baisieux; "A" Coy., under Lieut. W. H. C. Stanley, was to capture and mop up Marchipont and a wood lying to the left of that place, and then, if the Company on their left was held up, to push northwards through Petite Baisieux and assist the 12th Brigade by outflanking a village called Quiévrechain. "D" Coy., on the left, was to capture and "mop up" Maison Rouge and to push on, "mopping up" all the ground west of the Aunnelle River, keeping in touch with the 12th Brigade on the left and assisting, if necessary, in "mopping up" Quiévrechain. "B" Coy., which had suffered most heavily in the preceding offensive, was to remain in Support.

Zero Hour was 5.30 a.m. on the 6th November, and after a good barrage our troops moved forward, capturing the sunken road without difficulty. From this time onward they encountered stiff opposition. "A" Coy. captured Marchipont before 7.00 a.m., but found that the enemy was holding a wood on the right in strength; this had to be surrounded, and eventually the position was taken, yielding 30 prisoners, at least that many more having been killed. "D" Coy., on the left, was held up with the 12th Brigade by the enemy holding out fiercely in the outskirts of Quiévrechain, so the centre company, "A," pushed on as ordered and surrounded the town from the north, with the result that the place was surrendered, with 20 prisoners, four machine guns and four trench mortars. Meantime "C" Coy., on the right, was suffering from the failure of Imperials on their right to keep up; the flank was exposed to a withering machine gun fire, but by using one platoon as a defensive flank the company pushed on over the crest of the hill and gained the eastern bank of the Grande Honnelle. When this news was received Lieut. R. L. Gale, M.C., the Battalion Intelligence Officer, went forward to reconnoitre for possible means of crossing the river. He found that all the bridges were down and that wading was the only means by which the passage could be made. He therefore organized a party, consisting of himself, C.S.M. Dunn, D.C.M., of "C" Coy., two Scouts and a Lewis Gunner, waded across the river and established a post on the other side. The river was about fifteen feet wide and well over the knees. Pushing their way forward in face of heavy machine-gun fire, they obtained a footing in the near side of the first house. A message was then sent back to the balance of "C" Coy., who effected a crossing under cover of the fire of the solitary Lewis gun which was already on the eastern side. "B" Coy. was then ordered up from Supports to protect the right flank, the Imperials still being 3,000 yards behind, and this manoeuvre resulted in the complete capture of Baisieux and the total confusion of the enemy, who seemed to be wholly unprepared for such a rapid denouement. They could be observed running from the eastern outskirts of the town, and afforded easy targets for our Lewis gunners and riflemen, who were not slow to take advantage of same, causing heavy casualties. As an example of the complete surprise obtained it may be stated that a team and waggon suddenly appeared outside the sugar factory and commenced loading, apparently quite unaware of our presence in the vicinity; the waggon and sugar remained in our possession; the driver was shot and the horses bolted. After throwing out a screen of outposts "C" Coy. was ordered to stand firm and consolidate, our two flanks being already too much exposed to make a further advance advisable. Moreover, we had reached the "ultima Thule" of our objective. "B" Coy. was accordingly ordered to connect up with the Imperials on the right, who were still 2,500 yards in the rear, thereby affording the necessary protection for our right flank. We were relieved the same night by the 25th Bn., which arrived after nightfall; the darkness was so profound that relief was to some extent hampered, and it was not until early next morning that the last of the companies reached their billets back in Valenciennes. We had completed our last tour in the line, and to the Battalion in the Fourth Division, which had originally been raised in the most western districts of Canada, had fallen the honour of capturing the stronghold of the enemy lying furthest to the east of all that had been occupied by the Division. We had come from further west and gone further east than any other unit in the "Fighting Fourth."

During the past three weeks we had taken 80 prisoners, two field guns, four trench mortars and 26 machine guns. Our casualties had been comparatively light and were largely caused by gas shells, numbering in all: Killed or Died of Wounds—Capt. H. Dunlop, M.C., and six Other Ranks; Wounded—Lieuts. C. E. Henderson, R. L. Gale, M.C., G. V. Atkin, M.C., J. R. Wilson, M.C., J. Palmer, S. P. Martin, W. H. C. Stanley, and 50 Other Ranks.

CHAPTER XIII.

The Signing of the Armistice—We Move to Belgium—Mons and St. Symphorien—Christmas Day on the Edge of the World—Boitsfort—The Battle of Brussels—On Our Way—The Overseas Parade—Good-bye to "Over There"—Demobbed

ESTED, but dirty and bedraggled, we woke up on the 7th in Valenciennes, and promptly had our feelings badly hurt by being curtly ordered to remain indoors well out of sight, as the Prince of Wales was coming to town to inspect the 12th Brigade, and we did not look respectable enough to be seen. This was a piece of ultra-snobbishness on the part of the Higher Command; thank God our Royal Family are not similarly constituted; the Prince would not have minded seeing a few soldiers dirty from the Line, he's not that kind of a fellow, but no officer can ever bear to let a senior see one of his men except "in the pink," and if the 12th were clean for inspection and the 11th were dirty from action, well, the 11th had to keep out of sight; that was all there was to it. By 4.45 p.m., however, we were considered respectable-looking enough to march through Valenciennes to billets which had been provided for us at Anzin, a suburb of the city and connected with it by a long, unbroken street. We found first-rate accommodation and almost every man had a bed, but to emphasize the innate beastliness of the Hun mind and temperament the following incident is related; it is absolutely true and came under the personal observation of the writer. In one of the billets were found two vases full of flowers on the mantel-piece, and as flowers were scarce these were preserved. It was soon noticed, however, that a most unpleasant odour was pervading the atmosphere, and a close investigation showed that the vases had been carefully filled with urine by the late occupants, who had not been evicted so quickly that they were not able first to leave behind visible proofs of their degraded mentality. We were in Anzin when the news of the Armistice came through. At 9.09 a.m. on the 11th day of the 11th month of 1919 we were informed by Brigade that the Armistice terms had been accepted by Germany and that hostilities would cease at 11 a.m. This was immediately confirmed by an official wire.

It was a happy day for Major Ryan; first came the news of the Armistice, and shortly afterwards he was notified that he had been awarded the Distinguished Service Order for his services in connection with the 2nd Battle of Arras, and that he had been granted the Acting Rank of Lieut.-Colonel with authority to wear the insignia of the rank. That day massed bands played in the public square in Valenciennes in honour of Armistice, but there were no facilities for rejoicing on a good old-fashioned scale.

The following day we were notified that we should form part of the Army of Occupation in accordance with the terms of the Armistice, and when we left on the 15th, proceeding north towards Belgium, we understood that in the fullness of time we should go to the Rhine to relieve one or other of the Canadian Divisions. The anticipation did not exactly arouse enthusiasm amongst the troops, as it seemed probable that the whole distance would have to be covered on foot and in full marching order. It was a fine morning when we left Anzin, bright and cold, just the kind of weather for a march; but we soon found that though the weather was all right the roads were not. They were crowded to capacity with swarms of returning refugees, some in lorries loaned for the purpose by the Allies; some on foot, wheeling their belongings in every conceivable form of vehicle. As we were marching in Brigade formation we were held up interminably by this congestion and it was the middle of the afternoon before we reached our destination, Quiévrechain, a shell-shocked village which had figured prominently in the last offensive. Our blankets were still under guard at one of the many depots we had formed during the last months, and the night was bitterly cold, and not even the gay and festive life of one house at least in Quiévrechain could quite compensate for the lack of warmth. The next day we made an early start, but even so we could not avoid the traffic. Lorries by the hundred passed us on their way up to bring back refugees; others were detailed to go further still to assist in bringing back our returning prisoners from Hunland, and naturally the men wanted to know why the empty lorries going forward could not be utilized to take us on our way, or, at any rate, to relieve us of our packs. On this day we crossed the frontier into Belgium and at 3:30 p.m. reached the town of Paturages; here again we found excellent billets; the town was fully peopled and the inhabitants vied with each other in their hospitality. We were beginning to find that there are Belgians and Belgians, and the Belgians whom we met round Mons and Brussels were as different from those we had encountered round Ypres as cheese is from chalk. On the 19th of the month, the day before we left Paturages, Colonel Lister returned from England, fully recovered from the severe wounds he had sustained at Cambrai, and it is no exaggeration to say that he was welcomed back enthusiastically. St. Symphorien was our next halting-place, and here we remained for over three weeks in very fair billets; six months before we should have voted them "top-hole," but a few weeks spent in the territory which had been so hastily vacated by the enemy had enlarged our expectations. We often thought that for the Hun out of the line it must have been a very good war; he never had to "rest" in shell-shocked areas; he could always look forward with certainty to a good time in real towns, and could refresh both his physical and mental outlook a few miles behind the firing line with cities and countrysides which had not been ravaged by warfare. Moreover, he could always be sure of comfortable beds and all facilities for good cooking and messing. Our experience did not tend to show that the German soldier was badly fed, except when his supplies were cut off at the front; when in Reserve he must have had ample opportunities for "doing himself proud."

St. Symphorien is a little two-streeted village lying about three miles from the centre of Mons, and we had a very pleasant time there. Prices, of course, were terribly high in Mons, but it was good to be near a real town which had not lost its civil population and which showed no trace at all of enemy occupation. The two special features of interest are the Cathedral and Alva's Tower, the latter standing on an eminence above the town. This was used in the days of Spanish tyranny as a watch-tower, and an incredible number of stairs lead up through the massive walls to the summit, whence a wonderful view of the surrounding country can be obtained by the breathless climber. On the other side of St. Symphorien is a cemetery, of which one is bound to say that here the Germans paid suitable honour to their dead foemen as well as to their own men; the cemetery is beautifully arranged, the ground having been granted for the purpose by a local land-owner, and the Germans having erected grave-stones, etc. Here lie a large number of men from the Middlesex Regiment, who fell during the first days of the war. Whilst we were in St. Symphorien the air was full of stories of mutiny in various units of the Corps; one battalion was reported to have thrown down its arms and positively refused to march another step towards the Rhine; another was said to have shot its colonel; another still had been put under arrest by other units in its brigade. All these stories were utterly without foundation, and were almost certainly disseminated by enemy agents, who thus early after Armistice were sowing the seeds of strife and disunion in the ranks of their victorious foes. Towards the end of the month an opportunity was granted to a limited number of men to visit Brussels, as it was not then known that within a few weeks we should be quartered within walking distance of the capital. About this time it was generally recognized that the advance to the Rhine by the Fourth Division was likely to be greatly delayed, and an elaborate system of systematic training on military, educational and recreational lines was inaugurated. This was more fully developed later, when the Rhine project had been definitely abandoned, and will be dealt with in due course.

The month or six weeks which lapsed after the signing of the Armistice saw a great falling-off in the general service rendered by the Transport Branches. Up to this time one of the most amazing features of the whole Army organization had been the wonderful regularity with which supplies of all kinds had reached the Forward areas. Not only necessities but luxuries had been available through the Y.M.C.A. at most times, and it had been a rare thing for the postal service to be delayed. After Armistice, however, a reaction seemed to set in. It is true that a large number of lorries had been requisitioned for the use of refugees and returning prisoners, and that the railway line between Valenciennes and Mons had been badly damaged by the Hun on his final retreat, but in view of the fact that large quantities of munitions were no longer required in constant succession it is hard to understand why the Transport Services should have suddenly developed "dry rot." In the Fourth Division we only suffered inconvenience; tobacco was at a premium, and mail, both outgoing and incoming, was not only delayed but lost, "ditched" would perhaps be the better word; the First Division, however, which was pressing forward to the Rhine, suffered real hardships through this cause, and it was not until towards the end of December that normal conditions began to obtain.

One day passed very much like another at St. Symphorien. The mornings were devoted to physical training and two hours' military training of some description; the afternoons to football or some other form of athletics. There was not much to do in the evenings, but Mons was within an easy walk, and there was a certain satisfaction in the mere walking round the streets of a real town where the lights no longer had to be shielded from the heavens. Close by were first-class baths; these were to be found at Havre and were miners' baths of the same description as at Bruay.

On the 12th we fell in once more and departed from St. Symphorien on our way to the area which had been allotted us for Christmas; fortunately for our peace of mind on the march we none of us had any idea of what had been found good enough for the junior battalion. Our first halt was at La Louvrière, a good-sized town which made such a favourable impression on the unit that later on one man requested that his leave warrant be made out for this place, as he preferred it to "Blighty" or any place in France. We were now in the heart of the great industrial area of Belgium, and the people all looked prosperous. The following day we marched to Courcelles, a clean little town lying on the eastern fringe of the industrial area, and when we left it on the 14th we found ourselves gradually drawing away into the agricultural districts, where the cultivation of the beetroot seemed the be-all and end-all of existence. Fleurus was the last decent-sized town we saw, and it had in part been badly wrecked when the Hun, absolutely regardless of civilian life and property, had blown up an ammunition train prior to his departure. All along the route were evidences of the German military "débacle"; guns, either wrecked or abandoned, or parked or numbered amongst the evidences of good faith demanded by the Armistice terms, ruined tractors and anti-aircraft guns on their movable platforms. We spent that night in Sommebreffe, a village too small to contain our Battalion, in additions to the 87th, so "C" Coy. was quartered in Ligny, of 1815 fame, and most of Headquarters were billeted in a group of cottages midway between the two. The following day was a Sunday and a church parade in the local theatre attracted crowds of the inhabitants, who were evidently under the impression that our Protestant form of Service was some new kind of secular entertainment. Another day's march brought us to Perwez, and on the 17th we were introduced to our Christmas quarters. Two Christmas and New Year's Days had we spent in the line; the third was to be spent in an area which, if it ever figured in the general scheme of creation at all, must have been given form and substance in a fit of absentmindedness. It seemed to lie on the top of a curve of the earth's surface, and as we breasted the edge there was nothing to see on any side but a dull expanse of muddy fields stretching away into the horizon and gently perfuming the air with the subtle scent of rotting beetroot. Accommodation was so limited that the Battalion had to be split up amongst three different villages, Headquarters and "D" Coy. being billeted in Autre Eglise, "A" and "B" in Foix des Caves and "C" in Hedenge. The area was already crowded with French refugees, and to make matters worse, the civilian population was suffering from an epidemic of influenza. There were no facilities for recreation, no hall for lectures or entertainments. There was "No nothing." The other units in the Brigade were in much the same plight, as a result of which a spirited protest was forwarded to the proper quarters, and in course of time, as will be seen later, we had our compensation; but it was evidently the original intention of the Higher Command to leave the 11th Brigade all dumped on the end of the world, there to rot, physically and mentally, until such time as our corroded bodies could be shipped back to Canada.

Our new hosts were nice enough people as far as they went; but, to tell the truth, there was but little to choose between them and their beetroots; they had vegetated so long that they had partaken of the nature of the soil; to use a colloquialism, "there was nothing to them." They lacked the meagrest necessities of life, and when Christmas Day came it was difficult to raise enough plates to feed the men their Christmas dinner by Companies and Headquarters, even when all resources were pooled. It was a village tragedy when two members of Headquarters Staff slowly and not ungracefully subsided into two stacks of plates and broke the lot, because these plates simply could not be replaced within fifty miles. Their whole conception of life was based on the beetroot, from which they even distilled a peculiarly harmless but very distasteful form of beer. It was amid such surroundings as these that we spent the festive season, and though it is possible now to see the comic side of this experience, at the time we were much aggrieved that, with all France and Belgium to choose from, we should have been exiled to this wilderness at that particular time of year. If the war had been in active progress we should have regarded the thing differently.

On December 20th an historic "rout," to use a Regency term, was given by the Burgomaster, Sheriffs and Common Council of Brussels to the representatives of all the Allied Armies who were within reasonable reach. It was Brussels' official celebration of victory, and was a very splendid affair indeed. Col. Lister represented the 102nd Bn., and returned very much impressed with the scale on which the reception, which was followed by dancing. had been conducted. All the rooms opening off the Council Chamber in the wonderful "Hotel de Ville," or Town Hall of Brussels, were thrown open; the marvellous tapestries, the gorgeous paintings, the brilliant uniforms of the Diplomatic Corps mingling with the soberer khaki of the military, the exquisite toilettes of the women, all combined to make a spectacle as brilliant as it was impressive. Many a guest present, as he listened to the stirring strains of the Band of the Ier Regiment de Grenadiers must have thought of that other historic ball given in the same city just over 103 years before, when the Iron Duke was present on the eve of Waterloo, amidst the other revellers at the Duchess of Richmond's mansion. On this occasion the heroic M. Max was a central figure in the ceremonies.

Christmas Day and New Year's Day passed at Autre Eglise and the other two villages; it was found possible by dint of much careful planning and borrowing to arrange Christmas dinners, but though everything possible was done the festival lacked the proper spirit; Dickens himself could not have assumed the Christmas spirit in that dull neighbourhood ,and it was with a sigh of relief that we learned of a move which would take place early in the year. There were rumours that, like the Israelites of old, we were to be led into a land flowing with milk and honey; this time Rumour proved true; though we had not been forty years in the wilderness of Sinai we had been nearly three weeks in the "Beetroot" country, and it was the most cheerful Battalion in the world that marched gladly away on the morning of January 4th; we didn't know exactly where we were going, but we were on our way, and that was the main thing. This march was marked by the re-appearance of our Bugle Band; this had been disbanded when the unit first reached England, and many of the boys had done splendid service since that time as Battalion Runners; now the Bugles were reorgainzed and, under the efficient leadership of Sergeant-Drummer W. Miller they helped us on the march, playing alternately with the Brass Band. The country through which we passed improved with every step, and our spirits rose correspondingly. The first stop was at Melin, where Headquarters were established, but as this village was not large enough to accommodate the whole Battalion, "B" and "C" Coys. were billeted at Athuy. The following afternoon we reached Ottenburg, a purely Flemish village where few of the inhabitants even understood French, and then on January 6th we marched 13 miles on splendid roads over hilly country and found ourselves at Boitsfort, which for nearly three months was to be our home; and a grand home it was.

The official name of Boitsfort is the Commune de Watermael-Boitsfort, and it proved to be everything that we had hoped for. It is a fashionable suburb, or country resort, lying about five miles outside Brussels, with which it is connected both by train and car service. A good system of electric cars was in operation at frequent intervals, and throughout the whole of our stay we were always granted the privilege of riding in these cars free. The neighbourhood is most delightfully laid out in walks, driveways, boulevards and woodland trails, the late King Leopold having spent much money on beautifying the landscape. A race-course at Boitsfort is one of the attractions, there being still another one a couple of miles away at Groenendael, and during the season all fashionable Brussels flocks to Boitsfort, where most of the wealthy Bruxellois have their country homes. Here was the regular home of English jockeys riding for Belgian owners, and many of the civilians spoke excellent English. It may well be imagined that the Battalion just gave one big grunt of satisfaction, called everything square on the last deal, and proceeded to extract all the pleasure out of life which the time and opportunity afforded. So began the famous Battle of Brussels.

The next day was devoted to cleaning up and exploring our new location. In the middle of Boitsfort is a picturesque lake which swarms with carp of a gigantic size; these the licensee catches cold-bloodedly by the hundreds in nets. The place swarms with children, who are taught both French and Flemish in the schools. The amazing number of children throughout Belgium is worthy of remark; the kingdom may well claim to be one of the most densely populated countries in the world; they are very nice children, too, and we made great friends with them everywhere. The civilians generally abounded in hospitality; every man had a bed, and in many houses the men would hand over their rations to their hosts, who would then treat their visitors as boarding guests. Boitsfort has many first-rate hotels, and these were used both for billets and messes, the officers being quartered in "La Maison Haute," a really massive pile, standing in ample grounds of its own, Headquarters Sergeants using the "Hotel Beau Sejour," commanding a view of the lake, and the Companies all being equally well provided for.

A book might be written on the doings of the next three months, but it is not the purpose of this volume either to rival Baedeker or to emulate Boccaccio, but it may be remarked that it is now much easier to understand why it was that the Carthaginian army under Hannibal fell to pieces after their experiences in winter quarters in Capua. The big feature of our life during this time was the Educational Scheme, which was designed both to provide occupation for the moment and to help towards the fitting of men for civilian life; as to its merits on the latter count there is room for argument, but it certainly helped to fill in the mornings and was preferable to drill. A little Physical Exercise, followed by some form of Educational training, brought us to dinner-time; then games or a trip to Brussels passed away the afternoon; for the evenings there were billiard tables, dances, cards and—Brussels. The only difficulty was to keep in funds. Prices were uniformly high, and though a wise and beneficent Command made it possible to draw an extra hundred francs once in two months for the purpose of taking a 48-hour leave in Brussels, a hundred francs is only $20, and lasts just about half as long. Dances were very popular, and few evenings passed without some Company or detail arranging a dance in an excellent dance-hall known as "La Salle d'Harmonie."

Frequent lectures were given, and occasionally a theatrical performance would be staged by "The Maple Leaves" or some visiting English company.

March 25th figures as an important date, as on that day the 11th Brigade paraded at Groenendael for inspection by H.M. the King of the Belgians. On this occasion each Battalion paraded with its regimental colours for the first time. We had had to have our own Colours made for us in Brussels, and the firm responsible did very creditable work; but there was always the feeling that Regimental Colours should not have had to be bought by the Canteen Fund, and that some city or community in Canada had missed the chance of its life in not having come forward and donated the Colours with its blessing.

During the whole of this period the Battalion Orderly Room staff was kept busy in preparing documents for demobilization. More time, money and paper was wasted owing to Red Tape in this connection than the taxpayer would like to see presented in figures. After weeks of patient toil necessitating the use of reams of paper we completed all the documents as required; then, on our arrival later in England we were told that all these Nominal Rolls, etc., would have to be done again, as in England they worked under a different system from that adopted in France. One might be pardoned for supposing that the different systems were in use so as to have an excuse for keeping as many khakied "Cuthberts" working as possible. It is a fact that in Belgium we made out lists according to orders showing in which of about a dozen dispersal areas our men wished to be demobilized; on our arrival in England we were told positively that we should all be discharged in Toronto without any choice, and later we were divided into three dispersal areas. Talk about too many cooks spoiling the broth; the whole Demobilization Staff was "in the soup" all the time. And they had been working out the details for about two years!

It was on April 24th that we finally said "good-bye" to our kind hosts and friends at Boitsfort and left by train from Wavre for Le Havre, which we reached on the 26th. The train journey was slow, but there was plenty of room in the box-cars, and the food was both abundant and good. The Canadian Embarkation Camp at Le Havre was greatly overcrowded and very uncomfortable, but we were, of course, disposed to regard everything with a favourable eye at that time. But the bathing system was intolerable and deserves a word of censure. It had been laid down that every man should be "deloused," another verbal product of the war, meaning "freed from lice," before embarkation. A first-class system was accordingly inaugurated which would doubtless have proved most efficacious if it had not been negatived by subsequent proceedings. The men proceeded to the bath-house, stripped and hung all their outer clothing, including puttees and great-coats, on a travelling rack which passed through a disinfecting room full of chemicals and reached the men in another compartment where they went after the bath. Splendid idea! Why, then, should all the good effect have been taken away by issuing the men with washed underwear which in many cases was still verminous? The Army seemed unable to get it into its head that the laundries never did manage to get rid of vermin. As has been pointed out before, the laundries exterminated vermin theoretically: they rarely, if ever, did it practically, and there is not a man in the Canadian Corps who had experience with washed underclothing who will not bear out this statement.

On April 29th Capt. W. W. Dunlop, M.C., Adjutant, with 25 Other Ranks, left for England, the whole party under the command of Lieut.-Col. F Lister,. D.S.O., M.C., to take part in the great parade of Overseas Forces through London. Eight other officers also left for the same purpose, but on arrival it was found that each Battalion was to be represented by the Commanding Officer and the Adjutant only in addition to the Other Ranks. This party reached "A" Wing, Bramshott, on the evening of the 30th. May 3rd was a wonderful day for the Overseas Forces. We fell in at 3:45 a.m. and marched to Liphook where we entrained for Waterloo, which was reached by 6:30. Thence we marched to Hyde Park, where tea and sandwiches were served, after which we were at liberty to wander round the park until 11.00, when dinner was served. The troops fell in again at 12:45, and moved off at 1:40 along the following route: Stanhope Gate, Constitution Hill, Buckingham Palace, where the King took the salute, Buckingham Palace Road, Victoria Street, Parliament Street, Whitehall, Charing Cross, Strand, Australia House, which we circled, Aldwych, Kingsway, High Holborn, New Oxford Street, Oxford Street, Marble Arch and back to our starting place. Enormous crowds assembled and gave an enthusiastic reception. It was an inspiring event, though the early part of the march was spoiled for at least one member of the unit, who kept on wondering how he was ever going to manage to unfix his bayonet from the "slope," seeing that this was an operation which always worried him even when done from the "order." Our train left Waterloo at 8.00 p.m. and we were back in camp again an hour before midnight. The whole affair had been an unqualified success; it had given the troops an opportunity to realize for themselves the unbounded admiration and affection which the people of England entertained for them and their prowess; incidentally it had given them a new idea of a real London crowd.

The remaining days in England were not long in spending. The main body of the Battalion came over on May 4th, and thereafter the time was spent in passing Medical Boards and completing Demobilization returns, after which the last leave was enjoyed and on May 31st we left Liphook Station at 4.30 a.m. for Liverpool, reaching the Mersey port about 3.30 in the afternoon, when we immediately embarked on board the "Mauretania." On the following day, the anniversary of the great naval battle of "The Glorious First of June," the giant liner left her moorings and at 1.45 p.m. we crossed the bar on our way to Canada. Quarters on board were excellent, and even if they had not been it is not likely that much discontent would have been aroused; moreover, the sea was phenomenally calm, and after a voyage which was very nearly a record-breaker, we landed at Halifax at 10.30 a.m. on Friday, June 6th. An hour later the trains pulled out for Toronto, which was reached on the evening of Sunday. Here the big majority of the unit was demobilized, only some 125 Westerners bound for Revelstoke or Vancouver remaining for the final stage of the journey. And here a tribute of thanks and acknowledgment is due from the Westerners to the people of Toronto generally and to the Sportsmen's Patriotic Association in particular for the unbounded hospitality shown during the twenty-four hours spent in their midst. A free excursion was arranged for these men to visit Niagara Falls, and this included a luncheon at the Clifton Hotel and dinner on the boat during the return journey. It was a very graceful compliment to the Men of the West, and the latter were correspondingly grateful.

And so we came to the Golden West, leaving at Revelstoke on the 13th a few of our party, and spending that night at North Bend so that we might arrive in Vancouver at a reasonable hour on the morning of the 14th. A tremendous crowd had assembled in the Terminal

City to greet all that were left of the 102nd Battalion, which had been so largely recruited in the vicinity, and a vociferous welcome was accorded us as we passed up Granville Street on our way to be demobilized. On the following day those of us who still had another leg of the journey to complete embarked for Victoria, and then at long last the active history of the 102nd (North British Columbians) Battalion came to a close.

Just two more incidents must be recorded and then this history will also conclude. On Monday evening, June 15th, a banquet was held in the Vancouver Hotel, Vancouver given "in honour of Lieut.-Colonel Fred Lister, C.M.G., D.S.O., M.C. and Officers, Non-Commissioned Officers and Men of the 102nd Battalion upon the occasion of the return of the Battalion to British Columbia after their arduous and victorious campaign in defence of the Empire," and this banquet was tendered by the Province of British Columbia, the City of Vancouver, Old Comrades and Friends.

The last scene of all took place on Sunday, September 22nd, 1919, when the Battalion Colours were deposited in Christ Church, Vancouver, with all the pomp and ceremony which such an occasion demanded. The following account is taken from the columns of the "Vancouver Sun" of September 23rd, 1919, and with this introduction the historian takes leave of his readers.

UNIQUE CEREMONY AT CHRIST CHURCH

Regimental Colors of 102nd Are Deposited After Custom of Early Days in England

In accordance with a military custom that has its origin in the early days of England's history, a divine service was held on Sunday afternoon, September 22nd, in Christ Church, Vancouver, to mark the depositing of the regimental colours of the 102nd Battalion, "North British Columbians." The church was crowded to the doors with members of the Battalion and their relatives, friends and other spectators, who witnessed this impressive and simple service. The 29th Vancouver Battalion placed their colours in the same church some time ago.

The members of the Battalion assembled in the school room and formed up in file, with Lieut.-Col. Fred Lister, C.M.G., D.S.O., M.C., former officer commanding, and Major H. B. Scharschmidt, acting adjutant, leading, the colour party followed and with the members, proceeded to the west door. Halting at the foot of the stone steps the adjutant proceeded forward and knocked thrice on the door with the hilt of his sword and demanded admission. In the meantime the officiating clergyman, Rev. Dr. W. W. Craig, D.D., M.A., rector of Christ Church, with the members of the choir, had moved down the centre aisle of the church towards the door. The clergyman, accompanied by two wardens, awaited the demand for entrance.

Who Comes Here?

"Who comes here?" asked Rev. Dr. Craig, upon the door being opened.

The adjutant replied: "I have been commanded by Lieut.-Col. Fred Lister, C.M.G., D.S.O., M.C., the last commanding officer of the 102nd Battalion, 'North British Columbians,' to inform the authorities of this Church that he has repaired here today upon his return from the Great War with the colours of the Battalion, and desires admission to prefer a request that they be deposited here."

The clergyman answered, "Inform Col. Lister, commanding the 'North British Columbians,' that every facility will be afforded him in executing his most laudable purpose."

After the entry into the church the National Anthem was sung, and then the procession proceeded up the aisle. The clergyman and the wardens halted two paces beyond the top of the chancel steps and faced the congregation, while the officer commanding and colour party halted at the foot of the steps. Addressing Rev. Dr. Craig, Col. Lister said:

"Sir, on behalf of the officers and men of the 102nd Battalion, 'North British Columbians,' I have the honour to inform you these are colours of their Battalion, and to request that they be deposited here for safe-keeping, as a token of their gratitude to Almighty God, by Whom alone victory is secured, for His providential care and gracious benedictions granted them in the discharge of duty. In so acting they also desire to provide a memorial to the men of all ranks who served under these colours, and to afford an inspiration for patriotic service and sacrifice to all who may worship here for all time to come."

Rector's Words

Taking the colours from the officers of the colour party, Col. Lister passed them to the clergyman and he in turn gave them to the wardens. In accepting them the Rector said: "In the faith of Jesus Christ we accept these colours for the glory of God and in memory of those who were faithful, many of them even unto death, in the sacred cause of King and Country, and in confidence of the inspiration they will afford to all who may behold them. In the Name of the Father, and of the Son, and of the Holy Ghost. Amen."

The clergyman, followed by the wardens carrying the colors, proceeded to the altar and personally placed first the King's Colour and then the Regimental Colour in the permanent fixtures.

Taking as his text the second and third verse of the eighth chapter of Deuteronomy, Rev. Dr. Craig said that the thought that he had desired to bring before the minds of the people was summed up by the question, "What have you learned during the last five years?" People were put on earth to learn and life was the teacher. It disciplined the people and made them disciples. One thing that the War taught was the divine omnipotence of God. The war taught people to desire realities. The men who went through it are determined to have the reality of life. They cannot bear conventions and must have appreciation of the moral standards and issues. They would do away with sham and convention and demanded reality in personal religion.

Two Hundred of 102nd Present

The officer bearing the King's Colour was Capt. T. R. Griffiths, M.C., while the officer bearing the Regimental Colour was Lieut. R. D. Forrester. The other three members of the colour party were Regt.-Sergt.-Major W. H. Long, Reg. Sergt.-Major John Russell, D.C.M., and Sergt. R. W. Rayner, M.M. Right Rev. A. U. de Pencier, Bishop of New Westminster, assisted in the service, together with Major the Rev. C. C. Owen, former rector of Christ Church. There were nearly two hundred members of the 102nd present, and these came from all parts of the Province, from the Interior, Vancouver Island, and up the Coast.

APPENDIX A

FINAL ORDER

By Lieut.-Colonel Fred Lister, C.M.G., D.S.O., M.C., Commanding 102nd Infantry Battalion (North British Columbians).

"FOR close on three years the 102nd Canadian Infantry Battalion has endured the perils and hardships of war on the western front. Two years and eleven months ago we were on the high seas, but our faces were turned east; we were on the threshold of the Great Adventure. Today we are looking west, and our hearts are beating high in anticipation of a speedy reunion with our homes and loved ones.

"Many who sailed with us then are lying now on the several battlefields, or in the many cemeteries of France and Belgium, and their places were taken by others who did not shrink from making the supreme sacrifice. Many of our comrades, disabled by wounds or sickness, have already returned to Canada, and we are looking forward to meeting them once more, to tell them that we have not failed to maintain the traditions which they handed down to us.

"It is fitting, therefore, that before we disperse we take stock of our achievements on the battlefield, for the record of the 102nd Canadian Infantry Battalion is one of which any unit might surely well be proud. After only six months' organization in Canada the unit sailed for England, where it accomplished in six weeks the work which most Battalions took at least three months to perform. And so it came to France. During twenty-seven months of constant warfare we more than held our own. We can look back now and say that we never lost an inch of ground, that we never failed to take our objective, and to hold same when taken, and that no German ever set foot in our trenches save as a prisoner.

"We started out a British Columbia unit; we return an Ontario Battalion; but I defy anyone to note the point of cleavage. Welded together by many months of common danger, East and West have fused as one, and if the Battalion which set out in June, 1916, was a marvel of fitness, the reinforcements which have arrived from Ontario since August, 1917, have been all that the heart of man could desire.

"Within a few short days we shall be dispersed to our several homes, but I sincerely trust that the ties of friendship will never be broken. A Battalion Association has been formed for the set purpose of holding fast those ties, and I hope that each and all will keep in touch with this Association.

"Just a word of thanks and congratulation before we part. From my heart I congratulate the Battalion as a whole and each one of you individually for the gallant part taken by the 102nd Canadian Infantry Battalion in the Great War, and most sincerely do I thank every member of the unit for the sublime devotion to duty, and the loyal support of authority which has characterized the Battalion. Under Lieut.-Colonel J. W. Warden, D.S.O., you endured the horrors of the Somme and Passchendaele, and fought with fierce determination round Lens. When sickness forced his absence you gave the same unswerving loyalty to his second-in-command, Major (now Lieut.-Colonel) A. B. Carey, D.S.O., and gained the heights of Vimy Ridge. When special duty in Mesopotamia finally deprived us of the services of Lieut.-Colonel Warden, and I was honoured with your command, you extended to me the same whole-hearted support, adapting yourselves with courage and enthusiasm to the new conditions imposed by open warfare. When wounds compelled my temporary retirement you exhibited the same fine qualities of patience, obedience and endurance under the command in turn of my second, Major (now Lieut.-Colonel) E. J. Ryan, D.S.O. So many changes in command might well have taxed the discipline of older troops than you, but to the everlasting credit of the 102nd Battalion you gave to each and all a full measure of confidence and devotion.

"That happiness and prosperity may attend each one of you throughout your lives is my earnest wish. Good luck be with you all."

"FRED LISTER,
"Lieut-Colonel.
"Commanding 102nd Canadian Infantry Battalion.

"May 25th, 1919."

APPENDIX B

STATISTICAL TABLE

102nd Canadian Infantry Battalion

(NOTE—The following figures take no note of any ranks who joined the Battalion in Comox but were transferred or discharged prior to the departure of the unit overseas.)

TOTAL STRENGTH OF THE BATTALION

Total number of Officers	207
Total number of Other Ranks	3,656
	3,863

CASUALTIES

(NOTE—The following figures refer only to ranks still on the strength of the unit at the time of their casualty.)

Officers killed in action	31
Other Ranks killed in action	482
Officers died of wounds	6
Other Ranks died of wounds	117
Officers missing after action	1
Other Ranks missing after action	22
Officers died of sickness	0
Other Ranks died of sickness	17
Officers wounded	95
Other Ranks wounded	1,620
	2,391

DECORATIONS

Victoria Cross	1
Companion of St. Michael and St. George	1
Distinguished Service Order	5
Military Cross	38
Bar to Military Cross	6
Distinguished Service Medal	19
Military Medal	162
Bar to Military Medal	8
Meritorious Service Medal	9
Croix de Guerre (French)	1
Croix de Guerre (Belgian)	6
Medaille Militaire	1
Medaille d'Honneur avec Gliaves en Bronze	1
Cross of St. George, 4th Class (Russian)	3
Mentioned in Despatches	26
	287

APPENDIX C

Constitution and By-Laws of the 102nd Battalion Association

1. The name of this Association is the 102nd Battalion Association.

2. The Association is an independent Association, and will not be subservient to any political or other organization in Canada or elsewhere.

3. Active membership in the Association is limited to those members of the 102nd Canadian Infantry Battalion who actually served at any time with the unit in France or Belgium. Power is vested in the Branch Committees to elect honorary members.

4. The Association is divided into two branches, the Eastern Branch, with headquarters in Toronto, and the Western Branch, with headquarters in Vancouver; each Branch being controlled by a Committee of six, consisting of a Chairman, a Secretary, and four members, any three to form a quorum, and the Chairman to hold the deciding vote. The dividing line between the Branches will be the boundary line between Manitoba and Saskatchewan.

5. The organization of the Association consists of a President, a Vice-President, a General Secretary, and a Committee of twelve members, the

latter to consist of the governing bodies of the Eastern and Western Branches; any seven to form a quorum, and the Chairman to hold the deciding vote.

6. Officers of the Association and of the two Branches will be elected once a year at the annual meeting of the Branch members. The nominations for President, Vice-President, and General Secretary will be submitted to Branch Secretaries two months before the annual meeting, and a count of votes taken at the meeting will be forwarded to the last General Secretary, who will notify the incoming officers of their election. and will also notify the Branch Secretaries. The officers elected for the first year, however, will hold office until the second annual meeting.

7. The objects of the Association are as follows:—
   (a) To keep in contact old comrades, and to lend a helping hand where needed.
   (b) To keep alive the traditions of the 102nd Canadian Infantry Battalion, and to promote a spirit of loyalty and devotion to country in succeeding generations.
   (c) To work together in a true spirit of good citizenship for a better Canada.
   (d) To act as trustee for all Battalion trophies, Regimental Colours, documents, etc.
   (e) To work in concert for the establishment of the 102nd Canadian Infantry Battalion as a unit in the Canadian Permanent Forces, and to hand over to such unit, if formed, all existing Battalion property.
   (f) To raise money where needed for the relief of deserving cases of hardship endured by members or their dependents.
   (g) To keep in touch with the trustees of the Regimental Fund, for the purpose of recommending, through the Committee, cases deserving of relief.
   (h) To further the interests of all returned soldiers.

8. Both Branches of the Association will meet at least once a year on the same date, the place and date of the next meeting to be decided at this general meeting of each Branch. To prevent different dates being selected, the two Committees will come to an agreement beforehand by correspondence. In the event of disagreement the date will be selected by the President.

9. Each Committee will meet at least once a month, and will furnish the General Secretary with a copy of the Minutes. The General Secretary will file these with the Association records, and will forward to each Branch a copy of the Minutes forwarded by the other Branch.

10. A small Association button will be worn by members.

11. Each Branch will be responsible for the establishing and financing of its own headquarters.

OFFICERS OF THE ASSOCIATION

First Honorary President: H. S. Clements, Esq., M.P.
Second Honorary President: Lieut.-Colonel J. W. Warden, O.B.E., D.S.O.
President: Lieut.-Colonel F. Lister, C.M.G., D.S.O., M.C.
First Honorary Vice-President: Major R. J. Burde, M.C.
Second Honorary Vice-President: Capt. J. E. Thompson.
Third Honorary Vice-President: Major H. E. Homer Dixon.
Vice-President: Lieut.-Colonel E. J. Ryan, D.S.O.
General Secretary: Sergt. L. McLeod Gould, P.O. Box 721, Victoria, B.C.

Eastern Branch:

Chairman: Lieut. H. J. French, M.C.
Secretary: Sergt. E. H. Telfer, Woods and Forest Branch, Parliament Buildings, Toronto.
Members: Lieut. W. H. C. Stanley, M.C.; Sergt. F. G. Reeks, M.M.; Pte. W. Johnstone; Pte. H. L. Ross.

Western Branch

Chairman:- Major S. H. Okell, M.C.
Secretary: Major F. J. Brandt, 418 Rogers Bldg., Vancouver, B.C.
Members: C.S.M. H. A. Farris, M.M.; C.Q.M.S. W. S. Brown; Sergt. F. W. Hambleton; Sergt. R. G. Orr.

APPENDIX "D"

Nominal Roll of Officers and Other Ranks, 102nd Battalion

EXPLANATORY NOTE

The following Nominal Roll contains the names of:

(a) All Officers and Other Ranks who landed with the 102nd Battalion in England, June 29th, 1916:

(b) All Officers and Other Ranks who reinforced the 102nd in England and proceeded to France, August 11th, 1916.

(c) All Officers and Other Ranks who actually reported for duty as reinforcements in the field.

It does not include some hundreds of reinforcements who were sent over to France as drafts for the 102nd Battalion, but who were transferred in France to other units before they reported to the 102nd Battalion.

The names of places in brackets after a casualty show the battle front on which the casualty was incurred. Authorities for the award of decorations are also shown.

It must be remembered that after August, 1917, all who did not hail from Ontario were posted to other units on evacuation to England. It has been found impossible to give any details of the subsequent career of these men, except in rare instances. The words "to Eng." after a man's casualty denote that he was then struck off the strength of the battalion and that his subsequent history is unknown to the compiler of the Nominal Roll.

In every case Acting Rank has been credited to the individual. It has been felt that if a man was worthy of bearing acting rank in the field he is entitled to such rank in a Nominal Roll of this nature. Where reliable information has been received of the promotion of an Officer or Other Rank after he was struck off the strength of the Battalion he is credited with such promotion in the Nominal Roll.

The addresses given are for the most part those of the Next-of-Kin, as given to the Paymaster when reinforcements reported for duty. In too many cases these addresses are in Europe, whereas the man concerned is in Canada, but letters sent there will doubtless be forwarded.

The following abbreviations have been used:

Bde.	Brigade.
C.I.B.	Canadian Infantry Brigade.
C.C.A.C.	Canadian Casualty Assembly Centre.
C.C.C.	Canadian Corps Camp.
C.F.C.	Canadian Forestry Corps.
C.I.B.D.	Canadian Infantry Base Depot.
C.C.R.C.	Canadian Corps Reinforcement Camp.
C.G.B.D.	Canadian Garrison Base Depot.
C.L.T.M.B.	Canadian Light Trench Mortar Battery.
C.M.G.	Companion of the Order of St. Michael and St. George.
C.R.O.	Corps Routine Order.
C.R.T.	Canadian Railway Troops.
d.	Dated.
D.C.M.	Distinguished Conduct Medal.
Dec.	Decorated.
D.O.S.	Died of Sickness.
D.o.w.	Died of Wounds.
D.R.O.	Divisional Routine Order.
D.S.O.	Distinguished Service Order.
Ech.	Echelon.
Emp.	Employment.
Eng.	England.
Engr.	Engineer.
Evac.	Evacuated.
G.R.O.	General Routine Order.
K.i.a.	Killed in Action.
L.G.	London Gazette.
M.C.	Military Cross.
Men. in des.	Mentioned in Despatches.
M.G.C.	Machine Gun Corps or Company.
M.M.	Military Medal.
M.S.M.	Meritorious Service Medal.
Ret.	Returned.
Tr.	Transferred.
W.	Wounded (includes Gassed).

NOMINAL ROLL

OF

OFFICERS AND OTHER RANKS

OF THE

102nd Canadian Infantry Battalion

COMPLETE WITH CASUALTIES
AND ADDRESSES

NOMINAL ROLL OF OFFICERS

(Asterisk denotes original officers.)

RANK	NAME	CASUALTY.	ADDRESS OR THAT OF NEXT-OF-KIN.
Lt.-Col.	*Warden, J. W.	Granted auth. to raise unit. 3-11-15; dec. D.S.O. (Somme) L.G. 29898; mentioned in despatches, L.G. 30107, d. 1-6-17; tr. to Eng. for special service (Mesop.) 11-1-18; later tr. to Russia; later apptd. O.C. Russian Officers Training School, near Vladivostok.	427 Arnold St., Foul Bay, Victoria, B.C.
Lt.-Col.	*Lister, F.	O.C. "A" Co. 22-10-16; dec. M.C. (Somme) L.G. 29898; D.S.O. (2nd Triangle) L.G. 30281; 2nd. l.c. 22-5-17; mentioned in despatches, L.G. 30448, d. 28-12-17; C.O. 12-1-18; w. 27-9-18 (Cambrai) to Eng.; ret. 19-11-18; dec. C.M.G., L.G. d. 3-6-19; men. in des. L.G. d. 8-7-19.	Land Settlement Board, Creston, B.C.
Lt.-Col.	Carey, A. B.	Tr. from 67th Bn. 4-11-16; w. 20-11-16 (Somme); mentioned in despatches, L.G. 29890, d. 4-1-17; A.-O.C. 14-2-17 to 12-4-17; dec. D.S.O. (Vimy), L.G. 30234; tr. to command of 54th Bn. 23-5-17; dec. Bar to D.S.O. (Cambrai); C.M.G., L.G. d. 3-6-19; men. in des. L.G. d. 8-7-19.	Vancouver, B.C.
Lt.-Col.	Ryan, E. J. W.	Reptd. 16-3-17; mentioned in despatches, L.G. 30706, d. 7-4-18; O.C. "C" Co.; 2nd l.-c. 12-1-18; A.-O.C. 3-10-18 to 19-11-18; dec. D.S.O. (Valenciennes) L.G. 31183; mentioned in despatches, L.G. d. 8-7-19.	Suite 5, Fairfield Bg, 445 Granville St, Vancouver, B.C.
Lt.-Col.	*Worsnop, C. B.	2nd l.-c. to 15-12-16; dec. D.S.O. (Somme) L.G. 29898; tr. to 50th Bn. 15-12-16; tr. to command of 75th Bn.; tr. to Eng. as O.C. 16th Res. Bn. B.C.R.D.	741 Thurlow St., Vancouver, B.C.
Major	Armour, S. D.	Tr. from 67th Bn. 2-5-17; att. to Gen. Staff, 4th Div. 2-5-17; apptd. Staff Capt. with 12th Bde. 21-5-17; sec. as G.S.O. 3rd Gr. 4th Div. 6-3-18; dec. Croix de Guerre, Belgian, L.G. 30792, d. 9-7-18; men. in des. L.G. d. 8-7-19.	875 Chilco St., Vancouver, B.C.
Major	*Bailey, J. B.	Adj. from 2-12-16; tr. to 54th Bn. as 2nd l.-c. 13-7-17; dec. D.S.O. with 54th Bn.	Sandwick, Vancouver Island, B.C.
Major	Bapty, W.	Att. as M.O. from C.A.M.C. 12-3-17; w. 8-6-17; w. 2-11-17 to Eng.	1175 Fort St., Victoria, B.C.
Major	*Brandt, J. F.	O.C. "B" Co. (Vimy) att. to No. 7 P.O.W. Co. 22-5-17; tr. to Eng. 11-11-17.	418 Rogers Bldg., Vancouver, B.C.
Major	*Brydon, R. G. H.	Works Officer; O.C. "C" Co. (Vimv); mentioned in despatches, L.G. 30107, d. 1-6-17; k. l. a. 9-4-17 (Vimy).	Mrs. F. M. Brydon, 961 Howe St., Vancouver, B.C.
Major	*Burde, R. J.	Att. to 11th C.I.B. as Bombing Officer to 16-4-17; dec. M.C. (Somme), L.G. 29859; O.C. "C" Co. (Triangle and Lens) det. as 4th Div. Ammn. Off. 16-12-17; tr. from P.B. to Eng. 15-6-18.	Port Alberni, B.C.

Major	Christie, A. E.	Tr. from 67th Bn. 2-5-17; att. to 1st Army H.-Q. as P.B. Off. sec. as P.B. Off. Can. Corps, 24-10-17; tr. to Eng. 24-9-18	604 Linden Ave., Victoria, B.C.
Major	Dempster, G. L.	Reptd. 3-2-17; O.C. "A" Co. (Lens); evac. sick in Eng. 15-10-17	St. Hilda's Boarding Estmt., Ridgemont Rd., St. Albans, Eng. Coldstream, Vernon, B.C.
Major	*Dixon, H. E. H.	O.C. "B" Co.; w. 21-10-16 to Eng.	
Major	Gary, F. J.	Tr. from 67th Bn. 2-5-17; A.-Adj. (Lens); O.C. "B" Co. dec. M.C. (Lens), L.G. 30308; Bar to M.C. (Oppy). L.G. 30901; d. o. w. 2-9-18 (2nd Arras)	Mrs. F. J. Gary, Morningside, Sioux City, Iowa, U.S.A.
Major	Graham, A.	Reptd. from 29th Bn. 8-10-17; A.-Adj.; att. to 2nd Bn. C.M.G.C. 8-4-18	2900 Scott St., Vancouver, B.C.
Major	*Hagar, L. M. M.	Tr. to Base Co. 11-8-16	P.O. Box 1523, Victoria, B.C.
Major	*Halsey, J. C.	Adj. from 1-11-16 to 2-12-16; evac. sick 17-12-16 to Eng.; d. o. s. in Canada.	Mrs. Halsey, 212 Kamloops St., Vancouver, B.C.
Major	*Johnston, A. T.	O.C. "A" Co.; k. i. a. 2-9-16 (St. Eloi)	Mrs. Johnston, 1010 Salisbury Drive, Vancouver, B.C.
Major	*Mackenzie, K. G.	O.C. "D" Co. 22-10-16; k. i. a. 20-11-16 (Somme)	Mrs. Mackenzie, Box 40, Kamloops, B.C.
Major	*Matthews, J. S.	O.C. "C" Co. 2-5-17; O.C. "D" Co.; Adj. 20-12-17; dec. M.C., L.G. 30716, d. 31-5-18; w. 2-9-18 (2nd Arras); w. 27-9-18 (Cambrai) to Eng.	1343 Maple St., Kitsilano, Vancouver, B.C.
Major	*Okell, S. H.	Tr. from 67th Bn. 2-5-17; O.C. "D" Co.; Adj. 20-12-17; dec. M.C., L.G. 30716, d. 31-5-18; w. 2-9-18 (2nd Arras); w. 27-9-18 (Cambrai) to Eng.	702 Wilson St., Victoria, B.C.
Major	Ramsay, P. B. H.	Reptd. 30-1-17; tr. to 3rd Can. Pioneers, 10-4-17.	7 Gilford Court, Vancouver, B.C.
Major	*Rothnie, G.	O.C. "D" Co.; missing, believed k. i. a. 21-10-16 (Regina)	Mrs. Rothnie, 153 Victoria St., Kamloops, B.C.
Major	*Scharschmidt, H. B.	Adj. from 4-12-15 to 14-10-16; att. to 10th C.I.B. Staff 14-10-16 for 4 mos.; O.C. "D" Co.; w. 6-6-17 (2nd Triangle) to Eng.	1190 Salisbury Drive, Vancouver, B.C.
Major	Scudamore, T. V.	Reptd. 24-12-18 from 7th Bn.	c/o Cox & Co., Charing Cross, London, W.C., Eng.
Major	Trapp, T. D.	Reptd. from 131 Bn. 11-4-17; evac. sick 30-4-17 to Eng.	229 3rd Ave., New Westminster, B.C.
Major	Walwyn, W. McL.	Reptd. 4-4-18; O.C. "C" Co.; A.-2nd 1.-c. Valenciennes; dec. M.C., L.G. 31092, d. 1-1-19; Education Off. 11th C.I.B. after Armistice.	
Capt.	Atkin, I. C. R.	Reptd. 25-12-16; O.C. "A" Co.; dec. M.C. (Lens), L.G. 30355; Bar to M.C. (Amiens), L.G. 31043; w. 27-9-18 (Cambrai) to Eng.	c/o S. J. Moore, 142 Jameson Ave., Toronto, Ont.
Capt.	Barton, W. S.	Reptd. from 103rd Bn. 7-8-16; w. 27-8-16 (St. Eloi) to Eng.; prom. Capt. in Canada	1291 Davie St., Vancouver, B.C.
Capt.	Bell, W.	Reptd. from 103rd Bn. 7-8-16; w. 21-10-16 (Regina) to Eng. Staff Capt. H.-Q. Hastings. Bde. Maj Hastings; tr. to Argyle House as A.G.2D.	111 Pemberton Bldg., Victoria, B.C.
Capt.	Brimacombe, V. C.	Reptd. 24-12-16; O.C. "D" Co.; dec. M.C. (Amiens), L.G. 31043	1634 North Hampshire Rd., Victoria, B.C.
Capt.	*Colwell, T. C.	Chaplain (Meth.); tr. to Base Co. 11-8-16; Joined 1st Div. in France; dec. M.C.	c/o Bank of Montreal, New Westminster, B.C.
Capt.	Daniels, I. J. E.	Chaplain (R.C.) 17-8-16; tr. to Eng. 15-3-17	Kincardine, Ont.
Capt.	Dunlop, H.	Att. as M.O. from C.A.M.C. 2-11-17; dec. M.C. (Amiens), L.G. 31043; k. i. a. 2-11-18 (Valenciennes).	No address available. Mrs. H. Dunlop, c/o N. C. Taintor, 54 Niles Street, Hartford, Conn., U.S.A.

Capt. Dunlop, W. W.	Tr. from 67th Bn. 2-5-17; w. twice with 67th; prom. from Sgt. 23-5-17; w. 16-8-17 (Lens); w. 17-11-17 (Passchendaele); dec. M.C. (Passchendaele), L.G. 2nd Supp., d. 1-2-18; Adj. 27-9-18 to demob.; dec. Bar to M.C. (Cambrai), L.G. 31183		c/o Mr. Caldwell, 620 O'Farrell St., San Francisco, Cal.
Capt. *Fall, J.	Tr. to Base Co. 11-8-16		Hillbank P.O., Vancouver Island, B.C.
Capt. Fallon, C. A.	Chaplain (R.C.); reptd. 23-2-18; dec. M.C. (Cambrai), G.R.O. 418		
Capt. Fitzmaurice, R.	Reptd. from 11th C.M.R. 29-7-16; A.-O.C. "C" Co.; Intelligence Officer; Transport Officer; mentioned in despatches, L.G. 31089, d. 31-12-18.		211 Alfred St., Kingston, Ont.
Capt. *Gale, R. L.	Prom. from Pte. 28-4-17; Intelligence Officer; dec. M.C. (Oppy), L.G. 30950; Bar to M.C. (Valenciennes) C.R.O. 2040; w. 6-11-18 (Valenciennes)		Vernon, B.C.
Capt. Gook, E. J.	Reptd. from 11th C.M.R. 1-8-16; Adj. 14-10-16; det. to Base, Havre 30-10-16; evac. sick to Eng. 17-5-17		Smithers, B.C.
Capt. Graham, L. B.	Att. as M.O. from C.A.M.C. 6-11-16; evac. sick 19-2-17 to Eng.		Langford P.O., Vancouver Island, B.C.
Capt. *Griffith, T. R.	Transport Officer; dec. M.C. (Lens), L.G. 30450; O.C. "C" Co.; w. 2-9-18 (2nd Arras) to Eng.		No address available.
Capt. Henderson, C. E.	Reptd. from 227th 9-9-17; O.C. 11th C.I.B. Pack Train; O.C. "C" Co.; w. 18-10-18; dec. M.C. (Valenciennes), L.G. d. 3-6-19		Fraser Mills, Vancouver, B.C.
Capt. *Kirkpatrick, J. A.	Paymaster		Box 910, Sudbury, Ont.
Capt. Knight, J. G.	Reptd. from 131st Bn. 4-1-17; Works Officer; O.C. "B" Co.; dec. M.C. (2nd Triangle), L.G. 30287; Bar to M.C. (2nd Arras), L.G. 31183		543 Toronto St., Victoria, B.C.
Capt. Leeson, D.	Reptd. 2-3-19; tr. to Records List 3-5-19		Vernon, B.C.
Capt. Loudon, W. J.	Reptd. from 11th C.M.R. 29-7-16; att. to 11th C.I.B. as Camp Commandant. Dicklebusch, 24-8-16; w. 21-10-16 (Regina) to Eng.		c/o C. W. Derry, 23 Casmir Rd., Heralds Cross, Dublin, Ire.
Capt. Mann, J. A.	Reptd. from 225th Bn. 21-3-17; O.C. "A" Co.; dec. M.C. (2nd Arras), L.G. 31183; dec. Croix de Guerre, Belgian, (Cambrai) C.C.M.S. 409-19		No address available.
Capt. *Matheson, R. P.	Dec. M.C. (Regina), L.G. 29898; w. 10-11-16 (Somme) to Eng; mentioned in despatches, L.G. 30107, d. 1-6-17; prom. Capt. and Adj. R.M. Hospital, Esquimalt		123 North 3rd St., Hamilton, Ohio, U.S.A.
Capt. McAllister, H. C.	Att. as M.O. from C.A.M.C. 19-11-18		Royal Military Hospital, Esquimalt, B.C.
Capt. *McCualg, R.	Acc. w. 14-10-16 to Eng.; prom. in Canada		Ridgetown, Ont.
Capt. McDonald, P. A.	Chaplain (R.C.) 4-4-17; tr. to H.-Q. C.R.T. 23-3-18		Terminal City Club, Vancouver, B.C.
Capt. *McNeill, N. M.	M.O.; evac. sick 27-10-16		Glencoe, Vernon River, P.E.I.
Capt. Nicholls, R. W.	Reptd. from 74th Bn. 22-7-16; k. i. a. 23-10-16 (Regina)		Prince Rupert, B.C.
Capt. *O'Kelly, T. P.	Transport Officer; dec. M.C. (Lens), L.G. 30450; att. to 11th C.I.B. as Tpt. Off.; dec. Bar to M.C. (Passchendaele), L.G. 30530; evac. sick to Eng. 19-11-17		No address available.
Capt. Oldham, A. C.	Tr. from 67th Bn. 2-5-17; att. to 4th Div. School 2-5-17; tr. to Eng. 30-12-17		1218 Melville St., Vancouver, B.C.
			Headley, Epsom, Surrey.

Capt.	O'Leary, F. J.	Tr. from 53rd Bn. 29-7-16; att. to 11th C.I.B. as O.C. 11th C.L.T.M.B. 3-8-16; mentioned in despatches. L.G. 29890, d. 4-1-17; dec. M.C. (Vimy), L.G. 30111; att. to H.-Q. Branch, Can. Corps H.-Q. 31-1-18; tr. as Staff Capt. to 1st Can. Engineer Bde.	51 Mount-Nod-Road, Streatham, London, S.W.16, Eng.
Capt.	Paterson, G.	Tr. from 7th Bn. 31-8-16; att. to 11th C.I.B. 31-7-16; dec. M.C. (Somme), L.G. 29886; evac. sick 30-3-17 to Eng.	No address available.
Capt.	*Robbins, J.	W. 20-11-16 (Somme); prom. from Sgt. 29-11-16; w. 9-4-17 to Eng; prom. Capt. in Canada.	956 Logan Ave., Toronto, Ont.
Capt.	*Ross, J. H.	Tr. to Base Co. 11-8-16.	Pacific Club, Victoria, B.C.
Capt.	Schell, C. A.	Reptd. from 204th Bn. 9-9-17; w. 23-7-18 to Eng.	R.R. No. 3, Port Elgin, Ont.
Capt.	Scott, A. G.	Reptd. 18-6-16; att. to 11th C.I.B. as O.C. 11th C.M.G. Co. dec. M.C. (Lens), L.G. 30340; tr to C.M.G.C. 30-6-17	No address available.
Capt.	Spencer, G. J.	Reptd. from 75th Bn. 22-7-16; w. 21-10-16 (Regina) to Eng.	No address available.
Capt.	*Stead, F.	Quartermaster; mentioned in despatches, L.G. 30448, d. 28-12-17	1925 Pendrell St., Vancouver, B.C.
Capt.	Terry, S. D.	Tr. from 67th Bn. 2-5-17; k. i. a. 25-8-17 (Lens).	S. Terry, The Manse, Ashvale, Aldershot, Eng.
Capt.	Thomson, M. F.	Reptd. from 121st Bn. 11-4-17; att. to 11th C.I.B. as O.C. Tump-Line Section, 15-4-17; dec. M.C. (Lens), L.G. 30450; mentioned in despatches, L.G. 30706, d. 28-5-18	Duncan, B.C.
Capt.	Trousdale, A. C.	Reptd. from 74th Bn. 22-7-16; Scout Officer; w. 11-11-16 (Somme) to Eng.	Box 720, Auckland, New Zealand.
Capt.	*Whyte, H. E.	W. 31-8-16 (St. Eloi) to Eng; tr. to C.A.P.C. and prom. Capt. in Canada.	138 Robertson St., Victoria, B.C.
Capt.	Woodley, J. W.	Att. as M.O. from C.A.M.C. 8-2-17 to 12-3-17.	No address available.
Lieut.	Adams, R. A.	Reptd. from 58th Bn. 30-9-17; Scout Officer; tr. to Eng. to R.A.F. 4-6-18.	75 Spruce Hill Rd., Balmy Beach, Toronto, Ont.
Lieut.	Alexander, E. D.	Tr. from 67th Bn. 2-5-17; evac. sick 23-7-17 to Eng.	162 St. Luke St., Montreal, Que.
Lieut.	*Allum, G. G.	Prom. from Sgt. 1-4-17; Bombing Officer; w. 17-8-17 (Lens) to Eng.	6 College Terrace, Brighton, Eng.
Lieut.	*Alsen, G. O.	Prom. from Pte. 29-11-16; evac. sick 24-8-17 to Eng.	Suite 1. 2225 First Ave, Vancouver, B.C.
Lieut.	Archibald, S. W.	Reptd. 12-8-18; w. 27-9-18 (Cambrai) to Eng.	R.R. No. 4, Seaforth, Ont.
Lieut.	Ardron, J. E.	Reptd. from 244th Bn. 30-9-17; tr. to Eng. from P.B. 16-11-17	Suite 2, 23 Sussex Ave., Montreal, Que.
Lieut.	Askey, W. G.	Reptd. 11-12-16; evac. sick 28-2-17 to Eng.	Pincher Creek, Alta.
Lieut.	Atkins, G. V.	Prom. from Cpl. 11-8-18; Scout Officer; dec. M.C. (Cambrai), L.G. 31183; w. 6-11-18 (Valenciennes) to Eng.	703 28th Ave. E., Vancouver, B.C.
Lieut.	Banks, H.	Tr. from 67th Bn. 2-5-17; prom. from Sgt. 6-6-18; dec. M.C. (Cambrai), L.G. 31183; d.o.w.17-10-18 (Cambrai)	Mrs. A. Fletcher, Lilling, Yorks, Eng.
Lieut.	Baurle, G. A.	Tr. from 67th Bn. 2-5-17; evac. sick 20-6-17 to Eng.	518 West 135th St., New York, N.Y., U.S.A.
Lieut.	Beesley, L. F.	Tr. from 67th Bn. 2-5-17; att. to 1st Tramway Co. 24-11-17	South Fort George, B.C.
Lieut.	Bennett, H. M.	Reptd. 11-12-16; w. 9-4-17 (Vimy) to Eng.	10 Denmark Rd., Ealing, London, W., Eng.
Lieut.	Bettlson, L. J.	Reptd. from 11th C.M.R. 29-7-16; w. 23-10-16 (Regina); w. (acc.) 11-11-16; att. to 11th C.L.T.M.B. 7-3-17; w. 15-8-17 (Lens) to Eng.	No address available.

Rank	Name	Record	Address
Lieut.	Beveridge, A. R.	Reptd. 30-9-17; Scout Officer; tr. to Eng. to R.A.F. 8-4-18	c/o S. Price & Sons, Worcester House, Walbrook, London, E.C., Eng.
Lieut.	Birks, W. H.	Reptd. from 119th Bn. 30-5-18; Educ. Officer after Armistice.	20 Westgate, Ripon, Yorks, Eng.
Lieut.	Boyes, D. A.	Reptd. 22-1-17; k. i. a. 9-4-17 (Vimy)	F. D. Boyes, 1426 1st Ave. E., Vancouver, B.C.
Lieut.	Brechin, J.	Reptd. from 225th Bn. 30-4-17; tr. to C.F.C. 22-5-17	1986 St. Ann St., Victoria, B.C.
Lieut.	*Brighton, A. M.	W. 22-10-16 (Regina); prom. from Sgt. 27-4-18; k. i. a. 27-9-18 (Cambrai)	J. Brighton, 81 Nithsdale Drive, Glasgow, Scot.
Lieut.	Brown, J. R.	Prom. from L.-Sgt. 6-6-18; k. i. a. 27-9-18 (Cambrai)	Mrs. J. R. Brown, Purton, Wilts, Eng.
Lieut.	Buchan, A. C. A.	Reptd. 11-12-16; w. 9-4-17 (Vimy) to Eng.	No address available.
Lieut.	*Carss, A.	D. o. w. 21-10-16 (Regina)	Mrs. A. Carss, Prince Rupert, B.C.
Lieut.	Cartmel, J.	Reptd. from 225th Bn. 30-4-17; att. to 11th C.I.T.M.B. 14-8-17; w. 30-10-17 (Lens) to Eng.	Atlin, B.C.
Lieut.	Chagnon, E. S.	Reptd. 4-4-18; dec. M.C. (Amiens), L.G. 31043; w. 8-8-18; (Amiens) to Eng.	66 Maple Ave., Hamilton, Ont.
Lieut.	Chalifour, S. J. L.	Reptd. 30-4-17; w. 9-6-17 (2nd Triangle) to Eng.	306 Nelson St., Ottawa, Ont.
Lieut.	*Copp, T. P.	K. i. a. 23-10-16 (Regina)	A. O. Copp, 1817 Kitchener St., Vancouver, B.C.
Lieut.	Cox, T. H.	Reptd. 30-6-17; w. 9-9-17 (Lens) to Eng.	13 Grassendale Rd., Grassendale, Liverpool, Eng.
Lieut.	Cresswell, J. A.	Reptd. 5-8-17; w. 7-8-17 (Lens) to Eng.	Warwick Club, 21 St George's Sq., London, W., Eng.
Lieut.	Crothers, W. E.	Reptd. on prom. from L.-Cpl. 18-8-18; w. 1-10-18 (Cambrai) to Eng.	
Lieut.	Dakers, J.	Tr. from 67th Bn. 2-5-17; att. to C.R.T. 2-5-17; dec. M.C. (Lens), L.G. 30450; w. 15-9-17 (Lens) to Eng.	City Hall, San Francisco, Cal., U.S.A.
Lieut.	Davidson, D.	Tr. from 67th Bn. 2-5-17; w. 9-6-17 (2nd Triangle); reptd. on prom. from Sgt. 17-9-18; w. 1-10-18 (Cambrai); evac. sick 2-11-18 to Eng.	c/o H.M. Customs, Victoria, B.C.
Lieut.	Davidson, J.	Reptd. from 121st Bn. 4-1-17; Works Officer; w. 19-3-17 (Vimy) to Eng.	744 Front St., Victoria, B.C.
Lieut.	Davis, G.	Reptd. from 121st Bn. 29-4-17; evac. sick 10-6-17 to Eng.	516 Fourth St., New Westminster, B.C.
Lieut.	Dawson, J. K.	Reptd. 22-5-18; k. i. a. 8-8-18 (Amiens)	c/o Messrs. Davis, Marshall, Macneill & Pugh, Vancouver, B.C.
Lieut.	Dent, T. E.	Reptd. from 11th C.M.R. 29-7-16; Sigs. Officer; att. to 4th Div. Sigs. 7-7-17	J. A. Dawson, Rosthern, Sask.
Lieut.	Devine, M. R. K.	Reptd. 3-2-18; w. 6-11-18 (2nd Arras) to Eng.	Knowles St., Stockton-on-Tees, Eng.
Lieut.	Duncan, A. D.	Reptd. 2-7-18; w. 4-9-18 (2nd Arras) to Eng.	Renfrew, Ont.
Lieut.	Dimsdale, H. G.	Reptd. 11-12-16; Scout Officer; O.C. "D" Co.; w. 9-4-17; dec. M.C. (Vimy), L.G. 30111; att. to 3rd Bn. C.R.T. 21-7-17	Benarty, Kinnoul, Perth, Scot.
Lieut.	Fallls, E. B. J.	Prom. from L.-Sgt. 26-2-17; Scout Officer; k. i. a. 9-4-17 (Vimy)	602 Rideau Rd., Calgary, Alta.
Lieut.	Flynn, J. P.	Tr. from 67th Bn. 2-5-17; tr. to No. 2 Forest Camp 20-4-17; dec. M.C. (Lens) C.R.O. 1277	Rev. S. W. Fallls, Central Meth. Ch., Calgary, Alta.
Lieut.	Forrester, A.	Tr. from 67th Bn. 2-5-17; Town Major, Hallecourt; evac. sick 17-1-18 to Eng.	Huntington, Que.
Lieut.	*Forrester, R. D.	Att. to Can. Corps Baths. 17-10-17; tr. to C.F.C. 1-12-17.	Nelson, B.C.
Lieut.	Frame, W. L.	Reptd. from 121st Bn. 27-2-17; w. 9-4-17 (Vimy) to Eng.	Suite 1, 742 Broughton St., Vancouver, B.C.
Lieut.	French, H. J.	Reptd. 5-2-18; A.-O.C. "D" Co.; dec. M.C. (Oppy), L.G. 30950	1136 12th Ave. W., Vancouver, B.C.
			137 Bond St., Toronto, Ont.

Lieut.	Fyles, J. J.	Reptd. from 7th Bn. 30-4-17; dec M.M. 1916; w. 19-5-17 (1st Triangle); evac. sick 2-6-17 to Eng.	c|o Atty, E. J. Kenny, Duluth, Minn., U.S.A.
Lieut.	Gaunce, W. G.	Reptd. 3-11-18; w. 6-11-18 (Valenciennes) to Eng.	c|o 201 Hibben-Bone Bldg., Victoria, B.C.
Lieut.	Gleason, E. L.	Tr. from 67th Bn. 2-5-17; k. l. a. 9-8-17 (Lens)	Mrs. R. Gleason, 611 Superior St., Victoria, B.C.
Lieut.	Goodyear, H. J.	Reptd. 3-2-18; w. 7-4-18 (Oppy); dec. M.C. (Amiens), L.G. 31043; k. l. a. 22-8-18 (Amiens)	Mrs. L. Goodyear, Grand Falls, Newfoundland.
Lieut.	*Gordon, MacL.	K. l. a. 21-10-16 (Regina)	Dr. G. B. Gordon, Univ. of Penn., Philadelphia, U.S.A.
Lieut.	*Grant, J. H.	D. o. w. 20-12-16 (Regina)	J. Grant, Nelson, B.C.
Lieut.	Griffin, C. S.	Reptd. from 7th Bn. 18-5-17; dec. M.C. (2nd Triangle), L.G. 30287; w. 13-6-17 (2nd Triangle) to Eng.	Sidney, B.C.
Lieut.	Gritten, L. A.	Tr. from 67th Bn. 2-5-17; w. 7-6-17 (2nd Triangle) to Eng.	5 Elmbank Mansions, Barnes, London, S.W., Eng.
Lieut.	Hall, R. W.	Reptd. 14-8-18; evac. sick 29-8-18 to Eng.	Richmond Hill, Ont.
Lieut.	*Harker-Thomas, F. R.	Reptd. on prom. from Pte. 7-9-18; k. l. a. 27-9-18 (Cambrai)	M. Harker-Thomas, Brymyrddin, Beechwood Ave., Kew Gardens, Surrey, Eng.
Lieut.	Harrison, S.	Reptd. from 103rd Bn. 29-4-17; evac. sick 2-6-17 to Eng.	302 Fifth St. E, North Vancouver, B.C.
Lieut.	Hartman, R. R.	Reptd. 11-9-17; att. to 11th C.L.T.M.B. 8-11-17; k. l. a. 2-9-18 (2nd Arras)	I. J. Hartman, Aurora, Ont.
Lieut.	Harvey, B.	Reptd. from R.F.C. 19-4-17; evac. sick 6-6-17 to Eng.	Montagu House, Baring Rd., Cowes, I.O.W., Eng.
Lieut.	Henry, W.	Reptd. 14-8-18; k. l. a. 27-9-18 (Cambrai)	Mrs. W. Hall, 345 Markham St., Toronto, Ont.
Lieut.	Honeyman, P.D.I.	Tr. from 67th Bn. 2-5-17; w. 16-5-17 (1st Triangle) to Eng.	Kerrisdale, B.C.
Lieut.	Howard, W. J. E.	Reptd. from 11th C.M.R. 29-7-16; tr. to 44th Bn. 2-2-17; dec. M.C. with 44th, L.G. 30111, d. 4-6-17.	No address available.
Lieut.	Huggins, C. G.	Reptd. from 50th Bn. 13-11-16; k. l. a. 14-5-17 (1st Triangle)	Mrs. Huggins, 11432 87th St., Edmonton, Alta.
Lieut.	*Johnston, J.	Reptd. on prom. from Cpl. 27-3-19;	Rossland, B.C.
Lieut.	Jonsson, H.	Tr. from 67th Bn. 2-5-17; att. to 1st Tramway Co. 24-11-17	Kandahar, Sask.
Lieut.	Knight, S. F.	Reptd. from 131st Bn. 18-1-17; dec. M.C. (Vimy) C.R.O. 1277; evac. sick 13-4-17 to Eng.	96 Sixth St., New Westminster, B.C.
Lieut.	Lahiff, D. R.	Reptd. from 7th Bn. 13-3-19.	c|o Mrs. Hanrahan, 32 Windsor Rd., Rathmines, Dublin, Ire.
Lieut.	Lamrock, J. S.	Reptd. from 164th Bn. 18-5-18; w. 30-9-18 (Cambrai) to Eng.	W. A. E. MacKay, Pachesham Towers, Leatherhead, Surrey, Eng.
Lieut.	Ledingham, G.	Reptd. 11-10-16; tr. on command to Eng 12-1-17.	35 St. James Villas, Somerville Rd., Penge. Kent, Eng.
Lieut.	*Leese, R. V.	Reptd. on prom. from C.S.M. 27-10-17; w. 27-9-18 (Cambrai) to Eng.	113 Wellmeadow Rd., Catford, London, Eng.
Lieut.	Lester, E. G.	Reptd. 19-1-17; d. o. w. 25-6-17 (Vimy).	Mrs. C. B. B. Lester, 35 Monmouth House, Yesterway, 21st Ave, Seattle, Wash., U.S.A.
Lieut.	Lineham, A.	Reptd. from 143rd Bn. 18-2-17; d. o. w. 10-4-17 (Vimy)	F. Lineham, Turgoose P.O., Victoria, B.C.
Lieut.	Livingstone, A. T.	Reptd. from 34 Bn. 30-5-18; dec. M.C. (Amiens), L.G. 31043	Harriston, Ont.
Lieut.	*Lloyd, J. L.	Prom. from O.R.S. 24-12-16; Asst. Adj; 2nd i. c. "D" Co.: k. l. a. 8-8-18 (Amiens); prom. to Captaincy announced in London Times d. 27-6-19.	Mrs. R. L. Lloyd. Pentypark, Clarbeston Rd., Pembrokeshire, Wales.

Lieut.	Love, H.T.M.	Reptd. from 121st Bn. 21-3-17; w. 9.-4.-17 (Vimy) to Eng.	22 Grove Rd., Clapham Rd., London, S.W., Eng.
Lieut.	Lowrie, G.	Tr. from 67th Bn. 2-5-17; k. i. a. 8-6-17 (2nd Triangle)	Mrs. Lowrie, Ladysmith, B.C.
Lieut.	Lyall, G. T.	Reptd. from 4th C.M.R. 30-9-17; w. 18-11-17 (Passchendaele); dec. V.C. (Cambrai), L.G. 31067; evac. sick in Eng. 21-2-19	
Lieut.	Manning, J. E.	Tr. from 67th Bn. 2-5-17; w. 12-6-17 (1st Triangle) to Eng.	Turncroft, Darwen, Lancs., Eng.
Lieut.	Manning, V. Z.	Reptd. from 121st Bn. 11-4-17; Works Officer; w. 6-8-17 (Lens); w. 30-9-18 (Cambrai) to Eng.	Holsworthy, Devon, Eng.
Lieut.	Marsden, M. M.	Tr. from 67th Bn. 2-5-17; Scout Officer; w. 9-6-17 (2nd Triangle) to Eng.	Fort Fraser, B.C.
Lieut.	Massey, O.	Tr. from 67th Bn. 2-5-17; w. 8-6-17 (2nd Triangle); dec. M.M. (Triangle) L.G. 30259; prom. from Sgt. 27-4-18; w. 27-9-18 to Eng.	1723 Pendrell St., Vancouver, B.C.
Lieut.	*Martin, L. M.	C.S.M. "A" Co.; w. 23-11-16 (Somme) to Eng.; prom. from C.S.M. 29-11-16	Birtles, Chilford, Cheshire, Eng.
Lieut.	Martin, S. P.	Reptd. from 7th Bn. 1-10-18; w. 6-11-18 (Valenciennes) to Eng.	10 Elmsworth Rd., Shirley, Southampton, Eng.
Lieut.	Matier, R. B.	Reptd. 23-7-17; prom. from Sgt. 22-11-18.	General Delivery, Tucson, Ariz., U.S.A.
Lieut.	Meredith, J. F.	Tr. from 67th Bn. 2-5-17; evac. sick 7-5-17 to Eng.	Kilkeel, Co. Down, Ireland
Lieut.	Mitchell, F. L.	Reptd. 12-6-18; det. for duty with R.A.F. 17-11-18; reptd. again 28-2-19	19 King St., Kingston, Ont.
Lieut.	Mont, J.	Reptd. 11-10-16; tr. on command to Eng 14-1-17.	219 Wellington St., Sault Ste Marie, Ont.
Lieut.	Moore, S. G.	Tr. from 67th Bn. 2-5-17; Sig. sergt.; dec. D.C.M. L.G. 30176, d. 3-6-18; prom. Sigs. Officer 26-6-18; k. i. a. 27-9-18 (Cambrai)	Springfield Mines, Cumberland Co., N.S.
Lieut.	Morrison, A. M.	Reptd from 227th Bn. 10-10-17; w. 4-9-18 (2nd Arras) to Eng.	Mrs. Moore, P.O. Box 357, Didsbury, Alta.
Lieut.	Morrison, R.	Tr. from 67th Bn. 2-5-17; Adj. C.C.R.C; men. in des. 8-7-19	Sudbury, Ont.
Lieut.	Murphy, E. H.	Reptd. from 121st 18-9-18; w. 27-9-18 (Cambrai) to Eng.	22 Aird St., Portsoy, Scot.
Lieut.	Macbeth, D. J.M.	Reptd. 3-2-18; evac. sick 3-9-18 to Eng.	Foxwarren, Man.
Lieut.	MacCormick, J.M.	Prom. from Pte. 9-11-16 and tr. to No. 1 Tunnelling Co. W. 21-10-16 (Regina) to Eng.; d. o. s. in Vancouver.	Alexandra Apts., University Ave., Toronto, Ont.
Lieut.	*Macdonald, A. G.	Reptd. from 75th Bn. 23-2-17; w. 21-3-17 to Eng.	c/o R. Cunningham & Son, Hazelton, B.C.
Lieut.	Macpherson, C. W.	W. 17-11-17 (Passchendaele)	C. Macdonald, 2530 York St., Vancouver, B.C.
Lieut.	McClatchey, T.	6-4-6-18; k. i. a. 27-9-18 (Cambrai)	Kincardine, Sask.
Lieut.	McClenahan, H. D.	Reptd. 16-4-18; w. 2-9-18 (2nd Arras) to Eng.	Mrs. McClatchey, 28 Black Block, Regina, Sask.
Lieut.	McCrea, E.	Reptd. from 227th Bn. 9-9-17; w. 10-4-18 (Oppy) to Eng.	204 Herkimer St., Hamilton, Ont.
Lieut.	McDermid, C. W.	Reptd. 28-11-17; Scout Officer; w. 2-9-18 (2nd Arras) to Eng.	Sudbury, Ont.
Lieut.	McDonald, F. M.	Reptd. 5-12-17; att. to 4th Bn. M.G.C. 17-4-18.	Box 1037, Collingwood, Ont.
Lieut.	Niblett, E. J.	Reptd. 7-7-18; w. 8-8-18 (Amiens) to Eng.	Box 105, Ripley, Ont.
Lieut.	Norwood, E. J.	Tr. from 67th Bn. 2-5-17; k. i. a. 8-6-17 (2nd Triangle)	99 Duke St., Hamilton, Ont.
Lieut.	Ogilvie, J. M.	Tr. from 67th Bn. 2-5-17; Works N.C.O.; w. 1-11-17 (Passchendaele); prom. from Sgt. 11-8-18; dec. M.C. (Valenciennes) C.R.O. 2040.	W. E. Norwood, 5 Glebe Villas, Hove, Sussex, Eng.
Lieut.	Packman, C. H.	Prom. from Works Sgt. 15-5-17; Lewis Gun Officer; w. 10-8-17 (Lens); dec. M.C. (Cambrai), L.G. 31183.	1071 Comox Street, Vancouver, B.C.
			74 Sketty Rd., Enfield, Middlessex, Eng.

Lieut.	Pae, P. R.	Reptd. from 119th Bn. 6-7-18; d. o. w. 1-10-18 (Cambrai)	Mrs. A. Pae, Box 234, Barrie, Ont.
Lieut.	Palmer, J.	Reptd. from 164th Bn. 18-3-18; w. 2-9-18 (2nd Arras)	Box 222, Hamilton, Ont.
Lieut.	Peers, C. T.	w. 18-10-18 (Valenciennes) to Eng.	Mrs. F. J. Peers, 13 Close Ave., Toronto, Ont.
Lieut.	Peers, E. L.	Reptd. 5-5-18; k. i. a. 8-8-18 (Amiens)	c/o G. Wheaton, Amherst, N.S.
Lieut.	Peers, T. W.	Reptd. 19-1-17; w. 9-4-17 (Vimy) to Eng.	13 Close Ave., Toronto, Ont.
Lieut.	*Penreath, H. E. A.	Reptd. 15-5-18; w. 2-9-18 (2nd Arras) to Eng.	1940 Barclay St., Vancouver, B.C.
		Prom. from Pte. 1-1-17; reptd. 27-8-17; tr. to Corps 7-9-18; Area Cmdnt. Gagny 5-8-18.	
Lieut.	Perry, R. H.	Reptd. 30-9-17; Bombing Officer; dec. M.C. (Cambrai), L.G. 31183	3 Chadwell Ave., Ilford, Essex, Eng.
Lieut.	*Proctor, G. B.	Tr. to Base Co. 11-8-16; reptd. on prom. from C.S.M. 8-9-18; dec. M.C. (Cambrai), L.G. 31183; w. 1-10-18 (Cambrai) to Eng.	General Freight Office, C.P.R., Vancouver, B.C.
Lieut.	Rankin, J. S.		c/o Dominion Bank, London, Ont.
Lieut.	*Rant, N. W. F.	Tr. to Base Co. 11-8-16.	c/o Lands Dept., Parliament Bldgs., Victoria, B.C.
Lieut.	Richardson, F.	Reptd. from 225th Bn. 30-4-17; w. 9-6-17 (2nd Triangle) to Eng.	9 Onslow Rd., Liverpool, Eng.
Lieut.	Rodgerson, J. S.	Reptd. from 50th Bn. 13-11-16; k. i. a. 13-5-17 (1st Triangle)	Mrs. M. Rodgerson, c/o The Manse, Gordon, Berwickshire, Scot.
Lieut.	Rowland, J. J.	Reptd. from 4th C.M.R. 30-9-17; w. 1-11-17 (Passchendaele) to Eng.	Route 2, Centreville, Carleton Co., N.B.
Lieut.	Rush, C. T.	Reptd. from 11th C.M.R. 28-7-16; k.i.a. 22-10-16 (Regina)	No address available.
Lieut.	Scott, S. M.	Tr. from 196th Bn. 19-2-17; w. 30-10-17 (Passchendaele) to Eng.; prom. from L.-Sgt. 22-11-18; reptd. 28-2-19	395 14th Ave. W., Vancouver, B.C.
Lieut.	Smith, R. T.	Reptd. from 227th Bn. 9-9-17; det. for R.A.F. 11-6-18; ret. 28-2-19	Sudbury, Ont.
Lieut.	*Squires, B. P.	Att. to 11th C.I.B. as Bombing N.C.O. Aug. '16; dec. M.M. (Vimy), L.G. 29953; prom. from Sgt. 7-5-17; mentioned in despatches, L.G. 30706, d. 29-5-18	c/o Mrs. J. T. Hammond, Little Weldon, nr. Kettering, Northants, Eng.
Lieut.	Stanley, W. H. C.	Reptd. from 208th Bn. 18-2-18; w. 29-4-18 (Oppy) dec. M.C. (when A.-O.C. "A" Co. Valenciennes) C. R.O. 2040; w. 6-11-18 (Valenciennes)	88 Pricefield Rd., Toronto, Ont.
Lieut.	*Stalker, R. A.	W. 8-9-16 (St. Eloi); k. i. a. 9-4-17 (Vimy)	Mrs. C. Stalker, 37 Charles St., Ottawa, Ont.
Lieut.	Sturgeon, W. J.	W. 10-11-16 (Somme) to Eng.	119 18th Ave., Vancouver, B.C.
Lieut.	Thomas, H. M.	Tr. from 67th Bn. 2-5-17; att. to R.F.C. 2-5-17	1235 Harold St., Vancouver, B.C.
Lieut.	Traves, C. W.	Reptd. from 196th Bn. 19-12-17; dec. M.M. (Passchendaele) C.R.O. 1571; reptd. on prom. from Sgt. 4-6-18; att. to R.A.F. 10-9-18	522 Royal Ave., New Westminster, B.C.
Lieut.	Tunnard, C. C.	Reptd. from 11th C.M.R. 29-7-16; w. 21-11-16 (Somme); tr. to 54th Bn. 31-10-16.	1265 Pleasant Ave., Oak Bay, Victoria, B.C.
Lieut.	Turner, A. R.	Reptd. from 58th Bn. 30-9-17; w. 18-11-17 (Passchendaele) to Eng.	Bow St., Langport, Somerset, Eng.
Lieut.	Vancorbac, G.	Reptd. from 164th Bn. 18-3-18; dec. M.C. (Oppy), L.G. 30901; w. 1-10-18 (Cambrai) to Eng.	21 Baikal Rd., Shanghai, China.
Lieut.	Walte, F. J.	Tr. from 67th Bn. 2-5-17	Garendon St., Leicester, Eng.

Lieut. Ward, R. G.	Reptd. 24-12-16; Bombing Officer; w. 21-1-17 (Vimy); evac. sick 23-3-17 to Eng.	119 First St., New Westminster, B.C.
Lieut. Webster, D. E.	Reptd. from 74th Bn.; sigs. Sergt.; prom. Sig³. Officer 15-5-17; w. 31-10-17 (Passchendaele) to Eng.	122 Leith St., Edinburgh, Scot.
Lieut. West, C. de F.	Reptd. from 225th Bn. 26-4-17; k. i. a. 12-5-17 (1st Triangle)	Mrs. W. de F. West, Kelliher, Sask.
Lieut. *Whitehead, J. M.	Lewis Gun Officer; tr. to 11th C.M.G. Co. 26-4-17	779 Thurlow St., Vancouver, B.C.
Lieut. Whittaker, C. W.	Reptd. 5-6-17; evac. sick 6-6-17 to Eng.	c/o G.W.V.A., Vancouver, B.C.
Lieut. Williams, F. S.	Tr. from 67th Bn. 2-5-17; tr. to 1st Tramway Co. 10-11-17; mentioned in despatches, L.G. 30408, d. 28-12-17	Holt, Troubridge, Wilts, Eng.
Lieut. *Wilson, J. H.	W. 21-10-16 (Regina); A.-O.C. "A" Co.; k. i. a. 9-4-17 (Vimy)	W. J. Wilson, 1238 Tecumseh Ave., Shaughnessy Heights, Vancouver, B.C.
Lieut. Wilson, J. R.	Reptd. 29-11-17; A.-O.C. "D" Co.; dec. M.C. (Cambrai). L.G. 31183; w. 6-11-18 (Valenciennes) to Eng.	117 Rose Ave., Toronto, Ont.
Lieut. *Wright, R. S.	Prom. from C.S.M. 1-4-17; w. 9-4-17 (Vimy) to Eng.	R.M. Hospital, Esquimalt, B.C.
Lieut. Wylie, J. R.	Dec. M.M. (Passchendaele) C.R.O. 1606; reptd. on prom. from L.-Cpl. 17-9-18; mentioned in despatches, L.G. d. 8-7-19	Winchester, Ont.

NOMINAL ROLL OF OTHER RANKS

REGT'L NUMBER	NAME	RANK	CASUALTY — DECORATIONS	PRESENT ADDRESS, OR THAT OF NEXT OF KIN.
703429	Abbott, C.	Pte.	Bugler. Tr. to 51st Bn. 2-8-16	165 Joseph Street, Victoria, B.C.
703554	Abel, A.	L.-Sgt.	W. 8-8-18. Det. to Eng. (Amiens)	41 London St., Maindee, Newport, Wales.
306417	Abel, T. S.	Pte.		148 Stinson Street, Hamilton, Ont.
706456	Ablett, G. H.	Pte.	K. i. a. 9-4-17 (Vimy)	Mrs. I. C. Ablett, 1279 Centre Road, Victoria, B.C.
253019	Abraham, T.	Pte.	D. o. w. 17-4-17 (Vimy)	Mrs. M. A. Abraham, Drumnasengh, Pontadown, Co. Armagh, Ireland.
703099	Achishen, A.	Pte.	K. i. a. 1-9-16 (St. Eloi)	E. Achishen, 9346 106th Ave., Edmonton, Alta.
703162	Ackery, I.	Pte.	Bugler. Tr. to 51st Bn. 2-8-16	1028 Howe St., Vancouver, B.C.
663545	Adair, J. W.	Pte.	Dec. M.M. (2nd Arras) C.R.O. 1930	Oakville, Ont.
3105030	Adam, R. K.	Pte.	W. 27-9-18 (Cambrai) to Eng.	73 Cambridge St., Lawrence, Mass., U.S.A.
903146	Adams, H. D.	Pte.		22 Chatsworth Rd. West Norwood, London, Eng.
706895	Adams, J.	Pte.	W. 6-4-17 (Vimy) to Eng.	Grey Creek, Kootenay Lake, B.C.
252003	Adams, J. H.	Pte.	K. i. a. 11-5-17 (1st Triangle)	G. F. Adams, Chertsey, Surrey, Eng.
761074	Adamson, L.	Pte.		c/o J. Foster, Creelman, Sask.
161297	Addis, J.	Pte.	Tr. 25th Bn. 7-10-16	No address available.
219885	Adshead, T. E.	Pte.	To 11th T.M.B. 19-19-16	No address available.
252487	Affanato, J.	Pte.	To Hosp. 28-9-18	169 Vermont St., Newton, Mass., U.S.A.
703189	Ahlman, E. W.	Pte.	K. i. a. 9-4-17 (Vimy)	Miss S. Ahlman, Fraxton, Sweden.
1003552	Aiken, A. W.	Pte.	To Eng. 2-3-19	Gore Bay, Manitoulin Island, Ont.

703384	Ainsley, T.	Pte.		Westhouse Farm, Killingworth, Newcastle-on-Tyne.
2020209	Ainsworth, R.	Pte.		382 Manchester Rd., Warrington, Lancs, Eng.
3107414	Aird, T. R.	Pte.	To Div. A.P.M. 28-1-19	286 Wellington St., Brantford, Ont.
2527380	Alexander, H. G.	Pte.	W. 2-9-18 (2nd Arras) to Eng.	8 Trelawn Lane, St. Ste. Marie, Ont.
706202	Alexander, J. C.	Pte.	W. 2-9-18 (2nd Arras) to Eng.	443 26th Ave. E., Vancouver, B.C.
703542	Alger, R. H.	Pte.	Tr. to 51st Bn. 2-8-16.	1730 Stephen St., Vancouver, B.C.
540501	Algie, R. L.	Sgt.	Bombing Sgt. to Eng. for Commission. Posted to B.C.R.D. 31-10-18.	
102694	Allan, G.	Pte.	Dmr. Pipe Band; to Lbr. Pool 17-4-18	31 Havelock St., Toronto, Ont.
102210	Allan, J. R.	C.S.M.	W. 2-6-17 (2nd Triangle) to Eng.	1015 Fisgard St., Victoria, B.C.
703320	Allan, J. W.	Pte.		142 Abbot St., Victoria, B.C.
663004	Allen, C. H.	Pte.	K. i. a. 8-8-18 (Amiens)	936 Granville St., Vancouver, B.C.
3107787	Allen, F. O.	Pte.	D. o. w. 7-11-18 (Valenciennes)	Mrs. E. J. Allen, Box 113, Burlington, Ont.
850006	Allen, S. W.	L-C	Evac. sick 14-1-19	Mrs. N. Allen, R.R. No. 2, Caister Centre, Ont.
907439	Allin, R. A.	Pte.	K. i. a. 9-4-17 (Vimy)	Lundys Lane, Niagara Falls, Ont.
703661	Alway, H.	C.S.M.	W. 13-5-17 (1st Triangle); dec. D.C.M. (Amiens) C.R.O. 1930; k. i. a. 27-9-18 (Cambrai)	Mrs. G. F. Allin, Stoughton, Sask. Mr. H. Alway, 27 South St., Wellington, Eng.
2527386	Alyea, A. F.	Pte.		Carrying Place, Ont.
727258	Ament, S. S.	Pte.	W. 8-8-18 (Amiens) to Eng.	Brussels, Ont.
252510	Amerson, P.	Pte.	K. i. a. 9-4-17 (Vimy)	Mrs. Martunson, Stauggran St., Hauemer, Norway
225476	Amery, G. E.	Pte.		P.O. Box 11, Ridgeville, Ont.
220245	Ames, R. E.	Pte.	Tr. to 51st Bn. 2-8-16	No address available.
703229	Anderson, W.	Pte.	Evac. sick 24-10-18	Fredericksburg, Denmark.
184072	Anderson, A.	Pte.	W. 12-6-17 (2nd Triangle)	Gadsby, Alta.
703489	Anderson, F. V.	Pte.	Evac. sick 2-2-19	Prince Rupert, B.C.
1010064	Anderson, G. H.	Pte.	K. i. a. 11-5-17 (1st Triangle)	A. Anderson, Lockhouses, Preston, Kirkcudbrightshire, Scotland.
703606	Anderson, H. G.	Pte.	W. 21-10-16 (Regina) to Eng.	Bella Bella, B.C.
703741	Anderson, J.	Pte.	W. 1-9-16 (St. Eloi).	Pacific, B.C.
703764	Anderson, R.	Pte.	Tr. to 6th Can. Area Emp. Co. 22-8-17	Paxton, Berwick-on-Tweed, Scotland.
703230	Anderson, R.	Pte.	K. i. a. 11-5-17 (1st Triangle)	Mrs. A. Anderson, Fredericksburg, Denmark.
907569	Anderson, W. P.	L-C.	W. 9-4-17 (Vimy); k. i. a. 17-11-17 (Passchendaele)	
102209	Andrews, H. G.	Cpl.	W. 4-9-18 (2nd Arras) to Eng.	Mrs. J. C. Anderson, 2220 Angus St., Regina, Sask.
704012	Angel, W. H.	Pte.	W. 8-9-16 (St. Eloi) to Eng.	20 Butts Rd., Alton, Hants, Eng.
3108672	Angle, M. E.	Pte.	Evac. sick 9-11-18	237 14th Ave. W., Calgary, Alta.
3110624	Angus, C. A.	Pte.		R.R. No. 2, Welland Poll, Ont.
103011	Angus, H. McL.	L-C	Tr. to 25th Bn. 3-6-18	533 Clinton St., Toronto, Ont.
252004	Anstead, G.	Pte.		261 Langside St., Winnipeg, Man.
219155	Antoine, J.	Pte.	K. i. a. 8-5-17 (1st Triangle)	4 Durham Road, Canning Town, London, Eng.
3109903	Appleyard, E. W.	Pte.	W. 26-12-17 (Mericourt) to Eng.	F. Antoine, Mattawa, Ont.
1066073	Apps, W. D.	Pte	W. 1-10-18 (Cambrai) to Eng.	c/o Miss M. Thorn, Thornbury, Ont.
2529375	Archbold, W.	Pte.	W. 16-8-17 and 20-12-17 (Lens and Mericourt)	Glenwilliam, Ont.
180930	Archer, S.	Pte.	to Eng.	10808 Amor Ave., Cleveland, Ohio, U.S.A.
3030563	Archibald, D.	Pte.	Evac. sick 11-1-19	Alberni, B.C.
246257	Arcond, J. E.	Pte.	K. i. a. 8-8-18 (Amiens)	17 Loring St., Lawrence, Mass., U.S.A.
				Mrs. G. Arcond, Smith Falls, Ont.

Regt. No.	Name	Rank	Casualty	Address
226963	Arliss, H.	Pte.	W. 23-7-18 (Oppy) to Eng.	13 Edward St., Hamilton, Ont.
703553	Armishaw, H. A.	Pte.	W. 15-5-17 (1st Triangle) to Eng.	Sayward, B.C.
102352	Armour, E. B.	Pte.	W. 13-5-17 (1st Triangle) (Lens) to Eng.	
703251	Armour, J. H.	Pte.	W. 21-4-17 (Vimy) to Eng.	1205 Johnson St., Victoria, B.C.
3108897	Armstrong, F. S.	Pte.	Evac. sick 29-12-18.	833 Windermere St., Vancouver, B.C.
102088	Armstrong, J. C.	Pte.	Tr. to 4th Div. H.Q. 30-8-17.	937 Assington Ave., Toronto, Ont.
246631	Armstrong, V. E.	Pte.	W. 19-3-18 (Mericourt).	36 Hollyshaw Lane, Whitkirk, Leeds, Eng.
3108670	Armstrong, W. T.	Pte.	Tr. at Bramshott, 1916.	575 Somerset St., Ottawa.
703585	Ash, S. G.	Pte.	Dec. M.M (2nd Arras) C.R.O. 1930; w. 6-6-17 (2nd Triangle); w. 2-9-18 (2nd Arras) to Eng.	Bowen Road, Bridgeburg, Ont.
102740	Ashton, H. O.	Sgt.		979 10th Ave., Vancouver, B.C.
907806	Ashton, J. A.	Pte.	K. i. a. 6-4-17 (Vimy)	c/o Mrs. C. Hanna, 36 Parker St., Warrington, Eng.
703830	Ashton, T.	Pte.	Tr. to Lbr. Pool, 9-6-18; later joined C.M.G.C.	S. Burns (Friend), Walkerville, Ont.
2528457	Askin, D. J.	Pte.	Evac. sick 20-10-18.	606 Mill St., Nelson, B.C.
436680	Askwith, G. E.	Pte.	W. 12-5-17 (1st Triangle); w. 10-4-18 (Oppy) to Eng.; tr. to 31st Bn. 12-8-18.	726 Macey Ave., Brooklyn, N.Y., U.S.A.
703047	Astell, F. W.	Pte.	Tr. to Lbr. Pool 9-6-18.	26 Gladstone St., Crook, Co. Durham, Eng.
102788	Atkin, W. F. N.	L.-C.	Evac. sick 19-3-19.	c/o Mrs. S. McKay, 1610 4th Ave. E., Vancouver, B.C
703317	Atkinson, F.	Cpl	Tr. to C.C.R.C. 22-2-18.	c/o Mrs. Sharp, 4 Hulham Rd., Exmouth, Eng.
102331	Atkinson, H. P.	Pte.	W. (Lens) to Eng. 6-9-17.	453 7th Ave. W., Vancouver, B.C.
250084	Atwell, J. W.	Pte.	K. i. a. 2-9-18 (2nd Arras).	343 Pembroke St., Victoria, B.C.
252468	Ayers, H. A.	Pte.	Evac. sick 14-4-17.	W. G. Atwell, 30 Huron St., Toronto, Ont.
3109547	Babin, I. W.	Pte.		Vanguard, Sask.
760437	Badzief, T.	Pte.		Kent Bridge, Ont.
				Pembroke, Ont.
703439	Bailey, A. E.	Pte.	W. 27-9-18 (Cambrai) to Eng.	New Westminster, B.C.
703074	Bailey, J.	Pte.	W. 11-5-17 (1st Triangle); w. 17-8-17 (Lens), tr. to 71st Co. C.F.C. W. 21-10-16 (Regina) to Eng. W. ret. to unit 3-11-18.	59 Junction Rd., Romford, Essex, Eng. Blackwater, Enouscourthay, Courtclough, Wexford, Ireland.
1003681	Bailey, J. W.	Pte.	W. 27-9-18 (Cambrai) to Eng.	Rickinhall, Suffolk, Eng.
1004061	Bailey, R. E.	Pte.	W. 12-3-18 (Lens); k.i. a. 1-10-18 (Cambrai).	No address available.
200188	Baillie, G.	Pte.	W. 27-9-18 (Cambrai) to Eng.	3383 Triumph St., Vancouver, B.C.
706929	Baines, E.	Pte.	W. 11-5-17 (1st Triangle) to Eng.; d.o.s. 15-2-19	Mrs. Baines, 143 Petre St., Sheffield, Eng.
907778	Baird, R. J.	Pte.	K. i a. 9-4-17 (Vimy).	Mrs. A. Baird, Lumsden, Sask.
703422	Baker, C. T.	Pte.		Latchmere Farm, Bramley, Hants, Eng.
3108680	Baker, G. L.	Pte.	W. 10-8-18 (Amiens) to Eng.	119 Barton St., E., Hamilton, Ont.
127624	Baker, H. S.	Pte.		Tillsonburg, Ont.
907894	Baker, J.	Pte.	D. o. w. 20-5-17 (1st Triangle)	1 Oakleigh Villas, Mannamead, Plymouth, Eng.
703951	Baker, R. E. G.	Pte.	W. 10-8-18 (Amiens) to Eng.	T. Baker, Cookstown, Ont.
249166	Baker, S. R.	Pte.	Tr. to Lbr. Pool, 3-5-18.	3 Madrid Place, Toronto, Ont.
632229	Baker, W.	Pte.	W. 30-9-18 (Cambrai) to Eng.	Box 79. Smith Falls, Ont.
2529312	Balbone, V.	Pte.	Tr. to 4th M.G.C. 1-5-18.	24 Sydney Rd., Tilbury, Essex, Eng.
207596	Baldwin, A.	Pte.	Evac. sick 4-10-16.	39 Gold St., Toronto, Ont.
703192	Ball, A.	Pte.	W. 12-4-17 (Vimy); w. 17-11-17 Passchendaele); w. 8-8-18 (Amiens).	13 Chester Terrace, Brighton, Eng.
183932				
908129	Ball, H.	Pte.	W. 6-4-17 (Vimy) to Eng.	c/o G. W. Ball, Red Deer, Alta. c/o H. N. Nicol, Edgley, Sask.

Regt. No.	Name	Rank	Casualties, etc.	Next of Kin
3030641	Ball, W.	Pte.	Tr. to C.O.R.D. 9-1-19	394 18th Ave., Newark, N.Y., U.S.A.
703277	Ballantyne, W.	Pte.		Barkip, near Dalry, Ayrshire, Scotland.
703829	Ballard, O. B.	Pte.	Evac. sick 1-11-16	Sutton Veny, Westminster, Wilts, Eng.
838668	Ballard, T. W.	Pte.	W. 15-11-17 (Passchendaele); evac. sick 7-1-18 to Eng.	
703775	Ballingal, J. R.	Pte.	W. 20-11-16 (Somme); k. i. a. 9-1-17 (Vimy)	Meaford, Ont.
1003360	Ballintine, B.	Pte.	K. i. a. 17-11-17	Mrs. Ballingal, Norton Leven, Fife, Scotland.
183520	Bamford, G. W.	Pte.	K. i. a. 21-10-16 (Regina)	E. Ballintine, Manitowaring, Ont.
704121	Bancroft, C.	Pte.	W. 9-4-17 (Vimy) to Eng.	Mrs. J. B. Lyne, 2117 East Main St., Richmond, Va.
252399	Baragar, W.	Pte.	W. 9-4-17 (Vimy); k. i. a. 16-8-17 (Lens)	Mrs. Bancroft, Craven Edge, Halifax, Eng.
252400	Baragar, W.	Pte.	W. 9-4-17 (Vimy)	Mrs. M. A. Baragar, Gooding, Sask.
1090357	Barclay, R. N.	Pte.	Tr. to 4th C.M.G. 1-5-18	Pontleux, Sask.
760657	Bareham, G.	Pte.	K. i. a. 9-4-17 (Vimy)	Ashcroft, B.C.
252030	Barker, E. G.	Pte.	W. 13-4-17 (Vimy) to Eng.	Mrs. F. Bareham, 1528 Georgia St., E., Vancouver, B.C.
663045	Barker, J. H.	Sgt.	Prov.-Sgt. tr. to A.P.M. 21-5-18	Neidpath, Sask.
703002	Barker, J. W.	Sgt.	W. 31-7-18 (Oppy); w. 28-9-18 (Cambrai)	Box 548, Oakville, Ont.
240578	Barker, S. R.	Pte.	Evac. sick 30-10-16	c/o City Police Force, Vancouver, B.C.
703855	Barker, P.	Pte.	W. 22-10-16 (Regina); w. 5-6-17 (1st Triangle) to Eng.	175 Cannon St. W., Hamilton, Ont.
129718	Barkley, J.	Pte.		Box 111, Grand Forks, B.C.
3108909	Barlow, J. W.	Pte	Dec. M.M. (Valenciennes) C.R.O. 2028	No address available.
1020090	Barlow, N. P.	Pte	K. i. a. 8-6-17 (2nd Triangle)	17 Highland Ave., Hamilton, Ont.
225830	Barnard, G. H.	Pte	K. i. a. 1-11-17 (Passachendaele)	J. Barlow, 11 Pembroke Rd., Balsall H., Birm'g., Eng.
2528460	Barnes, R.	Pte	Tr. to Lbr. Pool 9-6-18	Mrs. Barnard, 128 Shaw St., Toronto, Ont.
225273	Barnett, D.	Pte		13 Rope St., Rochdale, Lancs., Eng.
760892	Barnett, J.	Pte	Dec. M.M. (Cambrai) C.R.O. 1989	37 Brent St., Cheetham, Manchester, Eng.
703140	Barr, H. C.	Pte	W. 1-11-17 (Passchendaele); k. i. a. 1-10-18 (Cambrai)	1860 Robson St., Vancouver, B.C.
102412	Barr, T.	Pte	W. 15-8-17 (Lens); w. 1-10-18 (Cambrai)	287 High St., Watford, Herts, Eng.
161121	Barr, W.	Pte	W. 8-8-18 (Amiens); w. 1-10-18 (Cambrai) to Eng.	c/o Wm. Anderson, Cloverdale, Maywood P.O., V.I.
703773	Barrass, G.	Pte	W. 14-10-16 (Somme) to Eng	605 "Ine Ave. W., Montreal, Quebec.
226972	Barrett, S.	Pte	W. 30-4-18 (Oppy)	1015 l'ike St., Seattle, Wash., U.S.A.
102771	Barrett, B. W.	Pte	Tr. to Lbr. Pool 3-5-18	134 Niagara St., Buffalo, N.Y., U.S.A.
249265	Barrett, G. W.	Pte	W. 8-8-18 (Amiens) to Eng	Eburne Station, B.C.
703660	Barrett, G. A.	Pte.	Evac. sick 12-12-16	20 linstedon St., Toronto, Ont.
931225	Barrie, W. G.	Pte.		Gordon Villa, Gordon Rd., S. Woodford, Essex, Eng.
3105428	Barter, D. C.	Pte.	W. 24-8-18 (Amiens)	72 Front St., Campbellford, Ont.
2528502	Bartlett, A.	Pte.	Tr. to 4th C.M.G.C. 18-3-18	c/o Mrs. E. Caluer, 14 Fortune Rd., W. Hampsteau, London, N., Eng.
1003939	Bartlett, H.	Pte.	W. 8-2-18 (Mericourt) to Eng.; evac. sick 29-5-17 to Eng	57 Sudell St., Manchester, Eng.
703381	Bartolemew, C.	Pte.	W. 19-8-16 (St. Eloi); evac. sick 29-5-17 to Eng	Spanish. Ont.
703248	Barton, H.	Pte.	Tr. to Lbr. Pool 9-1-18	Nanaimo, B.C.
180004	Barton, H.	Pte.	W. 9-6-17 (1st Triangle) to Eng	Cumberland Bay, New Brunswick.
1031192	Basham, F.	Pte.	W. 5-6-17 (1st Triangle) to Eng	Gen. Del., Victoria, B.C.
3107431	Bate, V. D.	Pte.		Gristhorpe, Filey, Yorks, Eng.
219832	Bate, W. D.	Pte.	W. 21-10-16 (Regina); w. 2-8-17 (Lens)	R.R. No. 9, Dunville, Ont.
3107432	Bateman, H. V.	Pte.		Mississippi Hotel, Carlton Place, Ont. Paris, Ont.

Number	Name	Rank	Notes	Address
703345	Bateman, W.	Pte.	W. 29-12-16 (Vimy) to Eng.	2376 7th Ave. W., Vancouver, B.C.
102369	Bates, F.	Pte.	W. 9-4-17 (Vimy); tr. to 54th Bn. 30-5-17; prom. Sgt.	1716 Davie St., Vancouver, B.C.
3314278	Bauer, W. H.	Pte.	W. 6-11-18 (Cambrai)	R.R. No. 1, Welland, Ont.
760783	Bawn, J.	Pte.	W. 9-4-17 (Vimy)	Hazelburghi Farm, Nr. Chesterfield, Eng.
3109057	Baxter, J. G.	Pte.		Walnut St., Collingwood, Ont.
3107419	Baxter, R.	Pte.	Evac. 8-2-19	R R. No. 1, Athlone, Ont.
2607377	Baylis, J. W.	Pte.		c/o Mrs. J. T. Tower, Millbrook, Duchess Co., N.Y.
907343	Bayne, T. A.	Pte.	W. 9-4-17 (Vimy) to Eng.	Hillsboro', Inverness Co., Nova Scotia.
3109206	Beach, R. N.	Pte.	D. o. s. 26-10-18	Mrs. Beach, R.R. No. 1, Humberstone, Ont.
541440	Beacock, E. R.	Pte.	Dec. M.M. (Cambrai) C.R.O. 1989	32 Dundonald St., Toronto, Ont.
703059	Beak, W. F.	Pte.	Pay Sgt. on command in Eng.; revt. to join unit 22-9-18	
252417	Beasley, J.	Pte.	K. l. a. 11-5-17 (1st Triangle)	Coln St. Denis, Chedworth, Glos., Eng.
703791	Beatty, H. J.	Pte.	D. o. w. 16-9-16 (Lens)	Mrs. M. Boxall, 136 N. Barnet Rd., New Barnet, Eng.
838740	Beatty, J. H.	Pte.	W. 3-9-18 (2nd Arras) to Eng.	A. Beatty, Hughhinden, Queensland, Australia.
240619	Beaumont, E. F.	Pte.	K. l. a. 27-9-18 (Cambrai)	572 Alpha St., W., Queen Sound, Ont.
2529316	Beaumont, G.	Pte.	K. l. a. 27-9-18 (Cambrai)	Mrs. E. Beaumont, 133 Clifton Ave., Hamilton, Ont.
102846	Beaumont, J.	Pte.	W. 4-9-17 (Lens) to Eng.	Mrs. M. A. Smith, Gatehouse, Denaby Main, Yorks.
183840	Bebbington, G.	Pte.	W. 20-4-17 (Vimy) to Eng.	464 Gorge St., Victoria, B.C.
1004000	Bebko, S.	Pte.	Tr. to 54th Co. C.F.C. 26-3-18	Crewe, Cheshire, Eng.
703761	Bechtel, W. W.	Cpl.	Mentioned in despatches L.G. d-8-7-19; evac. sick 4-4-18	No address available.
184203	Beck, P. G.	Pte.	K. l. 9-4-17 (Vimy)	1769 45th Ave. E., Vancouver, B.C.
1066287	Beckerley, H.	Pte.	W. 24-8-18 (Amiens)	Mrs. M. Beck, Hand Hills, Alta.
3107420	Beckett, A. E.	Pte.		Ashton, near Holston, Cornwall, Eng.
3109412	Beckett, B. A.	Pte.		18 McLeod St., North Bay, Ont.
636093	Bedell, R.	Pte.	W. 9-6-17 (2nd Triangle) to Eng.	R.R. No. 1, Ridgeville, Ont.
907180	Bedford, C.	Pte.		Herald, R.M.D., Hastings Co., Ont.
540230	Beer, H. E.	Pte.	W. 1-1-17 (Vimy) to Eng.	103 Rosebery Ave., Manor Park, London, Eng.
199093	Beer, S. A.	Pte.	K. l. a. 17-5-17 (1st Triangle)	No address available.
220071	Beeson, G.	Pte.	W. 12-5-17 (1st Triangle); w. 18-3-18 (Lens)	Mrs. H. Beer 15 King Edward St., Exeter, Eng
760256	Begg, H. K.	Sgt.	Evac. sick, 24-3-17	Badshokles, Farnham, Eng.
3110578	Behle, C.	Pte.		4218 Gladstone Rd., South Vancouver, B. C.
1004074	Beland, E.	Pte.	Evac. sick 28-3-18 to Eng.	11 Cross St., St. Catherines, Ont.
252023	Belbin, A. C. W.	Pte.	Evac. sick 14-4-17 to Eng.	333 Secec St., Ottawa, Ont.
105494	Belbin, J.	Pte.	Tr. to Eng. as Minor 20-7-17	20 Larkbere Rd., Sydenham, Eng.
541002	Belford, J. E.	Pte.	Tr. to 51st Bn. 2-8-16	33 High Park, Boulevarde, Toronto, Ont.
541030	Belford, R. W.	Pte.	W. 10-11-16 (Somme); tr. to 2nd Bde. C.F.A. 4-10-17	No address available.
703416	Belgrove, E. W.	Pte.	Evac. sick to Eng. 11-3-17	527 Gladstone Ave., Toronto, Ont.
1003331	Belisle, S.	Pte.	W. 8-8-18 (Amiens) to Eng.	Box 172 Schubert St., Vernon, B.C.
1004054	Beliveau, L.	Pte.		Webbwood, Ont.
703908	Bell, A.	Pte.	Tr. to 67th Bn. 8-7-16; ret. 3-5-17	Little River West, Gaspe, Que.
703856	Bell, A. C	Pte.		Cabbachs, Boharm, Banffshire, Scot.
1003045	Bell, M. O.	Pte.	Tr. to C.C.R.C. 22-2-18	Souris, Man.
3317266	Bell, R.	Pte.	W. 1-10-18 (Cambrai) to Eng.	14 Orchard Rd., Overton, Lanarkshire, Scotland.
703589	Bell, N. H.	Pte.	K. l. a. 8-9-16 (St. Eloi)	Box 52, Midland, Ont.
				Mrs. M. Bell, 11 Wensland Rd., Howick, Scot.

Number	Name	Rank	Details	Address
908037	Bellamy, J. W.	Pte.	K. l. a. 9-4-17 (Vimy)	G. Bellamy, Wilkie, Sask.
3105812	Bellantone, A.	Pte.		No address available.
703134	Bellour, S. R.	Pte.	W. 8-9-16 (St. Eloi); evac. sick 2-9-17 to Eng.	Prince George, B.C.
76043S	Benham, S. R.	Pte.	Evac. sick 22-5-17 to Eng.	Mr. J. Benham, Quincy, Wash., U.S.A.
3109409	Benner, C. M.	Pte.		R.R. 1, Bridgeburg, Ont.
703578	Bennett, D.	Pte.	K. l. a. 27-9-18 (Cambrai)	Mrs. Bennett, 117 Kaslo St., Vancouver, B.C.
3105876	Bennett, D.	Pte.	Evac. sick 9-12-18	c/o Miss Minnie Scheublin, 672 Fulton St., Brooklyn, N.Y., U.S.A.
441339	Bennett, J. E.	Pte.	W. 9-6-17 (2nd Triangle) to Eng.	Taber, Alta.
3106651	Bennett, P. E.	Pte.		3605 Ave 1, Brooklyn, N.Y., U.S.A.
3109066	Bennett, P. W.	Pte.	W. 23-10-17 (Passchendaele)	4 F. Block, Peabody Bldg., Camberwell, London, Eng.
226247	Bennett, R.	Pte.	Dec. M.M. (Passchendaele) C.R.O. 1606; w. 27-9-18; dec. Bar to M.M. (Cambrai) C.R.O. 1989	c/o Mrs. E. Benoit, Ruscomb, Ont.
144683	Bennett, W. W.	Pte.		
3110522	Benson, J. H.	Pte.	K. l. a. 19-10-16 (Somme)	138 Bolton Ave., Toronto, Ont.
703535	Bent, N.	Pte.		856 Western Rd., Mt. Denis, Ont.
1003258	Bentley, H. J.	Pte.	W. 31-10-16 (Somme) to Eng	I. Bent, 978 Granville St., Vancouver, B.C.
101264	Bentley, W.	Pte.	K. l. a. 8-8-18 (Amiens)	Webbwood, Ont.
2529998	Bergeron, R.	Pte.		No address available. Mrs. A. Bergeron, Shawnigan Falls, Village St. Onge, St. Maurice Co., Quebec.
1006727	Bergeron, R.	Pte.	Tr. to 4th C.M.G.C. 1-5-18	Fouquier, Ont.
249466	Bergin, W. J.	Pte.	W. 8-8-18 (Amiens) to Eng.	c/o Miss Anderson, 197 Riverdale Ave., Toronto, Ont.
703772	Berkeley, W. D.	Pte.	W. 21-10-16 (Regina); w. 17-8-17 (Lens) to Eng	Sandwick, Vancouver Island, B.C.
127271	Berlett, C.	Pte.	W. 20-11-16 (Somme) to Eng.	39 Mill St., Woodstock, Ont.
704148	Berridge, G. S.	Cpl.	Tr. to Eng. for Commission 25-2-17	Room 5, Driard Hotel, Pender St. W., Vancouver, B.C.
763690	Berry, A. W.	Pte.	Dec. M.M. (Cambrai) C.R.O. 1989	Walkers Point, Manitoulin Island, Ont.
764036	Berry, G. E.	L-S.	W. 27-9-18 (Cambrai) to Eng.	Kagawong, Manitoulin Island, Ont.
703759	Berteaux, R. C	Pte.	W. 9-4-17 (Vimy) to Eng.	24 Ryan Court, 10th Ave. W., Vancouver, B.C.
102450	Bertucci, J.	Pte.	W. 12-6-17 (2nd Triangle); w. 8-8-18 (Amiens)	1155 Mason St., Victoria, B.C.
102337	Bertucci, L.	Sgt.	Dec. M.M. (Cambrai) C.R.O. 1989; evac sick 15-12-18 to Eng.	
267014	Berven, T.	Pte.	W. 8-9-17 (Lens); tr. to C.C.R.C. 22-2-18	1155 Mason St., Victoria, B.C.
706044	Berwick, J.	Pte.	W. 9-4-17 (Vimy) to Eng.	c/o Miss Berven, Gran Hadland, Norway.
102889	Berwick, W.	Pte.	Tr. to 26th Bn. 25-3-18; w. 19-4-17 (Vimy)	2330 Trent St., Victoria, B.C.
220326	Besmartny, J.	Pte.	Tr. to 71st C. C.F.C. 9-4-18	1909 Turner St., Vancouver, B.C.
703466	Bessette, E. C	Pte.	Evac. sick 21-11-18 to Eng.	No address available.
703684	Bessette, J. C	Pte.	W. 31-8-16 (St. Eloi); k. l. a. 21-10-16 (Regina)	Summerland, B. C.
704098	Bessette, P.	Pte.	D. o. w. 16-9-16 (St. Eloi)	Mr. C. Bessette, Ibelle, Que.
440307	Best, J.	Pte.	W. 11-5-17 (1st Triangle) to Eng.	Mrs. E. Bessette, Lumby, B.C.
135977	Best, S.	L.-C.	Mentioned in Des. 1-1-18, L.G. 30448; w. 6-11-18 (Valenciennes) to Eng; dec. M.M. (Valenciennes) C.R.O. 2028	Karaston, Sask.
3106605	Best, T. A.	Pte.	W. 6-6-17 (2nd Triangle) to Eng.	Balteagh, Portadown, Ireland.
219547	Beston, J.	Pte.	W. 18-3-18 (Lens); w. 8-8-18 (Amiens) to Eng.	67 Fullerton Ave., Hamilton, Ont.
925368	Beswick, H.	Pte.	K. l. a. 9-4-17 (Vimy)	Toronto, Ont.
252026	Betchelder, W.	Pte.	W. 27-9-18 (Cambrai)	11 Clayton St., Manchester, Eng.
1001011	Betts, C.	Pte.		Mr. G. Betchelder, Tompkins, Sask. 373 Graham Ave., Winnipeg, Man.

931226	Beusline, F.	Pte.	D. o. w. 29-9-17 (Lens)	No relatives.
225362	Bevan, S.	Pte.	Evac. sick to Eng. 26-10-17	22 Dundurn St., Hamilton, Ont.
102219	Beynon, G. P.	Pte.	D. o. w. 10-6-17 (2nd Triangle)	Mrs. R. Beynon, 1929 Chambers St., Victoria, B.C.
252010	Biddulph, A.	Pte.	K. i. a. 9-4-17 (Vimy)	Mrs. Biddulph, Swift Current, Sask.
703356	Biggin, B.	Pte.	Tr. at Bramshott 8-8-16	Vernon, B. C.
183444	Biggs, W. S.	Pte.	W. 9-4-17 (Vimy) to Eng.	Innisfail, Alta.
761184	Bijl, A.	Pte.	W. 9-4-17 (Vimy) to Eng.	No address available.
2528492	Billet-Doux, J. M.	Pte.	W. 30-9-18 (Cambrai)	1249 East Lafayette Ave., Detroit, Mich., U.S.A.
296870	Billington, A. J.	Pte.	Evac. sick 26-10-17 to Eng.	10 St. Paul's St., St. Catherines, Ont.
267016	Billington, G.	Pte.	K. i. a. 1-11-17 (Passchendaele)	E. Billington, 349 Gladstone St., Peterboro, Eng.
219157	Billsborough, C. G.	Pte.	Tr. to 51st Bn. 2-8-16	No address available.
703433	Bincincan, N.	Pte.	Tr. to 51st Bn. 2-8-16	St. Joseph's Hospital, Comox, B.C.
691007		Pte.		244 McNab St., Hamilton, Ont.
161279	Binyon, H. W.	Pte.	K. i. a. 12-5-17 (1st Triangle)	Mrs. M. E. Binyon, Bank House, Wallingford, Berks, Eng.
3110524	Bird, S. H.	Pte.	Tr. to Can. Ordnance Corps 15-8-16	184 Englinton Ave., Toronto, Ont.
703101	Birkett, F. J.	Arm.-Sgt.	W. 28-9-18 (Cambrai) to Eng.	P.O. Box 1294, Victoria, B.C.
663498	Bishop, E. J.	Pte.	Tr. to 4th C.M.G.C. 1-5-18	Sparta, Ont.
838242	Bisson, A.	Pte.		126 Kent St., Hull, Que.
3107801	Bittorf, S. E.	Pte.		R.R. No. 1, Cedarville, Ont.
220220	Black, H. M.	Pte.	Tr. to 11th C.L.T.M.B. 19-7-16	No address available.
799603	Black, N. W.	Pte.	W. 8-8-18 (Amiens) to Eng.	137 Dovercourt Rd., Toronto, Ont.
925342	Blackburn, A.	Pte.	K. i. a. 18-2-17 (Vimy)	Mrs. Blackburn, Weyburn, Sask.
226871	Blacker, R. J.	Pte.	W. 16-11-17 (Passchendaele); d. o. w. 11-8-18 (Amiens)	
219589	Blackhurst, G. T.	Pte.		Mrs. E. Blacker, Clinton, Ont.
761038	Blacklock, A. W.	Sgt.	Tr. to 51st Bn. 2-8-16	No address available.
				c/o Allen's Grocery, 10th Ave. and 6th St., New Westminster, B.C.
135047	Blaind, W. A.	Pte.	Evac. sick 30-1-18 to Eng.	193 Sherbourne St., Toronto, Ont.
252660	Blair, A.	Pte.	Evac. sick, 13-12-18 to Eng.	52 North Bridge St., Crieff, Perthshire, Scotland.
703797	Blake, H.	Pte.	D. o. w. 10-4-17 (Vimy)	D. Mills, Charles Creek Cannery, Kingscombe Inlet, B.C. (Friend).
2591328	Blake, W. H.	Pte.		447 Main St., W., Hamilton, Ont.
703476	Blakemore, A. S.	S.-Sgt.	O.R.S. at G.H.Q. from Sept. 1917	Cor. Blanca Rd. and 4th Ave., Point Grey, Vancouver.
663079	Blampled, E. T.	Sgt.	W. 4-9-18 (2nd Arras)	c/o W. A. Chapman, Milton, Ont.
252600	Blanchard, J. T.	Pte.		Mrs. M. Blanchette, 152 Banning St., Pt. Arthur, Ont.
3110382	Blanchette, P.	Pte.	K. i. a. 9-4-17 (Vimy)	c/o W. A. Chapman, Milton, Ont.
1003893	Blaney, W. R.	Pte.	W. 6-11-18 (Valenciennes) to Eng.	Mrs. M. Blanchette, 152 Banning St., Pt. Arthur, Ont.
3314059	Blank, J. A.	Pte.	W. 2-9-18 (2nd Arras)	12 Grosvenor Ave., Ste S. Marie, Ont.
1003961	Blatchford, C.	Pte.	W. to 4th C.M.G.C. 1-5-18	165 Queenston St., St. Catherines, Ont.
907765	Blaylock, T. R.	Pte.	W. 9-4-17 (Vimy) to Eng.	Copper Cliff, Ont.
703687	Blight, A. W.	Pte.	Evac. sick 22-9-17 to Eng.	Regina, Sask.
3317005	Blight, G. A.	Pte.	W. 2-9-18 (2nd Arras) to Eng.	St. Mewan St., Anstell, Cornwall, Eng.
1003432	Bloom, E. Z.	Pte.	Evac. sick 7-12-18 to Eng.	Brooklin, Ont.
703467	Blower, F.	Pte.	Tr. to 51st Bn. 2-8-16	No address available.
703713	Blundell, F. H.	Pte.	W. 15-4-18 (Oppy) to Eng.	839 Pandora St., Victoria, B.C.
2108748	Blundell, T. H.	Pte.		Phoenix, B.C.
703223	Blythe, F. W.	Pte.	Evac. sick 2-6-17 to Eng.	c/o Mrs. Whitehead, 33 Frederick Ave., Hamilton, Ont. Box 556, Vancouver, B.C.

Number	Name	Rank	Notes	Address
926021	Boblo, W.	Pte.	K. l. a. 9-4-17 (Vimy)	No address available.
703905	Boddington, R.H.St.J.	Pte.	W. 21-10-16 (Regina) to Eng.	c/o P. G. Morey, Nelson, B.C.
703535	Bolderstone, A. R.	Pte.	W. 21-10-16 (Regina); w. 8-6-17 (2nd Triangle) to Eng.	
3106440	Boles, J. H.	Pte.	Evac. sick 1-4-19	Mersey Road, Rock Ferry, Cheshire, Eng.
145057	Bolin, R. A.	Cpl.	K. l. a. 21-10-16 (Regina)	116 Park St., Hamilton, Ont.
103444	Bolton, E. R.	L.-C.	W. 10-6-17 (2nd Triangle) to Eng.	No address available.
3109204	Bond, G. W.	Pte.		Cos-Cob, Connecticut, U.S.A.
102213	Bond, H.	Sgt.	To Eng. for commission 23-8-18	Niagara Falls, Ont.
3314102	Bond, R.	Pte.	W. l. a. 27-9-18 (Cambrai)	Okanagan Centre, B.C.
240387	Bonham, J. E.	Pte.	K. l. a. 27-9-18 (Cambrai)	Mrs. C. Bond, Niagara Falls, Ont.
703531	Bonnette, W. E. J.	Pte.	Acc. inj. 9-4-17	Miss Real, 316 Main St., Hamilton Ont. (Friend).
663543	Bontez, H. F. G.	Pte.	Acc. w. 9-8-18 to Eng.	Wingham, Ont.
102668	Bonus, M.	Pte.	Tr. to 4th C.M.G.C. 1-5-18	2414 Granville St., Vancouver, B.C.
253083	Bool, H. J.	Pte.	Tr. to 7th Canl. Area Emp. Co. 22-8-17	Acton West, Ont.
703919	Boon, E. L.	Pte.	W. 15-8-17 (Lens) to Eng.	Nanaimo, B.C.
850814	Boon, W. L.	Pte.	Evac. sick 3-1-18 to Eng.	East End, Sask.
3310573	Booth, G.	Pte.	W. 23-7-18 (Lens) to Eng	c/o Thos. Boon, c/o Coleman Co., Santa Anna, Texas.
3109989	Borrow, J.	Pte.	K. l. a. 30-9-18 (Cambrai)	330 Cumberland Rd., Denistown, Glasgow, Scot.
703700	Bossart, W. M.	Pte.		Mrs. Borrow, 143 Barland St., Orillia, Ont.
908088	Bouchart, W.	Pte.	Tr. to Lbr. Pool 3-5-18	R.R. No. 2, Stevensville, Ont
	Bounsall, A. H.	Pte.	W. 9-4-17 (Vimy); w. 9-6-17 (2nd Triangle) to Eng.	Chicoutimi, Que.
252701	Bourke, M.	Pte.	W. 9-4-17 (Vimy); w. 17-4-18 (Oppy) to Eng.	Bowmansville, Ont.
2528389	Bourque, T.	Pte.	Evac. sick 9-11-18 to Eng	Demgeal, Killorgen, Co. Kerry, Ireland.
703084	Bousfield, W.	Pte.	K. l. a. 22-10-16 (Regina)	1366 St. John's Place, Brooklyn, N.Y., U.S.A.
102729	Bowen, W. E.	Pte.	W. 7-6-17 (2nd Triangle) to Eng.	Mrs. Bousfield, 2180 38th Ave., Kerrisdale, B.C.
907495	Bowerman, L. S.	Pte.	W. 11-5-17 (1st Triangle) to Eng.	Bryahyfryd, Aberdorey, North Wales.
3110809	Bowers, R. N.	Pte.		Dewar Lake, Sask.
907442	Bowes, E. W.	Pte.	W. 9-4-17 (Vimy) to Eng	Loring P.O., Ont.
703643	Bowes, J. E.	Pte.	K. l. a. 21-10-16 (Regina)	Stoughton, Sask.
200076	Bowes, J. R.	Pte.	W. 23-7-18 (Oppy)	Mrs. E. Bowes, Uppertown, Wolsingham, Durham, Eng.
219725	Bowle, P.	Pte.	Tr. to 51st Bn. 2-8-16	581 63rd Ave. E., Vancouver, B.C.
757675	Bowlby, R. T. C.	Pte.	W. 8-8-18 (Amiens); w. 27-9-18 (Cambrai) to Eng.	No address available.
760355	Boxall, W.	Pte.	D. o. w. 8-8-17 (Lens)	117 Maple Ave., Hamilton, Ont.
1103403	Boyd, A. E.	Pte.	W. 17-11-17 (Passchendaele); w. 26-12-17 (Merlcourt) to Eng.	Mrs. F. Boxall, 137 Maple St., S. Vancouver, B.C.
200091	Boyd, C.	Pte.	Evac. sick 4-3-18 to Eng.	Kagawong, Manitoulin Island, Ont. c/o Cpl. F. Boyd, No. 19 Co, C.A.S.C., 91117 Seaton St., Vancouver, B.C.
541388	Boyd, H. j.	Pte.	Tr. to 11th C.L.T.M.B. 19-7-16	No address available.
227190	Boyle, A. j.	Pte.	W. 8-8-18 (Amiens) to Eng.	Hatt St. West, Dundas, Ont.
931764	Boyle, J.	Pte.	W. 23-12-17 (Merlcourt); tr. to Lbr. Pool 24-1-18	c/o Chief of Police, Kamloops.
3314057	Boyle, R. L.	Pte.	K. l. a. 27-9-18 (Cambrai)	Mrs. Boyle, 31 Queenston St., S. Catherines, Ont.
3109393	Boyle, U. C.	Pte.	Tr. to 4th Div. Sig. Co. 13-1-19	Hatt St., Dundas, Ont.
2528331	Boys, A. B.	Pte.	W. 24-8-18 (Amiens); w. 27-9-18 (2nd Arras)	332 Waverley Rd., Toronto, Ont.
3106411	Brabbs, J. W.	Pte.	W. 3-9-18 (2nd Arras); w. 27-9-18 (Cambrai) to Eng.	189 Queen St., Hamilton, Ont.

760574	Bracewell, M. W.	Pte.	W. 1-11-17 (Passchendaele); w. 28-3-18 (Lens); w. 30-9-18 (Cambrai)	21 Orchard St., Bury, St. Edmunds, Eng.
704080	Brackenridge, D.	Pte.	Tr. to Lbr. Pool, 9-6-18	8 Lambs Lane, Dundee, Scotland.
727242	Brackley, F. T.	Pte.	W. 24-8-18 (Oppy) to Eng.	11 Watrous Rd., Aylesbury, Eng.
219807	Bradley, C. C.	Pte.	W. 10-11-16 (Somme); w. 9-4-17 (Vimy) to Eng.	Edwards P.O. Carleton Co., Ont.
1090100	Bradley, C. E.	Pte.	Missing after action 27-9-18 (Cambrai)	Carson Bradley, 1416 10th Ave., Calgary.
760955	Bradley, E.	Pte.	Tr. to Eng. as a minor 13-4-17	2130 Parker St., Vancouver, B.C.
761283	Bradley, P. E.	Pte.	W. 9-4-17 (Vimy); w. 14-5-17 (1st Triangle) to Eng.	
540107	Bradley, P. F.	Pte.	Tr. to 11th C.L.T.M.B. 1-10-17, ret. 14-11-18	Grand Valley, Ont.
3106310	Bradley, T.	Pte.	Evac. sick 2-12-18 to Eng.	No address available.
850646	Bradshaw, A. A.	Pte.		226 Hess St., Hamilton, Ont.
3030917	Brady, G. C.	Pte.	W. 6-11-18 (Valenciennes) to Eng.	Lion Hill Cottage, Wooton, Woodstock, Eng.
703370	Brady, P. J.	Pte.	Tr. to Lbr. Pool 9-6-18	130 Madison Ave., Baltimore, Md., U.S.A.
1003531	Brady, R.	Pte.	W. to 4th C.M.G.C. 18-3-18	Marinora, Ont.
225216	Brady, W. A.	Pte.	W. 8-8-18 (Amiens) to Eng.	Garson Mine, Ont.
138256	Brain, A. J.	Cpl.	Tr. from 75th Bn. 22-7-16; tr. back 19-2-17	26 Fermanagh Ave., Toronto, Ont.
138228	Brain, A. St. G. W.	Sgt.	Evac. sick 14-12-16	No address available.
703742	Brand, A. C.	Cpl.	W. 21-3-17 (Vimy); tr. to 4th C.M.G.C. 1-5-18	2446 6th Ave., Vancouver, B.C.
541059	Brander, A.	Pte.	W. 17-11-17 (Passchendaele) to Eng.	Wallaceburg, Ont.
760341	Brandrith, C. P.	Sgt.	Evac. sick 30-1-19 to Eng.	Boundary Bay, B.C.
703636	Brankin, D. B.	Sgt.	W. 11-11-16 (Somme) to Eng.	1719 Yew St., Vancouver, B.C.
219956	Brant, A. A.	Pte.	W. 19-11-16 (Somme) to Eng.	Deseronto, Ont.
249627	Brapter, R.	Pte.	To Eng. for demob. 20-3-19	Corbeton, Ont.
3110383	Brass, A. M.	Pte.		29 Caroline St., S., Hamilton, Ont.
3314101	Bratley, C.	Pte.	K. i. a. 27-9-18 (Cambrai)	Niagara Falls, South, Ont.
249895	Bratt, F. J.	Pte.	W. 6-11-18 (Valenciennes) to Eng.	Mrs. Bratt, R.R. No. 3, Galt, Ont.
3030918	Bratt, H.	Pte.		c/o Bank of Nova Scotia, Hamilton, Ont.
663416	Bray, H.	Pte.		Burlington, Ont.
101725	Bready, E. G.	Pte.	Evac. sick 19-4-17 to Eng.	Coppice Hill, Alta.
760056	Brearley, G.	Pte.	W. 12-5-17 (1st Triangle) to Eng.	Headshill Rd., Haywood, Lancs., Eng.
183034	Bremner, A. C.	Pte.	Tr. to 11th Bde. M.G. Co. 10-12-16	No address available.
252349	Bremner, J.	Pte.	W. 27-9-18 (Cambrai) to Eng.	Auchnavast, Westfield, Thurso, Scot.
163292	Brennan, D. S.	Pte.	Tr. to 4th Div. Emp. Co. 11-5-17	No address available.
2255533	Brennan, M. A.	Pte.	W. 27-9-18 (Cambrai)	Gananoque, Ont.
226025	Brent, G. E.	Sgt.	W. 17-11-17 (Passchendaele); dec. M.M. (Amiens) C.R.O. 1899; tr. to Eng. 31-10-18 for commission	
195438	Brew, P. M.	Pte.	D. o. w. 13-5-17 (1st Triangle)	46 Glendale Ave., Hamilton, Ont.
703567	Brewer, C. V.	Sgt.	Dec. M.M. (Lens) C.R.O. 1419; w. 10-4-18 (Oppy Raid) C.R.O. 1772; dec. D.C.M. (Oppy Raid)	Mrs. Brew, Agneas-le-Laxey, Isle of Man.
704153	Brewer, W. F.	Pte.	D. o. w. 1-9-16 (Somme)	141 Brunswick St., Fredericton, New Brunswick.
540361	Bridgeman, F. W.	Pte.	K. i. a. 22-10-16 (Regina)	Mrs. Frank Ginn, Matherson, New Ontario.
240481	Bridgewater, G. V.	Pte.	Tr. to 8th Bn. C. E. 11-7-18	No address available.
3106203	Brigham, G.	Pte.	W. 1-10-18 (Cambrai)	Simcoe, Ont.
704009	Brill, R. H.	Pte.	Evac. sick 7-3-17 to Eng.	Bank of Nova Scotia, Hamilton, Ont. G.P.O., Vancouver, B.C.

Number	Name	Rank	Details	Address
703971	Britney, F. J.	Pte.	Evac. sick 12-9-18 to Eng.	Gibson, York Co., New Brunswick.
908122	Broad, H. C.	Pte.	Evac. sick 15-4-17 to Eng.	Cheddington Rectory, Tring, Herts, Eng.
1003993	Broadford, R.	Pte.	K. l. a. 3-9-18 (2nd Arras).	Mrs. Broadford, 139 East Hayward St., East Braintree, Boston, Mass., U.S.A.
102612	Broadhurst, J.	Pte.	Tr. to 4th Div. Emp. Co. 11-5-17.	444 Birchfield Rd., Birmingham, Eng.
226377	Brockwell, T.	Pte.		c/o Rev. Mother Superior Evangelist, St. George's Home, Ottawa, Ont.
925445	Brodie, C.	Pte.	W. 12-5-17 (1st Triangle) to Eng.	Beregin, Sask.
663047	Brodie, R. V.	Pte.	W. 8-8-18 (Amiens) to Eng.	Oakville, Ont.
3317275	Brodeur, S. J.	Pte.		Waubaushene, Ont.
925181	Bromage, R. F.	Pte.	K. l. a. 25-3-17 (Vimy)	Mrs. C. Flawn, Trossacks, Sask.
703719	Bromley, S.	Pte.	Dec. M.M. (Vimy) C.R.O. 1236; evac. sick on leave 15-9-17; ret. to 72nd Bn. in the field.	
1003534	Bronson, R. H.	L.-C.		4847 Argyll St., Vancouver, B.C.
907060	Brook, W.	Pte.	W. 9-1-17 (Lens); tr. to Lbr. Pool 20-4-18	Blind River, Ont.
3317276	Brooks, A.	Pte.	Evac. sick 23-11-18 to Eng.	Lumsden, Sask.
760251	Brooks, H. R.	Pte.	W. 9-4-17 (Vimy)	31 Rufford Rd., Bootle, Liverpool, Eng.
703758	Brooks, W.	Pte.	Evac. sick, 9-1-18.	2209 Graveley St., Vancouver, B.C.
101076	Brotherstone, A.	Pte.	K. i. a. 8-6-17 (2nd Triangle)	c/o A. Brooks, Martock, Somerset, Eng. I. Brotherstone, Tinton Barns, Drem, Haddingtonshire, Scotland.
252356	Brough, R.	Pte.	W. 22-4-18 (Lens) to Eng.	50 Grieve St., Dumfernline, Fifeshire, Scot.
160701	Brough, A. C.	Pte.	W. 22-10-16 (Lens); tr. to 6th Can. Area Emp. Co. 22-8-17	No address available.
703664	Brown, D.	Pte.	K. l. a. 8-9-16 (St. Eloi)	Mrs. D. Brown, 155 Raplock St., Larkhall, Lanarkshire, Scot.
3109912	Brown, E. A.	Pte.		Box 187, Acton Halton, Ont.
219931	Brown, E. C.	Pte.	W. 15-11-17 (Passchendaele); dec. M.M. (Passchendaele) C.R.O. 1606	Marshville, Ont.
183758	Brown, E. E.	Pte.	Tr. to 11th Bde. M.G.C. 10-12-16.	No address available.
2255343	Brown, E. J.	Pte.	Evac. sick, 30-4-18 to Eng.	c/o Mrs. C. A. Dixon, William St., Grananoque, Ont.
102414	Brown, F.	Pte.	Tr. to 12th Bde. 17-7-17.	67 Bloomfield St., Derby, Eng.
703485	Brown, F. P.	Pte.	W. 21-10-16 (Somme) to Eng.	1874 Argyll St., Vancouver, B.C.
135989	Brown, F. R.	Sgt.	K. l. a. 9-4-17 (Vimy)	Miss M. E. Brown, Locust Hill, R.R. No. 1, Ont.
703917	Brown, F. R.	Pte.	W. 21-10-16 (Somme); k. l. a. 23-3-17 (Vimy)	Mrs. H. Brown, Midway, B.C.
1003069	Brown, G. A.	Pte.	Tr. to Lbr. Pool 12-7-18.; dec. M.M. (1st Triangle)	256 Bruce St., S. S. Marie, Ont.
703991	Brown, G.	Pte.	W. 13-5-17 (1st Triangle); tr. to Lbr. Pool, (Amiens) C.R.O. 1930	
703986	Brown, G. C.	Pte.	W. 9-6-17 (2nd Triangle); tr. to Lbr. Pool, 3-5-18	Box 370, Cumberland, B.C.
703115	Brown, H.	Sgt.	W. 21-10-16 (Somme) to Eng.	c/o D. McCallum, Grand Forks, B.C.
1004112	Brown, H.	Pte.	W. 17-3-18 (Lens)	356 5th St. E., North Vancouver, B.C.
540289	Brown, H. J.	Pte.	Dec. M.M. (Somme) L.G. 29953; tr. to 11th C.I.T.M.B. 1-10-17.	Bigwood, Ont.
240232	Brown, H. McK.	Pte.	W. 29-9-18 (Cambrai)	Toronto, Ont.
219438	Brown, H. V.	Pte.	W. 26-1-18 (Mericourt) to Eng.	7 Walnut St., Hamilton, Ont.
1003737	Brown, H. W.	Pte.	D. o. s. 27-12-17	Napanee, Ont.
200121	Brown, J.	Pte.	W. 21-4-18 (Oppy) to Eng.	Mrs. M. Brown, Big Lake, Manitoulin Island, Ont. 1003 Hillside Ave., Victoria, B.C.
127718	Brown, J.	Arm.-Cpl.	Tr. to 51st Bn. 2-8-16.	598 Adelaide St., Woodstock, Ont.

Reg. No.	Name	Rank	Notes	Address
3108366	Brown, J. A.	Pte.		182 West Second St., Mount Hamilton, Ont.
3109769	Brown, J. E. C.	Pte.		23 MacCormack St., Welland, Ont.
240584	Brown, J. H.	Cpl.		397 Ottawa St., Hamilton, Ont.
2528356	Brown, L. B.	Pte.	W. 8-8-18 (Amiens) to Eng.	Bayfield, Ont.
703263	Brown, L. H.	Sgt.	K. l. a. 9-4-17 (Vimy)	Mrs. Brown, 3524 W. Point Grey Rd., Vancouver, B.C.
703085	Brown, M. M.	Sgt.	W. 21-10-16 (Regina), . . . to Eng; Dec. D.C.M. (Regina) D.R.O. 316	
907793	Brown, R.	Pte.	K. l. a. 9-1-17 (Vimy)	Northfield, Nr., Nanaimo, B.C.
422185	Brown, R. H.	Cpl.	Evac. sick. 14-2-17	Mrs. R. Brown, Tynan, Sask.
252315	Brown, S.	Pte.	K. l. a. 9-4-17 (Vimy)	Glenlieuh, Sandgate, Eng.
703276	Brown, T.	Pte.	K. l. a. 22-11-16 (Somme)	D. A. G. Brown, Lilbrury, Ont.
145306	Brown, W. A.	Pte.	Tr. to 77th Bn. 10-8-16.	F. G. Loane, Hastings Shingle Co., Vancouver, B.C.
703001	Brown, W. S.	C.Q.M.S.	C.Q.M.S. for H.-Q. Later N.C.O. i/c Canteen	Renfrew, Ont.
249177	Browning, L.	Pte.		39 Lewis St., Victoria, B.C.
761094	Brownlee, T. J.	Pte.	W. 9-4-17 (Vimy)	44 Bristol Ave., Toronto, Ont.
703096	Bruce, A.	Pte.	Evac. sick 17-10-17 to Eng	Burquitlam, B.C.
237326	Bruce, W. H.	Pte.	W. 27-9-18 (Cambrai)	Terrace, B.C.
703336	Bruce, W. McR	Pte.	Tr. to 6th Can. Area Emp. Co. 22-8-17	Lumsden, Aberdeenshire, Scot.
3109925	Bruneau, J. F.	Pte.		Inverurie, Scotland.
252013	Brunell, L. A.	Pte.	W. 9-4-17 (Vimy) to Eng.	112 Wellington St., W., Steelton, Ont.
3108674	Brush, J. A. L.	Pte.	Evac. sick 20-10-18 to Eng.	Cliffside, New Jersey, U.S.A.
850325	Bryant, F. T.	Pte.	W. 3-9-18; evac. sick 14-2-19 to Eng.	Fingal, Ont.
703486	Bryanton, R.	Pte.	W. 15-4-18 (Mericourt)	20 Richmond Ave., St. Catherines, Ont.
219286	Brydon, C. J.	Cpl.	D. o. w. 11-11-16 (Somme)	Mrs. Chas. Powell, Powell River, B.C.
760178	Bryson, R. P.	Pte.	K. l. a. 5-17-17 (1st Triangle)	No address available.
704022	Buchan, P.	Pte.	Evac. sick, 16-6-16	Mrs. R. Bryson, 1322 Broadway W., Vancouver.
663650	Buchanan, A. J.	Pte.	W. 3-9-18 (2nd Arras); evac. sick 21-2-19 to Eng	121 Laren St. E., Vancouver, B.C. Grand Valley, Ont.
240640	Buchanan, J.	Pte.	W. 8-9-18 (Lens) to Eng.	1032 Pennsylvania Ave., Detroit, Mich., U.S.A.
1003109	Bucholz, O. F.	Pte.		419 Robson St., Vancouver, B.C.
703023	Buckberry, W.	Pte.	W. 26-4-17 (Vimy) .W. 9-6-17 (2nd Triangle)	c/o Henry King & Co., 9 Pall Mall, London, Eng.
3109535	Buckerfield, R.	L.-S.		Parry Sound, Ont.
3109208	Buckingham, J. E.	Pte.		Stayner, Ont.
850152	Buckner, R.	Pte.		63 Fourth Ave., Niagara Falls, Ont.
648012	Buffam, W. J.	L.-C.	Tr. to Eng. 29-1-19	Lanark, Ont.
757888	Bull, C. S.	Pte.		19 Florence St., Hamilton, Ont.
3109068	Bulmer, M.	Pte.	Evac. sick 25-1-19 to Eng.	Dunedin, Ont.
1003662	Bunting, C. H.	Cpl.	Evac. sick 21-9-16 to Eng.	2823 4th Ave. S., Seattle, Wash., U.S.A.
1003585	Burch, W. H.	Pte.		418 Elm St., W. Sudbury, Ont.
1003119	Burd. J.	Pte.	Evac. sick 13-12-18 to Eng.	72 Church St., Micheldever, Hants, Eng.
703653	Burdett, H. B.	Pte.	K. l. a. 22-10-16 (Regina)	Mrs. G. McCall, Cricklewood, London, Eng.
703827	Burford, F. W.	Pte.	Tr. to 51st Bn. 2-8-16	12 Bath Rd., Buxton, Eng.
704042	Burge, C.	Pte.	Evac. sick 20-10-16 to Eng.	G. P. O., Vancouver, B.C.
703490	Burke, A. C.	Pte.	W. 13-10-16 (Somme) to Eng.	Keatley, Sask.
3314269	Burke, J. H.	Pte.	K. l. a. 27-9-18 (Cambrai) to Eng.	Mrs. Palmer, Charlotte St., Pt. Colbourne, Ont.
704004	Burke, W. T.	Pte.	W. 11-11-16 (Somme) to Eng.	56 Ann St., Philadelphia, Penn., U.S.A.
703857	Burkmar, T. S.	Pte.	W. 1-11-17 (Passchendaele); evac. sick 26-3-19	17 Ralph St., Union Rd. Borough, London, Eng.
907352	Burn, H. A.	Pte.	W. 9-4-17 (Vimy) to Eng.	1803 11th Ave. E., Vancouver, B.C.
663048	Burnet, A. C.	Pte.	K. l. a. 27-9-18 (Cambrai)	Mrs. Burnet, Oakville, Ont.

Regtl. No.	Name	Rank	Remarks	Address
3314262	Burnett, F.	Pte.		144 Summer St., Niagara Falls, Ont.
703063	Burnett, H. M.	Pte.		The Friary, Princess Ave., Grimsby, Eng.
3108870	Burns, A. E.	Pte.	Tr. to Can. Lbr. Pool 9-3-18	c/o Miss Sullivan, 117 Welland Ave., St. Catherines.
760838	Burns, A. E.	Pte.		A. E. Burns, 19 Albert Rd., Tonbridge, Eng.
703752	Burns, A. F.	Pte.	Missing, 13-6-17 (2nd Triangle)	Bancroft, Ont.
252700	Burns, J. F.	Pte.	Evac. sick 8-5-17 to Eng.	c/o Mrs. Allen, c/o Bank Montreal, Nelson, B.C.
249056	Burns, W. J	Pte.		124 Booth Ave., Toronto, Ont.
703445	Burrell, W. B.	Pte.	Tr. to Eng. 16-1-19	94 East St., Melrose, Mass., U.S.A.
2528472	Burridge, F.	Pte.		152 East 48th St., New York, U.S.A.
7037277	Burrington, G.	Pte.	Dec. M.M. (Regina) D.R.O. 375; k. l. a. 21-11-16 (Somme)	Mrs. Burrington, Hazelton, B.C.
220262	Burrows, F.	Pte.	K. l. a. 1-10-18 (Cambrai)	Mrs. Robertshaw, 222 Dudley Hill Rd., Andercliff, Bradford, Eng.
703477	Bush, H. G.	Sgt.	W. 22-11-16 (Regina) to Eng.	Hill Farm, Collier's End, Herts., Eng.
703622	Bush, W. A.	Pte.	Tr. to Eng. for commission 10-12-16	Holt, Morden, Surrey, Eng.
249244	Butchart, W. W.	Pte.		70 East Mount St., Toronto, Ont.
103394	Butcher, A.	Pte.	W. 9-6-17 (2nd Triangle); w. 8-8-18 (Amiens).	26 Windsor St., Holloway, London, Eng.
703636	Butcher, A.	Pte.	W. 2-11-17 (Passchendaele) to Eng.	Post Office Staff, Vancouver, B.C.
441044	Butler, F.	Pte.	Evac. sick 7-4-17 to Eng.	No address available.
703623	Butler, F.	Pte.	K. l. a. 7-8-17 (Lens)	Mrs. F. Butler, 7123 Quebec St., Vancouver, B.C.
135591	Butt, H. R.	Pte.	K. l. a. 9-4-17 (Vimy)	Mrs. E. Butt, Homestead Rd., Medstead, Hants, Eng.
426061	Butterworth, W. H	Sgt	Evac. sick 14-4-17 to Eng.	717 Saskatchewan West, Moose Jaw, Sask.
2591308	Buttrum, H. R.	Pte.		R.R. No. 1 (Box 25), Hamilton, Ont.
249417	Byers, R. B.	Pte.		243 Spadina Ave., Toronto, Ont.
102421	Byrnell, W. H.	Pte.	W. 11-5-17 (1st Triangle); w. 17-8-17 (Lens) to Eng.	
706996	Caddell, A.	Pte	K. l. a. 9-4-17 (Vimy)	1865 Graveley St., Vancouver, B.C.
703717	Cadenhead, J.	Pte.		Mrs. Caddell, Wilkerson Rd., Saanich, B.C.
240639	Cadman, E.	Pte.	K. l. a. 27-9-18 (Cambrai)	229 Guelph St., Vancouver, B.C.
226475	Caffrey, J. A.	Pte.	W. 3-9-18 (2nd Arras)	Mrs. Cadman, 20 Gordon St., Hamilton, Ont.
907882	Cahoon, T. H	Pte.	W. 12-5-17 (1st Triangle); w. 15-8-17 (Lens) tr. to Lbr. Pool 22-11-17	2 Ship St., Barrow, Eng.
3108693	Cain, L.	Pte.	W. 2-11-17 (Valenciennes); tr. to C.C.R.C. 12-2-19	c/o Mrs. C. Briggs, Broomhedge Cert Bridge, County Down, Ireland.
706573	Cain, W. J	Pte.	W. 9-4-17 (Vimy) to Eng.	R.R. No. 2, Niagara-on-the-Lake, Ont.
760335	Cairns, H.	Pte.	Tr. to Y.M.C.A. 27-8-17	27 Goldsmith St., Liverpool, Eng.
3110610	Calabresi, O.	Pte.		1737 13th Ave. E., Vancouver, B.C.
703209	Calder, G. D.	Sgt.	Dec. M.M. (Somme) D.R.O. 386; Tempy. Bandmaster	P.O. Box 25, Welland, Ont.
703798	Callaghan, O.	Pte.	Evac. 27-10-16 to Eng.	P.O. Box 243, Penticton, B.C.
1042752	Callahan, P. H	Pte.	W. 23-7-18 (Oppy) to Eng.	Point Grey P.O., Vancouver, B.C.
703449	Calland, A. A. F.	Pte.	Dec. M.M. (Amiens) C.R.O. 1899; retained in Eng. 2-1-19	18 North Woodside Rd., Glasgow, Scot.
704158	Callister, W. H	Pte.	W. 23-11-16 (Somme); evac. sick 11-5-17 to Eng.	c/o Bank of Montreal, 9 Waterloo Place, London, Eng.
3106066	Calvin, W. A.	Pte.		25 Michael St., Peel, Isle of Man.
3314103	Camber, I. J.	Pte.	W. 28-9-18 (Cambrai) to Eng.	547 Peachtree St., Atlanta, Ga., U.S.A. Stamford, Ont.

Number	Name	Rank	Service	Address
703225	Cameron, H.	Pte.	Tr. to 51st Bn. 2-8-16	Grand Hotel, Water St., Vancouver, B.C.
252662	Cameron, J. A.	Pte.	K. i. a. 6-6-17 (Somme Triangle)	Miss M. Cameron, Shillochan, Currieridge, Scot.
703353	Cameron, R. B.	Pte.	W. 20-11-16 (Somme) to Eng.	c/o Miss Cameron, Rob Roy P.O., Ont.
249703	Cameron, W. J.	Pte.	K. i. a. 2-9-18 (2nd Arras)	Mrs. Cameron, c/o Mrs. M. Bertram, Westmount Drive, Toronto, Ont.
103274	Campbell, C.	Pte.	Tr. to 26th Bn. 25-3-18	General Delivery, Victoria.
102676	Campbell, D.	Pte.	Tr. to 4th Div. H.-Q. 8-8-17	850 Broughton St., Victoria, B.C.
103014	Campbell, D. MacS.	Cpl.	W. 13-5-17; w. 9-6-17 (1st and 2nd Triangle); w. 17-8-17 (Lens) to Eng.	
3109223	Campbell, D. S.	Pte.	W. 1-10-18 (Cambrai) to Eng.	Campbelltown, Scotland.
803190	Campbell, E. W.	Pte.	W. 9-6-17 (2nd Triangle); k. i. a. 27-12-17 (Merlcourt)	Taylor St., Niagara Falls, Ont.
703946	Campbell, F.	Pte.		R.R. No. 1, Ailsa, Craig, Ont.
249012	Campbell, G.	Pte.	W. 2-9-18 (2nd Arras)	Robert Campbell, Debert, Colchester Co., N.S.
760505	Campbell, G. F.	Pte.	W. 9-4-17 (Vimy); k. i. a. 17-11-17 (Passchendaele)	1147 Dovercourt Rd., Toronto, Ont.
252363	Campbell, H. A.	Pte.		778 39th Ave. E., South Vancouver, B.C.
3110530	Campbell, J. A.	Pte.	W. 28-9-18 (Cambrai); evac. sick 14-12-18 to Eng.	H. A. Campbell, Pinkerton, Ont.
3314285	Campbell, J. A.	Pte.		c/o Mrs. Ferguson, The Cottage, Ballyconnell, Ire.
703718	Campbell, J. L.	Sgt.	Tr. to 4th Can. Base Depot, 1-7-17	Chaleur P.O., Bonaventure, Que.
703739	Campbell, N. J.	Pte.	Dec. M.M. (Passchendaele) C.R.O. 1606; w. 1-10-18 (Cambrai) to Eng.	1035 Broadway East, Vancouver, B.C.
249036	Campbell, R.	Pte.	Tr. to Lbr. Pool, 20-2-18	119 Cumberland St., New Westminster, B.C.
1103040	Campbell, R. A.	Pte.	W. 18-11-17 (Passchendaele) to Eng.	1147 Dovercourt Rd., Toronto, Ont.
703714	Campbell, R. J.	Pte.	Tr. to 4th Div. Emp. Co. 11-5-17	Alliston, Ont.
226883	Campbell, W.	Pte.	W. 8-8-18 (Amiens) to Eng.	P.O. Box 131, Nelson, B.C.
252440	Campbell, W.	Pte.	W. 9-4-17 (Vimy) to Eng.	George Terrace, Campbelltown, Falkirk, Scotland.
703196	Campbell, W. J.	Cpl.	Tr. to C.C.A.C. 51st Bn. 16-6-16	Saskatoon, Sask.
2528494	Campbell, W. R.	Pte.	W. 1-10-18 (Cambrai) to Eng.	36 Alexander Rd., Eastham, London, Eng.
931231	Canning, R. F.	Pte.	Tr. to Lbr. Pool, 14-6-18	37 Davies Ave., Toronto, Ont.
704173	Cannon, J.	Pte.	Evac. sick 24-11-16 to Eng.	c/o Mrs. H. Ivens, Prior's Marston, Warwickshire.
703298	Cannon, R.	Pte.	Tr. to 51st Bn. 2-8-16	108 Alpha St., Victoria, B.C.
225228	Cannon, W. J.	Pte.	W. 20-4-18 (Oppy)	108 Alpha St., Victoria, B.C.
252618	Capehart, H.	Pte.	W. 9-4-17 (Vimy) to Eng.	7119 Upland St., Pittsburg, U.S.A.
454935	Carl, D. H.	L.-S.	K. i. a. 21-10-16 (Regina)	New Brighton, Pa., U.S.A.
2250539	Carleton, W.	Pte.	Evac. sick in Eng. 16-2-19	No address available.
102306	Carlisle, W.	Sgt.	Tr. to 75th Bn. 4-6-17; granted a commission in latter unit	Sorel, Que.
931229	Carlson, A.	Pte.	W. 21-10-16 (Somme) to Eng.	22 Whitevale St., Dannistoun, Glasgow, Scot.
907659	Carlson, H. B.	Pte.	W. 2-9-18 (2nd Arras); w. 31-10-18 (Valenciennes) to Eng.	c/o Mrs. S. Carlson, Denver, Colo., U.S.A.
3110531	Carlyle, T.	Pte.		Halbright, Sask.
703314	Carmichael, J.	Sgt.	W. 7-6-17 (2nd Triangle); w. 8-8-18 (Amiens) to Eng.; dec. M.M. (Vimy) C.R.O. 1236	Town Head, Highton, Lockerbie, Scotland.
703767	Carmichael, W.	Pte.		Nelson, B.C.
3106288	Carmichael, W. K.	Pte.	Evac. sick 22-10-16 to Eng.	c/o Mrs. E. Pitt, North Vancouver, B.C.
219791	Carmody, C. M.	Pte.	Dec. M.M. (Valenciennes) C.R.O. 2028	Cobalt, Ont. c/o Miss K. Carmody, Gen. Hosp., Pembroke, Ont.

Number	Name	Rank	Service	Address
703186	Carnie, G. B.	L.-C.	W. 17-9-16 (St. Eloi); w. 10-11-17 (Passchendaele); k. l. a. 3-9-18 (2nd Arras)	Mrs. M. Doyle, Box 1287 N. Yakima, Wash., U.S.A.
240590	Carnie, R. H. G.	Pte.		15 Blythe St. Hamilton, Ont.
53550	Carpenter, H.	Sgt.	W. 27-9-18 (Cambrai) to Eng.	c/o Mrs. Bowman, Toledo, Ohio, U.S.A.
225356	Carpenter, P.	Pte.	Detained in England	Bronte, Ont.
703612	Carr, R.	Pte.	Tr. to 51st Bn. 2-8-16	c/o Bank of Montreal, Prince Rupert, B.C.
931228	Carrell, J. A.	Pte.	Tr. to 51st Bn. 2-8-16	Woodstock, Ont.
2507313	Carrigy, M.	Pte.	W. 28-9-18 (Cambrai) to Eng.	c/o Mrs. T. Harrison, 153 Clinton Ave., Brooklyn, N.Y.
3108654	Carroll, J. G.	Pte.	W. 27-9-18 (Cambrai) to Eng.	Carrickhay P.O., Ballycloughan, Co. Longford, Ire.
3314014	Carroll, J. J.	Pte.	K. l. a. 9-4-17 (Vimy)	c/o Bank of Ottawa, Pembroke, Ont.
907328	Carroll, T. A.	Cpl.	W. 22-10-17 (Passchendaele)	Mrs. Carroll, 1436 Garnet St., Regina, Sask.
225384	Carron, O.	Pte.		221 McNab St. North, Hamilton, Ont.
2529356	Carswell, H. C.	Pte.	W. 8-4-17 (Vimy); w. 19-8-18 (Amiens) to Eng.	Mrs. A. R. Carron, Achigan, Mile 41, A.C.R.Y., Ont.
183865	Carter, A.	Pte.	W. 22-8-18 (Amiens) to Eng.	Red Deer, Alta.
3105966	Carter, P.	Pte.	W. 27-9-18 (Cambrai) to Eng.	c/o Bank of Nova Scotia, Hamilton, Ont.
3105724	Carter, S.	Pte.	K. l. a. 27-9-18 (Cambrai)	Mount Pleasant, Utah, U.S.A.
2529330	Cartmell, T. S.	Pte.		31 Faraday Rd., Ipswich, Suffolk, Eng.
3314109	Case, H.	Pte.	W. 9-6-17 (2nd Triangle); w. 5-9-18 (2nd Arras); dec. M.M. (Cambrai) C.R.O. 1989.	Mrs. Cartmell, Queen and Elgin Sts., Thorold, Ont.
219721	Case, R. P.	Pte.		c/o S. Harp, Esq., 101 Leighton, Rd., Kentish Town, London, N., England.
3109731	Casey, J.	Pte.	W. 1-11-17 (Passchendaele) to Eng.	R.R. No. 2, Lawbanks, Ont.
1003539	Cash, J.	Pte.		Grand River, Gaspe Co., Quebec.
1003288	Cassel, N. S.	Pte.	W. 27-9-18 (Cambrai)	45 Bell St., Ottawa, Ont.
835152	Casserley, F. R.	Pte.	K. l. a. 27-9-18 (Cambrai)	J. Cassel, Bolinbroke, Ont.
164578				c/o Miss Casserley, 33 Westholme, Hamstead Garden Suburb, London, N.W., Eng.
703688	Cassidy, A.	Cpl.	Dec. M.M. (Vimy) C.R.O. 1236; tr. to Eng. 24-9-17	Dawson, Y.T.
258469	Cassidy, C.	Pte.	W. 1-11-17 (Passchendaele) to Eng.	Hollyburn P.O., West Vancouver, B.C.
706011	Cassidy, J. F.	Cpl.	Dec. M.M. (Amiens) C.R.O. 1899; w. 2-9-18 (2nd Arras) to Eng.	
1003257	Cassidy, T. E.	L.-C.	W. 2-9-18 (2nd Arras) to Eng.	c/o J. Smith, 1379 Seaview Ave., Victoria, B.C.
703100	Catchpole, J. D.	Pte.	Tr. to Eng. 8-1-19	Huntsville P.O., Ont.
103253	Cathcart, J. A.	Pte.	W. 17-8-17 (Lens); tr. to Can. Engrs. 17-8-18	Courtenay P.O., B.C.
225390	Cattin, L. A. A.	Pte.	W. 8-8-18 (Amiens) to Eng.	Chemainus, B.C.
3109072	Caughey, H. G.	Pte.	Evac. sick 3-1-19 to Eng.	c/o Union Bank, Hamilton, Ont.
1003312	Caughill, L.	Pte.	Evac. sick 26-10-17 to Eng.	Penetang, Ont.
907130	Caulderwood, A. D.	Pte.	D. o. w. 17-4-17 (Vimy)	Little Current, Ont.
102800	Cavanagh, J.	Pte.	Tr. to Lbr. Pool, 19-12-17.	Mrs. H. Caulderwood, 1232 Cameron St., Regina, Sask.
1003255	Cavanaugh, J. B.	Pte.	Tr. to 1st Can. Lbr. Bn. 14-9-17	c/o Mrs. Bull, Perdue, Sask.
703922	Cave, T. B.	Cpl.	D. o. w. 11-11-16 (Somme)	c/o W. Cavanaugh, North Bay, Ont.
3108373	Cavin, E.	Pte.		Mrs. Cave, Grand Forks, B.C.
504705	Cawley, R. H.	Pte.	Tr. to 4th Div. Sigs. 13-1-19	Paris, Ont.
3107004	Cawson, W.	Pte.		P.O. Box 1327, Victoria, B.C.
739805	Cayuga, J.	Pte.	Tr. to Eng. for duty. C.C.C. 28-1-19	Carter's Corners, Andover, Mass., U.S.A.
907933	Centurini, M.	Pte.		Hagersville, Ont.
3105877	Chadwick, F.	Pte.	W. 27-9-18 (Cambrai) to Eng.	Canton Ticino, Lugano, Switzerland.
				1 Roosevelt Ave., Benerly, Mass., U.S.A.

Reg. No.	Name	Rank	Service Details	Address
103432	Chadwick, F. S.	Pte.	Tr. to Eng. as minor, 8-6-17	c/o Mrs. Gilman, 481 Fraser St., Esquimalt, B.C.
703520	Challand, H. W.	L.-C.	W. 21-10-16 (Regina) to Eng.	c/o T. Challand, Elston, Newark, Notts. Eng.
103276	Chalmers, J.	Pte.	Tr. to 26th Bn. 25-3-18	c/o Mrs. M. McKellar, Sunnyside, Milton Bridge, Midlothian, Scotland.
925343	Chamberlain, G. W.	Cpl.	Tr. to Eng. (Compassionate grounds) 6-12-17	Querrin, Sask.
925440	Chamberlain, H.	Pte.	K. I. a. 9-4-17 (Vimy)	G. Chamberlain, Querrin, Sask.
703325	Chamberlaine, C. H.	Cpl.	W. 2-9-18 (2nd Arras) to Eng.	1743 First St., Victoria, B.C.
908131	Chambers, E. E.	Pte.	D. o. w. 13-6-17 (2nd Triangle)	Mrs. E. Chambers, St. Mary's Rd., Dundalk, Ire.
703191	Chambers, E. E.	Cpl.	W. 9-4-17 (Vimy) to Eng.	Claresholm, Alta.
1003368	Chambers, J. M.	Pte.	W. 30-10-17 (Passchendaele); w. 16-11-17 (Passchendaele) to Eng.	
225964	Chandler, F. O.	Pte.	W. 8-8-18 (Amiens) to Eng.	Rydal Bank, Rose Township, Ont. c/o Mrs. Pabey, 87A, Princess May, Stoke Newington, London, Eng.
761259	Chandler, H.	Pte.	Dec. M.S.M. (L.G. d-3-6-19)	451 64th Ave. E., South Vancouver, B.C.
907494	Chapin, C. H.	Cpl.	W. 27-9-18 (Cambrai) to Eng.	Newdorf, Sask.
249403	Chapman, C. J.	Pte.	K. i. a. 31-10-17 (Passchendaele)	22 Gilpin St., Peterboro', Ont.
135450	Chapman, E. C.	Pte.		Mrs. M. Chapman, 38 Pemberry Rd., Tottenham, London, N.E. Eng.
1004183	Chapman, G. S.	Cpl.	W. 8-8-18 (Amiens); acc. inj. 13-8-18 to Eng.	Blind River, Ont.
101130	Charbonneau, J.	Pte.	W. 10-11-16 (Somme); acc. inj. 13-8-18 to Eng.	11421 124th St., Edmonton, Alta.
838039	Chard, T.	Sgt.	Dec. M.M. (Oppy Raid) C.R.O. 1966: w. 4-9-18 (2nd Arras); tr. to Eng. for commission 31-10-18	
3105261	Charlesworth, T.	Pte.		Fisherton, Ont.
703004	Charlton, C. A.	L-C	W. 27-9-18 (Cambrai)	13 Graham St., Providence, Rhode Island, U.S.A.
226940	Charlton, G.	Pte.	W. 12-6-17 (2nd Triangle) to Eng.	306 Alberta St., New Westminster, B.C.
226926	Charlton, W. J.	Pte.	Tr. to 4th Bn. C.M.G. 18-3-18	2571 Hartel Ave., Buffalo, N.Y., U.S.A.
252957	Charman, E. W.	Pte.	Tr. to 4th Bn. C.M.G. 18-3-18	380 Sackwell St., Toronto, Ont.
249577	Charpontier, V. P.	Pte.	W. 9-4-17 (Vimy) to Eng.	c/o T. Charman, Guildford, Surrey, Eng.
252706	Chase, F. L.	Pte.	W. 27-9-18 (Cambrai) to Eng.	Sutton West, Ont.
240535	Chasty, J. F.	Pte.	W. 27-9-18 (Cambrai) to Eng.	3 Turner Rd., Norwich, Eng.
199088	Cheney, F.	Arm-Cpl	W. 6-11-18 (Valenciennes) to Eng.	91 Dundurn St., Hamilton, Ont.
3108374	Chenier, A.	Pte.		827 Minnesota St., Fort William, Ont.
931230	Cherkuz, A.	Pte.	Tr. to 51st Bn. 2-8-16	c/o Mrs. Causoley, 219 Elgin St., Sarnia, Ont.
226417	Cherry, J. A.	Pte.	Tr. to Eng. for demob. 23-2-19	Cranbrook, B.C.
907073	Chester, F.	Pte.	W. 10-5-17 (1st Triangle); evac. sick 13-8-17 to Eng.	94 Monmouth St., Walkerville, Ont.
703068	Chevigny, A. E.	Pte.	Evac. sick, 13-4-18 to Eng.	c/o Mrs. T. M. Chester, Galloway St., Edgehill, Liverpool, Eng.
663587	Childs, J.	Pte.	K. i. a. 9-4-17 (Vimy)	c/o A. Chevigny de la Chevrautiere, St. Albert, Alta. Milton, Ont.
252932	Chipperfield, H. T.	Pte.		G. Chipperfield, 82 St. Ames Rd., Stamford Hill, London, N., Eng.
703135	Chipunow, A.	L.-C.	W. 18-11-17 (Passchendaele) to Eng.	460 Keefer St., Vancouver, B.C.
102676	Chisholm, A.	Pte	Evac. sick, 9-11-18 to Eng.	1317 McNair St., Victoria, B.C.
3108687	Chrest, E.	Pte		South River, Ont.
1004233	Chretien, A.	Pte		27 St. Joseph St., St. Jerome, Que.
3317019	Christie, C.	Pte.	Evac. sick, 21-10-18 to Eng.	No address available.
838041	Christie, J. M.	Sgt.	Dec. M.M. (2nd Arras) C.R.O. 1930.	338 6th St. E, Owen Sound, Ont.

Reg. No.	Name	Rank	Service Notes	Address
540551	Christie, K. S.	L.-C.	W. 8-8-18 (Amiens) to Eng.; dec. M.M. (Amiens) C.R.O. 1899	40 Superior St., Victoria, B.C.
3317282	Christie, W. J. H.	Pte.	W. 1-10-18 (Cambrai) to Eng.	174 Severn St., Owen Sound, Ont.
252736	Christofferson, C. L.	Pte.	K. i. a. 9-4-17 (Vimy)	L. Christofferson, Peperwikia, Bakbregede, Christiana, Norway.
440881	Chucas, M. J.	Pte.	Evac. sick '23-7-17 to Eng.	204 Bute Rd., Cardiff.
3108690	Church, J. S.	Pte.	Acc. w. 21-9-17 at Corps Shoot; tr. to Lbr. Pool 25-10-17	c/o Miss M. Semple, 22 Minto Ave., Hamilton, Ont.
704175	Churchard, G. L.	Pte.	K. i. a. 8-8-18 (Amiens)	Marpole, B.C.
704147	Churchill, L. L.	L.-C.	W. 11-5-17 (1st Triangle); w. 1-10-18 (Cambrai)	Mrs. E. M. Churchill, Digby, Nova Scotia.
135049	Churchill, T. F.	Pte.		38 Riverdale Ave., Toronto, Ont.
3108796	Clark, C.	Pte.	W. 1-11-17 (Passchendaele) to Eng.	Brookfield, Ont.
226901	Clark, C. G.	Pte.	W. 11-5-17 (1st Triangle) to Eng.	51 Main St., Smith Falls, Ont.
925043	Clark, J.	Pte.		Estevan, Sask. Box 338.
226919	Clarke, A.	Pte.		c/o S. B. Marcelles, Cochrane, Ont.
103047	Clarke, C. K.	L.-C.	W. 11-6-17 (2nd Triangle); dec. M.M. (2nd Arras) C.R.O. 1989; w. 30-9-18 (Cambrai)	97 Loughboro' Rd., Brixton, London, S.W., Eng.
160066	Clarke, D. S.	Pte.	Tr. to Lbr. Pool 20-4-18	Oxgang Cottage, Kirkintulloch, Scotland.
703116	Clarke, G. S.	Pte.	Apptd. a trustee in acc. with regs. for Battalion Trust Funds.	P.O. Box 196, Penticton, B.C.
126706	Clarke, H.	C.S.M.	W. 21-10-16 (Regina) to Eng.	34 Oxford St., Woodstock, Ont.
3030818	Clarke, H. F.	Pte.	W. 27-9-18 (Cambrai) to Eng.	c/o Bank of Nova Scotia, Hamilton, Ont.
907140	Clarke, H. O.	Pte.	Evac. sick 17-4-17 to Eng.	151 Cudworth Rd., S. Willisboro, Ashford, Kent, Eng.
3314149	Clarke, J.	Pte.	K. i. a. 27-9-18 (Cambrai)	Mrs. Clarke, Stop 19, Welland, Ont.
3109418	Claus, R. C.	Pte.	Evac. sick 27-2-19	P.O. Box 119, Ridgeway, Ont.
3314175	Clay, C. A.	Pte.	W. 2-9-18 (2nd Arras) to Eng.	13 Calvin St., St. Catherines, Ont.
3107155	Cleaveland, F. M.	Pte.		St. Paul Hotel, New York City, N.Y., U.S.A.
252474	Cleghorn, W. L.	Pte.	W. 9-4-17 (Vimy); w. 17-8-17 (Lens) to Eng.	Newmains, Lanarkshire, Scot.
252593	Clemens, W. H.	Pte.	K. i. a. 18-11-17 (Passchendaele)	W. Clemens, Breslau, Ont.
1004213	Clement, A.	Pte.	W. 17-2-18 (Oppy); w. 2-11-18 (Valenciennes) to Eng.	
447469	Clements, H. A.	Pte.	W. 1-10-18 (Cambrai)	La Chute, Que.
763470	Clements, R.	Pte.	W. 7-4-17 (Vimy); w. 17-11-17 (Passchendaele) to Eng.	117 38th Ave., Parkhill, Calgary, Alta.
540232	Clendenning, C. E.	L.-C.		Bent River, Ont.
246379	Cleveland, C.	Pte.	W. 11-11-17 (Passchendaele) to Eng.	Markham, Ont.
249459	Cline, F.	Pte.	K. i. a. 27-9-18 (Cambrai)	Edmonton, Alta.
703581	Clinton, T.	Pte.	Evac. sick 29-1-19	Mrs. Cline, 17 Turner Ave., Toronto, Ont.
3108561	Clotworthy, S. D.	Pte.	Evac. sick 17-12-18 to Eng.	Ellison's P.O., Larkin, B.C.
102750	Clucas, G.	Pte.	W. 11-5-17 (1st Triangle) to Eng.	43 James St., Newtownards, Ireland.
703512	Clyde, W. T.	Pte.	Tr. to 51st Bn. 2-8-16	Lydene, Croukburne Rd., Douglas, Isle of Man.
317017	Clysdale, A.	Pte.	W. 2-9-18 (2nd Arras) to Eng.	c/o Mrs. G. H. Brown, Lacombe, Alta.
136435	Coatsworth, C. H.	Pte.	Evac. sick 13-11-16 to Eng.	Park Road, Oshawa, Ont.
727114	Cobb, F.	Pte.	K. i. a. 18-11-17 (Passchendaele)	No address available.
102707	Cochran, H. L.	Pte.		Mrs. Cobb, 1 Alfred St., Northampton, Eng.
3109939	Cochrane, C. R.	Pte.	W. 30-9-18 (Cambrai)	D. W. Cochran, Nanaimo River P.O., B.C.
814413	Cochrane, G. U.	Pte.		223 Gloucester St., Steelton, Ont. Miss Cochrane, St. Joseph's Convent, Hamilton, Ont.

Number	Name	Rank	Details	Address
1066068	Cochrane, R. A.	Pte.	Tr. to 31st Bn. 12-8-18	c/o Mrs. H. S. Cochrane, R.R. No. 3, Clifford, Ont.
907288	Cockwill, E.	Pte.	W. 5-11-17 (Passchendaele) to Eng.	Edgeley, Sask.
3314293	Cockhead, W. H.	Pte.		55 Kingsdown Rd., Upper Stratton, Nr. Swindon, Eng.
703969	Cody, H. T.	Pte.	Evac. sick 6-11-17 to Eng.	Cody's, New Brunswick.
1029905	Coe, C. H.	Pte.	W. 17-6-17 (1st Triangle) to Eng.	McKay's Postoffice, B.C.
138234	Coe, P. H.	Pte.	Tr. to 75th Bn 9-6-17	No address available.
455338	Cohun, J.	Pte.	W. 6-9-17 (Lens); w. 1-11-17 (Passchendaele) to Eng.	46 Red Lion St., Holborn, London, Eng.
226572	Colr, W. K.	Pte.	Acc. inj. 4-3-18 to Eng.	Morrisburg, Ont.
252573	Cole, F. W.	Pte.	W. 9-4-17 (Vimy) to Eng.	6 Stanhope Cove, Church End, Finchley, London, Eng.
703362	Cole, J. J.	Pte.	Tr. to 51st Bn. 2-8-16	21 Cuthbert St., Montreal, Que.
704010	Coleman, J.	Pte.	Att. 11th C.I.B. Bombers; to Eng. for commission 2-5-17	
220042	Coleman, W. F.	Pte.	W. 14-2-17 (Vimy) to Eng.	Courtenay, B.C.
760009	Collier, C. H.	Pte.	Evac. sick 4-6-17 to Eng.	Bell St. Carleton Place, Ont.
200149	Collier, G. A.	Pte.	Evac. sick 17-10-17 to Eng.	40 Sheridan Ave., Toronto, Ont.
761096	Collier, H. B.	Cpl.		2520 Wellington Ave., Collingwood East, Vancouver.
704162	Collier-Wright, J.R.C.	Pte.	W. 20-10-16 (Regina) to Eng.	1183 McMillan Ave. (Fort Rouge), Winnipeg, Man.
703459	Collins, C.	Pte.	Evac. sick 18-10-18 to Eng.	Parksville, V.I., B.C.
249897	Collins, D. W.	Pte.	Evac. sick 30-9-18 to Eng.	Chute, Standon, Hants, Eng.
703461	Collins, E.	Pte.	Evac. sick in Eng. 17-11-18.	c/o A. Pullman, The Coomb, Hespeller, Ont.
240237	Collins, F. J. G.	Pte.		Chute, Standon, Hants, Eng.
3317147	Collins, J. J.	Pte.		Creighton Rd., Dundas, Ont.
703858	Collins, W. C.	Pte.	Evac. sick 22-11-16 to Eng.	R.R. No. 1, Campbellford, Ont.
760364	Collss, R. H.	Pte.		P.O. Box 357, Grand Forks, B.C.
238155	Colman, A.	Pte.	Missing after action, 9-4-17 (Vimy)	2622 44th Ave., Collingwood East, Vancouver, B.C.
907161	Colwill, F.	Pte.		Colchester, Essex, Eng. (Mrs. Colman)
703833	Comerford, E. W.	Pte.	Tr. to 51st Bn. 2-8-16	Blackwater, Ont.
3317285	Compeau, F.	Pte.	W. 3-9-18 (2nd Arras)	c/o St. Joseph's Hospital, Comox, B.C.
703776	Conbery, T.	Pte.	Evac. sick 11-11-16 to Eng.	Midland, Ont.
102465	Conly, J.	Pte.	Tr. to 8th Can. Area Emp. Co. 27-9-17	27 Meadows St., Watertown, N.Y., U.S.A.
129019	Connell, A. G.	Pte.	Tr. to C.C.A.C. Folkestone 3-9-16	Gerteraigh Cottage, Millaston, Nr. Glasgow, Scot.
219113	Connor, R.	Pte.	Tr. to 11th C.L.T.M.B. 19-7-16	12 Redcliffe Rd., Westham, Essex, Eng.
703144	Conrod, H. B.	Sgt	W. 21-10-16 (Regina) to Eng.	No address available.
2527400	Conway, J. W.	Pte.		P.O. Box 278, Cumberland, B.C.
3109938	Conway, T. W.	Pte.	Evac. sick 15-12-18 to Eng.	27 Lockwood Rd., Toronto, Ont.
703415	Cook, D.	Pte.	Tr. to Lbr. Pool 9-3-18	224 Huron St., S. S. Marie, Ont.
663151	Cook, E.	Pte.	W. 1-10-18 (Cambrai)	664 Kingsway, Vancouver, B.C.
703323	Cook, E. V.	Pte.	W. 23-3-17 (Vimy) to Eng.	644 St. Clarence Ave., Toronto, Ont.
126014	Cook, H. G.	Pte.	Tr. to 51st Bn. 2-8-16	Alert Bay, B.C.
1003628	Cook, W.	Pte.		90 Wilson St., Woodstock, Ont.
249845	Cook, W.	Pte.	W. 6-9-18 (2nd Arras) to Eng.	Morrisville, Manitoulin Islands, Ont.
249726	Coombs, G. E.	Pte.	W. 1-10-18 (Cambrai) to Eng.	Elmwood Terrace, Collingham, Nr. Leeds, Eng.
703148	Cooper, A.	Sgt	W. 15-9-16 (St. Eloi); w. 21-10-16 (Regina) to Eng.	11 Morse St., Toronto, Ont.
252464	Cooper, H. A.	Pte.	W. 9-4-17 (Vimy); w. 18-11-17 (Passchendaele) to Eng.	c/o Victoria Whaling Co., Victoria, B.C.
760860	Cooper, W.	Pte.	Tr. to Lbr. Pool 24-1-18	Aupney-Crucis, Nr. Cirencester, Eng.
				5020 Walden St., South Vancouver, B.C.

706492	Copas, F.	Pte.	k. 1. a. 9-4-17 (Vimy)	O. Copas, 130 Menzies St., Victoria, B.C.
100259	Cope, F. H.	Pte.	Tr. to C.C.C. Inf. School 14-8-17	No address available.
703302	Copeland, J.	Pte.	W. 24-10-17 (Passchendaele)	Lillooet, B.C.
703254	Copeland, W.	Sgt.	Lewis Gun N.C.O. from 30-1-18	Langley Prairie P.O., B.C.
115518	Coppen, E. H.	Pte.	Tr. to Lbr. Pool 9-6-18	Clifford Place, Thundersleigh, Rayleigh, Essex, Eng.
540231	Coppin, C. S.	C.S.M.		c/o 37 Norway Ave., Toronto, Ont.
13091	Copus, C. W.	C.S.M.	Dec. D.C.M. (Cambrai) C.R.O. 2029	86 Mitcham Rd. West Croydon, Surrey, Eng.
703799	Corbett, T. E.	Pte.	W. 9-4-17 (Vimy) to Eng.	P.O. Box 171, New Westminster, B.C.
2529371	Corby, E. H.	Pte.	W. 8-8-18 (Amiens) to Eng.	c/o Mrs. Chas. Burgent, Cultus, Norfold Co., Ont.
1003382	Corby, W. R.	Pte.	D. o. s. 25-10-18	John Corby, Wellingsborough, Northants, Eng.
703363	Corcoran, J.	Pte.	W. 22-10-16 (Regina) to Eng.	62 Lee Bg., cor. Main & Broadway, Vancouver, B.C.
703859	Corcoran, W. G.	Pte.	W. 8-8-18 (Amiens) to Eng.	Mount Bridge, Ont.
228013	Cork, W. E.	Pte.	Tr. to Eng. (C1.B1) 13-12-18	528 College St., Toronto, Ont.
249401	Corless, F.	Pte.	Tr. to 61st Bn. 2-8-16	110 Greenlaw Ave., Toronto, Ont.
703066	Cormack, D.	Pte.	W. 9-4-17 (Vimy) to Eng.	c/o Mrs. J. Dixon, New Brunswick P.O., N.B.
760727	Cormack, J.	Pte.	Tr. to 54th Bn. 6-11-17	Somerlie, Wick, Scotland.
102010	Cory, S. C.	Sgt.	Tr. to 54th Bn. C.M.G. 13-3-18	Steveston, B.C.
739095	Cosens, W. E.	Pte.	W. 9-4-17 (Vimy) to Eng.	Cayuga, Ont.
704110	Costello, T.	Pte.		Georges St., Kiltimagh, Co. Mayo, Ire.
102741	Cothran, G. E.	L-S.	Dec. M.M. (2nd Arras) C.R.O. 1989; tr. to Eng. for commission 31-10-18	5312 Alki Ave., Seattle, Wash., U.S.A.
703468	Cotte, A.	Pte.	Acc. inj. tr. to C.C.A.C. 5-12-16	1033 Pender St. W., Vancouver, B.C.
220225	Couch, J.	Pte.	D. o. w. 2-11-17 (Passchendaele)	Mrs. Couch, 1102 Princess St., Victoria, B.C.
931511	Coughlan, C. A.	Pte.	D. o. w. 11-6-17 (2nd Triangle)	Mrs. Coughlan, 220 4th Ave. S., Saskatoon, Sask.
760602	Couling, E. H.	Pte.		2222 Powell St., Vancouver, B.C.
760507	Couling, W.	Pte.	Tr. to Eng. as minor, 17-6-17	2222 Powell St., Vancouver, B.C.
3317163	Coulter, G. H.	Pte.	D. o. w. 1-10-18 (Cambrai)	Mrs. Coulter, Novar P.O., Ont.
3314438	Coulter, J. G.	Pte.		19 Ontario Ave., Hamilton.
219328	Coulter, R.	Pte.	evac. sick 21-10-16 to Eng.	No address available.
145833	Coombes, H.	Pte.	Tr. to 77th Bn 10-8-16	P.O. Box 62, Renfrew, Ont.
2528507	Counsell, G. E.	Pte.	W. 5-9-18 (2nd Arras) to Eng.	13 Walkerside Dairy, Walkerville, Ont.
907142	Coupal, H.	Pte.	W. 9-4-17 (Vimy) to Eng.	St. Jacques-le-Mineur, Que.
907553	Cousins, J. R.	Pte.	Evac. sick in Eng. 24-12-17	Scott, Sask.
1003488	Coutch, J. W.	Pte.	Evac. sick 26-10-17 to Eng.; tr. to Eng. for R.N.W.M.P.	J75 3rd Ave. East, Owen Sound, Ont.
908105	Cowan, B. W.	L-C.	W. 9-4-17 (Vimy); tr. to Eng. for R.N.W.M.P. 13-1-19	
3314027	Cowan, W. M.	Pte.	W. 4-9-18 (2nd Arras)	Stoughton, Sask.
907568	Cowherd, J.	Pte.	W. 9-4-17 (Vimy); tr. Can. Corps Sigs. 6-12-17	27 Lappin Ave., Toronto, Ont.
180024	Cox, M. M.	Sgt.	W. 20-5-17 (1st Triangle) to Eng.	22 Regina Court, Regina, Sask.
760713	Crabb, C.	Pte.	W. 8-1-18 (Mericourt) to Eng.	523 King Edward Ave., Ottawa, Ont.
3106589	Crabb, J. G.	Pte.	Evac. sick 28-1-19	P.O. Box 157, Steveston, B.C.
540109	Crabbe, H. B.	Pte.	K. i. a. 22-10-16 (Regina)	R.R. No. 1, Linwood, Levensworth, Kansas, U.S.A.
703307	Craig, A. J.	Pte.	Tr. to Can. Sig. Pool, 8-3-18	No address available.
907066	Craig, C. B.	Pte.	W. 9-4-17 (Vimy); w. 31-10-17 (Passchendaele) to Eng.	Lillooet, B.C.
540507	Craig, G. A.	L-S.	Dec. M.M. (Somme) D.R.O. 375; k. i. a. 9-4-17 (Vimy)	Carstairs, Alta.
3108376	Craig, J. W.	Pte.		Mrs. D. Craig, 88 McKenzie Crescent, Toronto, Ont. Gowganda, New Ontario.

200209	Craig, W. A.	Pte.	W. 12-11-17 (Passchendaele) to Eng.	1172 Bidwell St., Vancouver, B.C.
703028	Craige, J. M.	Pte.	Tr. to Eng. 8-1-19	1845 23rd Ave. East, South Vancouver, B.C.
703061	Craige, J. M.	Pte.		1845 23rd Ave. East, South Vancouver, B.C.
200177	Craighead, W. J. P.	Pte.	K. l. a. 17-11-17 (Passchendaele)	Mrs. Craighead, 1019 6th St. New Westminster, B.C.
103074	Craigmyle, J.	Pte.	Tr. to 26th Bn. 25-3-18	1703 Lee Ave., Victoria, B.C.
703057	Cramer, T. L.	Pte.	W. 1-11-17 (Passchendaele) to Eng.	Courtenay, B.C.
3314072	Cramp, W. R.	Pte.	W. 4-9-18 (Vimy) to Eng.	Dunville, Ont.
3109895	Crane, J. H.	Pte.	W. 2-11-18 (Valenciennes) to Eng.	5 Pleasant Place, Church Rd., Tottenham, London.
225377	Crawford, C. E.	Pte.	W. 8-8-18 (Amiens) to Eng.	River Desert, Que.
3108795	Crawford, G. J.	Pte.	Evac. sick 21-10-17 to Eng.	451 King St. W., Hamilton, Ont.
703321	Crawford, H.	Pte.		1120 Robson St., Vancouver, B.C.
3110237	Crawford, J. S.	Pte.		P.O. Box 115, Dundas, Ont.
3317024	Crawford, P. R.	Pte.		Sterviacke, Nova Scotia.
	Crawford, R. E.	Cpl.		Rosseau P.O., Ont.
126360	Cree, C. E. H.	Pte.	W. 14-11-17 (Passchendaele)	21 Railway Ave., Stratford, Ont.
704161	Creech, S. H.	Pte.	Tr. to Eng. 22-11-17	Colquitz P.O., B.C.
704006	Creelman, A.	Pte.	Tr. to Lbr. Pool 9-6-18	Terrace, B.C.
706062	Creffield, C. S.	Sgt.	W. 30-9-18 (Cambrai); evac. sick 14-1-19 to Eng.	2549 Victor St., Victoria, B.C.
1003799	Cressey, E. R.	Pte	Evac. sick 12-3-18 to Eng.	Copper Cliff, Ont.
102097	Crewe, H.	L.-C.	W. 8-8-18 (Amiens) to Eng.	346 Oak St., Victoria, B.C.
219192	Crickett, H. J.	Pte.	Tr. to 51st Bn. 2-8-16.	No address available.
3109554	Crocker, C. F.	Pte.		Parry Sound, Ont.
908073	Crompton, F.	Pte.	W. 9-4-17 (Vimy) to Eng.	251 Newbay Rd., Newbey, Nr. Rochdale, Lancs., Eng.
907607	Crone, A. D.	Pte.	W. 19-8-18 (Amiens) to Eng.	Richardson, Sask.
703637	Crook, F. J.	Cpl.	Men. In Despatches L.G. 1-1-19	7 Norfolk St., Bolton, Lancs., Eng.
706027	Crookston, G.	Sgt.	Tr. to Eng. for commission 23-8-18	16 Chichester Rd., Seaford, Sussex, Eng. (Bayside), Burnaby, B.C.
706937	Cross, A. N.	Pte.	W. 8-8-18 (Amiens) to Eng.	680 Princess St., Woodstock, Ont.
127274	Cross, J. T.	Pte.	Tr. to 51st Bn. 2-8-16	Little Current, Ont.
754165	Crossley, A. S.	Pte.	W. 24-3-18 (Lens) to Eng.	725 Princess St., New Westminster, B.C.
703698	Crouse, W.	Pte.	Dec. M.M. (Valenciennes) C.R.O. 2028	R.R. No. 2, Elindale, Ont.
3108113	Crowe, A. E.	Pte.	D. o. s. 6-1-19	Mrs. J. Crowe, P.O. Box 33, Cranbrook, B.C.
703945	Crowe, G.	Pte.	D. o. w. 2-10-18 (2nd Arras)	J. Crowe, Milton, Ont.
3314292	Crowe, J. W.	Pte.	D. o. w. 2-10-18 (2nd Arras)	c/o Mrs. Saberton, 245 B, Queen's Rd., Battersea Pk., London, Eng.
1004193	Crowley, E.	Pte.	W. 2-9-18 (2nd Arras) to Eng.	
180450	Crowshaw, W. H.	L.-C.	W. 9-6-17 (2nd Triangle) to Eng.	21 Maple Rd., Chisworth, Derbyshire, Eng.
183328	Cummer, H. E.	Pte.	W. 1-10-18 (Cambrai) to Eng.	1218 First St. E., Calgary, Alta.
3314287	Cunliffe, L.	Pte.		18 Upper Coomber Rd., South Croydon, London, Eng.
160563	Cunliffe, H.	Pte	W. 23-7-16 (Somme) to Eng.	No address available.
1003406	Cunningham, A. A.	Pte.	Tr. to 4th C.M.G.C. 1-5-18	228 Cathcart St., Steelton, Ont.
252714	Cunningham, R. J.	Pte.	Evac. sick 16-2-17 to Eng.	No address available.
681090	Cunningham, W. J.	Pte.	Evac. sick 16-6-18 to Eng.	192 Jarvis St., Toronto, Ont.
1003359	Curran, J.	Pte.	K. l. a. 18-11-17 (Passchendaele)	Mrs. J. Curran, Ardoch P.O., Ont.
760185	Currie, A. B.	Pte.	Tr. to Lbr. Pool, 8-11-17	3436 27th Ave. E., Vancouver, B.C.
908194	Currie, J. C.	Pte.	K. l. a. 9-4-17 (Vimy)	Mrs. A. J. Currie, Kenora, Ont.

3105292	Currie, J. W.	Pte.	Missing after action, 1-10-18 (Cambrai); believed taken prisoner	Miss J. Currie, New Row, Coleraine, Co. Derry, Ire.
663084	Currie, R. H.	Pte	W. 8-8-18 (Amiens) to Eng	Milton Heights, Ont.
1003875	Currier, J. A.	Pte.	K. i. a. 4-9-18 (2nd Arras)	T. Currier, Wabashine, Simcoe Co., Ont.
1003330	Currier, P.	Pte.	Evac. sick 9-11-17 to Eng	Webbwood, Ont.
704122	Curtis, J. M.	Pte.	Tr. to Eng. 8-10-17	11 Cook St., Victoria, B.C.
3105653	Curtis, T. L.	Pte.	D. o. w. 29-9-18 (Cambrai)	T. S. Curtis, 1231 First St. N.E., Washington, D.C.
703117	Curwain, S. T.	Pte.	Tr. o to 3rd Can. Pioneers, 4-6-17	c/o Miss Curwain, 30 Cavendish Rd., Mill Rd., Cambridge, Eng.
18636	Cuthbert, J.	Pte.	K. i. a. 17-11-17 (Passchendaele)	J. Cuthbert, Graybank House, Perth, Scot.
1003891	Cyr, D.	Pte.	W. 31-10-17 (Passchendaele); w. 15-3-18 (Lens)	c/o Mrs. H. Couture, L'Aise du Cap, Que.
703513	Dade, H.	Pte		95 Falmouth Ave. East, Highman's Park, Essex, Eng.
760929	Daem, L.	Pte	W. 26-1-18 (Mericourt); w. 2-11-18 (Valenciennes) to Eng	
788560	Dagg, W. A. R.	Pte.	W. and missing 13-6-17 (2nd Triangle)	Box 453, Revelstoke, B.C.
1003658	Daggett, A.	L-C	W. 23-7-18 (Oppy)	Portage-le-Forte.
478917	Dahlin, G. A.	Pte.	W. 27-9-18 (Cambrai)	Garston Mine, Ont.
727463	Dahm, L. W.	Cpl	W. 2-9-18 (2nd Arras) to Eng	Mount Vernon, Washington, D.C., U.S.A.
1003493	Daimpre, A. D.	Sgt.	Dec. M.M. (Cambrai) C.R.O. 1989	11 Park St., Kitchener, Ont.
540136	Deines, C. C.	Pte.	K. i. a. 15-10-16 (Somme)	Colbrook, Devon, Eng.
703860	Daly, F.	Pte.	W. 15-8-17 (Lens); w. to Eng. 13-5-18 (Oppy)	No address available. c/o Mrs. Carey, "The Alliance," W. Hampstead, London, Eng.
907259	Daly, J.	Pte.	W. 11-5-17 (1st Triangle) to Eng	26 Pine Grove, Bootle, Liverpool, Eng.
703396	Daly, W.	Pte.	Tr. to 51st Bn. 2-8-16	1132 Empress Ave., Victoria, B.C.
1003164	Danak, J.	Pte.	Tr. to 71st Can. Forestry Corps 9-4-18	No address available.
703440	Dancy, B. M.	Pte.	W. 21-10-16 (Regina): w. 1-10-18 (Cambrai) to Eng	
180037	Dandridge, J.	Pte.	W. 11-5-17 (1st Triangle)	1460 12th St., Detroit, Mich., U.S.A.
2529353	D'Angelo, P.	Pte.	K. i. a. 4-9-18 (2nd Arras)	East Hanney, Berks, Eng.
703800	Daniels, H. T.	Pte	Tr. to 11th Field Co. C.E. 11-5-17	E. D'Angelo, Offida, Ascoto, Piceno, Italy.
219248	Dann, G. F.	Pte.		Point Grey P.O., Vancouver, B.C.
138265	Darby, E. P.	Cpl.	Tr. to 75th Bn. 9-6-17	c/o A. D. Mason, 48 Bedford Ave., Buffalo, N.Y., U.S.A.
1090130	Darling, S. C.	Pte.	W. a. 27-9-18 (Cambrai)	No address available.
472186	Darlow, P. J.	Pte.	W. 6-11-18 (Valenciennes) to Eng.	Mrs. F. Darling, Lyn, Ont.
706112	Darrah, W. F.	Pte.	W. 1-11-17 (Passchendaele) to Eng.	2 Froghall, Finchley Rd., Hampstead, London, Eng.
3106230	Dart, R.	Pte.	W. 30-9-18 (Cambrai) to Eng	532 6th Ave. W., Vancouver, B.C.
249858	Davidson, J.	Pte.	W. 27-9-18 (Cambrai)	c/o Borden Ranch, Grady, New Mexico, U.S.A.
703852	Davidson, R. S.	Pte.		28 Scotland St., St. Ansoni, Conn., U.S.A.
440932	Davies, E.	Pte.	W. 4-6-17 (2nd Triangle) to Eng	East Drive, Mount Denis, York Twp., Ont.
240077	Davies, J. C.	Pte.	W. 27-9-18 (Cambrai) to Eng	Phoenix, B.C.
3314299	Davies, M. P.	Pte.		3 St. Michael's Ct., Castle Forgate, Shrewsbury, Eng.
704065	Davies, R.	Cpl.	W. 9-4-17 (Vimy) to Eng	269 King William St., Hamilton, Ont.
161272	Davies, S.	Pte.	K. i. a. 9-4-17 (Vimy)	Dunlavin, Wicklow, Ireland.
226864	Davies, T. E.	Pte.	W. 25-10-17 (Passchendaele) to Eng.	156 Logar Ave., Toronto, Ont.
220494	Davies, W.	Pte.	W. 21-10-16 (Regina); evac. sick 3-5-17 to Eng	T. Davies, 8 Wye Terrace, Bullth, Wales.
3030960	Davis, E. C.	Pte.		13 Lower Cathedral Rd., Cardiff, Wales.
3106424	Davis, S. R.	Pte.	K. i. a. 30-9-18 (Cambrai)	No address available. S. Davis, Richmond Ave., Morgantown, Va., U.S.A. Severn Bridge, Nuskoka, Ont.

Regt. No.	Name	Rank	Remarks	Address
703615	Dawe, J.	Pte.		Prince Rupert, B. C.
1003068	Dawkins, I. U.	Pte.		J. Dawkins, Blind River, Ont.
1003047	Dawkins, B.	Pte.	K. l. a. 6-4-18 (Lens)	Blind River, Ont.
703364	Dawson, B.	Pte.	K. l. a. 6-6-17 (2nd Triangle)	Mrs. P. D. Austin, 7 Windsor Ter., Newcastle, Eng.
703371	Dawson, W. E.	Pte.	W. 11-11-16 (Somme) to Eng.	North Vernon, Ind., U.S.A.
3317025	Deadman, A. J.	Pte.	W. 2-9-18 (2nd Arras) to Eng.	Crooksbury, Farnham, Surrey, Eng.
3106501	Dean, D. A.	Pte.	K. l. a. 4-9-18 (2nd Arras)	Mrs. A. Dean, P.O. Box 2, Dundas Rd., Hamilton, Ont.
226413	Dean, E. C.	Pte.	Tr. to 4th C.M.G.C. 13-5-18	P. O. Box 235, Port Dover, Ont.
2527403	Death, E. C.	Pte.	W. 27-9-18 (Cambrai) to Eng.	Garson Mines, Ont.
850034	Delaney, R. J.	Pte.		141 Russell Ave. St. Catherines, Ont.
663757	De Largie, G. M.	Pte.	Evac. sick 10-1-19 to Eng.	Freeman, Ont.
478841	Deleiko, M.	Pte.	W. 15-8-17 (Lens) to Eng.	No address available.
703999	De Lisle, A. W.	Pte.	D. o. w. 16-9-16 (St. Eloi)	C. A. De Lisle, Quyon P.O., Que.
3109238	Dell, H. C.	Pte.		R.R. No. 1, Port Robinson, Ont.
3108382	Delore, P.	Pte.	Evac. sick 10-3-19	Tweed, Ont.
1003991	Delpinto, P.	Pte.	W. 31-7-18 (Oppy)	No address available.
3105524	De Mello, M.	Pte.	Evac. sick 15-12-18 to Eng.	Southampton, West Bermuda, B.W.I.
540352	De Mill, F.	Pte.	K. l. a. 9-4-17 (Vimy)	J. De Mill, 36 Casaloma Bldg., Winnipeg, Man.
703483	Dendoff, L.	Pte.	Acc. w. 3-11-18 to Eng.	511 Milton St., Nanaimo, B.C.
2529381	Denis, G. A.	Pte.	W. 4-9-18 (2nd Arras)	414 Broadway, Lowell, Mass., U.S.A.
129618	Denman, D. L.	L-C	Evac. sick 15-8-17 to Eng.	Can. War Records Office, Ottawa.
219307	Denning, C. R. J.	Pte.	W. 11-11-16 (Somme) to Eng.	No address available.
704018	Denning, W. E.	Cpl.	Acc. w. 11-1-17; tr. to Eng. for commission 12-1-18	c/o Miss Denning, 59 Trafalgar Rd., Egremont, Cheshire, Eng.
663541	Denyes, M.	Pte.	K. l. a. 2-9-18 (2nd Arras)	Miss M. B. Denyes, Milton, Ont.
1003355	Depew, C.	Pte.	Tr. to Eng. for R.A.F. 30-7-18.	White River, Ont.
1096204	Deremo, G. F.	Pte.	W. 3-9-18 (2nd Arras) to Eng.	c/o Mrs. M. Baldwin, Gen. Del., West Toronto, Ont.
2252292	Dernier, G. J.	Pte.	W. 4-9-18 (2nd Arras) to Eng.	c/o Miss E. Powers, 4607 3rd Ave., Brooklyn, N.Y.
3108385	Deschamps, E.	Pte.		P.O. Box 194, Blind River, Ont.
102937	Deschamps, H.	Pte.		c/o Mrs. Harrison, Quesnel, B.C.
161266	Deschene, E. A.	Pte.	W. 19-2-17 (Vimy); tr. to 11th C.L.T.M.B. 1-10-17	
3108513	Desjardine, G.	Pte.		No address available.
3109081	Desrochers, I.	Pte.	W. 10-4-18 (Oppy); w. 8-8-18 (Amiens); evac. sick 5-2-19	Milford Haven, St. Joseph's Island, Ont.
648241	Desson, G. E.	Pte.		Lafontaine, Ont.
703397	De Tessier, A.	Pte.	Tr. to Eng. for commission 25-4-17; killed during training with R.A.F. in Eng.	1433 15th St. E., Calgary, Alta.
1003097	Dever, W. J.	Pte.	Tr. to 4th C.M.G.C. 1-5-18	Baron de Tessier, 6 Eccleston Sq., London, S.W., Eng.
467466	Devine, J. H.	Pte.	Evac. sick 4-4-18 to Eng.	c/o Mrs. H. Hodgins, Sudbury, Ont.
3109431	Devinnell, G. H.	Pte.	Evac. 2-1-19 to Eng.	Edmonton, Alta.
103056	Devlin, S.	Pte.	W. 27-9-18 (Cambrai) to Eng.	Elmvale, Ont.
2205089	De Vries, L.	Pte.	Evac. sick 26-6-18 to Eng.	Nanaimo, B.C.
3317289	Dick, J.	Pte.	K. l. a. 2-9-18 (2nd Arras)	604 Albert St., Ottawa, Ont.
703025	Dick, J.	L-C	Dec. M.M. (Somme) D.R.O. 386; tr. to Eng. for demob. 11-1-19	Mrs. F. Wood, Midland, Ont. Herlot Bay, B.C.

Regt. No.	Name	Rank	Notes	Address
102233	Dick, R. P.	Sgt.	Dec. M.M. (Amiens) C.R.O. 1899; tr. to Eng. for commission 23-5-18	1014 McCaskill St., Victoria, B.C.
219121	Dickason, R.	Pte.	Evac. sick 26-5-17 to Eng.	No address available.
252050	Dickie, T. H.	Pte.	K. i. a. 9-4-17 (Vimy)	O. S. Dickie, Maple Creek, Sask.
102774	Dickinson, C.	Pte.	W. 2-8-17 (Lens) to Eng.	1433 22nd Ave. S, Vancouver, B.C.
103370	Dickson, H. B.	Pte.	W. 14-5-17 (1st Triangle) to Eng.	27 North Ellen St., Dundee, Scot.
3110657	Digby, G. A.	Pte.		Fesserton, Ont.
703654	Diggle, J.	Cpl	W. 1-9-16 (St. Eloi); w. 14-11-17 (Passchendaele); w. 4-9-18 (2nd Arras) to Eng.	38 Marlborough Rd., Watford, Eng.
907724	Dillon, W. R.	Pte.	K. i. a. 9-4-17 (Vimy)	Mrs. M. Dillon, Wolseley, Sask.
102435	Dineen, J.	Pte.	Tr. to 7th Can. Area Emp. Co. 22-8-17	Milltown Cottage, Limerick, Ire.
3317290	Diotte, G.	Pte.	W. 27-9-18 (Cambrai) to Eng.	c/o Miss Bertha Richard, Penetang, Ont.
703450	Dixon, A.	Pte.	K. i. a. 8-6-17 (2nd Triangle)	Mrs. Dixon, 692 South Alvarado St., Los Angeles, Cal.
763242	Dixon, C.	Pte.	Evac. sick 15-8-18 to Eng.	Port Carling, Ont.
925450	Dixon, G. H.	Pte.	Evac. sick 1-4-18 to Eng.	Glasrevin, Sask.
3314301	Doan, J. W.	Pte.	W. 4-9-18 (2nd Arras) to Eng.	152 Davidson St., Welland, Ont.
703696	Dobb, H. T.	Cpl	W. 19-11-16 (Somme), Provost-Corporal	632 55th Ave. East, South Vancouver, B.C.
102435	Dobson, G. H.	Pte.	K. i. a. 14-11-17 (Passchendaele)	Mrs. S. Dobson, Bruce Mines, Ont.
1003653	Dobson, J. F.	Pte.	D. o. w. 6-6-17 (2nd Triangle)	P. Dobson, 54 Merchiston Ave., Edinburgh, Scot.
102228	Dodd, A. C.	Pte.	W. 12-6-16 (St. Eloi) to Eng.	326 Elm St., P.O. Vernon, B.C.
703993	Dodd, H. R. F.	Cpl.	Post-Corporal	Okanagan Mission, B.C.
706029	Dodds, C. W.	L.-C.		Warrigal, Victoria, Australia.
704097	Dodds, E. G.	Pte.	W. 11-11-16 (Somme) to Eng.	New Westminster, B.C.
790616	Dodds, J. P.	Pte.	Evac. to Eng. from P.B. 15-3-17	1811 River Drive, New Westminster, B.C.
703256	Dodson, O. A.	Pte.	Tr. to 4th C.M.G.C. 1-5-18	200 Holton Ave. S., Hamilton, Ont.
679009	Doherty, P.	Pte.	K. i. a. 22-10-16 (Somme)	F. Doherty, Ardmonmieu, Killorqui, Co. Kerry, Ire.
704020	Doherty, R. R. T.	L.-C.	K. i. a. 11-11-16 (Somme)	Mrs. Doherty, 227 10th St., North Vancouver.
704094	Doherty, W. R.	Pte.	Tr. to Lbr. Pool, 3-5-18.	Sault Ste. Marie, Ont.
1004197	Dolby, A.	Pte.	W. 22-3-17 (Vimy) to Eng.	Sub P.O. 5, cor. 5th and Yew Sts., Kitsilano, Van., B.C.
703316	Dolby, E.	Pte.	W. 15-11-17 (Passchendaele) to Eng; dec. M.M. (Passchendaele) C.R.O. 1571	
703315	Dominity, J.	L.-C.	K. i. a. 27-9-18 (Cambrai)	2175 13th Ave. W., Vancouver, B.C.
184076	Donahue, W. D.	Pte.	W. 21-10-16 (Regina); w. 23-6-17 (2nd Triangle); tr. to 1st Lbr. Bn. 14-9-17	Mr. Dominity, Standorf, Alta.
3108565	Donaldson, J. R.	Pte.	Evac. sick 17-9-16 to Eng.	c/o Mrs. E. Griffiths, R.R. No. 4, Welland, Ont.
703158	Donnelly, E.	Pte	W. 27-9-18 (Cambrai) to Eng.	Burdett, Alta.
703693	Donnelly, F. S.	Pte	W. 30-9-18 (Cambrai); k. i. a. 2-11-18 (Valenciennes)	P.O. Box 16, Fort George, B.C.
851125	Donovan, M.	Pte.	Evac. sick 24-11-16 to Eng.	35 Clarendon St., Glasgow, Scot.
3105437	Donville, L. T.	Pte.	K. i. a. 9-4-17 (Vimy)	Miss M. Donovan, 818 Rush St., Chicago, Ill.
135466	Doolin, M.	Pte	Tr. to Lbr. Pool 29-3-18.	No address available.
252055	Doray, A.	Pte	W. 10-6-17 (2nd Triangle); w. 2-8-17 (Lens)	E. Doolin, Newport, Vermont, U.S.A.
703168	Dott, R. McK.	Pte.	W. 7-1-17 (Merlcourt) to Eng.	Moose Creek, Ont.
219441	Doucett, J.	Pte.	Tr. to 11th C.I.T.M.B. 1-10-17; ret. 14-11-17; dec. M.M. (Cambrai) C.R.O. 1989	No address available.
703682	Douglas, A.	Cpl.	Tr. to 51st Bn 2-8-16	Bellingham, Wash., U.S.A.
703306	Douglas, A.	Pte.	Evac. sick 21-10-18 to Eng.	c/o A. Douglas, Aronbridge, Stirlingshire, Scot.
703444	Douglas, F. J.	Pte.		No address available.
2528460				309 Columbia St., Utica, N.Y., U.S.A.

126019	Douglas, H. F.	Sgt.	W. 20-10-16 (Regina) to Eng.	372 Buller St., Woodstock, Ont.
703208	Douglas, J. A.	Pte.	W. 20-10-16 (Regina) to Eng.	795 Thurlow St., Vancouver, B.C.
249350	Douglass, J.	Pte.	Tr. to 4th C.M.G.C. 1-5-18.	225 Concord Ave., Toronto, Ont.
703978	Dow, W. J.	Pte.	Tr. to 67th Bn. 8-7-16.	111 Robert St., Toronto, Ont.
3106346	Dowd, D. F.	Pte.	Evac. sick 5-3-19.	227 McCauley St., Toronto, Ont.
703309	Dowd, M.	Pte.	W. 19-10-16 (Somme); tr. to Lbr. Pool 17-9-18.	c/o M. M. O'Dowd, 400 W. 14th St., New York City
417953	Dowhaniuk, D.	Pte.	W. 8-6-17 (2nd Triangle) to Eng.	No address available.
703563	Dowling, F.	Pte.	W. 2-9-16 (St. Eloi); w. 22-10-16 (Regina) to Eng.	
225235	Dowsley, J. D.	Pte.		Prince Rupert, B.C.
704099	Doyle, C.	Pte.	Dec. M.M. (Vimy) C.R.O. 1142; w. 15-8-17 (Lens); tr. to Lbr. Pool 31-10-17.	Strasburgh P.O., Penn., U.S.A.
160069	Doyle, C. S.	Pte.	Evac. sick 14-12-16 to Eng.	1831 Robson St., Vancouver, B.C.
908085	Dragasilly, J.	Pte.	W. 4-5-17 (1st Triangle).	No address available.
1006207	Dragon, J.	Pte.		No address available.
1023316	Drinkwater, J. P.	Pte.	D. o. w. 12-6-17 (1st Triangle).	P.O. Box 138, Denis, Richelieu River, P.Q.
1004015	Driscoll, J.	Pte.	W. 16-11-17 (Passchendaele) to Eng.	A. Drinkwater, Alberni, B.C.
907794	Drobot, N.	Pte.	W. 1-11-17 (Passchendaele) to Eng.	c/o Mrs. J. Boucher, Ramsay, Ont.
907686	Drolet, J.	Pte.		Drobot, Sask.
103180	Dryhurst, F.	Pte.	W. 16-8-17 (Lens); d. o. w. 9-8-18 (Amiens).	Keystown, Sask.
				Mrs. J. H. Wensley, 65 Howe St., South Hill, Moose Jaw, Sask.
219952	Duby, G.	Pte.	W. 25-10-16 (Somme) to Eng.	No address available.
2528445	Dubey, M. L.	L.-C.	Evac. sick 27-3-19 to Eng.	40 Delzeele St., Detroit, Mich., U.S.A.
907628	Duchesneau, D.	Cpl.		Estevan, Sask.
3109433	Duckworth, E. S.	Pte.		13 Court St., Dundas, Ont.
2527308	Duckworth, H.	Pte.	Acc. inj. 18-7-18.	773 South 13th St., Newark, N.J., U.S.A.
706496	Dudley, A. A.	Pte.	K. i. a. 9-4-17 (Vimy).	Mrs. M. Dudley, 24 Vincent Rd., Dorking, Eng.
3317069	Duff, F. L.	Pte.	W. 1-10-18 (Cambrai) to Eng.	c/o Mrs. Stoneburg, 157 Sumach St., Toronto, Ont.
931232	Duff, R. J.	Pte.	W. 2-9-18 (2nd Arras) to Eng.	c/o C.P.R., Golden, B.C.
103087	Duffield, A.	Pte.	K. i. a. 6-6-17 (2nd Triangle).	Mrs. S. J. Duffield, Calamut Ave., Cloverdale, Maywood P.O., Victoria, B.C.
703402	Duguid, G.	Pte.	K. i. a. 3-9-18 (2nd Arras).	Mrs. J. Craig, Marpole Station, B.C.
183078	Duhamel, J.	Pte.	Tr. to 11th M.G.C. 10-12-16.	No address available.
703464	du Jardin, F. G.	Cpl.	Tr. to Record Office 11-8-16; tr. to 29th Bn. 10-4-18.	
3317026	Duncan, C. H.	Pte.	W. 4-9-18 (Vimy) to Eng.	C.P.R. Hotel, Sicamous, B.C.
135666	Duncan, G. L.	Pte.	Evac. sick 21-10-16 to Eng.	107 Richmond St., Oshawa, Ont.
703586	Duncan, F.	Pte.	Dec. M.M. (Vimy) C.R.O. 1236.	No address available.
703746	Duncan, J.	Pte.	Evac. wounded to Eng. 8-12-17 (Passchendaele)	138 6th Ave. E., Vancouver, B.C.
703214	Duncan, R. G.	Sgt.	N.C.O. Medical Detail; dec. M.M. (2nd Arras) C.R.O. 1930; d. o. w. 28-9-18 (Cambrai)	209 King St., Broughty Ferry, Scotland.
649070	Duncan, T. R.	Pte.	Evac. sick 16-11-17 to Eng.	Rev. W. Duncan, Sandwick, V.I., B.C.
1103732	Duncanson, J. F.	Pte.	Evac. sick 14-7-18 to Eng.	22 Salcott Rd., Clapham, London, Eng.
931268	Dunn, J. H.	C.S.M.	Dec. D.C.M. (Amiens) C.R.O. 1930.	Silver-Water, Manitoulin Islands, Ont.
703571	Dunn, J. J.	C.S.M.	Tr. to 11th M.G.C. 8-2-17.	107 Cedar St., Boston, Mass., U.S.A.
2529322	Dunn, J. W.	Pte.	K. i. a. 30-9-18 (Cambrai).	c/o Bank of Commerce, Prince Rupert, B.C.
				J. Dunn, 11 Holborn Terrace, Ryton-on-Tyne, Northumberland, Eng.
1004244	Dunn, V. W.	Pte.	Sick in Eng. 11-10-18.	Oshawa, Ont.

249319	Dunning, J.	Pte.	W. 11-4-18 (Oppy) to Eng.	83 Solway St., Belfast, Ireland.
907186	Dunphy, P. A.	Sgt.	W. 2-9-18 (2nd Arras); k. i. a. 2-11-18 (Valenciennes).	
727081	Dunsmore, A. J.	Sgt.	K. i. a. 8-8-18 (Amiens).	Mrs. E. Dunphy, 1445 Retallack St., Regina, Sask.
3106113	Dupree, J.	Pte.	K. i. a. 27-9-18 (Cambrai).	Mr. J. Dunsmore, R.R. No. 1, St. Paul, Ont.
2528371	Durbin, W. H.	Pte.	W. 3-9-18 (2nd Arras); w. 27-8-18 (Cambrai).	Mrs. L. S. Swain, 771 Polk Ave., Memphis, Tenn.
703334	Durham, C.	Pte.	Tr. to 51st Bn. 2-8-16.	Mrs. B. Boncelle, Oak Harbour, Wash., U.S.A.
704057	Durnford, F. H.	Pte.		Kitselas, Vancouver, B.C.
907546	Durnin, G. C.	Pte.	W. 11-6-17 (2nd Triangle); evac. sick 27-11-17 to Eng.	717 So. L, Tacoma, Wash., U.S.A.
226981	Durrell, J. S.	Pte.	W. 2-9-18 (2nd Arras).	Stoughton, Sask.
102776	Dutot, P. D.	Pte.	W. 12-5-17 (1st Triangle) to Eng.	188 McIntyre St., North Bay, Ont.
225853	Dwight, A.	Pte.	Evac. sick 4-5-18 to Eng.	1246 Fort St., Victoria, B.C.
207146	Dwyer, P.	Pte.	W. 9-6-17 (2nd Triangle) to Eng.	118 Clinton St., Toronto, Ont.
2528311	Dyer, P.	Pte.	W. 3-9-18 (2nd Arras); tr. to C.C.R.C. 12-2-19.	Carrigaholt, Clare Co., Ireland.
102962	Dyson, A.	Pte.	W. 6-5-17 (1st Triangle; dec. Cross of St. George, Cl. IV. (Russian) Lond. Gaz. 30467 14-1-18.	c/o Mrs. Gray, 3 Birch Ave., Hamilton, Ont.
703514	Eagleson, M. J.	Pte.	Tr. to 11th C.L.T.M.B. 1-10-17.	c/o Mrs. C. A. Burros, Fraser Mills, B.C.
220284	Eames, H. D.	L.-C.	W. 1-9-16 (St Eloi) to Eng.	Lillooet, B.C.
249727	Early, G. J. A.	Pte.	Tr. to 4th C.M.G.C. 1-5-18.	No address available.
2528462	Earnshaw, J. S.	Pte.	Tr. to 4th C.M.G.C. 1-5-18.	72 Spruce St, Toronto, Ont.
3030701	East, G. T.	Pte.		129 Rebecca St., Stratford, Ont.
3110210	Easton, W. P.	Pte.		5 Margueretta Ter., Oakley St., Chelsea, Eng.
703265	Eastwood, A. R.	Pte.	Tr. to 231st Bn. 1916.	P.O. Box 141 Brantford, Ont.
703864	Eaton, C.	Pte.	Tr. to 11th Can. Area Emp. Co. 22-8-17.	c/o Mrs. J. Aspinal, 2 Raincliffe Tce., Leeds, Eng.
703863	Eaton, E. G.	Pte.	W. 9-4-17 (Vimy) to Eng.	c/o S. I. Eaton, Martley, Worcestershire, Eng.
704019	Eby, E.	Sgt.	Evac. sick 16-3-19, Post-Sergeant.	P.O. Box 423, Grand Forks, B.C.
3105944	Eckenrod, W. W.	Pte.		Terrace, B.C.
663087	Eden, H.	Pte.	W. 27-9-18 (Cambrai) to Eng.	P.O. Box 15, Uniontown, Penn., U.S.A.
183806	Edgar, H.	Pte.	Tr. to 11th M.G.C. 10-12-16.	Bartonville, Hamilton, Ont.
925404	Edgar, H. W.	Pte.	W. 13-4-17 (Vimy) to Eng.	No address available.
931233	Edgington, A.	Pte.	W. and missing after action 9-4-17 (Vimy).	Wroxeter, Ont.
760982	Edmond, R. E.	Pte.		2608 Ontario St., Vancouver, B.C.
703446	Edmonds, J. S.	Pte.	W. 9-8-16 (St. Eloi); w. 20-10-16 (Regina) to Eng.	Mrs. M. E. Edmond, 615 8th Ave. E., Vancouver, B.C.
103362	Edwards, A.	Pte.	Dec. M.M. (2nd Triangle) C.R.O. 1335; k. i. a. 6-9-17 (Lens).	Vernon, B.C.
103085	Edwards, G.	Pte.	W. 12-5-17 (1st Triangle); w. 27-9-18 (Cambrai) to Eng.	Mrs. A. Edwards, 1619 Denman St., Victoria, B.C.
255057	Edwards, G. A.	Pte.	W. 14-5-17 (1st Triangle) to Eng.	c/o Mrs. J. Getthings, 135 Raleigh Rd., North St., Ashton Gate, Bedminster, Bristol, Eng.
1032662	Edwards, J H.	Pte.	W. 8-8-18 (Amiens); to Eng.	Freecastle, Breconshire, Wales.
6492220	Edwards, M. R.	Pte.	W. 3-9-18 (2nd Arras); evac. sick 18-10-18 to Eng.	Walford, Ont.
908298	Edwards, N T.	Pte.	W. 9-4-17 (Vimy) to Eng.	Thornloe, Ont.
126746	Edward, W. B.	Pte.	K. i. a. 8-8-18 (Amiens).	Findlater, Sask.
3106545	Egan, W.	Pte.	W. 1-10-18 (Cambrai) to Eng.	Mrs. Edwards, Lakefield, Ont.
				Dayton, Ont.

210345	Eggett, C.	Cpl.	K. 1. a. 13-3-18 (Lens)	Mrs. J. Eggett, 682 Princess Ave., London, Ont.
703703	Eldridge, C. K.	Cpl.	W. 14-9-16 (St. Eloi) to Eng.	Beaver Harbour, New Brunswick.
3109242	Eller, I.	Pte.		R.R. No. 1, Fonthill, Ont.
183163	Elliott, C.	Pte.	W. 9-4-17 (Vimy); w. 1-11-17 (Passchendaele) to Eng.	1437 2nd St., N.W., Calgary, Alta.
102805	Elliott, G. B.	L.-C.	W. 30-9-18 (Cambrai); men. in despatches, L.G. 8-7-19.	
760085	Elliott, J.	Pte.	Tr. to Lbr. Pool, 17-9-18	703 Fort St., Victoria, B.C.
703669	Elliott, R.	Pte.		2127 Stephen St., Kitsilano, Vancouver, B.C.
2250721	Ellis, F. L.	Pte.	Tr. to Eng. from P.B. 8-1-19	c/o Miss S. Elliott, 612 Gollowgate, Glasgow, Scot.
907625	Ellis, H.	Pte.	Sick in Eng. on leave 29-11-17	763 Bird Ave., Buffalo, N.Y., U.S.A.
				c/o Mrs. K. Bedwell, 10 Eldon Rd., High St., Walthamstow, London, Eng.
703902	Ellis, J. B.	Pte.	W. 18-11-16 (Somme); tr. to Eng. from P.B. 11-1-19	Bellevue Cottage, Cookham, Maidenhead, Eng.
3314143	Ellis, P. W.	Pte.	W. 27-9-18 (Cambrai) to Eng.	Moulinette, Ont.
200206	Ellis, S. E. W.	Pte.	W. 2-9-18 (2nd Arras)	514 Sturdee St., Esquimalt, B.C.
103291	Elms, O. W.	Pte.	W. 9-4-17 (Vimy) to Eng.	2525 7th Ave. W., Vancouver, B.C.
703338	Elmsile, A.	Sgt.	Tr. to Can. Corps Gas Services 27-2-18	C.A.P.C., Drill Hall, Victoria, B.C.
3106418	Elving, R. R.	Pte.	Evac. sick 5-12-18 to Eng.	c/o Mrs. A. Fox, 381 Victoria Ave., Hamilton, Ont.
180039	Ely, R. H.	Pte.	W. 10-6-17 to Eng.	1249 Fairfield Rd., Victoria, B.C.
2528305	Emory, G.	Pte.	W. 27-9-18 (Cambrai) to Eng.	13 Bishop St., Toronto, Ont.
2226961	England, W. W.	Pte.	Evac. sick 14-12-18 to Eng.	R.R. No. 4, St. Catherine's, Ont.
907396	English, M.	Sgt.	W. 9-4-17 (Vimy); evac. sick 5-12-18 to Eng.	1409 4½ St. E., Calgary, Alta.
3106460	Enright, J.	Pte.	W. 27-9-18 (Cambrai) to Eng.	55 Cannon St. W., Hamilton, Ont.
3317293	Evans, A.	Pte.	W. 27-9-18 (Cambrai); evac. sick 2-11-18 to Eng.	R.R. No. 1, Midland, Ont.
663090	Evans, A. J.	Pte.	W. 1-10-18 (Cambrai) to Eng.	58 Ontario St., Guelph, Ont.
907748	Evans, A. S.	Pte.	Tr. to Lbr. Pool 9-6-18	c/o Mrs. O. Wallis, Wimbleton, London, Eng.
911755	Evans, C. S.	Pte.	Tr. to Eng. for R.A.F. 7-4-18; ret. 5-11-18; to Eng. for course 1-3-19.	
3105689	Evans, G. E.	Pte.	K. l. a. 27-9-18 (Cambrai)	1336 13th Ave. W., Vancouver, B.C.
3317294	Evans, I.	Pte.	W. 27-9-18 (Cambrai) to Eng.	Mrs. A. Evans, Cootocook, New Hampshire, U.S.A.
703851	Evans, J.	L.-C.	K. l. a. 22-10-16 (Regina)	Victoria Harbour, Ont.
				Mrs. S. A. Evans, Bosworth, Poplar Ch. P.O., Kootenay, B.C.
240084	Evans, J. D.	Pte.	W. 10-4-18 (Oppy) to Eng.	45 Roy St. N., Hamilton, Ont.
715584	Evans, J. J.	Pte.	W. 12-5-17 (1st Triangle) to Eng.	c/o Mrs. J Grencon, Half-way Cove, Greysboro Co., Nova Scotia.
160447	Evans, J. O.	Pte.	W. 22-10-16 (Regina); w. 15-8-17 (Lens)	c/o Mr. Baldwin, Appleford School, nr. Abingdon, Berks, Eng.
126619	Evans, T.	Pte.	Tr. to 51st Bn. 2-8-16	24 Whliton St., Bridgemouth, Eng.
703372	Evans, T.	Pte.	W. 9-4-17 (Vimy); w. 12-6-17 (2nd Triangle) to Eng.	19 Rawley Grove, Stafford, Eng.
663414	Evans, T. A.	Pte.	W. 1-10-18 (Cambrai)	105 Logan Ave., Toronto, Ont.
102595	Evanson, S.	Sgt.	W. 17-8-17 (Lens) dec. M.M. (Amiens) C.R. O. 1899.	c/o Mrs. J. Cotton, Sandy Bank, Whixall, nr. Whitchurch, Salop, Eng.
3110221	Everett, G.	Pte.	W. 2-11-18 (2nd Arras) to Eng.	13 Ward St., nr. Cuthorpse, Grimsby, Eng.
703778	Ewing, R. C.	Pte.	K. l. a. 22-10-16 (Regina)	A. H. Ewing, Woodstock, Ont.

Number	Name	Rank	Notes	Address
703691	Exell, E. R.	L.-C.	W. 11-11-16 (Somme) to Eng.	962 61st St., Oakland, Cal., U.S.A.
3314303	Eymann, A.	Pte.	W. 30-9-18 (Cambrai) to Eng.	Mont Pelham, Ont.
907896	Facey, E. W.	Pte.	W. 9-3-17 and 9-4-17 (Vimy) to Eng.	Sutcombe, Eng.
3106335	Fagan, B.	Pte.	W. 27-9-18 and 30-9-18 (Cambrai)	93 E. 33rd St., Mount Hamilton, Ont.
3314114	Faggetter, W.	Pte.	W. 2-9-18 (2nd Arras) to Eng.	c/o R. Maybee, Wellman's Corners, St. Catherines.
703594	Faherty, S.	Pte.	W. 9-8-17 (Lens) to Eng.	Renoyle, Co. Galway, Ireland.
102040	Faichen, T.	Pte.	Evac. sick 19-11-18 to Eng.	40 Eccles Rd., Clapham, London, S.W. 11, Eng.
2528336	Fair, W.	Pte.	W. 27-9-18 (Cambrai) to Eng.	c/o E. Henderson, Beamsville, Ont.
703777	Fairbank, C. S.	Pte.	Evac. sick 25-3-18 to Eng.	G.W.V.A., Vancouver, B.C.
761271	Falk, J. E.	Pte.	K. 1. a. 2-9-18 (2nd Arras).	Mrs. E. Falk, R.R. No. 2, Cloverdale, B.C.
3109574	Fanning, A. E.	Pte.		269 Herkimer St., Hamilton, Ont.
931234	Farby, E.	Pte.	Evac. sick 15-12-17 to Eng.	Bismark, North Dakota, U.S.A.
1004206	Farley, S.	Pte.	W. 7-5-18 (Oppy); w. 6-11-18 (Valenciennes).	c/o Mrs. G. Westacott, R.R. No. 1, Shelbourne, Ont.
126456	Farmer, E. W.	Pte.	K. 1. a. 9-4-17 (Vimy)	Miss R. Farmer, 100 Winn's Ave., Walthanstow, Essex, Eng.
663386	Farmer, H.	Pte.	W. 16-8-18 (Amiens)	Oakville, Ont.
3109960	Farmer, W. J.	Pte.	K. 1. a. 22-10-16 (Regina)	R.R. No. 2, Sault Ste. Marie, Ont.
161020	Farr, C.	Pte.		No address available.
3106017	Farrant, E.	Pte.	K. 1. a. 27-9-18 (Cambrai)	Mrs. E. Farrant, 433 Washington St., Dorchester, Mass., U.S.A.
727185	Farrant, F. C.	Cpl.	W. 30-10-17 (Passchendaele); w. 2-11-18 (Valenciennes) to Eng.	Mitchell, Ont.
706958	Farrant, G.	Pte.	W. 9-4-17 (Vimy) to Eng.	31 Kings Rd. Hollyhead, Wales.
931804	Farrar, W. J.	Pte.	Dec. D.M. (Lens) C.R.O. 1466; evac. sick 19-9-17 to Eng.	
703627	Farris, H. A.	C.S.M.	W. 12-6-17 (2nd Triangle); dec. M.M. (Amiens) C.R.O. 1899.	1216 E. 28th St., Tacoma, Wash., U.S.A.
226685	Faulkner, A.	Pte.	W. 8-8-18 (Amiens); w. 27-9-18 (Cambrai) to Eng.	6 Market Meadows, St. Mary Cray, Kent, Eng.
540554	Faulkner, W. C.	Pte.	Tr. to 11th C.L.T.M.B. 19-7-16.	c/o Royal Bank, King's St. W., Hamilton, Ont.
2528488	Fauville, C.	Pte.	Tr. to Lbr. Pool 12-7-18.	No address available.
2529324	Fawcett, A. F.	Sgt.	Tr. to Eng. as minor 29-5-18.	P.O. Montreal, Que.
3103182	Fedderm, F. S.	Sgt.	Tr. to 1st Can. Lbr. Bn. 16-7-17	248 Mary St., Hamilton, Ont.
1066159	Feltis, F. N. C.	Pte.	K. 1. a. 1-10-18 (Cambrai)	10 Holmes Rd., Twickenham, London, Eng.
663667	Fennell, M. H.	Pte.	Evac. sick 24-11-17 to Eng.	Mrs. J. Feltis, R.R. No. 3, Owen Sound, Ont.
760660	Fenton, C. W.	Pte.	W. 24-10-17 (Passchendaele) to Eng.	Grand Valley, Ont.
757058	Fenton, E. W.	Pte.	W. 2-9-18 (2nd Arras); dec. M.M. (2nd Arras) C.R.O. 1930; tr. to Eng. for Canada 23-3-19	McKay Postoffice, B.C.
103278	Ferguson, A. B. M.	Pte.	Evac. sick 29-11-18 to Eng.	91 Stuart St., E., Hamilton, Ont.
227193	Ferguson, C.	Pte.	W. to Eng. 23-11-17 (Passchendaele)	Pritchard, B.C.
103388	Ferguson, D.	Pte.	Evac. sick 4-5-17 to Eng.	St. Paul St. W., St. Catherines, Ont.
925452	Ferguson, D. B.	Pte.	K. 1. a. 9-4-17 (Vimy)	Pritchard, B.C.
907450	Ferguson, D. G.	Cpl.	D. o. w. 10-4-17 (Vimy)	Mrs. Chas. Sled, Regina, Sask.
219731	Ferguson, D. R.	Pte.	K. 1. a. 6-6-17 (2nd Triangle)	Miss E. M. Ferguson, Gen. Hosp., Regina, Sask.
703526	Ferguson, E.	Pte.		Mrs. A. Ferguson, Napanee, Ont.
104230	Ferguson, J.	Pte.	K. 1. a. 31-10-17 (Passchendaele)	9 Ash St., Harpurley, Manchester, Eng.
706157	Ferguson, R.	Pte.	W. 6-9-17 (Lens); tr. to Lbr. Pool 10-5-18	Mrs. M. Ferguson, 2362 16th Ave., Regina, Sask.
				131 Five Roads, Kilwenning, Scot.

Reg. No.	Name	Rank	Service Notes	Address
761153	Ferguson, T. H.	Pte.	W. 26-5-17 (1st Triangle) to Eng.	No address available.
704091	Ferguson, W.	Sgt.	W. 27-9-18 (Cambrai); tr. to Eng. for demob. 19-1-19	Gattonside, Melrose, Scotland.
838282	Ferguson, W. B.	Pte.	W. 2-5-18 (Lens); w. 1-10-18 (Cambrai); tr. to 31st Bn. 12-8-18	108 Norris St., Port Arthur, Ont.
3109096	Ferguson, W. E.	Pte.	Evac. sick 23-12-18 to Eng.	Dunedin, Ont.
703176	Ferrero, D.	Pte.		No address available.
663439	Ferrier, A.	Pte.	W. 8-8-18 (Amiens) to Eng.	Abernethy, Sask.
2528397	Ferris, R.	Pte.	K. i. a. 27-9-18 (Cambrai)	Mrs. L. Ferris, R.F.D. No. 7, Iona, Mich., U.S.A.
3106209	Fiddes, A. W.	Pte.	Evac. sick 3-1-19 to Eng.	28 Chester Ave., Westerley, Rhode Island, U.S.A.
219930	Fiddler, F.	L.-C.	W. 11-5-17 (1st Triangle); evac. sick 1-9-17 to Eng.	c/o A. Joy, Richmond P.O., Ont.
3314116	Field, C.	Pte.	D. o. w. 29-9-18 (Cambrai)	Mrs. C. Field, 1139 2nd Ave. E., Owen Sound, Ont.
703060	Field, F.	Sgt.	O.R.S. at H.Q. 3rd Ech. till Aug. 1917; tr. to Eng. for commission 5-10-17.	Courtenay, B.C.
102968	Fieldsted, J.	Pte.	W. 9-8-17 (Lens); tr. to 11th T.M.B. 7-3-16.	4231 Lyndale Ave. S., Minneapolis, U.S.A.
252944	Fildes, W. W.	Pte.		No address available.
850056	Findlay, J.	Pte.	K. i. a. 12-5-17 (1st Triangle)	5 Lowell Ave., St. Catherines, Ont.
703673	Finlayson, R.	Pte.	Evac. sick 27-2-19	D. Finlayson, Loch Carron, Rosshire, Scot.
2529334	Finnegan, W. J.	Pte.		c/o Miss Finnegan, 1 Austin Corners, 12 Wormersley Rd., London, N., Eng.
160113	Fisher, L.	Pte.	W. 23-1-17 (Vimy); w. 17-8-17 (Lens) to Eng.	24 Eaton Rd., Norwich, Eng.
225427	Fisher, W. J.	Pte.	Tr. to 4th M.G.C. 1-5-18	Grimsby, Ont.
102472	Fishwick, J. A.	Pte.	W. 9-6-17 (2nd Triangle) to Eng.	83 Tylketh St., Southport, Eng.
703029	Fiske, W. A.	Pte.	K. i. a. 24-9-17 (Lens).	Mrs. W. Fiske, c/o Mrs. Turnbull, Melrose, Casahova Fauquier Co., Va., U.S.A.
225807	Fitton, W. L.	Pte.	W. (Passchendaele) to Eng. 2-12-17.	29 Harcourt Ave., Toronto, Ont.
3030844	Fitzgerald, E.	Pte.	K. i. a. 21-10-16 (Regina).	2109 West 12th St., Chicago, Ill., U.S.A.
703990	Fitzgerald, J. W.	Pte.	W. 15-5-17 (1st Triangle); k. i. a. 25-8-17 (Lens)	J. A. Fitzgerald, Courtenay, B.C.
703308	Fitzgerald, S.	Pte.		
3314046	Fitzgerald, T. J.	Pte.		J. M. Fitzgerald, 24 Mt. Zion Place, Brighton, Eng.
3314205	Fitzpatrick, V. C.	Pte.	K. i. a. 4-9-18 (2nd Arras).	40 Elizabeth St., St. Catherines, Ont.
663387	Fitzsimmons, E.	Cpl.		Mrs. J. Fitzpatrick, Missoula, Que.
1004060	Fleming, E. I.	Pte.	Tr. to Eng. as minor 30-3-18.	Oakville, Ont.
160035	Fleming, G.	Pte.	W. 9-4-17 (Vimy) to Eng.	Owen Sound, Ont.
160887	Fleming, T. W.	Pte.	W. 21-10-16 (Regina) to Eng.	13 Queen's Rd., Ilford, Essex, Eng.
648316	Fletcher, T. C.	L.-S.	Tr. to 11th T.M.B. 19-7-16.	No address available.
219633	Fletcher, W.	Pte.	W. before tr. from 6th Bn.; tr. to Lbr. Pool 11-3-18	Rorke Ave., Halleybury, Ont.
102630	Flint, F. B.	Pte.	W. (Passchendaele) to Eng 26-11-17	No address available.
838070	Flintoff, S. A.	Pte.	W. 2-9-18 (2nd Arras)	245 14th Ave. E., Vancouver, B.C.
3317032	Foley, J. B.	Pte.	Evac. sick 30-1-17 to Eng.	112 8th St. E., Owen Sound, Ont.
219871	Foley, F. G.	L.-C.	Dec. M.M. (Cambrai) C.R.O. 1989; w. 6-11-18 (Valenciennes) to Eng.	35 Elgin St., Oshawa, Ont.
135476				c/o Mrs. J. McAllister, Vancroft, Ont.
226493	Foley, J. T.	Pte.	Evac. sick 8-12-18 to Eng.	13 Seaforth Ave., Toronto, Ont. 91 Sherman Ave., Hamilton, Ont.

Number	Name	Rank	Service	Address
3107482	Folville, A. J.	Pte.		Cayuga, Ont.
3108139	Foran, J.	Sgt.		Cornac, Ont.
703866	Forbes, A.	Pte.	k. l. a. 9-4-17 (Vimy)	Mrs. M. Forbes, 18 Jute St., Aberdeen, Scot.
252686	Ford, B.	Pte.	W. 9-4-17 (Vimy) to Eng.	Exeter, Ont.
252207	Ford, H. E.	Pte.	W. 9-4-17 (Vimy) to Eng.	55 Bexhill Rd., Eastbourne, Eng.
703284	Ford, J.	Pte.	Tr. to 7th Can. Area Emp. Co. 3-9-17	22 Portland Sq., Hamilton, Lanarkshire, Scot.
663090	Ford, J. A.	L.-S.	W. 27-9-18 (Cambrai)	Milton, Ont.
183254	Ford, J. E.	Pte.	W. 9-4-17 (Vimy) to Eng.	Gordonville, Ont.
3106388	Ford, N. G.	Pte.	Evac. sick 8-12-18 to Eng.	Milton, Ont.
3109963	Ford, W. E.	Pte.		R.R. No. 4, Milton, Ont.
2528455	Forham, C. H.	Pte.	D. o. w. 26-8-18 (Amiens)	J. Forham, 58 Ashleigh St., Springfield, Mass.
225214	Forrest, R. J.	Pte.	W. 3-9-18 (2nd Arr.. .o Eng.	c/o Miss Ballantyne, Boat Tankerton, Scot.
907426	Forrester, F. D.	Pte.	W. 9-4-17 (Vimy) tt Eng.	Clinton, Ont.
225483	Forster, W. E.	Pte.	W. 27-9-18 (Cambrai) to Eng.	36 Pine St., Welland, Ont.
252903	Forsythe, G.	Pte.	W. 9-4-17 (Vimy) to Eng.	Hill Head, Frandaugh, Aberdeenshire, Scot.
850052	Forsythe, M. R.	Pte.	K. l. a. 1-10-18 (Cambrai)	Mrs. A. Forsythe, Niagara Falls, Ont.
250069	Fortescue, R.	Arm-Cpl.	W. 2-9-18 (2nd Arras)	c/o Miss R. Pierce, 89 Logan Ave., Toronto, Ont
1004186	Forth, J. A.	Pte.	Tr. to Lbr. Pool 14-6-18	Church St., Parry Sound, Ont.
1003086	Fortier, J. J.	Pte.	K. l. a. 15-11-17	Riviere du Loup, Temiscouata, Que.
225214	Fortin, A.	Pte.	W. 20-10-16 (Regina) to Eng.	Mrs. E. Fortin, 29 Salibilsle St., St. Roch, Que.
1004008	Fosmo, J.	Pte.	W. 7-6-17 (2nd Triangle) to Eng.	Albas, B.C.
703941	Foss, E.	Pte.	W. 9-4-17 (Vimy) to Eng.	P.O. Box 214, Nelson, B.C.
703822	Foster, G.	Pte.	Tr. to 51st Bn. 2-8-16.	Earl Grey, Sask.
115509	Foster, G.	Pte.		P.O. Box 1033, Nanaimo, B.C.
703551	Foster, J.	Pte.	W. 18-2-17 (Vimy); w. 25-6-17 (2nd Triangle); dec. M.M. (Lens) C.R.O. 1491; 15-11-17 (Passchendaele); w. 30-9-18 (Cambrai)	
908196				
907086	Fowler, H.	Pte.	D. o. w. 16-4-17 (Vimy)	Stoughton, Sask.
761103	Fowler, J.	Pte.	W. 13-4-17 (Vimy) to Eng.	Mrs. M. H. Fowler, 1124 Athol St., Regina, Sask.
703275	Fowler, J. R.	Pte.	W. 9-6-17 (2nd Triangle); tr. to Eng. 31-12-18	1221 18th Ave. E., Vancouver, B.C.
1003511	Fox, H.	Pte.		West Branch, River John, Picton Co., N.S.
3110416	Fox, J. A.	Pte.	Tr. to 4th Div. Engrs. 27-7-16.	Manotick, Ont.
703955	Fox, W. F.	Pte.	D. o. w. 26-10-17 (Passchendaele)	Coburg, Ont.
907327	Francis, R. J.	Pte.	W. 12-5-17 (1st Triangle); w. 18-3-18 (Lens) to Eng.	Elsing, Norfolk, Eng.
102441	Frank, G.	Pte.		Mrs. M. Cornett, Glenavon, Sask.
102357	Frankham, C. F.	Pte.	Evac. sick 14-5-17 to Eng.	Keatings, B.C.
703734	Franklin, G. V. H.	Pte.	Evac. sick 22-11-16 to Eng.	Happy Valley, B.C.
3314309	Franklin, H. L.	Pte.	W. 27-9-18 (Cambrai) to Eng.	McKay, B.C.
227113	Franklin, L. L.	Pte.	W. 8-8-18 (Amiens) to Eng.	R.R. No. 2, Beamsville, Ont.
931812	Fransvold, J.	Pte.	W. 15-8-17 (Lens) to Eng.	465 West 162nd St., New York, N.Y., U.S.A.
145173	Fraser, A. H.	Pte.	Tr. to 77th Bn. 10-8-16.	c/o M. O. Rund, Barton, North Dakota, U.S.A.
1003818	Fraser, A.	Pte.	W. 20-8-18 (Amiens) to Eng.	129 Lees Ave., Ottawa, Ont.
2529462	Fraser, E.	Pte.		Massey Station, Ont.
443198	Fraser, F. W.	Pte.	Evac. sick on leave in Eng. 2-4-18.	43 St. George St., Steelton, Ont.
219560	Fraser, J. A.	Pte.	Tr. to 51st Bn. 2-8-16.	Kelowna, B.C.
706547	Fraser, M.	Pte.	K. l. a. 9-4-17 (Vimy)	No address available. J. Fraser, Inverness, Scotland.

1024422	Fraser, McK. M.	Pte.	Tr. to Eng. 9-2-19	40 Breadalbane St., Toronto, Ont.
703164	Fraser, N. C.	Pte.	W. 9-4-17 (Vimy), to Eng.	c/o Mrs. McDonald, 1340 George St., Victoria, B.C.
3107867	Fraser, W. H.	Pte.		Bancroft, Ont.
2527384	Fraser, W. H.	Pte.		1186 King St. E., Hamilton, Ont.
3317299	Fray, B. A.	Pte.	W. 27-9-18 (Cambrai)	No address available.
136643	Frazer, G. F.	Pte.	W. 22-10-16 (Regina) to Eng.	No address available.
704038	Frazer, J.	Pte.	W. 3-9-16 (Somme) to Eng.	c/o Mrs. A. Brown, St. John's, N.B.
240093	Frazer, W. T.	Pte.	W. 4-9-18 (2nd Arras) to Eng.	52 Florence St., Hamilton, Ont.
2528386	Freeman, E.	Pte.	Evac. sick 25-7-17 to Eng.	c/o Miss C. Campbell, Fremont Hotel, Nelson, B.C.
931138	French, E.	Pte.	W. 27-9-18 (Cambrai) to Eng.	No address available.
103234	French, H. C.	L.-C.	K. i. a. 1-11-17 (Passchendaele)	A. E. French, R.M.D. No. 3, Victoria, B.C.
931719	Freymouth, J. M.	Pte.	K. i. a. 6-8-17 (Lens)	Mrs. P. Freymouth, 310 Mission St., Vernon, B.C.
249924	Friers, A. E.	Pte.	W. 8-8-18 (Amiens) to Eng.	173 Marguereta St., Toronto, Ont.
703801	Froud, R. W.	Pte.	W. 19-10-16 (Somme) to Eng.	2576 6th Ave. W., Vancouver, B.C.
703181	Fry, E. S.	Pte.	Evac. sick 8-4-17 to Eng.	P.O. Box 57, South Fort George, B.C.
430723	Fryer, F. C.	Sgt.	W. 18-11-17 (Passchendaele) to Eng.	1342 Johnston St., Victoria, B.C.
703177	Fryer, J. P.	Pte.		Fort Kells, B.C.
540015	Fuller, A.	Pte.	Tr. to 11th C.L.T.M.B. 23-3-18	c/o Mrs. W. J. Chapman, 130 Medland St., Toronto.
102798	Fuller, H. W.	L.-C.	Evac. sick 3-8-17 to Eng.	42 Buffalo Ave., Niagara Falls, N.Y., U.S.A.
252329	Fuller, R. D.	Pte.	Evac. sick 28-5-17 to Eng.	Waldech, Sask.
2527307	Furlong, A. F.	Pte.	K. i. a. 1-10-18 (Cambrai)	D. Furlong, Sheenboro', Que.
3107250	Fysh, J. W.	Pte.		Utterson, Ont.
703420	Fyvie, J.	Pte.	Tr. to Eng. 15-4-18	193 6th Ave. W., Vancouver, B.C.
180047	Gadd, A.	Pte.	K. i. a. 27-9-18 (Cambrai)	J. Gadd, 1101 6th Ave. W., Vancouver, B.C.
703290	Gage, G. H.	Pte.	W. 9-6-17 (2nd Triangle); k. i. a. 23-7-18 (Oppy)	
703005	Gage-Cole, T. S.	Sgt.	W. 11-11-16 (Somme); tr. to Lbr. Pool 6-12-17	Mrs. W. Gage, Comox, B.C.
2529380	Gagne, E.	Pte.	W. 4-9-18 (2nd Arras)	3250 Sophia St., Vancouver, B.C.
703821	Gagne, O. G.	Pte.	Evac. sick 23-10-16	c/o A. Paquiatte, 1323 City Hall Ave., Montreal, Que.
1004075	Gagnon, A.	Pte.	Tr. to 4th M.G.C. 18-3-18	c/o Mrs. A. Ray, St. Andrews, Co., Comaraska, Que.
1004045	Galney, M. J.	Pte.	W. 31-10-17 (Passchendaele); evac. sick 4-6-18 to Eng.	569 Rue Louis Veuolleut, Longue Pointe, Montreal.
161072	Galavan, G. H.	Pte.	Evac. sick 21-10-16 to Eng.	c/o Miss E. Galney, 81 19th St. W., Buffalo, N. Y.
727461	Gale, A.	Sgt.	Tr. to Eng. for commission 23-8-18	c/o Mrs. J. Smith, Vericanna P.O., Alta.
226934	Gale, C.	Pte.	W. 8-8-18 (Amiens) to Eng.	R.R. No. 3, Stratford, Ont.
226933	Gale, G. G.	Pte.	W. 21-10-16 (Regina) to Eng.	Sweetwater, Texas, U.S.A.
240695	Gale, W.	Pte.	K. i. a. 4-9-18 (Vimy)	J. C. Gale, Sweetwater, Texas, U.S.A.
703867	Galineau, A. W.	Pte.		Smithville, Ont.
703906	Galipeau, J.	L.-C.	W. 3-9-17 (Lens) to Eng.	P.O. Box 56, Grand Forks, B.C.
704151	Gallacher, W. G.	Pte.	W. 22-10-16 (Regina) to Eng.	P.O. Box 56, Grand Forks, B.C.
3314651	Gallagher, T. J.	Pte.	K. i. a. 4-9-18 (2nd Arras)	4 Newton St., Paisley, Scot.
703349	Gallant, F.	Pte.	Missing after action 11-11-16 (Somme); believed taken prisoner.	Miss N. Gallagher, 35 Centre St., St. Catherines, Ont.
703628	Gallichan, A. J.	Pte.	W. 9-6-17 (2nd Triangle) to Eng.	c/o Mrs. A. E. Collier, Chemainus, B.C.
907111	Gallienne, C. A.	Pte.	Acc. w. 18-11-17 to Eng.	Bank of Commerce, Hastings St., Vancouver, B.C.
252838	Galloway, R. J.	Pte.	K. i. a. 9-4-17 (Vimy)	17 Mount Durant, Guernsey, Channel Islands, Eng.
3317040	Gamble, E. B.	Pte.		D. Galloway, Cabol, Sask.
226897	Garbutt, G. J.	Pte.	W. 6-11-18 (Passchendaele)	93 Agnes St., Oshawa, Ont.
				168 Markland St., Hamilton, Ont.

Reg. No.	Name	Rank	Remarks	Address
931238	Garbutt, J.	L.-S.	W. 21-10-16 (Regina) to Eng.	8 Appleton Rd., Linthorpe, Middlesboro, Eng.
838077	Gardhouse, R. N.	Pte.	W. 2-11-18 (Passchendaele)	142 5th St. E., Owen Sound, Ont.
850578	Gardiner, H. J.	Sgt.	Dec. M.M. (Valenciennes) C.R.O. 2028	Springfield Rd., Westfield, N.J., U.S.A.
727861	Gardner, C. H.	Pte.	Evac. sick 11-6-18 to Eng.	Milton Heights, Wellington Co., Ont.
704123	Garelinko, A.	Pte.	K. i. a. 8-9-16 (St. Eloi)	No address available.
2528469	Garlough, E.	Sgt.	Dec. M.M. (Cambrai) C.R.O. 1989.	Morrisburgh, Ont.
2528470	Garlough, L.	Pte.		Morrisburgh, Ont.
1003751	Garneau, F.	Pte.	W. 8-8-18 (Amiens) to Eng. w. 2-11-18 (Valenciennes)	Moulais Bay, Ont.
1003802	Garner, C. J.	Pte.	W. 24-10-17 (Passchendaele)	General Delivery, Saulte Ste. Marie, Ont.
703672	Garnet, W. P.	L.-C.	W. 20-10-16 (Regina) to Eng.	7 Lytton Ave., Corners Green, London, Eng.
703163	Garnham, S.	Sgt.	Left at Bramshott 10-8-16.	c/o Granby Consolidated M. & S. Co., Ltd., Vancouver.
1003074	Garrison, F. R.	Pte.	D. o. w. 22-7-18 (Oppy)	J. Garrison, Deseronto, Ont.
907844	Gaskell, J.	Pte.	W. 2-9-18 (2nd Arras); tr. to Lbr. Pool 11-10-18	West Lodge, Lymepark, Disley, Eng.
703965	Gates, H. B.	Sgt.	Dec. M.M. (Triangle) C.R.O. 1335.	60 Hugh St., London, S.W., Eng.
102014	Gatus, D. A.	Cpl.	W. 8-8-18 (Amiens)	Chemainus, B.C.
931236	Gaudery, H.	Pte.	W. 19-10-16 (Somme)	St. Norbert, Man.
226478	Gaudette, A. J.	Pte.	W. 27-9-18 (Cambrai); D.C.M. (Cambrai) L.G. d-3-6-19	5 Cadillac St., Ford, Ont.
703745	Gaudreau, J.	Pte.	Evac. sick 21-10-16 to Eng.	c/o J. Tremblay, Murray Bay, Que.
1003516	Gauthier, A.	Pte.	W. 21-4-18 (Oppy) to Eng.	Massey, Ont.
250087	Gaw, T.	L.-C.	W. 29-9-18 (Cambrai)	57 Welland Ave., Moore Park, Toronto, Ont.
1267769	Geddes, C. G.	Pte.	Evac. sick 22-1-19.	7 Clinton St., Guelph, Ont.
240490	Geddes, J.	Pte.	W. 2-9-18 (2nd Arras) to Eng.	366 John St., N., Hamilton, Ont.
126002	Gee, L.	Pte.	W. 21-10-16 (Regina) to Eng.	R.R. No. 5, Ingersoll, Ont.
703634	Gee, W.	Pte.	W. 22-10-16 (Regina) to Eng.	c/o Mrs. G. Ardley, Comox, B.C.
208373	Gelfond, D.	Pte.	Tr. to Can. Corps Wireless, 25-1-17	Victoria, B.C.
3030739	Geller, C.	Pte.	W. 12-6-17 (2nd Triangle) to Eng.	2624 Alberni Ave., Chicago, Ill., U.S.A.
249667	Gent, A. D.	Pte.	Evac. sick 26-12-18 to Eng.	44 Herman Block, Frome, Somerset, Eng.
916255	Gentle, J. E.	Pte.	W. 2-9-18 (2nd Arras) to Eng.	16 Crown St., Barbourne, Worcester, Eng.
760389	George, A. E.	Pte.	Evac. sick 7-5-17 to Eng.	18 Armstrong Ave., Toronto, Ont.
703820	George, F. A.	L.-C.	Evac. sick 18-11-16 to Eng.	Campslaugh, Chilliwack, B.C.
703846	Georges, R. E.	Pte.	W. 31-10-16 (Somme); d. o. w 8-6-17 (Triangle)	South Slocan, B.C.
703260	Georges, R. J.	Pte.		
703260	Georgeson, D. W.	C.S.M.	Dec. M.M. (Somme) D.R.O. 375; dec. Bar to M.M. (Vimy) C.R.O. 1236; tr. to Eng. for commission 19-12-17	Mrs. H. H. Georges, South Slocan.
622955	Gerard, P.	Pte.	Tr to 1st Can. Lbr. Bn. 8-8-17	2136 Guelph St., Vancouver, B.C.
3106072	Germaine, G. W.	Pte.	W. (Valenciennes) to Eng. 1-10-18	Forget, Sask.
249153	Gibbons, W. P.	Pte.		Mallory P.O., Oswego Co., N.Y., U.S.A.
704176	Gibbs, F. A.	Cpl.	W. 21-10-16 (Regina)	123 Lippincott St., Toronto, Ont.
703286	Gibbs, H. I.	Pte.	Evac. sick 21-8-16 to Eng.	38 Wellington Hill, Horsfield, Bristol, Eng.
1003602	Gibson, A.	Pte.	W. 23-10-17 (Amiens) to Eng.	Lillooet, B.C.
931100	Gibson, H.	Sgt.	W. 8-8-18 (Amiens) to Eng.	c/o Mrs. J. Riley, Lusville, Que.
703484	Gibson, J. T.	Pte.	Evac. sick in Eng. 27-5-19	Keewatin, Ont.
850771	Gibson, L. A.	L.-S.	W. 6-8 (Oppy) to Eng. (St. Eloi); dec. Scout Sergt., w. 14-9-16 (Lens) L.G. 30945. Medaille Militaire	c/o L. Gould, P.O. Box 721, Victoria, B.C.
703730				Port Dalhousie, Ont. G.P.O., Vancouver, B.C.

Number	Name	Rank	Notes	Address
1003946	Gibson, M. H.	Pte.		Bracebridge, Ont.
663267	Giddings, B.	Pte.		Milton Heights, Ont.
703937	Giddings, W.	Cpl.		c/o A. W. Jackson, City Hall, Kamloops, B.C.
907791	Giggs, A. J.	Pte.	W. 8-8-18 (Amiens) to Eng.	15 Victoria St., Newbury, Berks, Eng.
663719	Gilbert, C. V.	Pte.	W. 21-10-16 (Regina) to Eng.	Burlington, Ont.
225350	Gilbert, L. A.	Pte.	Evac. sick 30-5-17 to Eng.; W. 27-9-18 (Cambrai) to Eng.; W. 1-11-17 (Passchendaele); w. 6-11-18 (Valenciennes); dec. M.M. (Valenciennes) C.R.O. 2028	
250092	Giles, A.	Pte.	K. i. a. 6-11-18 (Valenciennes)	819 Bloor St., Toronto, Ont.
2529463	Giles, L.	Pte.		Mrs. M. A. Giles, Granske, Castlemine, Co. Kerry, Ire.
430540	Gill, A. W.	Pte.	W. 17-11-17 (Passchendaele) to Eng.	17 Cathcart St., Ottawa, Ont.
154218	Gillespie, J. McL.	Pte.	K. i. a. 17-11-17 (Passchendaele)	8 Alexander Rd., Lydenham, London, Eng. Mrs. E. Gillespie 17 Highworth St., Marylebone, London, Eng.
703996	Gillis, J. J.	Pte.	W. 19-5-17 (1st Triangle); dec. M.M. (Passchendaele) C.R.O. 1606; w. 23-7-18 (Oppy); w. 2-9-18 (2nd Arras) to Eng.	Doctors' Brook, Antigonish, N.S.
703190	Gillis, J. N.	Pte.	W. 13-5-17 (1st Triangle) to Eng.	Orivell, P.E.I.
2021944	Gillson, H. H.	Pte.		1938 Lakewood Drive, Vancouver, B.C.
1003501	Gilroy, R. J.	Pte.		Gore Bay, Ont.
225268	Glonet, E.	Pte.	Dec. M.M. (Valenciennes) C.R.O. 2028	St. Paul, Middle Caraquet, N.B.
160790	Girdler, L.	Pte.	W. 21-10-16 (Regina) to Eng.	No address available.
755067	Giverman, A.	Pte.	K. i. a. 1-11-17 (Passchendaele)	H. Giverman, Hull, Que.
773105	Glass, J. H.	Pte.	Evac. sick 24-11-18 to Eng.	Paris, Ont.
303423	Glauber, R. H.	Pte.	W. 16-11-17 (Passchendaele) to Eng.	1240 Commercial Drive, Vancouver, B.C.
3110076	Gleason, H.	Pte.	Evac. sick 9-12-18 to Eng. for demob. 9-1-19	No address available.
443156	Glendinning, W. L.	Pte.	D. o. w. 8-11-18 (Valenciennes)	Mrs. Glendinning, Inglewood, E. Farleigh, Kent, Eng.
200200	Glenn, B.	Pte.	K. i. a. 31-10-17 (Passchendaele)	J. G. Glenn, 1416 10th Ave. E, Vancouver, B.C.
703678	Glennie, J.	Pte.	W. 9-6-17 (2nd Triangle); w. 2-9-18 (2nd Arras) to Eng.	
704137	Glithero, C.	Pte.	Tr. to 11th C.L.T.M.B. 1-10-17; ret. 14-11-18; tr. to Eng. to R.N.W.M.P. 13-1-19	c/o Jas. Petrie, Anchenbreddie, Insch, Aberdeen, Scot. c/o Mrs. S. Glithero, 320 Fidalgo St., Georgetown, Wash., U.S.A.
675725	Glover, T. H.	Pte.	W. 14-5-17 (1st Triangle) to Eng.	232 King St. E., Hamilton, Ont.
199199	Godchere, T.	Pte.	Dec. M.M. (Vimy) C.R.O. 1236; k. i. a. 9-4-17 (Vimy)	Mrs. M. Godchere, Longuelac, Ont.
240513	Goddard, L.	Pte.	Tr. to 44th Bn. 12-8-18	641 Barton St. E., Hamilton, Ont.
1003566	Goddard, P. H.	Pte.		P.O. Box 1123 Sudbury, Ont.
2528497	Godfrey, J. E.	Pte.		25 Radnor St., N. Woodbury Rd. Nottingham, Eng.
703128	Godin, J. F.	Pte.	D. o. w. 28-11-16 (Somme)	Mrs. W. Shiels, Minitonas, Man.
760850	Godwin, C.	Pte.	W. 15-8-17 (Lens); tr. to Lbr. Pool 22-11-17	Newton, nr. Vowchurch, Pontrilas, Hereford, Eng.
706421	Goetz, J. J.	Pte.	W. 27-9-18 (Cambrai) to Eng.	Franklin Hotel, Hamilton, Ont.
1075327	Gold, J.	Pte.	Evac. sick 11-5-17 to Eng.	32 Highbury Gardens, Ilford, Essex, Eng.
240696	Golden, J. L.	Pte.	W. 10-4-18 (Oppy); tr. to 4th Bn. C.M.G.C.	
181181	Goldie, W. L.	Pte.	K. i. a. 12-6-17 (2nd Triangle)	Cheepston, Ont.
163032	Gooch, A. B.	Pte.	W. 18-10-16 (Somme); tr. to 75th Bn. 9-6-17	Mrs. M. Goldie, Maywood P.O., Saanich, B.C.
489667	Gooch, F. E.	Pte.	W. 1-11-17 (Passchendaele) to Eng.	No address available. c/o J. Defresne, Fort St. James, Stewart Lake, B.C.
164669	Gooch, J.	Pte.	Tr. to 75th Bn. 9-6-17	No address available.

Number	Name	Rank	Service Details	Address
249999	Good, C. W.	Pte.	W. 3-9-18 (Cambrai) to Eng.	278 Gladstone Ave., Toronto, Ont.
252071	Good, L. R.	Pte.	K. i. a. 6-4-17 (Vimy)	Thos. Good, Tompkins, Sask.
249513	Goode, A. E.	Pte.	Missing after action 1-10-18 (Cambrai)	31 Garnoch Ave., Toronto, Ont. (Mrs. A. Good).
253118	Goodfellow, T.	Pte.	W. 29-4-17 (Lens); w. 8-8-18 (Amiens) to Eng.	Wauerton, nr. Wigton, Cumberland, Eng.
703394	Goodick, H. B.	Pte.	W. 5-6-17 (2nd Triangle) to Eng.	c/o Mrs. F. Prior, 38 Beacané St., Gloucester, Mass.
703868	Goodin, H. L.	Pte.	W. 21-10-16 (Regina); k. i. a. 27-12-17 (Merlcourt)	Mrs. M. E. Ellis, Cody, Nebraska, U.S.A.
703224	Gooding, G. G.	Pte.	K. i. a. 22-10-16 (Regina)	Mrs. C. S. Pearne, 160 Douglas St., Stratford, Ont.
703677	Goodlet, W.	Pte.	W. 9-8-17 (Lens) to Eng.	14 Constitution St., Leith, Scotland.
703557	Goodman, A.	Pte.	W. 21-10-16 (Regina); w. 13-4-17 (Vimy) to Eng.	
1003411	Goodman, W. G.	Pte.	Tr. to 4th Bn. C.M.G.C. 1-5-18	1929 Chambers Street, Victoria, B.C.
3106882	Goodmurphy, M.	Pte.	K. i. a. 8-9-16 (St. Eloi)	c/o Mrs. A. Glade, 38 Evans Rd., Copper Cliffe, Ont.
703065	Goodrich, G.	Pte.	W. 9-4-17 (Vimy) to Eng.	Cockburn Island, Ont.
252963	Goodwin, T. G.	Pte.	Tr. to 67th Bn. 8-7-16.	A. Goodrich, Clavimont Trad. Co., Clavimont, Alta.
703613	Goodwin, W. J.	Pte.	Tr. 1-10-18 (Passchendaele) to Eng.	17 Anerley Park, Anerley, London, Eng.
249765	Goodyear, C. L.	Pte.	Tr. to Eng. for commission, 16-3-17.	46 Cecil Street, Toronto, Ont.
541063	Gordon, D. A.	Pte.	Tr. to Eng. for commission, 16-3-17.	No address available.
1003284	Gordon, J. N	Pte.	W. 1-10-18 (Cambrai); evac. sick 20-10-18 to Eng.	No address available.
3109251	Gordon, O. P.	Pte.		Thessalon, Ont.
249185	Gordon, T. S.	Pte.		R.R. No. 3, Welland, Ont.
2528340	Gore, P. J.	Pte.	W. 1-10-18 (Cambrai) to Eng.	228 Fairview Ave., West Toronto, Ont.
704100	Gorman, R. A.	Pte.	K. i. a. 23-10-16 (Regina).	Bank of Nova Scotia, King and Sherman Sts., Hamilton, Ont.
703519	Gosse, W. G.	Sgt.	Tr. 3-11-16 to Can. Corps Officers' Training School; prom. R.S.M.; later granted commission at Corps School	Mrs. H. P. Gorman, Forrest City, Ark., U.S.A.
703043	Gothard, A. F.	Sgt.	Dec. M.M. (Lens) C.R.O. 1419; w. 16-11-17 (Passchendaele) to Eng.	119 St. Patrick's St., New Westminster, B.C.
703706	Gott, F.	Pte.	Evac. from P.B. to Eng. 15-3-17.	Bella Coola, B.C.
703008	Gould, L. McL.	Sgt.	Dec. Croix de Guerre, Belgian (Passchendaele) C.R.O. 1645; dec. M/S.M. L.G. d-3-6-19	Lillooet, B.C.
1003311	Gould, S. H.	Pte.	Tr. to Lbr. Pool, 16-9-18.	P.O. Box 721, Victoria, B.C.
249174	Goulding, T. J.	Pte.	D. o. w. 27-9-18 (Cambrai)	Tehkummah, Manitoulin Islands, Ont.
225380	Goulet, E. J.	Pte.	Tr. to 4th Div. M.G.C.	2 Nassau Place, Toronto, Ont.
907506	Graham, C. T.	Pte.		Mrs. A. Goulet, 16 O'Mera St., Ottawa, Ont.
103379	Graham, J. A.	L.-C.	W. 9-6-17 (2nd Triangle) to Eng.	P.O. Box 661, Regina, Sask.
102269	Graham, J. McC.	Cpl.	W. 9-6-17 (2nd Triangle); w. 15-8-17 (Lens); tr. to Lbr. Pool 24-1-18; d. o. s. in Canada, 26-2-19	362 Sylvia St., Victoria, B.C.
103263	Graham, O. F.	Pte.	Acc. inj. 12-5-18 to Eng.	Milner, B.C.
102780	Graham, S. J.	Pte.		Miss V. Graham, 362 Sylvia St., Victoria, B.C.
3314313	Graham, T. N.	Pte.		North Lonsdale, Gen. Delivery, N. Vancouver, B.C.
102765	Graham, V. R.	Cpl.	W. 12-6-17 (2nd Triangle); d. o. w. (acc.) 30-8-17	640 7th St. A.E., Owen Sound, Ont.
				Mrs. Beamish, 25 Binden Rd., Shepherd's Bridge, London, Eng.

907435	Grain, J. R.	Pte.	W. 2-9-18 (2nd Arras) to Eng.	Kerrobert, Sask.
2395602	Grainger, A. H.	Pte.	W. 27-9-18 (Cambrai)	1 Church St., Willenhall, Staffs, Eng.
226979	Grant, C. E.	Pte.	Tr. to 4th Bn. C.M.G.C. 18-3-18	c/o Mrs. L. Broughton, R.R. No. 2, Caister Cen., Ont.
252077	Grant, D.	Pte.	W. 2-9-18 (2nd Arras)	Swift Current, Sask.
703562	Grant, E.	Pte.	Tr. to 51st Bn. 2-8-16	2514 Napier St., Vancouver, B.C.
703393	Grant, G. H.	Pte.	Evac. sick 4-1-17 to Eng.	c/o J. Bazett, Duncan, B.C.
1013208	Grant, G. W.	Pte.	W. 24-3-18 (Lens) to Eng.	Carlingford, Ont.
703665	Grant, H. H.	Sgt.	Sergeant Tailor	4120 14th Ave. W., Point Grey, Vancouver, B.C.
2015166	Grant, J.	Pte.	W. 8-8-18 (Amiens) to Eng.	1918 4th Ave. W., Vancouver, B.C.
703389	Grant, J. F.	Pte.		39 North St., Forfar, Scotland.
703044	Grant, S. G.	Pte.	W. 24-10-17 (Passchendaele) to Eng.	1150 Howe St., Vancouver, B.C.
703161	Grant, W. G.	Pte.		565 Main St., Shettleston, Glasgow, Scot.
252331	Gray, M. M.	L.-C.	W. 8-1-18 (Mericourt); tr. to Lbr. Pool 10-4-18	79 Main St., Caran, Ireland.
706073	Gray, T.	Pte.	W. 1. a. 8-5-17 (1st Triangle)	Mrs. M. Gray, 1404 Bay St., Victoria, B.C.
703210	Gray, W.	Pte.	W. 22-10-16 (Regina) to Eng	1649 8th Ave. E., Vancouver, B.C.
160655	Green, A. E.	Pte.	Tr. to Lbr. Pool 24-1-18.	Austin Villas, Ballyckhmore, Co. Down, Ire.
219135	Green, A. E.	Pte.	K. i. a. 21-10-16 (Regina).	No address available.
707023	Green, C. J.	Pte.	W. 9-4-17 (Vimy) to Eng.	F.O. Box 674, Nanaimo, B.C.
249443	Green, F. J.	Pte.	D. o. w. 28-9-13 (Cambrai)	Mrs. M. Green, 26 Torrence Ave., Toronto, Ont.
704013	Green, G.	Pte.	W. 6-9-17 (Lens) to Eng.	c/o Miss Chilcox, Rock Creek, B.C.
760125	Green, G.	Pte.	K. i. a. 9-4-17 (Vimy).	Mrs. L. M. Green, 5250 6th Ave. E., South Vancouver.
3105690	Green, H. J	Pte.	Tr. to Eng. for demob. 9-1-19	c/o Bank of Nova Scotia, Hamilton, Ont.
102107	Green, H. J.	Pte.	Evac. sick in Eng. 15-2-18	928 Bay St., Victoria, B.C.
760054	Green, J.	Pte.	W. 27-9-18 (Cambrai) to Eng.	c/o Mrs. S. Almeen, Van Anda Island, B.C.
102596	Green, W.	Pte.	Tr. to Eng. from P.B. 24-9-17	c/o Mrs. Cryer, 14 Greenhill Yard, Burnley, Eng.
226942	Greenaway, W.	Pte.	W. 1. a. 8-8-18 (Amiens)	M. Greenaway, 40 Mercer St., Toronto, Ont.
225473	Greene, E. S.	Pte.	D. o. w. 16-9-18 (2nd Arras)	S. Greene, Grand Bend, Ont.
3105970	Greene, M.	Pte.	W. 2-11-18 (2nd Arras) to Eng.	Broome, Que.
103155	Greenlees, M. G.	Pte.	W. 13-5-17 (1st Triangle) to Eng.	54 New Broad St., London, Eng.
2527363	Greenslade, L. G.	Pte.	W. 1-10-18 (Cambrai) to Eng.	Caledonia, Ont.
703680	Greer, E. J.	Pte.	Acc. inj. 5-5-17 to Eng.	826 Homer St., Vancouver, B.C.
174983	Grey, S.	Pte.	W. 9-3-17 (Vimy); evac. sick 31-5-17 to Eng.	39 Pearl St. N., Hamilton, Ont.
706799	Grieve, C.	Pte.	W. 15-11-17 (Passchendaele) to Eng.	c/o Mrs. A. Tweed, Courtenay, B.C.
102979	Grieve, D.	Pte.	to Eng. 22-8-17 (Lens)	Middlesboro, B.C.
703036	Grieve, H.	Pte.	W. 6-6-17 (2nd Triangle)	c/o Mrs. A. Tweed, Courtenay, B.C.
252074	Griffin, C. D.	Cpl.	W. 1-10-18 (Cambrai) to Eng	c/o Mrs. A. Baskerville, Burnham, Sask.
1003676	Griffin, J.	Pte.	W. 4-9-18 (2nd Arras) to Eng.	St. John's, Newfoundland.
102108	Griffiths, L. G.	Sgt.	W. 9-6-17 (2nd Triangle); w. 13-11-17 (Passchendaele) to Eng.; prom. Sergt. in Eng.	1020 Caledonia Ave., Victoria, B.C.
2528334	Grigora, J.	Pte.	K. i. a. 2-9-18 (2nd Arras)	No address available.
703342	Grist, A. W.	Pte.	W. 11-11-16 (Somme)	Comox, B.C.
1045805	Grivakis, H.	Pte.	W. 27-7-18 (Oppy); w. 8-8-18 (Amiens) to Eng.	Arhames, Crete, Greece.
704073	Grose, C. R.	Pte.	W. 19-3-18 (Lens); w. 8-8-18 (Amiens) to Eng.	Rossland, B.C.
225367	Grove, J. J.	Pte.	Evac. sick 5-12-17 to Eng.	62 Crosby Ave., St. Catherines, Ont.
703243	Grundy, A.	Cpl.	Tr. to Eng 4-4-17 for commission, R.A.F.	28 S.C.P. Lane, Astley, Manchester, Eng.
1003266	Guard, J.	Pte.	Evac. sick 14-10-17 to Eng.	c/o C. Guard, Carnie, Nenominee Co., Mich., U.S.A.

704111	Guegan, T. H. H.	Pte.	W. 1-9-16 (St. Eloi) to Eng.	c/o Mrs. L. Hagedorn, Selah, Wash., U.S.A.
250108	Guerin, J.	Pte.	W. 1-11-17 (Passchendaele) to Eng.	St. Simeon, Port au Quilles, Conte Charlevoin, Que.
755010	Guiney, J. S.	Pte.	K. i. a. 9-4-17 (Vimy)	Milford Haven, Ont.
253040	Gunn, H.	Pte.	W. 9-6-17 (2nd Triangle) to Eng.	J. E. Gunn, Corriander P.O., Anerold, Sask.
931237	Gunrud, A.	Pte.	W. 1-10-18 (Cambrai) to Eng.	Cranbrook, B.C.
704017	Gushue, C.	Pte.	K. i. a. 21-10-16 (Regina)	c/o N. Gushue, Bacon Cove, Harbourmain, Disk, Nfd.
931079	Gustafson, J.	Pte.	W. 11-11-16 (Somme) to Eng.	Miss A. Gustafson, 3310 Osgood St., Chicago, Ill.
703491	Gustavson, H.	Pte.	Evac. sick 20-11-18 to Eng.	c/o F. Hendriks, Bella Coola, B.C.
2108736	Guy, F. A.	Pte.	K. i. a. 9-4-17 (Vimy)	Carn Friars, St. Mary's, Scilly, Cornwall, Eng.
253130	Hadden, R. G.	Pte.	Evac. sick 23-8-18 to Eng.	J. Hadden, 374 Van Norman St., Port Arthur, Ont.
703030	Hadden, T.	Pte.	W. 11-11-16 (Somme) to Eng.	Courtenay, B.C.
703869	Haddon, G. M. M.	L.-C.	W. 17-5-17 (1st Triangle); w. 6-6-17 (2nd Triangle) to Eng.	8 Penywern Rd., Earlscourt, London, S.W., Eng.
219177	Haden, J. J.	Pte.		
703645	Hadfield, B.	Pte.	W. 19-8-16 (St. Eloi); evac. sick 6-7-17 to Eng	474 Salem St., Toronto, Ont.
931239	Hagarty, A.	Pte.	W. 22-10-16 (Somme); evac. sick 16-11-17 to Eng.	c/o Miss Hadfield, Goldieland, Settle, Yorks, Eng.
1003215	Hagan, N. N.	Pte.	W. 8-8-18 (Amiens) to Eng.	c/o Mrs. K. Stevenson, Powasson, Ont.
102049	Haggerty, W. J.	L.-C.	Dec. M.M. (Cambrai) C.R.O. 1989; evac. sick in Eng. 18-11-18	Thessalon, Ont.
253029	Haggis, E.	Pte.	Dec. M.M. (Lens) C.R.O. 1419; w. 17-8-17 (Lens) to Eng.	Tamworth, Ont.
703704	Halcrow, W.	Pte.	K. i. a. 22-2-16 (Regina)	Bedham Farm, Tettleworth, Sussex, Eng.
704167	Hale, R. H.	Pte.	W. 31-10-16 (Somme) to Eng.	R. Halcrow, Cumberland, B.C.
931494	Hale, V. H.	Pte.	W. 27-9-17 (Lens); tr. to Lbr. Pool 3-5-18.	33 Dudley St. W., Bromwich, Eng.
200227	Halford, F.	Pte.	Evac. sick 14-9-17 to Eng.	Kisby, Sask.
3107068	Halket, J.	Pte.		1568 Comox St., Vancouver, B.C.
703189	Hall, A. G.	Pte.	W. 21-3-18 (Lens)	170 East Superior St., Chicago, Ill., U.S.A.
2527383	Hall, G. E.	Pte.	W. 4-9-18 (2nd Arras) to Eng.	Prince Rupert, B.C.
3106020	Hall, H. D.	Pte.		525 Wall St., Scranton, Penn., U.S.A.
1102610	Hall, H. D.	Pte.	W. 9-6-17 (2nd Triangle); k. i. a. 17-8-17 (Lens)	c/o Bank of Nova Scotia, Hamilton, Ont.
1003533	Hall, J.	Pte.	Evac. sick 13-2-18 to Eng.	J. Hall, Perkins, Mich., U.S.A.
101167	Hall, J. A.	Cpl.	N.C.O. l|c Bn. Runners from 4-6-17; dec. M.M. (Vimy) C.R.O. 1236.	c/o Mrs. T. Morrison, Copper Cliffe, Ont.
703792	Hall, R. N.	C.Q.M.S.	C.Q.M.S. ''A" Co.	1125 27th St., Edmonton, Alta.
760680	Hall, W. G.	Pte.	W. 9-4-17 (Vimy) to Eng.	P.O. Box 694, Revelstoke, B.C.
706209	Hall, W. G.	Pte.	W. 9-4-17 (Vimy) to Eng.	Joyce P.O., Vancouver, B.C.
703469	Hall, W. T.	Pte.	Evac. sick 6-4-17 to Eng.	522 Simcoe St., Victoria, B.C.
703803	Hallas, F.	R.Q.M.S.	Dec. M.S.M. L.G. 30750	The Island, West End, Steeple Clayton, nr. Winslow, Bucks, Eng.
703979	Hallett, S.	Pte.	Evac. sick 15-4-17 to Eng.; tr. to 7th Bn. and k. i. a.	152 Dallas Rd., Victoria, B.C.
925054	Halliday, A.	Pte.	W. 9-4-17 (Vimy) to Eng.	Gringle House, Wellston, Northants, Eng.
703195	Halliday, A.	Sgt.	W. 22-11-16 (Somme) to Eng.	Estevan, Sask.
703465	Halliday, H.	Pte.	W. 21-10-16 (Regina); w. 19-11-16 (Somme) to Eng.	c/o B.N.A., Prince Rupert, B.C.
467139	Hallsall, E.	Pte.	W. 21-10-16 (Regina) to Eng.	c/o Bank of Montreal, Enderby, B.C. No address available.

Reg. No.	Name	Rank	Notes	Address
703470	Halstead, W.	L.-C.	W. 8-9-16 (St. Eloi) to Eng.	Hazelton Hall, Wakefield, Eng.
252248	Halverson, M.	Pte.	W. 9-4-17 (Vimy) to Eng.	Kincorth, Sask.
703278	Hambleton, F. W.	Sgt.	Sergeant Cook; dec. Croix de Guerre, French C.R.O. 1299	
225429	Hamburg, W. A.	Pte.	W. 27-9-18 (Cambrai); dec. M.M. (Valenciennes) C.R.O. 2028	5638 Nanaimo St., Vancouver, B.C.
240675	Hamilton, H.	Pte.		c/o Mrs. P. Montgomery, 127 Mulberry St., Hamilton, Ont.
703804	Hamilton, J. W. F.	Pte.	W. 2-10-16 (St. Eloi) to Eng.	30 Gilmour St., Glasgow, Scot.
226950	Hamilton, L.	Pte.		141 Shields Rd., Glasgow, Scot.
240114	Hamilton, R. L.	Pte.		c/o Mrs. G. Hill, 42 Ritchie Ave., Toronto, Ont.
663370	Hamilton, R. R.	Pte.	W. 17-3-18 (Lens); k. i. a. 27-9-18 (Cambrai)	Mrs. Hamilton, Allenburg P.O., Ont.
220488	Hamp, W. G. H.	Pte.	W. 9-8-17 (Lens) to Eng.	Milton Heights, Ont.
252837	Hampson, J.	Pte.	W. 17-7-18 (Oppy); w. 27-9-18 (Cambrai)	Brunswick Cottage, Worcester Park, Surrey, Eng.
701101	Hampton, F.	Cpl.	W. 13-10-16 (Somme)	57 Weaver Ave., Bloomfield, N.J., U.S.A.
703090	Hampton, F.	Cpl.	Evac. sick 25-10-16 to Eng.	27 Hobson St., Bolton, Eng.
				c/o Miss D. Shelborn, 16 Windmill Rd., Hampton Hill, Middlessex, Eng.
225279	Handsfield, J. C.	Pte.	W. 27-9-18 (Cambrai) to Eng.	c/o J. Handsfield, 101 Miller Ave., Toronto, Ont.
703571	Handsley, J.	Pte.	Tr. to Lbr. Pool 2-1-18	57 Montague St., Lincoln, Eng.
704034	Hankin, F. A.	Pte.	Evac. sick 18-10-18 to Eng.	c/o Y.M.C.A., Cordova St., Vancouver, B.C.
703982	Hanley, C.	Pte.	Evac. sick 5-2-19	c/o Mrs. W. Watts, South Bank, Durham, Eng.
3108953	Hanna, J. A.	Pte.	W. 6-11-18 (Valenciennes) to Eng.	R.R. No. 2, Mona Rd., Ont.
3314086	Hannah, W. H.	Pte.		23 Raymond St., St. Catherines, Ont.
3317167	Hannant, L.	Pte.		Itterlingham, Norfolk, Eng.
704154	Hansen, C.	Pte.	K. i. a. 31-10-17 (Passchendaele)	Mrs. M. Hansen, 29 Albert St., Ottawa, Ont.
931210	Hanson, G.	Pte.	Tr. to 1st Can. Div. Emp. Co. 5-7-17	Cranbrook, B.C.
704046	Hanson, H.	Pte.	W. 21-10-16 (Regina) to Eng.	R.R. No. 1, New Westminster, B.C.
784489	Hanson, H. E.	Pte.	W. 31-10-17 (Passchendaele) to Eng.	Homeside P.O., Ont.
701103	Hanson, L.	Pte.	K. i. a. 9-4-17 (Vimy)	Miss M. Foster, 22 Eldon Place, Brighton, Eng.
2527319	Hanson, O. W.	Pte.	Acc. w. 14-8-18; w. 18-10-18 (Valenciennes)	c/o C. Christiansen, 63 Albert St., Regent's Park, London, Eng.
703528	Harbidge, F.	Pte.	Evac. sick 20-6-17 to Eng.	Smithers, B.C.
703570	Harbidge, G.	Pte.	W. 21-10-16 (Regina); w. 9-8-17 (Lens) to Eng.	Smithers, B.C.
703070	Harbridge, A.	Pte.	W. 8-9-16 (St. Eloi); w. 18-11-17 (Passchendaele) to Eng.	
2527343	Hardie, W. McK.	Pte.	Evac. sick 30-8-18 to Eng.	1140 13th Ave. E., Vancouver, B.C.
907801	Harding, W. P.	Pte.	W. 8-4-17 (Vimy) to Eng.	R.R. No. 3, Owen Sound, Ont.
703352	Hardman, J.	Pte.	W. 22-11-16 (Somme); w. 12-4-17 (Vimy)	80 Bath Rd., Bristol, Eng.
760737	Hardman, S.	Pte.	Tr. to 4th Div. Emp. Co. 12-1-18	Barrington, Cambridge, Eng.
703154	Hardy, A.	Pte.	W. 1-11-17 (Passchendaele) to Eng.	601 Hamilton St., Vancouver, B.C.
704024	Hardy, F. D.	Pte.	W. 21-10-16 (Regina) to Eng.	P.O. Box 878, Prince Rupert, B.C.
704124	Hardy, J.	Pte.	W. 21-10-16 (Regina) to Eng.	P.O. Box 878, Prince Rupert, B.C.
703285	Hardy, J. C.	Pte.	W. 1-10-16 (St. Eloi) to Eng.	c/o J. Johnson, 702 6th St., Oakland, Cal., U.S.A.
103300	Harknett, P.	Pte.	W. 12-6-17 (2nd Triangle) to Eng.	R.R. No. 2, Cloverdale, B.C.
907804	Harley, S.	Pte.	Tr. to 6th M.G.C. 1-1-17	Hillbank Station, V.I., B.C.
2591113	Harley, T. E.	Pte.		No address available.
3317055	Harriden, J.	Pte.	W. 2-9-18 (2nd Arras) to Eng.	Raglan, Ont.
703994	Harner, P. W.	Pte.	Evac. sick 8-9-17 to Eng.	929 Cotton Drive, Vancouver, B.C.

907103	Harrington, J.	L.-C.	W. 12-6-17 (2nd Triangle); w. 27-9-18 (Cambrai) to Eng.	20 Flower St., Carlisle, Eng.
703595	Harrington, T.	Pte.	K. i. a. 21-10-16 (Regina)	Mrs. Harrington, Newton, Sola, Co. Limerick, Ire.
249787	Harris, E.	Pte.	W. 2-9-18 (2nd Arras) to Eng.	44 McPherson Ave., Toronto, Ont.
145092	Harris, G.	Pte.	Tr. to 77th Bn. 10-8-16	212 Colbourne Ave., Kingston, Ont.
760840	Harris, J. G.	Pte.	W. 12-6-17 (2nd Triangle) to Eng.	Blacktall P.O., Stanley, Alta.
220120	Harris, N. B.	Pte.	Tr. to 4th C.M.G.C. 1-5-18	1248 11th Ave. W., Vancouver, B.C.
931381	Harris, S.	Pte.	Evac. sick 14-9-17 to Eng.	Grand Forks, B.C.
703152	Harris, S. A.	Pte.	W. 21-10-16 (Regina); K. i. a. 8-6-17 (2nd Triangle)	F. A. Harris, Box 6, Stanley Park, Vancouver, B.C.
907623	Harris, S. G.	Cpl.	W. 9-8-17 (Lens); tr. to Eng. for commission 23-8-18	c/o Y. Bryan, Colty Rd., Bridgend, S. Wales.
703201	Harrison, G.	Pte.	W. 21-10-16 (Regina) to Eng.	1061 Howe St., Vancouver, B.C.
126477	Harrison, J.	Pte.	W. 9-4-17 (Vimy) to Eng.	Nottingham Rd., Kegworth, Derby, Eng.
226828	Harrison, J. A.	Pte.	W. 1-10-18 (Cambrai) to Eng.	123 Lower Bagget St., Kingston, Ont.
706107	Harrison, W. F.	Pte.	W. 7-9-17 (Lens) to Eng.	912 Fairfield Rd., Victoria, B.C.
160647	Harrold, J. T.	Pte.	Evac. sick 26-11-16 to Eng.	No address available.
226999	Hart, A. R.	Pte.	W. 23-7-18 (Oppy) to Eng.	Uxbridge, Ont.
850509	Hart, J. W.	Pte.		Port Dalhousie, Ont.
225478	Hartin, M.	Pte.	W. 1-10-18 (Cambrai)	c/o Mrs. T. Jones, Weston P.O., Ont.
907374	Hartley, J. M.	Pte.	W. 1-4-17 (Vimy) to Eng.	St. John's, Newfoundland.
129034	Hartridge, R. C.	Sgt.		230 3rd St. W., North Vancouver, B.C.
540517	Hartup, F.	L.-C.	W. 11-6-17 (2nd Triangle) to Eng.	No address available.
1003241	Harvey, H.	Pte.	Evac. sick 22-9-17 to Eng.	Thessalon, Ont.
103049	Harvey, P.	Pte.	Tr. to Can. 8th Area Emp. Co. 27-9-17.	Linlithgow, Scotland.
3105096	Harvey, S. T.	Pte.	K. i. a. 2-11-18 (Valenciennes)	Mrs. J. Hendry, 1208 N. 62nd St., Terre Haute, Ind.
252679	Harvey, W.	Pte.		c/o C. Middleton, Gen. Ave., Treelon, Sask.
226472	Harwood, R. C.	Pte.	Tr. to 4th C.M.G.C. 1-5-18	R.R. No. 1, Chatham, Ont.
160974	Haskins, K.	Pte.	Evac. sick 29-8-16 to Eng.	No address available.
907525	Haslett, W. T.	Pte.	Tr. to 16th M.G. Co. 1-1-17	No address available.
907685	Haug, W. H.	Pte.	W. 25-3-17 (Vimy); dec. M.M. (Passchendaele) C.R.O. 1571; w. 4-9-18 (2nd Arras) to Eng.	Tiverton, Bruce Co., Ont.
703732	Havard, R. J.	Cpl.	Sanitary N.C.O., evac. sick 23-10-17 to Eng.	c/o Mrs. J. Rich, "The Walk," Merthyr Tydvil, Wales.
907421	Haward, H. H.	Pte.	W. 6-9-17 (Lens); w. 15-3-18 (Lens) to Eng.	1127 Rae St., Regina, Sask.
663637	Hawes, J.	Pte.	W. 23-7-18 (Oppy) to Eng.	Burlington, Ont.
103366	Hawkins, W. F.	Pte.	K. i. a. 10-6-17 (2nd Triangle)	Mrs. Hawkins, 61 Islip Rd., Oxford, Eng.
225374	Hawley, F. A.	Pte.	Evac. sick 31-10-17 to Eng.	51 Emily St., Brantford, Ont.
703584	Hawson, H.	Pte.	W. 20-11-16 (Somme); tr. to 8th Can. Area Emp. Co. 27-9-17.	
663095	Hawthorne, R. B.	Pte.	W. 10-4-18 (Oppy) to Eng.	Travellers Hotel, Vancouver, B.C.
703492	Hay, A. E.	Pte.	K. i. a. 19-10-16 (Somme)	553 Sherbourne St., Toronto, Ont.
907987	Hay, D. H.	Pte.	Evac. sick 29-3-17 to Eng.	Mrs. J. Hay, 10 Palmeny St., Leith, Scotland.
249921	Hayden, H.	Pte.	W. 23-3-18 (Lens) to Eng.	Yellowgrass, Sask.
703246	Havens, H.	C.Q.M.S.	Dec. M.M. (Passchendaele) C.R.O. 1571; tr. to Eng. for commission 23-8-18.	215 Oak St., Toronto, Ont.
907203	Hayes, R. J.	Pte.	Tr. to 16th M.G. Co. 1-1-17	P.O. Box 1034, Vancouver, B.C.
663171	Hayes, O. D.	Pte.	W. 1-10-18 (Cambrai) to Eng.	No address available. c/o Mrs. E. McCallum, 223 Perth Ave., Toronto, Ont.

102652	Haynes, A. C.	Pte.	K. i. a. 15-5-17 (1st Triangle)	A. L. Haynes, 284 45th Ave. E., Vancouver, B.C.
703471	Haynes, E. B.	Pte.	W. 9-4-17 (Vimy) to Eng.	c/o Seebach & Hubble, Trescombe Portage, Willow River, B.C.
126523	Haynes, C. J.	Pte.	Tr. to C.A.M.C. 14-7-16	No address available.
704165	Hayward, E. F.	Pte.	Tr. to 51st Bn. 2-8-16	2820 Blackwood St., Victoria, B.C.
761198	Hayward, H. A.	Pte.	W. 9-4-17 (Vimy) to Eng.	c/o E. Bennett, 4004 Commercial St., S. Vancouver.
103173	Hayward, P. J.	Pte.	Tr. to 8th Bn. 30-6-17	2056 Milton St., Victoria, B.C.
160681	Hazelwood, H.	Pte.	K. i. a. 18-5-17 (1st Triangle)	No address available.
703840	Hazen, C. T.	Pte.	K. i. a. 9-4-17 (Vimy)	G. L. Hazen, 1419 Queen St., Toronto, Ont.
541333	Hazlett, C. H.	Pte.	W. 30-10-16 (Somme) to Eng.	No address available.
703985	Headdon, H. B.	Pte.	W. 17-9-16 (St. Eloi); w. 21-10-16 (Regina) to Eng.	93 Grosvenor Rd., St. Paul's, Bristol, Eng.
252290	Heal, R. W.	Pte.	W. 12-6-17 (1st Triangle) to Eng.	Torrington, Eng.
761219	Hearn, F. J.	Pte.	Tr. to 7th Can. Lbr. Co. 16-8-17	723 Cordova St. E., Vancouver, B.C.
760755	Hearnden, G. P.	C.S.M.	Dec. D.C.M. (New Year's Hon. Desp. 1-1-19)	Joyce P.O., Collingwood, B.C.
703871	Heaven, A. G.	Cpl.	Dec. M.M. (Somme) D.R.O. 375; w. 9-4-17 (Vimy) to Eng.	
102573	Hedges, W. H.	Pte.	W. 11-11-16 (Somme) to Eng.	P.O. Box 266, Grand Forks, B.C.
703943	Heffer, A.	Pte.	Evac. sick 24-11-16	c/o Mrs. C. Cline, 608 Broadway Bldg., Portland, Ore.
703686	Hellscher, R.	Pte.		Fairvak Terrace, Maindee, Newport, Wales.
249128	Helmrich, H.	L-C.		Midway, B.C.
703600	Helland, C.	Pte.	W. 21-10-16 (Regina); w. 12-6-17 (2nd Triangle); tr. to 44th Bn. 12-8-18	Kitchener, Ont.
102743	Henderson, A. C.	Pte.	K. i. a. 20-6-17 (1st Triangle)	Prince Rupert, B.C.
704102	Henderson, A. H.	Pte.	Att. from C.A.M.C. to Water Detail	Mrs. Henderson, 4221 Elgin St., South Vancouver, B.C.
908153	Henderson, G. M.	L-C.	W. 17-5-17 (1st Triangle); dec. M.M. (Oppy) C.R.O. 1755; w. 27-9-18 (Cambrai)	Bank of Commerce, Courtenay, B.C.
908225	Henderson, H. F. K.	Pte.	Evac. sick 20-1-17 to Eng.	Oak River, Man.
102766	Henderson, H. H.	Pte.	Tr. to Lbr. Pool 16-9-18	No address available.
703458	Henderson, J. P.	Cpl.	W. 11-11-16 (Somme); Sanitary N.C.O.	c/o Mrs. Farley, 7 Foxcote Rd., Bedminster, Eng.
727824	Henderson, J. P.	Sgt.	W. 11-11-16 (Somme); Sanitary N.C.O.	Hill St., Lisburn, Co. Antrim, Ireland.
252767	Henderson, N.	Pte.	Evac. sick 18-9-18 to Eng.	694 Waterloo St., London, Ont.
102239	Henderson, R. C.	Pte.	Tr. to 2nd Can. Lbr. Co. 16-8-17	48 Banknock, Stirling, Scot.
703872	Henderson, W. H.	L-C.	D. o. w. (acc.) 29-9-16	2016 Blanchard St., Victoria, B.C.
703753	Henley, S. V.	Pte.	Evac. sick 18-11-16 to Eng.	Mrs. W. Robertson, P.O. Box 484, Hedley, B.C.
226426	Henrich, G. L.	Pte.	Tr. to Eng. for R.N.W.M.P. 27-1-19	38 Walnut St., Nanaimo, B.C.
838985	Henry, G. E.	Pte.	Dec. M.M. (2nd Arras) C.R.O. 1930; tr. to Eng. for demob. 9-2-19	145½ Church St., Toronto, Ont.
703155	Heppell, R.	Pte.	Evac. sick 29-7-16	Flesherton, Ont.
703441	Herbert, S. A.	C.S.M.	W. 9-6-17 (2nd Triangle); tr. to Lbr. Pool 25-10-17	c/o Mrs. J. Matte, Rimouski, Que.
226818	Hermiston, K.	Pte.	W. 14-11-17 (Passchendaele) to Eng.	67 Richmond Rd., Ilford, Essex, Eng.
706516	Herrington, A.	Pte.	Evac. sick 19-9-17 to Eng.	84 Collingwood St., Kingston, Ont.
850080	Hetherington, C.	Cpl.	Evac. sick 26-8-18 to Eng.	Duncan, B.C.
252088	Hetherington, P.	Pte.	W. 2-8-17 (Lens); w. 27-9-18 (Cambrai) to Eng.	Dundas, Ont.
704035	Hevenor, J. H.	L-C.	W. 31-8-16 (St. Eloi) to Eng.	Caunamore, Ont.
3031156	Hewitt, L.	Pte.	K. i. a. 27-9-18 (Cambrai)	Hazelton, B.C.
1004120	Hewson, R. A. C.	Pte.	W. 24-10-17 (Passchendaele) to Eng.	John Hewitt, Greenwood Rd., Leeds, Eng.
				Gore Bay, Ont.

Number	Name	Rank	Service Record	Address
760841	Heyes, G.	Pte.	Evac. sick 15-6-17 to Eng.	815 Burrard St., Vancouver, B.C.
703188	Heyes, H.	Pte.	W. 22-10-16 (Regina); w. 7-8-17 (Lens) to Eng.	132 Salisbury St., Liverpool, Eng.
703618	Hickes, R. T.	Sgt.	Medical Sergeant; evac. sick in Eng. 10-12-16.	P.O. Box 364, Nelson, B.C.
219481	Hickey, E. L.	L.-C.	W. 14-5-17 (1st Triangle) to Eng.	Picton, Ont.
103157	Hickey, T. M.	Sgt.	W. 8-6-17 (2nd Triangle); tr. to Lbr. Pool 31-10-17	
237657	Hicks, N.	†Pte.		715 Cook St., Victoria, B.C.
225928	Hicks, J. S.	Pte.	Tr. to Fort Garry Horse 11-4-18	612 Delaware Ave., Toronto, Ont.
3109591	Higginson, W. E.	Pte.		Allanburg, Ont.
183917	Higgins, P. W.	Pte.	Evac. sick 9-12-16 to Eng.	Inholmes, Ont.
704061	Higgs, C. C.	Sgt.	K. i. a. 1-9-16 (St. Eliot).	No address available.
703956	Hill, A. J.	Pte.	D. o. w. 23-10-16 (Regina).	Mrs. C. W. Higgs, Lima P.O., O.R.C., South Africa.
174855	Hill, C.	Pte.	Tr. to 11th M.G.C. 10-12-16	Mrs. J. A. Hill, Andover, South Dakota, U.S.A.
3109260	Hill, G.	Pte.	K. i. a. 2-11-18 (Valenciennes).	No address available.
226980	Hill, H. C.	Pte.	W. 3-9-18 (2nd Arras)	W. Hill, R.R. No. 2, Marshville, Ont.
907406	Hill, J. R.	Pte.	W. 9-4-17 (Vimy); evac. sick 2-11-17 to Eng.	728 Elgin St., Smith Falls, Ont.
907213	Hillis, T. J.	Cpl.	W. 9-4-17 (Vimy); evac. sick 29-4-17 to Eng.	Ethelbert, Sask.
252950	Hillman, J.	Pte.	W. 3-9-18 (2nd Arras) to Eng.	295 Donegal Rd., Belfast, Ire.
145774	Himes, A. E.	Pte.	W. 18-3-18 (Lens); tr. to 51st Bn. 12-8-18.	Lockbridge, Ohio, U.S.A.
164104	Hinchcliffe, R. E.	Pte.	W. 27-9-18 (Cambrai); evac. sick 4-1-19 to Eng	187 McGillivra St., Ottawa, Ont.
703511	Hinds, J. T.	Cpl.	K. i. a. 11-11-16 (Somme)	19 Jepson St., Niagara Central, Ont.
722454	Hing3t, E. J.	Pte.	Evac. sick 28-12-17 to Eng.	Mrs. Hinds, 217 Kennedy St., Nanaimo, B.C.
703493	Hinkley, H. R.	Pte.	Tr. to 51st Bn. 2-8-16.	Mitchel, Ont.
102705	Hinksman, D.	Pte.	W. 13-6-17 (2nd Triangle); dec. M.M. (Lens) C.R.O. 1419; dec. Bar to M.M. (2nd Arras) C.R.O. 1930; w. 1-10-18 (Cambrai) to Eng.	c/o Mrs. Handley, P.O. Box 17, Route 5, Ifills-borough, Ore., U.S.A.
219869	Hinton, G. J.	L.-C.	W. 27-9-18 (Cambrai) to Eng.	General Delivery, P.O. Nanaimo, B.C.
761280	Hobbs, C. H.	Pte.	W. 9-6-17 (2nd Triangle) to Eng.; k. i. a. 17-8-17 (Lens)	c/o Mrs. J. Leslie, Domville, Ont.
102695	Hobbs, R. A.	Sgt.	Sergeant Shoemaker	Mrs. Hobbs, 80 Starr St., Edgeware Rd., London, Eng.
704411	Hodge, F.	Pte.		1020 Arnot Ave., The Gorge, Victoria, B.C.
704174	Hodgson, A.	Pte.	K. i. a. 20-10-16 (Regina).	Tandridge, nr. Oxted, Surrey, Eng.
252566	Hodgson, H.	Pte.		Mrs. Hodgson, cor. 12th St. and St. George's Ave., N. Vancouver, B.C.
3110249	Hodgson, T. E.	Pte.		Brooklyn, Guildford Rd., S. Farnborough, Eng.
3105399	Hoeg, E. C. P.	Pte.	W. 27-9-18 (Cambrai) to Eng	Cayuga, Ont.
3030545	Hogan, J.	Pte.	Tr. to 11th C.L.T.M.B. 1-10-17.	c/o Bank of Nova Scotia, Hamilton, Ont.
907592	Hogg, A.	Pte.		2728 Prairie Ave., St. Louis, Mo., U.S.A.
703901	Holbrook, E. W.	Sgt.	Dec. D.C.M. (Somme) D.R.O. 375; tr. to Lbr. Pool 4-11-17	Menden, Ont.
103226	Holburn, R.	L.-C.	W. 27-9-17 (Passchendaele) to Eng.	Grand Forks, B.C.
106810	Holden, W. J.	Sgt.	Bandmaster	c/o Mrs. A. Ormiston, 49 Prospect St., Methuen, Mass.
703233	Holder, F. A.	Pte.	Tr. to 51st Bn. 2-8-16.	8 Page St., St. Catherines, Ont.
208079	Holland, F.	Pte.	Tr. to 11th M.G.C.	826 Dominion Rd., Victoria, B.C.
203080	Holland, H.	L.-C.	Dec. M.M. (Passchendaele) C.R.O. 1571; tr. to Eng. Demob. duty 14-3-19	c/o Mrs. A. Sendall, 181 Crawley Rd., Horsham, Eng.
703874	Holland, F. C.	Pte.	Evac. sick 24-11-16 to Eng.	c/o Miss Lowden, 24 Highgate, Kendal, Eng. Greenacres, Wash., U.S.A.
3108702	Holland, W. H.	Pte.		P.O. Box 810, Thorold, Ont.

Number	Name	Rank	Service Record	Address
506558	Hollins, T. A.	Pte.	Evac. sick 5-3-18 to Eng.	Maywood P.O., Victoria, B.C.
2528321	Hollis, H. I.	Pte.	W. 6-9-18 (2nd Arras) to Eng.	727 Anaheim St., Pittsburg, U.S.A.
835738	Hollowood, F.	Pte.	D. o. w. 2-11-17 (Passchendaele)	T. Hollowood, Sharbot Lake, Ont.
907620	Hollowell, W. S.	Pte.	K. i. a. 10-4-17 (Vimy)	Thos. B. Hollowell, 84 Broadway, Northampton, Eng.
703674	Hollyer, W.	Cpl.	Att. P.B. Engr. Unit 11-7-17.	27 Montpelier Rd., Twickenham, Eng.
911759	Holmes, A. T. F.	Sgt.	W. 9-4-17 (Vimy) to Eng.	956 11th Ave. E., Vancouver, B.C.
703981	Holmes, G.	Pte.	Tr. to 51st Bn. 2-8-16	c/o E. N. Holmes, Creston, B.C.
1003600	Holmes, L. A.	Pte.	K. i. a. 27-9-18 (Cambrai)	Mrs. M. Holmes, 33 Highland Ave., Hamilton, Ont.
703348	Holman, C.	Sgt.	W. 11-11-16 (Somme) to Eng.; ret. 8-7-17; evac. sick 3-10-17 to Eng.	
703306	Holt, E. S.	Pte.	Tr. to 6th Can. Area Emp. Co. 22-8-17.	Upper Musquodoblh, Halifax Co., N.S.
438270	Holt, G. C.	Cpl.	W. 30-9-18 (Cambrai) to Eng.	c/o Val. Holt, Ampfield, Hants, Eng.
102114	Holt, H.	Pte.	W. 12-6-17 (2nd Triangle); w. 8-8-18 (Amiens) to Eng.	14 St. Mary's Place, Bury, Lancs, Eng.
761160	Holt, J.	Pte.	W. 13-5-17 (1st Triangle); w. 17-11-17 (Passchendaele)	1048 Pandora St., Victoria, B.C.
2528348	Homan, W. E.	Pte.	W. 8-8-18 (Amiens)	1129 Woodland Drive, Vancouver, B.C.
2528491	Honeywell, A.	Pte.	Tr. to 4th M.G.C. 1-5-18	84 Ilford Rd., Toronto, Ont.
250085	Honsinger, E. J.	Pte.	W. 16-3-18 (Lens); dec. M.M. (2nd Arras) C.R.O. 1930	927 Albert St., Watts, Cal., U.S.A.
102474	Hood, D.	Pte.	W. and missing after action 11-6-17; reported as prisoner of war.	R.R. No. 3, Moorefield, Ont.
102606	Hook, J. A.	Sgt.	W. 7-6-17 (2nd Triangle); w. 8-8-18 (Amiens) tr. to Eng. for commission 31-10-18	c/o Mrs. McCulloch, 40 New Rd, Ayr, Scot.
160465	Hooks, C.	Pte.	W. 23-9-17 (Lens) to Eng.	Boundary Bay, Ladner, B.C.
931125	Hopkins, A.	Pte.	Tr. to Lbr. Pool 28-6-18.	7 Jubilee St., Walsend-on-Tyne, Eng.
763064	Hopkins, W.	Pte.	W. 2-9-18 (2nd Arras) to Eng.	c/o W. Hopkins, Colwynstone, Wales.
1003007	Hopkins, W. F.	Sgt.		c/o J. Keeler, Bracebridge, Ont.
850430	Horner, T. W.	Pte.	W. 1-10-18 (Cambrai) to Eng.	Sylvan Valley, Algoma, Ont.
703221	Horrobin, W. B.	Pte.	W. 8-8-18 (Amiens); w. 6-11-18 (Valenciennes) to Eng.	3 Woodland Place, East Greenwich, London, Eng.
669213	Horsfield, J.	Pte.	W. 27-9-18 (Cambrai) to Eng.	1290 Burrard St., Vancouver, B.C.
703211	Horwood, E. R.	Pte.	Tr. to Eng. Demob. duty 29-1-19.	175 Lisgar St., Toronto, Ont.
703104	Horwood, W. J.	Sgt.	Lewis Gun N.C.O.; tr. to Eng. for commission in R.A.F. 30-1-18.	P.O. Box 202, Cumberland, B.C.
226492	Hoskins, H. A.	Pte.	W. 27-9-18 (Cambrai) to Eng.	103 Holloway, Bath, Eng.
2527341	Hough, F. N.	Pte.	W. 2-9-18 (Cambrai) to Eng.	191 Royce Ave., Toronto, Ont.
102752	Houghton, J.	L.-S.	Tr. to 4th M.G.C. 3-5-18	Emily St., Paris, Ont.
226877	Houle, A.	Pte.	K. i. a. 1-11-17 (Passchendaele).	14 Norwood Grove, Leeds, Eng.
760714	Hourston, W. B.	Pte.	W. 9-4-17 (Vimy)	A. Houle. Hoberdean, Que.
703494	House, A. R.	Pte.	Tr. to 51st Bn. 16-7-16.	c/o Mrs. McKie, Ryehill Ave., Leith, Scot.
703938	Houston, E.	Sgt.	Dec. M.M. (Amiens) C.R.O. 1899; d. o. w. 4-9-18 (2nd Arras)	Leighton Rd., Oak Bay, Victoria, B.C.
540518	Houston, T.	Pte.	W. 11-11-16 (Somme) to Eng.	T. Houston, Arnprior, Ont.
220371	Howard, J.	Pte.	D. o. w. 6-6-17 (2nd Triangle)	No address available.
703009	Howden, J. C.	Cpl.	Evac. sick 20-4-17 to Eng.	N. Howard, Manchester, Eng.
703299	Howe, J.	Pte.	Tr. to Strathcona's Horse 11-4-18.	460 Gorge Road, Victoria, B.C.
703733	Howe, W. E.	Pte.	W. 9-3-17 (Vimy); d. o. w. 4-11-18 (2nd Arras)	Murrayville P.O., B.C.
				Mrs. L. Howe, Port Haney, B.C.

Number	Name	Rank	Details	Address
704002	Howitt, M. H.	Sgt.	Dec. M.M. (Cambrai) C.R.O. 1989; evac. sick to Eng. 16-1-19.	104 George St., Hamilton, Ont.
136258	Hubbard, A.	Pte.	K. i. a. 15-9-16 (St. Eloi).	No address available.
3105430	Hubbard, H.	Pte.	Evac. sick 25-2-19 to Eng.	Bigheart, Okla., U.S.A.
703203	Huck, W. E.	Cpl.	K. i. a. 20-10-16 (Regina).	Mrs. W. E. Huck, Whaleton P.O., B.C.
703010	Hudson, H.	Pte.	Evac. sick 11-3-19.	Capilano P.O., North Vancouver, B.C.
126099	Hudson, H.	Pte.	D. o. w. (acc.) 4-1-18.	Mrs. Rominger, 10 King St., Kitchener, Ont.
703280	Hudson, R. E.	Pte.	Dec. M.M. (Somme) D.R.O. 316; evac. sick 5-2-17 to Eng.	Mrs. Lumley, 2537 Forbes St., Victoria, B.C.
443952	Hudspith, R.	Pte.	Evac. sick 17-11-17 to Eng.	c/o Mrs. L. Ashmore, 18 Dene View, Benwell, Newcastle, Eng.
160215	Huggins, F. W.	Pte.	Tr. to Eng. as minor 27-6-17.	No address available.
2527401	Hughes, D. K.	Pte.	W. 1-10-18 (Cambrai) to Eng.	11 Hill St. Douglas, Isle of Man.
249565	Hughes, E. R.	Pte.	W. 10-4-18 (Oppy) to Eng.	334 Mont Rose Ave., Toronto, Ont.
160981	Hughes, J.	Pte.	W. 9-4-17 (Vimy) to Eng.	1405 4th St. W., Calgary, Alta.
908190	Hughes, R.	L.-C.		Lunnford, Alta.
103374	Hughes, T. B.	Pte.	Evac. sick 25-4-19 to Eng.	Box 447, Nanaimo, B.C.
252429	Hughes, W. J.	Pte.	K. i. a. 9-4-17 (Vimy).	Mrs. D. Hughes, Baxterville, Ont.
703737	Hulbert, F. H.	Pte.	Tr. to 51st Bn. 16-7-16.	Mrs. Hume, 1046 Harwood St., Vancouver, B.C.
252667	Hulbig, F. H.	Pte.	K. i. a. 9-4-17 (Vimy).	Mrs. L. Hulbig, c/o J. H. C. Eddy, 36 Hart Ave., Winnipeg, Man.
925259	Hull, S. E.	Pte.	W. 9-4-17 (Vimy) to Eng.	c/o H. Spilsbury, Amulet. Sask.
703515	Hume, A.	Pte.	K. i. a. 11-5-17 (1st Triangle).	Mrs. J. Hume, 1046 Harwood St., Vancouver, B.C.
931776	Humphrey, J. F.	Pte.	Tr. to Eng. as minor 18-10-17.	c/o Mrs. J. Humphrey, 1317 Cook St., Victoria, B.C.
1003292	Humphrey, R. W.	Pte.	Evac. sick 1-12-17 to Eng.	2 Wells St., 4 Gulan, Wales.
1003588	Humphrey, L. C.	Cpl.		220 Kenilworth Ave., Toronto, Ont.
2523222	Hunt, C.	Pte.	Evac. sick 14-2-17 to Eng.	Waldeck, Sask.
703544	Hunt, L. E.	Pte.	W. 23-10-16 (Somme) to Eng.	837 Broadway E., Vancouver, B.C.
253021	Hunter, D. A.	Sgt.	K. i. a. 9-4-17 (Vimy).	R.R. No. 3, Cars, Ont.
911777	Hunter, E. A.	Pte.	Evac. sick 29-12-17 to Eng.	Mrs. Hunt, Astley Vicarage, Shropshire, Eng.
226863	Hunter, K. L.	Pte.	W. 20-3-18 (Lens); k. i. a. 1-10-18 (Cambrai).	c/o Mrs. F. Leonard, 308 Joseph St., Utica, N.Y., U.S.A
761315	Hunter, R. P.	Pte.	W. 12-5-17 (1st Triangle) to Eng.	Mrs. L. Hunter, Armstrong, B.C.
103016	Hunter, T. J.	Pte.	K. i. a. 8-9-16 (St. Eloi).	Mrs. Scott, 2023 4th Ave. E., Vancouver, B.C.
220050	Hunter, W. R.	Pte.	K. i. a. 24-8-18 (Amiens).	No address available.
1003294	Huntington, A. S.	Cpl.	W. 19-8-16 (St. Eloi) to Eng.	I. Hunter, Hilly Grove, Ont.
220153	Huntington, E. F.	Pte.	Evac. sick 18-10-18.	No address available.
703103	Hurlburt, H. S.	Sgt.	W. 9-4-17 (Vimy) to Eng.	1133 Hornby St., Vancouver, B.C.
911258	Hurn, B.	Pte.		McLeod, Alta.
1003980	Hurrell, S. R.	Pte.	W. 9-6-17 (2nd Triangle) to Eng.	Gore Bay, Ont.
703854	Hussey, E. S. L.	Pte.	W. 20-11-16 (Somme); tr .to Lbr. Pool 27-10-17	Pensilra, nr. Liskard, Cornwall, Eng.
703875	Hutchings, G. S.	R.Q.M.S.	Men. in des. L.G. 30448: tr. to Eng. on exchange, 27-11-17.	c/o G.W.V.A. Vancouver, B.C.
703658	Hutchings, H. J.	Pte.	Tr. to 2nd C.M.G. 22-11-18.	69 57th Ave. W., South Vancouver, B.C.
907229	Hutchinson, C. B.	L.-C.		20 Whitbred Rd., Brockley, Kent, Eng.
2521102	Hutchison, G. O.	Pte.	W. 30-10-17 (Passchendaele) to Eng.	P.O. Box 154, Digby, N.S.
160207	Hutton, H. J.	Pte.	W. 9-4-17 (Vimy) to Eng.	Balmadie, Aberdeenshire, Scotland.
160979	Hutton, W. J.	Pte.	Evac. sick 13-11-17 to Eng.	628 12th St., Lethbridge, Alta.

Number	Name	Rank	Event	Address
931242	Hyde, F. L.	Pte.	K. i. a. 19-8-16.	Mrs. L. Hyde, R.R. No. 3, Waterford, Ont.
252415	Hydon, M.	Pte.	W. 27-9-18 (Cambrai) to Eng.	25 Monteith St., Detroit, Mich., U.S.A.
250139	Hynes, E. J.	Pte.	W. 27-9-18 (Cambrai) to Eng.	c/o Mrs. Roirdon, Arthur St., Toronto, Ont.
226977	Iles, L.	Pte.	W. 4-9-18 (2nd Arras) to Eng.	350 Crawford St., Toronto, Ont.
2237199	Iliffe, A.	Pte.		c/o Mrs. Hamilton, 213½ Davenport Rd., Toronto, Ont.
907857	Illyw, B.	Pte.	Tr. to 8th Can. Area. Emp. Co.	No address available.
252675	Ince, F.	Pte.	K. i. a. 9-4-17 (Vimy).	A. Ince, G.P.O., Clare, Suffolk, Eng.
1003082	Inch, H.	Pte.		36 Blucher St., Saulte Ste. Marie, Ont.
136412	Inkster, J. L.	Pte.	W. 1-11-17 (Passchendaele) to Eng.	Goderich, Ont.
704095	Irasik, A.	Pte.	K. i. a. 8-9-16 (St. Eloi).	No address available.
240016	Ireland, G. M.	Pte.	W. 10-4-18 (Oppy) to Eng.	32 Wentworth St., Hamilton, Ont.
703787	Irish, R. J.	Pte.	Evac. sick 2-4-18 to Eng.	Coleman, Ont.
240126	Irvine, W.	Pte.		86 Mars Ave. N., Hamilton, Ont.
1003947	Isherwood. R.	Pte.		13th Ave. E., Vancouver, B.C.
1023401	Iversen, J.	Pte.	Tr. to Lbr. Pool 14-9-18.	No address available.
703269	Iverson, W. J.	C.Q.M.S.		Capliano P.O., Vancouver, B.C.
907063	Jack, J. W. C.	Pte.	Tr. to 16th M.G.C. 1-1-17.	No address available.
200178	Jacklin, A.	Pte.		1534 Redfern St., Victoria, B.C.
850375	Jacklin, G. E.	Pte.	W. 6-9-18 (2nd Arras) to Eng.	193 Main St., Niagara Falls, Ont.
703977	Jacks, G. E.	Pte.	W. 21-10-16 (Regina); tr. to Eng. from P.B. 13-12-18	
703913	Jackson, A. B.	Pte.	W. 1-10-18 (Cambrai) to Eng.	c/o L.S.B., Creston, B.C.
252871	Jackson, J. McN	Pte.	K. i. a. 9-4-17 (Vimy).	1626 13th Ave. E., Vancouver, B.C.
704112	Jackson, N.	L.-C.	W. 11-11-16 (Somme); d. o. w. 12-4-17 (Vimy)	Mrs. C. Jackson, 57 Approach Rd., Margate, Eng.
663463	Jackson, W. J.	Pte.	D. o. w. 8-10-18 (Cambrai).	J. W. Jackson, 593 E. 23rd St., Paterson, N.J., U.S.A.
901177	Jacobs, A. E.	Pte.	K. i. a. 9-4-17 (Vimy).	Mrs. W. Alexander, Alton, Ont.
907157	Jacques, J.	Pte.	W. 9-4-17 (Vimy) to Eng.	F. Jacobs, Adanac, Sask.
907237	Jacques, L.	Pte.	Tr. to 16th M.G.C. 1-1-17.	c/o G. Monkley, Underwood, Jocksdale, Notts, Eng.
2529437	Jalbert, L. L.	Pte.	W. 1-10-18 (Cambrai) to Eng.	No address available.
703137	James, A. L.	Pte.	K. i. a. 8-6-17 (2nd Triangle)	Naughton, Ont.
706076	James, G. O.	Sgt.	Evac. sick 1-9-16 to Eng.	Mrs. James, Kerrisdale P.O., Vancouver, B.C.
	James, M. P.	Pte.	W. and missing after action 5-8-17 (Lens)	983 53rd Ave, E., Vancouver, B.C.
706851	James, W. H.	Pte.		Mrs. James, 359 Sandy Combe Rd., Kew Gardens, London, Eng.
760057	Jamieson, A. B.	Pte.	Evac. sick in Eng. 23-2-18.	c/o Mrs. Jas. March, 828 Old Esquimalt Rd., Victoria.
703587	Jamieson, D.	Pte.	Dec. M.M. (Passchendaele) C.R.O. 1571	Ardley P.O., Vancouver, B.C.
3109601	Jardine, C. L.	Pte.	Tr. to 4th Div. A.P.M. 28-1-19.	630 Burrard St., Vancouver, B.C.
703430	Jarratt, R. H.	Pte.		Powasson, Ont.
3107513	Jarrett, C. F.	Pte.	Evac. sick 6-1-19 to Eng.	558 Hornby St., Vancouver, B.C.
3108332	Jarrett, G.	Pte.	Evac. sick 14-12-18 to Eng.	c/o J. Lampman, Box 320, Wellandsport, Ont.
703143	Jarvis, I. W. Y.	Sgt.	Tr. to 51st Bn. 2-8-16.	170 Queen St. N., Hamilton, Ont.
1045905	Jarvis, W.	Pte.	Acc. w. 26-8-18 to Eng.	2380 6th Ave. W., Vancouver, B.C.
850426	Jeffreys, E. F.	Pte.	K. i. a. 1-10-18 (Cambrai)	R.R. No. 1, Decatur, Texas, U.S.A.
1003825	Jenkins, G. J.	Pte.	D. o. w. 15-4-18 (Oppy).	Mrs. J. McKinley, R.R. No. 1, Erin, Ont.
				Geo. Jenkins, Western Mill, Reynoldstone, Glamorganshire, Wales.
703930	Jennings, A.	Pte.	W. 11-11-16 (Somme); k. i. a. 9-4-17 (Vimy).	Mrs. E. R. Jennings, Appledale, Nelson, B.C.
760230	Jennings, G. H.	Pte.		1321 Point St., Victoria, B.C.
704103	Jensen, C.	Pte.	Evac. sick ex 11th C.L.T.M.B. 30-9-17 to Eng.	No address available.

903107	Jeremy, S. W.	L.-C.	W. 9-4-17 (Vimy) to Eng.	48 Geere Rd., Westham, Essex, Eng.
2529388	Jerman, J. A.	Pte.		179 Fulton Ave., Toronto, Ont.
3110677	Jewell, L.	Pte.		Gravenhurst, Ont.
704068	Jewitt, W. E.	Pte.		Gen. Del., Rossland, B.C.
1003508	Jewitt, L.	Pte.	W. 23-9-17 (Lens) to Eng.	Walford, Ont.
703383	John, W.	Pte.	Tr. to 61st Bn. 2-8-16.	12 Haliburton St., Nanaimo, B.C.
102768	Johncox, W.	Pte.	W. 5-6-17 (2nd Triangle) to Eng.	1055 12th St. E., Vancouver, B.C.
703207	Johnson, A.	Pte.	D. o. w. 10-1-17 (w. Somme).	No address available.
703932	Johnson, A. H	Pte.	W. 31-10-16 (Somme) to Eng.	c/o Mrs. Jas. Hardy, Box 140, Grand Forks, B.C.
704092	Johnson, E. H.	Pte.	W. 31-10-16 (Somme) to Eng.	Prince George, B.C.
2202570	Johnson, G. H.	Pte.	Dec. M.M. (Passchendaele) C.R.O. 1571	26 Bank St., Toronto, Ont.
135751	Johnson, H. H.	L.-C.	W. 8-8-18 (Amiens) to Eng.	11 Davidson St., Galt, Ont.
784084	Johnson, H. J.	L.-C.		200 Oak St., Toronto, Ont.
704060	Johnson, J. F.	Pte.	W. 1. a. 21-10-16 (Regina) to Eng.	173 McNab St. N., Hamilton, Ont.
931243	Johnson, J.	Pte.	W. 9-6-17 (2nd Triangle) to Eng.	No address available.
249348	Johnson, M.	Pte.	K. l. a. 23-7-18 (Oppy)	Alexandria, Ont.
252656	Johnson, T. W.	Pte.	W. 9-4-17 (Vimy) to Eng.	No address available.
200078	Johnson, W. R.	Cpl.	Tr. to Eng. for commission 31-10-18	Mrs. E. Kelly, R.R. No. 3, Fenelon Falls, Ont.
3107008	Johnson, W. W.	Pte.		3321 6th Ave. W., Vancouver, B.C.
2528471	Johnson, A.	Pte.	W. 24-8-18 (Amiens) to Eng.	3500 5th Ave., Pittsburg, Pa., U.S.A.
207166	Johnston, C.	Pte.	W. 13-5-17 (1st Triangle) to Eng.	290 John St. N., Hamilton, Ont.
926040	Johnston, F.	Pte.	K. l. a. 16-5-17 (1st Triangle)	Warner, Wisconsin, U.S.A.
252553	Johnston, G. V.	Pte.	K. l. a. 9-4-17 (Vimy)	L. Johnston, Madison Lake, Minn., U.S.A.
703574	Johnston, G. V.	Pte.	W. 21-10-16 (Regina); d.o.w. 16-11-16 (Somme)	Mrs. C. Johnston, P.O. Box 33, Abbey, Sask.
207435	Johnston, J.	L.-C.	W. 27-9-18 (Cambrai) to Eng.	Mrs. C. H. Johnston, 1601 Robson St., Vancouver, B.C.
102116	Johnston, P.	Pte.	W. 17-5-17 (1st Triangle); w. 8-6-17 (2nd Triangle) to Eng.	Moorefield, Ballymena, Co. Antrim, Ire.
1003782	Johnston, R. McW	Pte.	Evac. sick 11-4-18 to Eng.	Stone Falls, Berwickshire, Scot.
704113	Johnston, T.	Pte.	Tr. to 61st Bn. 2-8-16.	Copper Cliff, Ont.
761083	Johnston, T.	Pte.	W. 9-4-17 (Vimy) to Eng.	c/o J. Mayell, Kingston, Ont.
931476	Johnstone, A. A.	Cpl.	W. 8-8-18 (Amiens) to Eng.	938 12th Ave. W., Vancouver, B.C.
102809	Johnstone, S.	Pte.	Tr. to 4th Lbr. Bn. 4-8-17	c/o Mrs. M. McClenaghan, Swift Current, Sask.
703516	Johnstone, W.	Sgt.	W. 20-11-16 (Regina) w and missing after action 11-6-17 (2nd Triangle)	c/o Chas. Johnstone, Crown Mansions, Aberdeen, Scot.
703638	Johnstone, W.	Pte.		Mrs. J. McIntyre, Eastfield, Selkirk, Scot.
126052	Jolley, A. J.	Sgt.	K. l. a. 22-10-16 (Regina).	2587 Powell St., Vancouver, B.C.
645063	Jones, A. E.	Sgt.		Mrs. Jolley, 14 Strange St., Guelph, Ont.
703666	Jones, A. N.	L.-C.	Evac. sick 23-10-16 to Eng.	Big House Ranch, Windermere, B.C.
907037	Jones, A. R.	Pte.	W. 9-4-17 (Vimy) to Eng.	41 Pythian St., Liverpool, Eng.
225382	Jones, C. R.	Pte.	W. (Passchendaele) to Eng 20-12-17	1459 Albert St., Regina, Sask.
2528464	Jones, H. J.	Pte.	1-10-18 (Cambrai) to Eng.	R.R. No. 2, Dunville, Ont.
704114	Jones, H. P.	Pte.	W. 22-10-16 (Regina) to Eng.	c/o John D. Jones, Casenovia, N.Y., U.S.A.
703075	Jones, I. H.	Pte.	Tr. to R.A.F. 3-6-18.	Melville St., Vancouver, B.C.
761257	Jones, S.	Pte.	D. o. w. 17-4-17 (Vimy)	Park, Wexford, Ireland.
703655	Jones, T.	Pte.	Tr. to 11th C.I.T.M.B. 1-10-17	Mrs. Jones, 2063 13th Ave. E., Vancouver, B.C.
760494	Jones, T. O.	Pte.	Evac. sick 15-4-17 to Eng.	c/o Mrs. Lindel, 129 Commercial St., Portland, Maine.
703877	Jones, W.	Pte.	W. 22-11-16 (Somme) to Eng.	4 Crougochton Tce., Llanfair P.G., Wales. c/o S. T. Larson, Rock Creek, B.C.

649365	Jones, W. J.	Pte.	W. 6-8-17 (Lens); w. 12-8-17 (Lens) to Eng.	Haileybury, Ont.
102336	Jones, W. P.	Pte.	W. 11-5-17 (1st Triangle) to Eng.	Lake Buntzen, Vancouver, B.C.
703931	Jorgensen, A.	Pte.	Tr. to 21th Bn. 8-7-16	c/o A. Johnson, Princeton, B.C.
703443	Jowowich, K.	Pte.	D. o. w. 11-4-17 (Vimy)	O. Jowowich, Cumberland, B.C.
1015570	Juraskovich, M.	Pte.	Tr. to Lbr. Pool 26-12-17	No address available.
1004077	Kaiden, P.	Pte.	W. 22-10-17 (Passchendaele); tr. to 71st Co. C.F.C. 9-4-18	
1003635	Karmple, J. W.	Cpl.	Tr. to 51st Bn. 2-8-16	No address available.
704037	Kane, W. J.	Pte.	W. 1-10-18 (2nd Arras) to Eng.	P.O. Box 153, Copper Cliff, Ont.
226946	Kastner, H.	Pte.	Tr. to Lbr. Pool 31-10-17	Port Moody, B.C.
706426	Kavanagh, J. P.	Pte.	W. 9-4-17 (Vimy); tr. to Eng. on demob. duty 14-3-19	Sebringville, Ont.
135775	Kay, J.	Pte.		45 Milton Rd, Hoe St., Walthamstowe, London, Eng.
760647	Kay, T.	Pte.	W. 9-4-17 (Vimy) to Eng.	23 Maryfield, Abbey Hill, Edinburgh, Scot.
138323	Kayes, J.	Pte.	Acc. inj. 22-9-16 to Eng.	40 Prospect Ave., Chicapoo, Mass., U.S.A.
252969	Kearns, J.	Cpl.	Tr. to Eng. demob. duty 20-3-19	No address available.
1066161	Kearns, R. P.	Pte.	Evac. sick 19-3-18 to Eng.	c/o Bk. of N. S., King & Sherman Sts., Hamilton, Ont.
703980	Keddie, A.	Pte.	Tr. to Lbr. Pool 14-10-18	321 7th St. E, Owen Sound, Ont.
754499	Keefer, M. B.	Pte.	Tr. to 31st Bn. 12-8-18	Guardridge, Fife. Scotland
226424	Keeling, H. T.	Pte.	W. 15-7-18 (Oppy) to Eng.	Wiarton, Ont.
907549	Keenan, E.	Pte.	W. 9-4-17 (Vimy) to Eng.	76 A. Marshall St., Folkestone, Eng.
2507409	Keene, E.	Pte.	Evac. from P.B. to Eng. 13-12-18	Groggan P.O. Randalstown, Co. Antrim, Ire.
1003535	Keetch, C.	L-C.	Evac. sick 21-10-18 to Eng.	No address available.
200129	Keir, A.	Pte.	W. 8-8-18 (Amiens) to Eng.	Portage la Prairie, Man.
103308	Kelly, A. E.	Pte.	W. 31-10-17 (Passchendaele) to Eng.	North Lansdale P.O., North Vancouver, B.C.
760204	Kelly, G.	Pte.	W. 9-4-17 (Vimy) to Eng.	435 14th Ave., Vancouver, B.C.
761314	Kelly, J. T.	Pte.	W. 9-6-17 (2nd Triangle) to Eng.	11 Metropole Mansions, Douglas, Isle of Man.
760206	Kelly, M.	Pte.	Evac. sick 25-5-17 to Eng.	c/o Mrs. A. Craston, East Hartpool, Eng.
				c/o Miss A. Wallerdyne, Y.M.C.A., Dunsmuir St., Vancouver, B.C.
240318	Kelly, R. C.	Pte.	Tr. to 4th C.M.G.C. 1-5-18	411 Herkimer St., Hamilton, Ont.
3030765	Kelly, W. H.	Pte.		c/o Michael Kelly, Glebe St., Birr, Kings Co., Ire.
1003568	Kelly, W. O.	Pte.	Evac. sick 12-10-17 to Eng.	Sudbury, Ont.
253085	Kelman, J.	Pte.	W. 4-9-17 (Vimy); d. o. s. 22-10-18	W. Kelman, Indian Head, Sask.
127372	Kendall, F.	Sgt.		683 Princess St., Woodstock, Ont.
703279	Kendall, L. D.	Pte.	Evac. sick 31-10-17 to Eng.	319 11th St. E, North Vancouver, B.C.
1003723	Kendrick, M. C.	Pte.	Tr. to 51st Bn. 2-8-16	Usk, B.C.
103613	Kendrick, H. W.	Pte.	W. 3-9-18 (2nd Arras) to Eng.	23 Trelawne Ave., Saulte Ste. Marie, Ont.
			W. 1-11-17 (Passchendaele); w. 17-11-17 (Passchendaele) to Eng.	
703365	Kennedy, D.	Pte.	Tr. to 51st Bn. 2-8-16	Gore Bay, Ont.
1003740	Kennedy, D.	Pte.	Dec. M.M. (Valenciennes) C.R.O. 2028; w. 31-10-18 (Valenciennes)	2766 4th Ave. W., Vancouver, B.C.
1090039	Kennedy, D. H.	Cpl.	K. i. a. 9-4-17 (Vimy)	71 Chambly St., Montreal, Que.
761285	Kennedy, H.	Pte.	W. 9-4-17 (Vimy); w. 27-9-18 (Amiens); tr. to Eng. demob. duty 2-1-19	14 Oldfield Ave., Montreal, Que.
760916	Kennedy, J.	Pte.		W. Kennedy, Guysboro, Nova Scotia.
1003218	Kennedy, J. B.	Pte.		3741 Larnark St., South Vancouver, B.C.
760398	Kennedy, L. l.	Cpl.	Evac. sick 19-9-17 to Eng.	Thessalon, Ont.
				1946 Victoria Drive, Vancouver, B.C.

Number	Name	Rank	Notes	Address
221183	Kenney, R.	Pte.		224 Brunswick Ave., Toronto, Ont.
760837	Kenny, H. H.	Sgt.	W. 5-8-17 (Lens); w. 27-9-18 (Cambrai)	Box 993, Nanaimo, B.C.
703720	Kent, T.	Pte.	Tr. to Eng 17-6-18	Mrs. M. A. Kent, Sandy, Beds, Eng.
703630	Kent, W. J.	Pte.	Evac. sick 9-11-17 to Eng.	Cor. 59th Ave. and Montcalm St., Marpole, B.C.
663101	Kerns, D. S.	Pte.		Burlington, Ont.
663592	Kerns, W. K. A.	Pte.	Evac. sick 4-10-18 to Eng.	Burlington, Ont.
225233	Kerr, G. J.	Pte.	K. i. a. 4-9-18 (2nd Arras)	Mrs. A. S. Crawford, Harriman, Orange Co., N.Y.
703311	Kerr, H. P.	Pte.	Tr. to 51st Bn. 2-8-16.	Dominion, No. 4, Bridgeport, Cape Breton.
102737	Kerr, J.	Pte.	W. 5-6-17 (2nd Triangle); w. 17-8-17 (Lens) to Eng.	
907753	Kerr, J.	Pte.	K. i. a. 9-4-17 (Vimy)	Marksboro', Warren Co., N.J., U.S.A.
907814	Kerr, J. C.	Pte.	Missing after action 9-4-17 (Vimy)	Mrs. N. Kerr, Roby, nr. Liverpool, Eng.
249712	Kerr, R. J.	Pte.	Tr. to 4th C.M.G.C. 18-3-18.	Mrs. A. E. Kerr, 1350 Rae St. Regina, Sask.
907427	Kerr, W. J.	Pte.	K. i. a. 7-6-17 (2nd Triangle).	25 Bathurst St., Toronto, Ont.
116766	Kerridge, A. E.	Sgt.	Att. 11th C.I.B. H.-Q.; men. in des. L.G. 30706; dec. Medaille d'Honneur avec gliaves en bronze C.R.O. 1989.	W. G. Kerr, Elora, Ont.
760049	Kershaw, W. J.	Pte.	Evac. sick 12-5-17 to Eng.	745 Burrard St., Vancouver, B.C.
219511	Ketcheson, R. S.	Pte.	W. 23-1-17 (Vimy); k. l. a. 2-9-18 (2nd Arras)	Whonnock P.O., B.C.
835155	Keyes, W.	Pte.	Evac. sick 18-11-17 to Eng.	H. Ketcheson, Madoc, Ont.
703098	Keys, G. C.	Pte.	Tr. to 51st Bn. 2-8-16.	c/o W. Ferguson, N. Augusta Rd., Brockville, Ont.
931156	Kidd, R.	C.S.M.	Dec. D.C.M. (Oppy) C.R.O. 1878; tr. to Eng. for commission 31-10-18.	504 Central Bldg., Victoria, B.C.
160137	Klevill, A. L.	Pte.	W. 22-10-16 (Regina) to Eng.	c/o Imperial Bank, Nelson, B.C.
704152	Kilpatrick, W. F.	Pte.	Tr. to Eng. from P.B. 17-6-18	No address available.
226486	Killrose, T.	Pte.	W. 28-9-18 (Cambrai) to Eng.	742 Nelson St., Vancouver, B.C.
760201	Kinch, G. S.	Pte.	D. o. w. 24-5-17 (Vimy)	c/o Miss H. Kilroe, 198 East First St., Superior, Wis.
				Mrs. E. L. Kinch, 206 Waterloo Rd., Wolverhampton,
463996	King, J. S.	Pte.		2 Charlemont Ave., Kingston, Ireland.
240598	King, F. W.	Pte.	Evac. sick 22-8-18 to Eng.	253 Herkimer St., Hamilton, Ont.
226880	King, G. H.	Pte.	K. l. a. 2-9-18 (2nd Arras)	62 Wilson St., Hamilton, Ont.
1003604	King, H. L.	Pte.		Mrs. A. King, Hugill Warren, Sudbury, Ont.
907423	King, H. L.	Pte.		2231 Halifax St., Regina, Sask.
183688	King, H. N.	Pte.	W. 10-6-17 (2nd Triangle) to Eng	Trochut, Alta.
292258	King, J. J.	Sgt.	Tr. to Can. Mil. Police 21-5-18	c/o A. Smith, Dand, Man.
445708	King, J. J.	Pte.	W. 17-8-17 (Lens); evac. sick 21-3-18 to Eng.	No address available.
2528444	King, P. E.	Pte.	K. i. a. 1-10-18 (Cambrai)	No address available.
663027	King, R.	Pte.	Evac. sick 29-1-19 to Eng.	No address available.
706834	Kingsley, J. E.	Cpl.	W. 24-3-18 (Lens) to Eng.	Parksville P.O., B.C.
703403	Kinnear, A. R.	Pte.	W. 21-10-16 (Regina); dec. M.M. (Cambrai)	
225956	Kinnear, J. W.	Cpl.	W. 2-11-18 (Valenciennes) to Eng; dec. M.M. (2nd Arras) C.R.O. 1930.	1857 Union St., Vancouver, B.C.
225946	Kirby, A. H.	Pte.	W. 30-9-18 (Cambrai); tr. to Lbr. Pool 25-10-18	184 Belmont Ave., Hamilton, Ont.
703027	Kirby, D. S.	Sgt.	Dec. M.S.M., L.G. d-1-1-19.	c/o Dr. Langrill, 227 King St. W., Hamilton, Ont.
703757	Kirby, E. V.	Pte.	K. i. a. 9-4-17 (Vimy)	Crowstone, Blake Hall Rd., Wanstead, London, Eng.
2527376	Kirby, R. L.	Pte.	D. o. w. 4-9-18 (2nd Arras)	R. Kirby, 4350 14th Ave. W., Vancouver, B.C.
252117	Kirby, R. P.	Pte.	W. 4-9-18 (Vimy)	Mrs. G. M. A. Kirby, R.R. No. 1, Dayton, Ont.
				Swift Current, Sask.

703313	Kirby, Z.	C.S.M.	Dec. D.C.M. (Triangle) C.R.O. 135; w. 8-8-18 (Cambrai)	Suite 106, Holly Lge., 1210 Jervis St., Vancouver, B.C.
540241	Kirk, T. J.	Pte.	W. 8-9-16 (St. Eloi) to Eng	No address available.
703555	Kirkland, G. H.	Pte.	Tr. to 3rd Lbr. Bn. 6-7-17	Stragglesthorpe, Notts, Eng.
703564	Kirkland, G. W.	Pte.	Tr. to 51st Bn. 2-8-16	Stragglesthorpe, Notts, Eng.
703639	Kirkwood, T.	Pte.	W. 27-9-18 (Cambrai) to Eng	2105 Oxford St., Vancouver, B.C.
2529405	Kirtland, A.	Pte.	Evac. sick 6-11-18 to Eng	c/o Mrs. D. Harris, St. Catherines, Ont.
2527387	Kite, E. H.	Pte.	Evac. sick 30-1-18 to Eng	152 Dufferin Ave., Stratford, Ont
1003397	Kittle, H. C.	Pte.	W. 5-8-17 (Lens)	Cheyboygan, Mich, U.S.A.
252516	Kivell, H.	Pte.	W. 31-8-16 (St. Eloi); w. 22-10-16 (Regina) to Eng.	Clarkson, Ont.
704039	Kiziskey, M.	Pte.		
101644	Klassen, P. A.	Pte.	D. O. w. 4-11-16 (Regina)	Prince Rupert, B.C.
1003702	Klement, A.	Pte.	W. 22-10-17 (Passchendaele) to Eng	No address available.
2528493	Kline, J.	Pte.	W. 27-9-18 (Cambrai) to Eng	c/o C. F. Russell, Yorkhaven, Pa., U.S.A.
704088	Kluss, H.	Pte.	K. l. a. 16-9-16 (St. Eloi)	No address available.
704089	Kluss, M.	Pte.	W. 11-5-17 (1st Triangle); evac. sick 23-5-17 to Eng.	No address available.
2529377	Knight, A. H.	Pte.	Evac. sick 20-8-18 to Eng	c/o Mrs. Harrison, Redlynch, Churchill Rd., Upper Parkstone, Dorset, Eng.
2529335	Knight, J. F.	Pte.	W. 27-9-18 (Cambrai) to Eng	c/o Mrs. K. Knight, 7 Gladstone Rd., Upper Parkstone, Dorset, Eng.
220052	Knight, T.	Pte.	Tr. to 51st Bn. 2-8-16	No address available.
226982	Knocker, D.	L-S.	W. 2-9-18 (2nd Arras)	206 Market St., Hamilton, Ont.
219014	Knowles, H. L.	Pte.	K. l. a. 9-4-17 (Vimy)	No address available.
219949	Knowles, W. G.	L-C.	K. l. a. 9-4-17 (Vimy)	H. Knowles, Merrickville, Ont.
1031129	Knox, A. S.	Pte.	Tr. to 26th Bn. 25-3-18	1023 Caledonia Ave., Victoria, B.C.
925708	Knox, C. V.	Pte.	K. l. a. 9-4-17 (Vimy)	Mrs. Knox, Foxhollow, Eugene, Laine Co., Ore., U.S.A.
1066235	Knox, W. J.	Pte.	Evac. sick 20-10-18 to Eng	R.R. No. 1, Proton, Ont
704168	Knudson, P.	Pte.	W. 21-10-16 (Regina); tr. to 3rd Lbr. Bn. 11-7-17	
100137	Knutson, E.	Pte.	W. 15-11-16 (Somme) to Eng	No address available.
931244	Kononuk, A.	Pte.	K. l. a. 16-9-16 (St. Eloi)	No address available.
240319	Konkle, H. McD.	Sgt.	Dec. D.C.M. (Valenciennes) L.G. d-3-6-19	Box 284, Grimsby, Ont.
1003428	Koral, S.	Pte.	Tr. to No. 2 H.-Q. C.F.C. 9-4-18	No address available.
703527	Korner, C. H.	Pte.	Evac. sick 26-4-17 (Vimy); dec. Cross of St. George, Cl. IV. (Russian); evac. sick 13-10-17 to Eng.	34 Ancaster Drive, Annesland, Glasgow, Scot.
252492	Kowalske, K.	Pte.	W. 9-4-17 (Vimy)	
506034	Kowalski, F.	Pte.	W. 1-11-17 (Passchendaele)	c/o J. H. Bogart, Nadinville, Sask.
703319	Kreiger, H. C.	Pte.	Tr. to 51st Bn. 2-8-16	792 Magnus Ave., Winnipeg, Man.
474013	Kreutzwieser, R.	Pte.	K. l. a. 21-10-16 (Regina)	c/o J. R. Smith, 1873 Nelson St., Vancouver, B.C.
703094	Kultula, W.	Pte.	Evac. sick 22-7-17 to Eng	No address available.
760555	Kurso, J.	Pte.	K. l. a. 9-4-17 (Vimy)	Prince Rupert, B.C.
101056	Lacaille, D. E.	Pte.	W. 9-4-17 (Vimy) to Eng	No address available.
2525971	Lackey, H.	Pte.	Evac. sick 24-10-16 to Eng	c/o H. Brown, 356 5th St. E, N. Vancouver, B.C.
2528463	La Crosse, P. H.	Pte.	W. 9-4-17 (Vimy) to Eng	c/o R. Manning, Rutland, Vermont, U.S.A. Search Mouth, Ont.
1003863	Lafontaine, A. C. J.	Pte.	W. 27-9-18 (Cambrai) to Eng	Gracefield, Que.

Number	Name	Rank	Details	Address
184228	Lagrow, J. P.	Cpl.	W. 30-9-18 (Cambrai) to Eng.	c/o E. Demas, R.M.R. No. 1, Red Deer, Alta.
3107091	Laidlaw, W. P.	Pte.	W. 1-10-18 (Cambrai) to Eng.	1666 Hopo St., Providence, R.I., U.S.A.
663001	Laidman, J. R.	Pte.	W. 8-8-18 (Amiens) to Eng.	22 Ashley St., Hamilton, Ont.
907566	Lake, C. B.	Pte.	W. 8-9-16 (St. Eloi); k. i. a. 22-10-16 (Regina)	Stoughton, Sask.
703064	Lalumiere, N.	Pte.		G. Lalumiere, St. Brimo, Que.
3106561	Lalonde, A.	Pte.		Hanmer, Ont.
258474	L'Amie, W. G.	Pte.	Evac. sick 6-12-16 to Eng.	828 23rd Ave., Vancouver, B.C.
100214	Lamont, J.	Pte.	Tr. to Lbr. Pool 5-12-18.	No address available.
704027	Lamping, V. J.	Pte.		1326 Granville St., Vancouver, B.C.
3109279	Lampman, O. O.	Pte.		Marshville, Ont.
907974	Lander, J. B.	Pte.	W. 9-4-17 (Vimy) to Eng.	Saltcoats, Sask.
2627313	Landry, L. J.	Pte.	W. 3-9-18 (2nd Arras) to Eng.	Grand Anse, Gloucester Co., New Brunswick.
703011	Langford, J. B.	Sgt.	Pioneer Sergeant; evac. sick 19-9-17 to Eng.	321 Seaforth St., Victoria, B.C.
703333	Langdon, P.	Pte.	W. 21-10-16 (Regina); tr. to 4th C.M.G.C. 1-5-18	c/o C. Tizzard, c/o Messrs. M. Taylor & Son, High St., Fareham, Eng.
440892	Langran, C. S.	Pte.	Evac. sick 10-1-18 to Eng.	Carlow, Co. Carlow, Ireland.
703398	Lanoitt, J.	Pte.	Tr. to 51st Bn. 2-8-16.	Lake Langdon, Mich., U.S.A.
704169	Lansdowne, B. G.	Pte.	Tr. to Eng. demob. duty 8-1-19.	3 Hayes Block, Yew St., Vancouver, B.C.
760737	Lapointe, J.	Pte.	W. 27-9-17 (Lens); evac. sick 23-10-17 to Eng.	Little Peebles, Galpie Co., Que.
704166	Larmer, W. H.	Pte.		Box 176, Portage la Prairie, Man.
703805	Larson, C.	Pte.	W. 24-8-18 (Amiens) to Eng.	c/o P. Larson, R.R. No. 1, New Westminster, B.C.
703215	Lasser, R.	Pte.	W. 22-10-16 (Regina); w. 9-4-17; dec. M.M. (Vimy) C.R.O. 1236; evac. sick 13-5-17 to Eng.	c/o Otto Lasser, Powell River, B.C.
161285	Latham, C. A.	Pte.	W. 22-11-16 (Somme); w. 7-9-17 (Lens); tr. to Mil. Police 28-9-18.	c/o H. T. Latham, City Hall, Moose Jaw, Sask.
704160	Latimer, G. B.	Sgt.	Dec. M.M. (Cambrai) C.R.O. 1989.	1076 Robson St., Vancouver, B.C.
737318	Latter, E. A. R.	Pte.	Dec. M.M. (Cambrai) C.R.O. 1989; evac sick 25-1-19 to Eng.	
1012440	Latour, A.	Pte.	W. 30-9-18 (Cambrai) to Eng.	35 Guelph St., Stratford, Ont.
252993	Laurie, A.	Pte.	W. 9-4-17 (Vimy) to Eng.	103 Loretta Ave., Ottawa, Ont.
850085	Lavelle, J.	Pte.	W. 2-9-18 (2nd Arras) to Eng.	Cadillac, Sask.
264655	Lavigny, E.	Pte.	Tr. to Lbr. Pool 16-9-18.	177 Fountain Bridge, Edinburgh, Scot.
161143	Law, A.	Pte.	Dec. M.M. (Vimy) C.R.O. 1236; Bar to M.M. (2nd Triangle) C.R.O. 1329; w. 17-11-17 (Passchendaele); d. o. s. 25-10-18.	514 Plesse St., Montreal, Que.
2529432	Law, I. A.	Pte.	W. 1-10-18 (Cambrai) to Eng.	Mrs. A. Law c/o Mrs. Hodge, Main St., Lime Kilns, nr. Dumfermline, Fifeshire, Scot.
703510	Lawler, J.	Pte.	Dec. M.M. (Cambrai) C.R.O. 1989.	Port Dover, Ont.
703829	Lawler, T.	Pte.	K. i. a. 22-10-16 (Regina).	2224 Larch St., Vancouver, B.C.
				Mrs. Lawler, 54 South Dean Gardens, Wimbledon Park, London, Eng.
161089	Lawrence, G. E.	Pte.	Tr. to 1st Can. Emp. Co. 5-7-17.	Mrs. Lawrence, Conchehay, Bath, Eng.
208155	Lawrence, A.	Pte.	W. 9-6-17 (2nd Triangle) to Eng.	Rowantree House, Stromness, Orkneys, Scot.
263110	Lawrence, A. J.	Pte.	K. i. a. 9-4-17 (Vimy)	Mrs. J. J. Gilchrist, Rosetown, Sask.
925615	Lawrence, G. H. R.	Pte.	K. i. a. 12-6-17 (2nd Triangle).	Mrs. St. Ames, 26 Shaftesbury Bldg., Lower Church St. West Croydon, Eng.
907743	Lawrence, R.	Pte.	K. i. a. 12-5-17 (1st Triangle).	Mrs. A. Lawrence, San Toy, Vandyke Rd., Leighton-Buzzard, Eng.

Regt. No.	Name	Rank	Remarks	Address
760718	Lawrence, W.	Pte.	W. 11-5-17 (1st Triangle) to Eng.	c/o Mrs. W. Gule, 844 21st Ave. E., Vancouver, B.C.
225945	Lawrence, W.	Pte.	W. 30-9-18 (Amiens)	66 Beechwood Ave., Hamilton, Ont.
2529404	Lawson, H. A.	Pte.	Evac. to Eng. as minor 1-6-18.	Thorold Park, Thorold, Ont.
703239	Lawson, R.	Pte.	W. 6-9-17 (Lens) to Eng.	18 Grange St., Grangemouth, Scot.
931482	Lazzer, A.	Pte.	K. i. a. 27-9-18 (Cambrai)	No address available.
2528325	Leaky, E.	Pte.	W. 2-9-18 (2nd Arras) to Eng.	Carleton Place, Ont.
220040	Leaky, G. O.	Pte.	Acc. w. 26-10-16 to Eng.	No address available.
703391	Leatherdale, J.	Pte.	Dec. Croix de Guerre, Belgian, C.C.M.S. 409-19	c/o Dep. C. Leatherdale, Police Sta., Vancouver, B.C.
3030948	Le Blanc, J.	Pte.	Acc. inj. 3-10-18 to Eng.	43 Nickie St., Gardiner, Mass., U.S.A.
100914	Lee, G. P.	Pte.		9560 105th Ave., Edmonton, Alta.
703841	Lee, W. G.	Cpl.	W. 21-10-16 (Regina) to Eng.	c/o Imperial Bank, Nelson, B.C.
704076	Leeson, A. G.	Pte.	K. i. a. 21-10-16 (Regina)	Mrs. Leeson, Danville, Contra Costa Co., Cal., U.S.A.
703142	Lefley, T.	Pte.	K. i. a. 15-9-16 (St. Eloi)	Mrs. M. Aldred, Wissepp, nr. Hallworth, Suffolk, Eng.
225993	Legge, J. A.	Pte.	Tr. to Eng. as minor 15-1-18	c/o Mrs. H. Hendrie, 169 Claremont St., Toronto, Ont.
1106201	Leggett, J. B.	Pte.	W. 1-10-18 (Cambrai) to Eng.	Markdale, Ont.
3030847	Legon, C.	Pte.	W. 23-1-17 (Vimy); w. 11-5-17 (1st Triangle); w. 12-11-17 (Passchendaele)	2528 N. Ashland Ave., Chicago, Ill., U.S.A.
925061	Lein, M. P.	L.-C.		
907555	Lemond, S. A.	Pte.	W. 9-6-17 (2nd Triangle); w. 11-8-17 (Lens) to Eng.	c/o Mrs. M. Hicks, Quesnel, B.C.
907098	Lemprière, E. P. J.	Pte.	Tr. to 4th C.M.G.C. 1-5-18	Vares, Ont.
838114	Lenahan, J. K.	Pte.		Miss E. Lemprière, 1936 Garnett St., Regina, Sask.
101634	Lendrum, J.	Pte.	W. 22-10-16 (Regina)	727 5th Ave. E., Owen Sound, Ont.
1003112	Lennox, C. S.	Pte.	W. 4-9-18 (2nd Arras)	248 Amelia St., Fort William, Ont.
226939	Leroux, A.	Pte.	W. 27-9-18 (Cambrai) to Eng.	Steelton, Ont.
907298	Leschinski, V.	Pte.	Tr. to 16th M.G. Co. 1-1-17	Isle Perrot, South Co., Vaudreuil, Que.
250091	Leslie, A. Y.	Pte.	Tr. to 4th C.M.G.C. 1-5-18	No address available.
540126	Leslie, D.	Sgt.	Tr. to 4th Div. Sigs. 2-8-16	Brighton, Ont.
704033	Leslie, I. Y.	Pte.	D. o. w. 1-9-16 (St. Eloi)	No address available.
103064	Leslie, W. K.	Sgt.	Dec. M.M. during service with 67th Bn; k. i. a. 5-6-17 (2nd Triangle)	Mrs. C. A. Leslie, 31 Court Yard, Eltham, Kent, Eng.
703963	Lett, A.	Pte.	K. i. a. 22-10-16 (Regina)	Mrs. M. Leslie, 2430 Richmond St., Victoria, B.C.
703291	Letts, G. F. C.	Pte.	Tr. to Lbr. Pool 9-6-18.	F. Lett, Johnston St., Birmingham, Eng.
3314350	Levere, P.	Pte.	W. 27-9-18 (Cambrai)	Box 567, Prince Rupert, B.C.
3106364	Lewis, A. H.	Pte.		Mrs. Lewis, Port Colbourne, Ont.
225294	Lewis, A. S.	Pte.	W. 1-10-18 (Cambrai) to Eng.	197 Victoria Ave. S., Hamilton, Ont.
704114	Lewis, C. S.	Pte.	Evac. sick 23-8-16 to Eng.	c/o A. H. Taylor, 14 Ripley Place, Buffalo, N.Y.
252281	Lewis, F. B.	Pte.	Evac. sick 15-1-17 to Eng.	Enchant, Alta.
703974	Lewis, H.	Ptu.	Tr. to 4th Div. Emp. Co. 11-5-17	Maple Creek, Sask.
703120	Lewis, H. G.	Pte.		Creston, B.C.
703024	Lewis, J. P.	Pte.	Tr. to Lbr. Pool, 3-5-18.	Sayward P.O., Salmon River, B.C.
219229	Lewry, G. J.	Pte.	W. 8-8-18 (Amiens) to Eng.	42 East Dulwich Rd., London, S.E., Eng.
703659	Lewtas, F. G.	Sgt.	Tr. to Eng. for commission 7-4-17	483 King St. E., Toronto, Ont.
907473	Leybourne, D. J.	Pte.	W. 2-8-17 (Lens) to Eng.	1126 McClure St., Victoria, B.C.
1004081	Liddle, E. C.	Pte.	W. 1-11-17 (Passchendaele) to Eng.	Coolkenno, Co. Wicklow, Ireland.
3203	Lidstone, H. J.	Pte.	K. i. a. 30-10-17 (Passchendaele)	130 Albert St., Saulte Ste. Marie, Ont.
490567	Lightly, T. K.	Pte.	W. 30-10-17 (Passchendaele) to Eng.	J. Lidstone, Laird, Ont.
703390	Limb, A.	Pte.	Tr. to 67th Bn. 8-7-16.	237 Templeton Drive, Vancouver, B.C.
				Box 99, Merritt, B.C.

903071	Liminison, W.	Pte.	Evac. sick 25-10-17 to Eng.	No address available.
925762	Lindbloom, F.	Pte.	W. 5-6-17 (2nd Triangle); tr. to Lbr. Pool 16-5-18	No address available.
164652	Lindley, C.	Pte.	W. 17-5-17 (1st Triangle) to Eng.	c/o Mrs. A. Honyleton, 390 Glenwood Ave., Buffalo, N.Y., U.S.A.
850409	Lindley, R.	Pte.	Evac. sick 8-7-18 to Eng.	256 John St., Niagara Falls South, Ont.
3314348	Lindsay, R. D.	Pte.	W. 6-11-18 (Valenciennes) to Eng.	10 Emerson Place, Buffalo, N.Y., U.S.A.
706135	Lindsay, W.	Pte.	W. 31-7-18 (Oppy); evac. sick 17-10-18 to Eng.	1340 George St., Victoria, B.C.
1003115	Lingwood, A.	Pte.	Dec. D.C.M. (2nd Arras) G.R.O. 410; w. 4-9-18 (2nd Arras) to Eng.	c/o Miss C. V. Clement, 286 Bruce St., S. S. Marie, Ont.
704040	Linn, A.	L.-S.		
3110689	Linton, C. M.	Pte.	K. i. a. 9-4-17 (Vimy)	c/o Nels Olsen, 5 Sandback, Sjobs Skane, Sweden.
907126	Lintott, S. E.	Pte.	W. 27-9-18 (Cambrai)	c/o T. W. Brown, R.R. No. 1, Agincourt, Ont.
1025588	Lister, G.	Pte.	Evac. sick 7-12-18 to Eng.	Mrs. A. Lintott, 1013 Rae St., Regina, Sask.
2529379	Little, J.	Pte.	W. 9-6-17 (2nd Triangle); k. i. a. 27-9-18 (Cambrai)	1120 Vancouver St., Victoria, B.C.
102244	Little, R. S.	L.-C.		2 Flower St., Carlisle, Eng.
102597	Littlejohn, W.	Pte.	Tr. to 3rd Lbr. Bn. 11-7-17	Mrs. J. Little, Box 867, Victoria, B.C.
126249	Livens, J. A.	Pte.	K. i. a. 19-8-16 (St. Eloi)	2653 Scott St., Victoria, B.C.
102757	Livingston, D.	Pte.	W. 5-6-17 (2nd Triangle) to Eng.	Mrs. M. Lewis, 52 Elmwood Ave., London, Ont.
145778	Livingstone, J. G.	Pte.	Tr. to 77th Bn. 10-8-16	59 Laoon Fern, Balychulish, East Argyleshire, Scot.
2015176	Lloyd, L. M.	Pte.	Tr. to Eng. on demob. duty 6-1-19	Renfrew, Ont.
2531163	Lobb, J.	Pte.	W. 14-5-17 (1st Triangle) to Eng.	No address available.
103195	Lock, G. H.	Pte.	Dec. M.M. (Passchendaele) C.R.O. 1606; dec. Bar M.M. (Cambrai) C.R.O. 1989; w. 1-10-18 (Cambrai)	Box 777, Swift Current, Sask.
704155	Locke, J. A.	Pte.	Tr. to 11th C.L.T.M.B. 1-10-17	Edgehill, Norfolk, Eng.
907236	Loco, E.	Pte.	D. o. w. 4-9-18 (2nd Arras)	Woodbridge, Ont.
252268	Loeppky, A.	Pte.	K. i. a. 9-4-17 (Vimy)	Mrs. L. Loco, Cymbric P.O., P.E.I.
136671	Logan, G.	R.S.M.		P. Loeppky, Waldeck, Sask.
81522	Logan, G.	R.S.M.	W. 9-4-17 (Vimy) to Eng.	230 Perth Ave., Toronto, Ont.
102374	Logle, A.	Pte.	Evac. sick 14-10-17 to Eng.	45 Netherfield Rd., Nelson, Lancs.
850763	Lomas, J. F.	Pte.	W. 27-9-18 (Cambrai) to Eng.	2620 Belmont Ave., Victoria, B.C.
140618	Long, E. A.	Pte.	Evac. sick 21-1-17 to Eng.	c/o Mrs. A. Nish, 122 Everton Rd., Con-Medlock, Manchester, Eng.
703561	Long, G. A.	Sgt.	W. 21-10-16 (Regina) to Eng.	No address available.
703050	Long, H. W.	R.S.M.	Regimental Sergeant-Major to 20-6-17; att. to Corps School as Instr. to 27-3-18; tr. to Lbr. Pool 27-3-18; tr. Eng. for duty April 1918	1382 29th Ave. E., Vancouver, B.C.
703984	Long, J.	Pte.	Evac. sick 7-9-17 to Eng.	2022 William St., Vancouver, B.C.
1003510	Long, L. S.	L.-C.		Erickson, B.C.
3105495	Loveland, W.	Pte.	W. 30-9-18 (Cambrai) to Eng.	Blind River, Ont.
907573	Lovell, A.	Pte.	K. i. a. 9-4-17 (Vimy)	c/o Bank of Nova Scotia, Hamilton, Ont.
252475	Loudon, T.	Pte.	W. 9-4-17 (Vimy) to Eng.	A. Lovell, Titterworth, Suffolk, Eng.
102672	Low, J. J. B.	Pte.	Tr. to 26th Bn. 25-3-18	Clelland, Lanarkshire, Scot.
102397	Lowry, G. B.	Pte.	W. 13-5-17 (1st Triangle); tr. to Eng. on demob. duty 20-3-19	1420 Denman St., Victoria, B.C.
				1811 Crescent Rd., Foul Bay, Victoria, B.C.

703472	Lowry, W.	Pte.	Evac. inj. 20-1-17 to Eng.	Donegore House, Dunadry, Belfast, Ireland.
1033191	Lowther, F.	Pte.	Evac. sick 28-5-17 to Eng.	Van Anda, Texada Island, B.C.
2529382	Lozelle, W.	Pte.	W. 8-8-18 (Amiens) to Eng.	214 Atlantic St., Bay City, Mich, U.S.A.
1003465	Lozier, A.	Pte.	Evac. acc. inj. 13-9-17 to Eng.	Tracadee, New Brunswick.
703283	Lumley, M. N.	Pte.	Tr. to 51st Bn. 2-8-16.	537 Forbes St., Victoria, B.C.
541176	Lundy, W. M.	Pte.	W. 19-8-16 (St. Eloi) to Eng.	No address available.
135771	Luxton, T. J.	Pte.	Evac. sick in Eng. 13-11-18.	62 Windway Rd., Victoria Park, Cardiff, Wales.
404972	Luxton, W. J.	Cpl.	Missing after action 27-9-18 (Cambrai); believed taken prisoner of war.	
703640	Lyle, E. H.	Pte.	K. i. a. 22-10-16 (Regina).	19 Brook Rd., Ely, Cardiff, Wales.
102739	Lynch, J. J.	Pte.	Evac. sick 13-5-17 to Eng.	S. Lyle, Alberni, B.C.
3105719	Lynch, J. J.	Pte.	W. 2-11-18 (Valenciennes).	c/o Mrs. M. Angle, 2111 Carlton St., Philadelphia.
3106212	Lynch, T. J.	Pte.	W. 2-9-18 (2nd Arras).	c/o Miss M. Lynch, 4535 2nd Ave., Hazelwood, Pa.
3106213	Lynch, V. D.	Cpl.	K. i. a. 2-10-16 (Regina).	21 S. 20th St., Flushing, L. I., New York, U.S.A.
703398	Lynn, G. S.	Pte.	W. 21-10-16 (Regina); w. 27-12-16 (Vimy); d. o. w. 1-11-17 (Passchendaele)	c/o Bank of Nova Scotia, Hamilton, Ont.
704171				Mrs. B. Lynch, Parry Sound, Ont.
102245	Lynn, N.	Pte.	W. 20-10-16 (Regina); tr. to 54th Bn. 8-6-17	Mrs. B. Papworth, 1420 14th St., Oakland, Cal., U.S.A.
2527131	Lyons, H. T.	Pte.	W. 9-4-17 (Vimy) to Eng.	1314 Pembroke St., Victoria, B.C.
761049	Maars, J.	Pte.	W. 9-4-17 (Vimy) to Eng.	Drincoe, Mount Charles, Co. Donegal, Ireland.
761050	Maars, M.	Pte.	W. 2-9-18 (2nd Arras) to Eng.	42 Cordova St. E., Vancouver, B.C.
1008842	Maddeloni, D.	Pte.		No address available.
2499168	Madgett, D. K.	Pte.		Revelstoke, B.C.
761010	Madigan, J. A.	Pte.	W. 9-4-17 (Vimy); dec. M.M. (Oppy) C.R.O. 1755; dec. Bar M.M. (Cambrai) C.R.O. 1989; Tr. to Eng. for demob. duty 9-2-19.	North Huron St., Toronto, Ont.
3020480	Madsen, G.	Pte.	Evac. sick 24-1-19.	R.R. No. 1, Cobden, Ont.
703541	Magee, J. H.	Pte.	Tr. to Lbr. Pool 3-5-18.	c/o Miss B. Cranston, 213 May St., E. Hamilton, Ont.
226949	Maheux, W.	Pte.	W. 5-9-18 (2nd Arras).	Free Press, Nanaimo, B.C.
706838	Mahon, C.	Pte.	Evac. sick 1-12-17.	Kingsfield, Franklin Co., Maine, U.S.A.
704126	Main, R.	Pte.	W. 21-10-16 (Regina); tr. to C.G.B.D. 20-5-17	3915 Midvale Ave., opp. 39th Ave., Seattle, Wash.
703495	Mair, G.	Pte.	Dec. M.M. (Oppy) C.R.O. 1755; w. 19-8-18 (Amiens) to Eng.	Bonnington Falls, B.C.
760797	Mair, W. J.	Pte.	Transport Sergeant; dec. M.M. (Lens) C.R.O. 1520; tr. to Eng. 2-12-18.	c/o Mrs. J. Stewart, 9 Ferry Rd., Torry, Aberdeen, Scot.
703041	Maitland, T. R.	Sgt.		2145 Yukon St., Vancouver, B.C.
706658	Maitland-Dougall, H. K.	Pte.	K. i. a. 9-4-17 (Vimy).	Creston, B.C.
226468	Makowsky, H. E.	Cpl.	W. 6-11-18 (Valenciennes) to Eng.	Mrs. W. Maitland-Dougal, Ucluelet, B.C.
908162	Malesku, G.	Pte.	K. i. a. 2-9-18 (2nd Arras).	70 Mouland St., Little Falls, N.Y., U.S.A.
3107941	Malloy, E. J.	Pte.		Mrs. C. Malesku, 1720 Quebec St., Regina, Sask.
703914	Malone, P.	Pte.	Tr. to 51st Bn. 2-8-16.	64 Queenston St., St. Catherines, Ont.
102801	Maloney, P.	Pte.	W. 9-8-17 (Lens) to Eng.	Cosmopolitan Hotel, New Westminster, B.C.
1033132	Maniguall, T. K.	Pte.	Tr. to 4th Div. Emp. Co. 22-2-18.	134 Alberta St., Sapperton, New Westminster, B.C.
160585	Manley, H. J.	Pte.	K. i. a. 25-10-16 (Regina).	The Grange, Audlem, Cheshire, Eng.
540459	Manlove, S. H.	Pte.	W. 19-8-16 (St. Eloi); tr. to C.C.R.C. 22-2-18.	No address available.
703442	Mann, K. A.	Pte.	Evac. sick 21-9-16 to Eng.; dec. M.S.M.	Ann Arbour, Mich., U.S.A.
703014	Manning, W. H.	Sgt.	Signal Sergeant from 26-6-18; dec. M.S.M. L.G. d-3-6-19	c/o Mrs. K. Pratt, West Point Grey, Vancouver, B.C.

Number	Name	Rank	Details	Address
703715	Mansfield, T. A.	Pte.		Nelson, B.C.
102330	Manuel, A. D.	L.-C.	W. 5-6-17 (2nd Triangle) to Eng.	Exploit, Newfoundland.
103152	Manwood, H.	L.-C.	W. 6-11-18 (Valenciennes); men. in des. L.G. d-8-7-19; tr. to Eng. for disch. 31-3-19.	
931803	Marcovitch, J.	Pte.	Tr. to 51th Co. C.F.C. 26-3-18.	Thompson Cross, Staly Bridge, Cheshire, Eng.
850616	Marinelli, A.	Pte.		No address available.
252430	Marjerison, J. L.	Pte.	Evac. sick 7-12-18 to Eng.	Thorold, Ont.
850105	Markle, G. R.	Pte.	W. 30-9-18 (Cambrai).	Nevill, Sask.
3106377	Markle, N. A.	Pte.	K. i. a. 27-9-18 (Cambrai).	614 Niagara St., Niagara Falls, N.Y., U.S.A.
703975	Marks, T.	Pte.	W. 20-11-16 (Somme); men. in des. L.G. 30107; evac. sick 11-5-17 to Eng.	A. Markle, 18 Myrtle Ave., Galt, Ont.
184179	Marles, G. W.	Pte.	Tr. to 11th M.G.C. 10-12-16.	c/o Robt. Marks, Hope, B.C.
703712	Marlow, R.	Pte.	W. 21-1-18 (Mericourt) to Eng.	No address available.
931608	Marquet, C.	Pte.	Evac. sick 9-12-17 to Eng.	Talbot P.O. Coronation, Alta.
252144	Marr, J.	Pte.	Evac. sick 23-5-17 to Eng.	No address available.
				Cabri, Sask.
760741	Marrlette, J. W.	Pte.	K. i. a. 9-4-17 (Vimy).	Mrs. A. Marrlette, 3588 Georgia St. E., Vancouver, B.C.
703608	Marrin, P.	Pte.	Men. in des. L.G. 30107; evac. sick 23-5-17 to Eng.	
669282	Marriott, A. S.	Sgt.	W. 27-9-18 (Cambrai) to Eng.	Mrs. M. Morton, Deer Harbour, Orkis Is., Wash
226482	Marriott, C. N.	Pte.	W. 8-8-18 (Amiens); d.o.w. 28-9-18 (Cambrai)	577 Ontario St., Toronto, Ont.
219674	Marriott, J.	Pte.	Tr. to Lbr. Pool 19-2-18.	I. Marriott, R.R. No. 2, Wyoming, Ont.
703842	Marrison, F.	Pte.	K. i. a. 24-10-16 (Regina).	Scalford, Leicestershire, Eng.
703816	Marrison, H.	Pte.	K. i. a. 9-4-17 (Vimy).	W. Marrison, Columbia Gardens, B.C.
703880	Marrone, A.	Pte.	Evac. sick 11-6-18 to Eng.	Mrs. E. Marrison, Columbia Gardens, B.C.
240152	Marshall, F.	Pte.		Shaughnessy Hospital, Vancouver, B.C.
226138	Marshall, F. O.	Pte.	W. 1-10-18 (2nd Arras).	No address available.
126649	Marshall, H.	Pte.	Evac. sick 23-10-16 to Eng.	Dunville, Ont.
103186	Marshall, H.	Pte.	W. 21-11-17 (Passchendaele) to Eng.	Ayr, Ont.
704082	Marshall, J.	Pte.	W. 9-4-17 (Vimy) to Eng.	4 Harrop St., Greenheys, Manchester, Eng.
528099	Marshall, T. H.	Pte.		185 A. Lexington Ave., San Francisco, Cal., U.S.A.
226997	Marshall, W. W.	Pte.		402 Westmoreland Ave., Toronto, Ont.
				12 Victoria Crescent, Lisburn, Co. Antrim, Ire.
760988	Marsland, R.	Pte.	K. i. a. 9-4-17 (Vimy).	H. Marsland, 856 Georgia St. E., Vancouver, B.C.
703071	Martel, A. J.	Pte.	W. 3-9-16 (St. Eloi); k. i. a. 12-6-17 (2nd Triangle)	
1066276	Martell, W.	Pte.		W. Martel, Villeneuve, Alta.
931246	Martin, C. H.	Pte.	W. 11-11-16 (Somme) to Eng.	Corbetton, Ont.
907520	Martin, E.	Pte.	K. i. a. 1-11-17 (Passchendaele).	Wardner, B.C.
249077	Martin, E. A.	Pte.		Mrs. H. Martin, Evesham, Sask.
1004907	Martin, G. N.	Pte.	Evac. sick 20-11-17 to Eng.	26 Winifred Ave., Toronto, Ont.
226988	Martin, J. A.	Pte.		c/o Mrs. Alvis, 332 E. 29th St., New York City, N.Y.
249411	Martin, J. D.	Pte.	Tr. to Eng. as minor 27-8-18.	North Bay, Ont.
1015578	Martin, P. J.	Pte.	W. 31-7-18 (Lens); k. i. a. 27-9-18 (Cambrai)	570 Adelaide St. W., Toronto, Ont.
925662	Martin, R.	Pte.	W. 8-8-18 (Amiens) to Eng.	Mrs. P. D. Bourgouin, 54 Lima St., Vegreville, Alta.
250035	Martin, R. H.	Pte.	W. 1-10-18 (2nd Arras) to Eng.	Ratcliff, Sask.
240160	Martin, V. E.	Pte.	W. 31-7-18 (Oppy) to Eng.	286 Harvie Ave., Toronto, Ont.
160292	Martin, W. B.	Pte.	K. i. a. 22-10-16 (Regina).	11 Sherman Ave. N., Hamilton, Ont.
703487	Maskell, A.	Pte.	Tr. to Eng. 19-5-17.	No address available.
760007	Mason, E.	Pte.	K. i. a. 10-6-17 (2nd Triangle).	3532 Pine St., Vancouver, B.C.
				Mrs. J. Mason, 46 26th Ave. W., South Vancouver, B.C.

No.	Name	Rank	Notes	Address
226443	Mason, H. G.	Pte.	D. o. w. (acc.) 13-12-18	Mrs. O. Riopel, 183 B. Amherst St., Montreal, Que.
138246	Mason, W. B.	Pte.	Tr. to 75th Bn. 9-6-17	No address available.
703146	Mason, W.	C.S.M.	Dec. M.M. (Vimy) C.R.O. 1236; evac. sick 12-7-17	
703815	Massey, G.	Pte.	Tr. to 4th Div. Emp. Co. 10-6-18	18 Kincardine St., Dundee, Scot.
703556	Massie, W.	Sgt.	Dec. M.M. (Vimy) C.R.O. 1236; w. 9-4-17 (Vimy) to Eng.	Nelson, B.C.
252658	Master, H.	Pte.	Evac. sick 27-3-17 to Eng.	1538 37th Ave. E., Vancouver, B.C.
2527349	Matheson, E. W.	Pte.	K. i. a. 16-5-17 (1st Triangle)	High St., Whaddon, Bucks, Eng.
102128	Matthews, F. S.	Pte.	W. 9-6-17 2nd Triangle) to Eng.	P.O. Rydal Bank, Ont.
252562	Matthews, G.	Pte.	K. i. a. 2-9-18 (2nd Arras)	G. M. Matthews, Oleary, P.E.I.
3031028	Matthews, T.	Pte.	W. 2-9-18 (2nd Arras) to Eng.	70 Yarmouth Rd., Toronto, Ont.
703106	Mathewson, W.	Pte.	W. 6-11-18 (Valenciennes)	Mrs. C. Frost, 1308 S. 29th St., Philadelphia, U.S.A.
252143	Mathieson, H. W.	Pte.	W. 9-4-17 (Vimy) to Eng.	22 Blackhall St., Paisley, Scot.
907611	Maunders, E.	Pte.		Sorrento, B.C.
704026	May, C.	Pte.	W. 28-8-16 (St. Eloi); evac. sick 20-4-17 to Eng.	c/o Miss E. Capps, Huntsville, Ont.
252134	May, C. R.	Pte.	W. 9-4-17 (Vimy) to Eng.	c/o Miss Bourne, 31 Belmont Rd., Southampton, Eng.
907969	Maybin, J.	L-S.	W. 9-4-17 (Vimy) to Eng.	Windthorst, Sask.
763354	Mayes, W. J	Pte.	Tr. to Lbr. Pool 14-10-18	25 St. Albins Rd., Seventings, Essex, Eng.
252272	Maynard, L.	Pte.	W. 9-4-17 (Vimy) to Eng.	Bracebridge, Ont.
931318	Mecredy, T.	Pte.	Evac. sick 2-12-17 to Eng.	Main St., Upbridge, Ont.
252745	Meek, A. W.	Pte.	W. 9-4-17 (Vimy) to Eng.	142 Robertson St., Foul Bay, Victoria, B.C.
703344	Melghen, E.	L-S.	Tr. to Eng. for commission 30-1-18	Shaunavon, Sask.
1003881	Melcher, F.	Pte.	K. i. a. 27-9-18 (Cambrai)	St. Mary's, Ont.
704081	Mellish, M.	Pte.	W. 21-10-16 (Regina) to Eng.	M. Melcher, Eagerville, Ont.
226986	Mellor, D.	Pte.	Evac. sick 30-11-18 to Eng.	Armstrong, B.C.
907668	Melton, F.	Pte.	W. 9-6-17 (2nd Triangle)	41½ Sherman Ave., East New York, U.S.A.
3107946	Mendels, D. M	Pte.		Eldorado City, Ark., U.S.A.
703238	Mennie, G. M	Pte.		989 Tupper St., Montreal, Que
200186	Menzies, W.	Pte.	W. 1-10-18 (Cambrai) to Eng.	Fern Cottage, Granton-on-Spey, Morayshire, Scot.
1003614	Merrick, W. R.	Pte.		c/o Mrs. E. Dobbins, 971 Nicola St., Vancouver, B.C.
3110758	Merrill, W.	Pte.	Evac. sick 24-7-17 to Eng.	Gore Bay, Ont.
703394	Merryfield, C. A.	Sgt.	Tr. to Lbr. Pool 30-8-18	c/o Mrs. G. Emmis, 24 Elliott St., Birmingham, Ont.
219197	Mews, L.	Pte.		1238 Rudlin Ave., Victoria, B.C.
3108711	Michener, K. D.	Pte.		c/o Robt. Mews, Shelburne, Ont.
703328	Middlemis, W.	L-S.	K. i. a. 10-6-17 (2nd Triangle)	R.R. No. 2, Marshville, Ont.
253111	Middleton, C.	Pte.	Evac. sick 26-5-17 to Eng.	Mrs. A. King, 32 Heatherlee St., Selkirk, Roxburghsire, Scot.
1015583	Mijuskovich, W.	Pte.	W. 25-10-17 (Passchendaele) to Eng.	c/o Mrs. J. Angus, 172 Crown St., Aberdeen, Scot.
1015584	Mijuskovich, W.	Pte.	W. to Eng. 6-9-18 (2nd Arras)	Juneau, Alaska.
760395	Miles, P.	Pte.	K. i. a. 6-9-17 (Lens)	Dawson, Y.T.
908103	Miller, A.	Pte.	W. 9-4-17 (Vimy) to Eng.	Mrs. E. Miles, 64 Cromwell Rd., Wimbledon, Eng.
911754	Miller, A. H	Sgt.	W. 9-4-17 (Vimy) to Eng.	Newbury, Berks, Eng.
907560	Miller, C. C.	Pte.	W. 13-5-17 (1st Triangle); evac. sick 30-5-17 to Eng.	737 14th Ave. E., Vancouver, B.C.
334255	Miller, C. E.	Pte.	W. 8-8-18 (Amiens) to Eng.	Regina, Sask.
102811	Miller, H.	Pte.	W. 8-6-17 (2nd Triangle); d. o. s. 31-1-18	Wardsville, Ont.
907608	Miller, R.	Pte.	W. 30-10-17 (Passchendaele) to Eng.	Mrs. O. Walter, 51 King St. Leamington, Eng. Scott, Sask.

Regt. No.	Name	Rank	Notes	Address
3039951	Miller, T. W.	Pte.	D. o. w. 21-10-16 (Regina)	123 Blossom St., Fitchburg, Mass., U.S.A.
703312	Miller, W.	L.-C.		Mrs. J. Kneale, Queen's Hotel, Ramsey, Isle of Man.
703411	Miller, W.	Sgt.	Sergeant Drummer	934 Hillside Ave., Victoria, B.C.
907244	Miller, W. J.	Pte.	W. 9-4-17 (Vimy) to Eng.	Superb, Sask.
160325	Millership, W. E.	Pte.	W. 20-10-16 (Regina) to Eng.	No address available.
240260	Millican, H.	Pte.	W. 3-9-18 (2nd Arras) to Eng.	c/o Mrs. B. Walker, 9 Aurora St., Hamilton, Ont.
850952	Milliken, J. J.	Sgt.	W. 24-3-18 (Lens) to Eng.	James St., Port Dalhousie, Ont.
931746	Millington, W.	Pte.	W. 26-7-18 (Oppy); w. 27-9-18 (Cambrai) to Eng.	
1063153	Millon, J.	Pte.	K. i. a. 27-9-18 (Cambrai)	L.S.B., Creston, B.C.
				W. Millon, 235 Windsor Ave., Montreal, Que.
102657	Mills, A. J.	Pte.	K. i. a. 30-10-17 (Passchendaele)	Mrs. E. Mills, 36 Calthorpe St., Grey's Inn Rd., London, E.C., Eng.
703579	Mills, C.	Pte.	Dec. M.M. (Somme) D.R.O. 316.	2428 Venables St., Vancouver, B.C.
226357	Mills, F. J.	Pte.	Evac. sick 30-10-17 to Eng.	Cope Ave., Homeside P.O., Ont.
703273	Mills, G. J.	L.-C.	W. 19-11-16 (Somme) to Eng.	1314 36th Ave. E., South Vancouver, B.C.
225257	Mills, T.	Pte.		c/o Mrs. E. Maxner, Adams St., Lexington, Mass.
250081	Millward, W. A.	Pte.	Evac. sick 13-2-19 to Eng.	29 Melville St., Dingle, Liverpool, Eng.
837761	Milne, N. D.	Pte.	W. 3-9-18 (2nd Arras) to Eng.	Elmwood, Ont.
103305	Milton, S.	Pte.	D. o. w. 20-5-17 (1st Triangle)	F. C. Milton, 15 West Ave., Pennsylvania, Exeter, Eng.
3102293	Miner, H. L.	Pte.	Evac. sick 21-12-18 to Eng.	Port Colborne, Ont.
252939	Mingot, G. F.	Pte.	W. 9-4-17 (Vimy); d. o. w. 2-10-18 (Cambrai)	G. F. Mingot, Divide, Sask.
703156	Minnis, S.	Pte.	K. i. a. 21-10-16 (Regina)	Mrs. M. Minnis, 1928 Oak Bay Ave., Victoria, B.C.
252146	Minty, S. E.	Pte.	Evac. sick 19-4-17 to Eng.	96 Langland Rd., Poole, Dorset, Eng.
102252	Mirams, A. J.	R.S.M.	Regimental Sergeant-Major from 20-6-17; dec. M.S.M. L.G. 30750.	
225389	Misener, F. J.	Pte.	W. 1-10-18 (Cambrai)	1814 Oak Bay Ave., Victoria, B.C.
703081	Misonivitch	Pte.	K. i. a. 8-9-16 (St. Eloi)	32 Welland Ave., St. Catherines, Ont.
1003057	Mitchell, C. V. A.	Pte.		No address available.
220146	Mitchell, G.	Pte.	W. 12-6-17 (2nd Triangle) to Eng.	301 Park St., Peterboro, Ont.
703150	Mitchell, T. M.	Sgt.	Sergeant Tailor; tr. to Lbr. Pool 10-5-18	23 Clark St., Toronto, Ont.
1003798	Mitchell, W.	Pte.	Tr. to 4th Bn. M.G.C. 18-3-18; dec. M.M. (Oppy) C.R.O. 1765; d. o. w. 28-9-18 (Cambrai)	184 12th Ave. W., Vancouver, B.C.
102066	Mitchell, W. J.	Cpl.	W. 16-11-17 (Passchendaele)	Cockburn Island, Ont.
760597	Moffat, B. H.	Pte.	W. 27-9-18 (Cambrai) to Eng.	C. Mitchell, Tillicum P.O., Victoria, B.C.
540524	Moffat, G.	Pte.	K. i. a. 1-10-18 (Cambrai)	No address available.
703478	Moffat, J.	Pte.	Evac. sick 10-11-16 to Eng.	Mrs. Moffat, 104 Alexander St., Toronto, Ont.
703340	Mogg, A. B.	Pte.	K. i. a. 19-8-16 (St. Eloi)	1542 1st Ave., Vancouver, B.C.
				Rev. H. H. Mogg, Bishops Cannings Vicarage, nr. Devizes, Wilts, Eng.
706986	Mogridge, W. J.	Pte.	W. to Eng. 7-5-18 (Oppy)	Solihull, Warwickshire, Eng.
540524	Money, E. C. K.	Pte.	W. 30-4-18 (Oppy)	513 10th St., New Westminster, B.C.
727726	Money, O.	Pte.	W. 31-7-18 (Oppy) to Eng.	55 East Ave., Oxford, Eng.
706940	Monk, H. N.	Sgt.	W. 31-10-17 (Passchendaele); O.R.S. in the Field from 28-9-18; dec. M.S.M. L.G. d-3-6-19	
727529	Monteith, J. C.	Pte.	W. 4-9-18 (2nd Arras) to Eng.	c/o Box 721, Victoria, B.C.
784105	Montgomery, A. R.	Pte.	W. 10-4-18 (2nd Arras) to Eng.	126 John St., Stratford, Ont.
252140	Montgomery, D. A.	Pte.	W. 9-4-17 (Vimy) evac. sick 18-11-17 to Eng.	171 Elgin St., Hamilton, Ont.
703013	Montgomery, F. J.	Sgt.	Sergeant Butcher	Larriston, New Castleton, Roxburghshire, Scot.
				c/o Mrs. M. E. Fleming, 742 Nelson St., Vancouver.

Reg. No.	Name	Rank	Casualty	Address
103190	Montgomery, H. E.	Pte.	W. 27-9-18 (Cambrai) to Eng.	4134 Dumfries St., South Vancouver, B.C.
1004215	Montgomery, R. C.	Pte.	W. 23-1-18 (Mericourt) to Eng.	Grimsthorpe, Manitoulin Islands, Ont.
249147	Montgomery, R. J.	Pte.	W. 3-9-18 (2nd Arras) to Eng.	15 Wellesley Ave., Toronto, Ont.
225284	Montgomery, T. R.	Pte.	K. i. a. 1-10-18 (Cambrai).	Mrs. S. P. Montgomery, 48 Castlereagh St., Belfast, Ireland.
240259	Montgomery, W. H.	Pte.	W. 5-9-18 (2nd Arras) to Eng.	54 Fairleigh Ave., Hamilton, Ont.
225342	Moody, J.	Pte.	W. 4-9-18 (2nd Arras) to Eng.	5 Highfield Rd., Scarborough, Eng.
2528405	Moon, J.	Pte.	Tr. to 4th M.G.C. 18-3-18.	12 Park Ave., Barnaldswick, Yorks, Eng.
1004118	Mooney, J. M.	Pte.	W. 8-8-18 (Amiens) to Eng.	Massey Station, Ont.
3110094	Moore, D.	Pte.		105 Thorold Ave., St. Catherines, Ont.
907230	Moore, G.	Pte.	W. 3-9-18 (2nd Arras) to Eng.	c/o Mrs. M. Young, c/o Mrs. Wagstaff, Guildford Rd., Montlowly, Perth, West Australia.
706482	Moore, J.	Pte.	W. 9-4-17 (Vimy); w. and missing after action 13-6-17 (2nd Triangle)	Mrs. Moore, Half Moon Inn, Wrekenton, Gateshead-on-Tyne, Eng.
163631	Moore, J.	Pte.	Tr. to Lbr. Pool 18-4-18.	60 Wellington St., Stratford, Ont.
910929	Moore, J.	Sgt.	k. i. a. 9-4-17 (Vimy).	Rev. W. S. Moore, 214 First Ave. E., Prince Albert, Sask.
703679	Moore, J. W.	Pte.	Dec. M.M. (Cambrai) C.R.O. 1989.	Suite 2, Colonial Apts., Burrard St., Vancouver, B.C.
252309	Moore, P. R.	Pte.	W. 9-4-17 (Vimy) to Eng.	c/o Mrs. D. Godfred, 48 Brighton Rd., Darlington, Eng.
3110021	Moore, P. R.	Pte.		Box 57, MacLennan, Ont.
760151	Moore, S.	Pte.	W. 8-8-18 (Amiens).	Forrester St., Truro, Nova Scotia.
2527378	Moore, S. W.	Pte.	W. 24-8-18 (Amiens) to Eng.	R.R. No. 1, Saulte Ste. Marie, Ont.
760865	Moore, C.	Pte.	W. 7-9-17 (Lens) to Eng.	Bellingham, Wash., U.S.A.
703479	Morgan, A.	Pte.	Evac. sick 30-8-16 to Eng.	McKay P.O., West Burnaby, B.C.
252598	Morgan, E. G.	Pte.	W. 2-9-18 (2nd Arras) to Eng.	1 China Tce., Cross St., West Cowes, Isle of Wight.
703699	Morgan, F. C.	Sgt.	W. 1-11-17 (Passchendaele) to Eng.	P.O. Box 28, Nanaimo, B.C.
3105180	Morgan, H.	Pte.	W. 27-9-18 (Cambrai) to Eng.	c/o E. Bowyer, 3 Rifle Green, Blaenadon, Mon., Wales.
2528330	Morgan, I.	Pte.	Tr. to Lbr. Pool 13-1-18.	3 Derwen Rd., Alltwen, Swansea Valley, Wales.
925299	Morin, J. F. S.	Pte.	W. i. a. 30-10-17 (Passchendaele).	7 Lansdowne Terrace, Cheltenham, Eng.
704063	Morrison, J. W.	Pte.	W. 21-10-16 (Regina); tr. to Eng. for commission 31-10-18.	Metlakatla, B.C.
703424	Morkill, G. H.	Pte.	Evac. sick 21-10-16 to Eng.	19 Gore St., Vernon, B.C.
907563	Morley, A. H.	Sgt.	Dec. M.M. (Vimy) C.R.O. 1236; N.C.O. Medical Detail from 27-9-18.	
703521	Morris, A.	Pte.	K. i. a. 6-6-17 (2nd Triangle).	R.R. No. 1, Granton, Ont.
850538	Morris, J. A.	Pte.	W. 6-9-18 (2nd Arras) to Eng.	Miss H. Bridges, Sandwick, B.C.
195956	Morris, J.	Pte.	K. i. a. 30-10-17 (Passchendaele).	Carleton St., St. Catherines, Ont. Mrs. M. Morris, 46 Harwood Rd., Lewisham, London, S.E., Eng.
3030680	Morris, R.	Pte	W. 1-10-18 (Cambrai) to Eng.	137 Westlawn Ave., Pawtucket, R.I., U.S.A.
907606	Morrisey, T. F.	Pte	Evac. sick 27-2-17 to Eng.	1232 Powell St., Vancouver, B.C.
908232	Morrish, W. L.	Pte.	W. 9-4-17 (Vimy) to Eng.	Oxleow, Sask.
103286	Morrison, W.	Pte.	K. i. a. 12-6-17 (2nd Triangle)	A. Murray, Skegerstaness, Stornoway, Lewis, Scot.
136100	Morrison, D. A.	Pte.	W. 18-11-16 (Somme)	82 Ashburnham Rd., Toronto, Ont.
703481	Morrison, J.	Pte.	Tr. to Eng. as minor 28-3-17.	852 17th Ave. W., Vancouver, B.C.
706337	Morrison, J. S.	Cpl.	Evac. sick 23-7-17 to Eng.	2052 Chaucer St., Victoria, B.C.
931849	Morrison, M.	Pte.	Tr. to 31st Bn. 12-8-18.	R.R. No. 2, Cloverdale, B.C.
703480	Morrison, T.	Pte.	Evac. sick 16-11-16 to Eng.	852 17th Ave. W., Vancouver, B.C.

Regt. No.	Name	Rank	Service	Address
3108592	Morrison, W.	Pte.	....	c/o Bank of Nova Scotia, King and Sherman Sts., Hamilton, Ont.
704143	Morrissey, E.	Cpl.	W. 20-10-16 (Regina); evac. sick 17-8-17 to Eng.	
2015172	Morrow, A.	Pte.	W. 1-10-18 (Cambrai) to Eng.	47 Blackington Rd., Seaford, Sussex, Eng.
931817	Morrow, A. T.	Pte.	Tr. to 4th M.G.C. 13-5-18.	c/o Mrs. Snubb, 301 J. St., Hoquiam, Wash., U.S.A.
850100	Morrow, C.	Pte.	Evac. sick 24-11-16 to Eng.	R.R. No. 2, New Westminster, B.C.
219649	Morton, A.	Pte.	Tr. to 11th C.L.T.M.B. 1-10-17.	127 Palmer Ave., Niagara Falls, Ont.
541452	Morton, G. N.	Pte.	Tr. to Lbr. Pool 9-6-18.	No address available.
240629	Morton, J.	Pte.		No address available.
2160987	Morton, S. W.	Pte.		204 Hunter St. W., Hamilton, Ont.
703881	Moseley, A. I.	L.-C.	K. i. a. 21-10-16.	c/o W. Patterson, Oxford Mills, Ont.
703814	Mosscrop, R.	Pte.	W. 11-11-16 (Somme) to Eng.	Mrs. A. Moseley, Victoria St., Nelson, B.C.
220871	Mouck, M. S.	Pte.	Tr. to 51st Bn. 2-8-16.	c/o Royal Bank, Nelson, B.C.
249495	Mountjoy, F. C.	Pte.	W. 23-7-18 (Oppy) to Eng.	16 Kingston Rd., Toronto, Ont.
703806	Mowat, A.	Pte.	W. 11-11-16 (Somme); k. i. a. 9-4-17 (Vimy).	A. Mowat, Harvey Station, New Brunswick.
703882	Mowat, A. N.	Sgt.	W. 9-4-17 (Vimy) to Eng.	No. 2 Prince of Wales Apts., Oldfield Ave., Montreal.
2499311	Muckler, J.	Pte.		414 Gold St., Buffalo, N.Y., U.S.A.
102068	Mudge, A. E.	Pte.	W. 8-6-17 (2nd Triangle); W. 10-4-18 (Oppy); tr. to 31st Bn. 12-8-18.	
703754	Muir, G.	Pte.	Tr. to 2nd Can. Tun. Co. 6-2-17.	Crown Hill, Plymouth, Eng.
703114	Muir, J.	Pte.	Tr. to 2nd Co. C.F.C. 24-5-18.	Prideau St., Nanaimo, B.C.
183757	Muldrew, W. H.	Pte.	K. i. a. 9-4-17 (Vimy).	Roseburn, Edinburgh, Scot.
703575	Mulhern, J.	Pte.	W. 18-10-16 (Somme); w. 6-4-18 (Vimy); w. 2-9-18 (2nd Arras) to Eng.	Mrs. J. Muldrew, Red Deer, Alta.
145558	Mulligan, M.	Pte.	Tr. to 77th Bn. 10-8-16.	Pasqua, Sask.
3030792	Mulloy, P.	Pte.	W. 27-9-18 (Cambrai) to Eng.	107 Concord St., Ottawa, Ont.
225271	Mulloy, C. B.	Pte.	W. 27-9-18 (Cambrai) to Eng.	Brillica, Mass., U.S.A.
2528473	Mundy, W. M.	Pte.	Acc. w. 18-8-18 to Eng.	4 Briar Close, Evesham, Eng.
707134	Munro, J.	Pte.	W. 9-4-17 (Vimy) to Eng.	102 Convent Ave., New York, U.S.A.
252650	Munroe, P.	Pte.		470 Constance Ave., Esquimalt, B.C.
252612	Murchie, R.	Pte.	K. i. a. 4-9-17 (Vimy).	Box 38, Waldeck, Sask.
183746	Murdoch, E. J.	Cpl.	W. 15-5-17 (1st Triangle); d. o. w. 4-9-18 (2nd Arras).	D. Murchie, Kilmary P.O., Isle of Arran, Scot.
703701	Murphy, A. R.	Pte.	W. 27-9-18 (Cambrai) to Eng.	J. Murdoch, 1252 6th Ave. S., Lethbridge, Alta.
3314182	Murphy, C. L.	Pte.	W. 27-9-18 (Cambrai) to Eng.	c/o Mrs. D. Morand, Lumby, B.C.
3310182	Murphy, D. N.	Pte.	W. 23-1-18 (Merlcourt) to Eng.	R.R. No. 1, Cayuga, Ont.
1004106	Murphy, J.	Pte.	W. 1-11-17 (Passchendaele) to Eng.	Simcoe, Ont.
1003362	Murphy, P. J.	Pte.	Tr. to 51st Bn. 2-8-16.	Box 561, Saulte Ste. Marie, Mich., U.S.A.
219276	Murphy, W.	Pte.	Dec. Croix de Guerre, Belgian, C.C.M.S. 409-19	Aylmer, Wright Co., Que.
703685	Murphy, W. E.	Pte.		No address available.
252149	Murray, A.	Pte.	W. 3-9-18 (2nd Arras).	Lumby, nr. Vernon, B.C.
101573	Murray, C.	Pte.	W. 20-10-16 (Regina) to Eng.	10 Ellengowan Rd., Shawlands, Glasgow, Scot.
252148	Murray, C. S.	Pte.	W. 6-4-17 (Vimy) to Eng.	Tolland, Alta.
703369	Murray, D.	Pte.	W. i. a. 10-10-16 (Somme).	Morse, Sask.
219277	Murray, D.	Pte.	W. 15-8-17 (Lens) to Eng.	Mrs. Murray, 101 7th Ave. W., Vancouver, B.C.
252753	Murray, H.	Pte.	Tr. to 51st Bn. 2-8-16.	No address available.
246086	Murray, H. J.	Pte.		No address available.

Reg. No.	Name	Rank	Notes	Address
160951	Murray, J.	Pte.	Acc. w. 11-6-18; tr. to Lbr. Pool 1-11-18	Whitefish, Mont., U.S.A.
252969	Murray, P.	Pte.	W. 9-4-17 (Vimy) to Eng.	Helmsdale, Sutherlandshire, Scot.
703592	Murray, T. C.	Pte.	Tr. to 9th Can. Area Emp. Co. 25-7-18	2192 Queen St., Toronto, Ont.
1021311	Murray, W. McI.	Sgt.	W. 27-9-18 (Cambrai) to Eng.	Ladysmith, B.C.
908042	Murray, W. R.	Pte.	W. 9-4-17 (Vimy) to Eng.	Usherville, Sask.
907057	Musto, A. O.	Pte.	Evac. sick 9-9-17 to Eng.	874 Lawd St., Regina, Sask.
703736	Muyleart, B.	Pte.	W. 2-9-18 (2nd Arras) to Eng.	219 Cordova St., Vancouver, B.C.
763163	Myers, L. L.	Pte.		Gravenhurst, Ont.
703681	Myhill, L. E.	Pte.	K. i. a. 15-9-16 (St. Eloi)	Mrs. Myhill, 69 Station Rd., Hanwell, London, Eng.
3109138	Myler, H.	Pte.		No address available.
703602	McAfee, G. G.	Cpl.	Dec. M.M. (Oppy) C.R.O. 1755; w. 10-4-18 (Oppy) to Eng.	Returned Soldiers Club, Vancouver, B.C.
703618	Macdonald, A. H.	Pte.	Evac. sick in Eng 16-6-16	901 Metropolitan Bldg., Vancouver, B.C.
760936	MacDonald, A. K.	Pte.	K. i. a. 6-6-17 (2nd Triangle)	Mrs. M. MacDonald, 706 Vernon Dve., Vancouver, B.C.
102476	MacDonald, C. C.	Pte.	Evac. sick 24-5-17 to Eng.	Sidney, B.C.
703708	MacDonald, C. J.	Pte.		1302 Seymour St., Vancouver, B.C.
160861	MacDonald, D.	Pte.		No address available.
3105053	MacDonald, J. M.	Pte.	D. o. w. 19-5-17 (1st Triangle)	A. MacDonald, c/o Byn Co., White Horse, Yukon.
704126	MacDonald, N. A.	Pte.	W. 20-10-16 (Regina); w. 8-8-18 (Amiens)	139 E. George St., Providence, R.I., U.S.A.
859361	MacDonnell, D. E.	Pte.	W. 30-9-18 (Cambrai)	22 Crossboat Locks, Stornoway, Scotland
240514	MacFarlane, J. W.	Pte.		348 Pacific Ave., Toronto, Ont.
931163	MacIntosh, W. M.	Cpl.		555 King St. E., Hamilton, Ont.
252150	Mackay, A. R.	Pte.	W. 9-4-17 (Vimy) to Eng.	Eli, Fifeshire, Scot.
225461	Mackay, C. W.	Pte.		Vidora, Sask.
704135	Mackay, D. R.	Cpl.	Evac. sick 19-1-17 to Eng.	1420 Washburn St., Scranton, Pa., U.S.A.
249330	Mackay, J. B.	Pte.	K. i. a. 4-9-18 (2nd Arras)	Pittentrail, Broomfield, Rogat, Sutherland, Scot.
210648	MacKay, V. E.	L.-C.		Mrs. E. MacKay, Sparkhall Ave., Toronto, Ont.
704025	Mackendrick, J. W.	Pte.	Tr. to 51st Bn. 2-8-16	Winona, Ont.
703795	Mackenzie, J.	Pte.	Evac. sick 21-4-17 to Eng.	Campbelltown, New Brunswick
862974	Mackenzie, J. S.	Pte.	W. 2-9-18 (2nd Arras) to Eng.	855 Davie St., Vancouver, B.C.
706133	Mackenzie, S.	Pte.	W. 1-11-17 (Passchendaele) to Eng.	180 Monro St., Toronto, Ont.
252743	MacKenzie, T.	Pte.	W. 9-4-17 (Vimy); w. and missing after action 9-8-17 (Lens)	Box 702 Snohomish, Wash., U.S.A.
703437	MacKenzie, W. C.	Pte.	W. 21-10-16 (Regina); evac. sick 16-7-17 to Eng.	A. MacKenzie, Obigacil, Rosshire, Scot.
3030116	MacKie, J.	Pte.	K. i. a. 1-10-18 (Cambrai)	1686 Georgia St., Vancouver, B.C.
2393408	Mackintosh, A.	Pte.	D. o. w. 29-11-18 (Cambrai)	Mrs. MacKie, 99 Old Row, Drougan, Ayrshire, Scot.
703948	MacLachlan, D. A.	Pte.	K. i. a. 21-10-16 (Regina)	Mrs. E. Mackintosh, 2525 7th Ave. E, New York City.
1003567	MacLachlan, P.	Cpl.	W. 2-9-18 (2nd Arras)	Mrs. A. MacLachlan, West Bay, Cape Breton, N.S.
141962	Maclellan, A. G.	Pte.	K. i. a. 30-9-18 (Cambrai)	Box 465, Sudbury, Ont.
760787	MacLeod, A. G.	Pte.	Tr. to Can. Corps H.Q. 15-7-18	D. Maclellan, Bruichladdich, Islay, Scot.
103327	Macleod, J.	Pte.	Evac. sick 26-16-17 to Eng.	2242 8th Ave. W., Vancouver, B.C.
3106415	Macleod, M.	Pte.		Balanlan, Stornoway, Scot.
102382	MacMaster, R. MacL.	Sgt.	Tr. to Eng. on duty 11-2-19	Stornoway, Scot.
3315623	MacMillan, T. J.	Pte.		Vicosa P.O., South Vancouver, B.C.
102620	MacNeil, L.	Pte.	W. 16-8-17 (Lens) to Eng.	2756 Helen St., Philadelphia, U.S.A.
703843	MacPhee, A.	Pte.	W. 19-10-16 (Somme); tr. to 11th C.L.T.M.B. 1-10-17	c/o Bank of Montreal, Greenwood, B.C.

Number	Name	Rank	Notes	Address
225496	MacRae, D. L.	Pte.	Missing after action 27-9-18 (Cambrai); believed taken prisoner of war	K. MacRae, 18 Birch St., Sherbrooke, Que.
1003834	McAdam, D. C.	Pte.	Tr. to Eng. as minor 4-11-17	Chapleau, Ont.
2527376	McAllister, S.	Pte.		26 Alexander St., Saulte Ste. Marie, Ont.
703488	McAlpine, W. N.	Pte.	Evac. sick 1-9-16 to Eng	c/o Mrs. Huckin, 1274 Burrard St., Vancouver, B.C.
102767	McArdle, M.	Cpl.	Dec. M.M. (Cambrai) C.R.O. 1989	679 Broadway, Vancouver, B.C.
83038	McArthur, G. C.	Pte.	W. 7-9-17 (Lens); tr. to Eng. for commission 20-9-17	
225599	McArthur, J.	Pte.	Tr. to Lbr. Pool 25-10-17	c/o the City Engineer, Guelph, Ont.
760844	McArthur, J. J.	Pte.	D. o. w. 13-4-17 (Vimy)	Annan, Gray Co., Ont.
703425	McArthur, R. B.	Pte.	Tr. to 67th Bn. 8-7-16	T. McArthur, 43 Strickland St., Nanaimo, B.C.
703705	McAuley, W. M.	Pte.	Tr. to 51st Bn. 2-8-16; dec. M.M. (Passchendaele)	48 Muir Ave., Toronto, Ont.
907440	McBean, K.	Pte.	W. 2-8-17 (Lens); dec. M.M. (Passchendaele) C.R.O. 1571	c/o A. Chisholm, Smithers, B.C.
3105641	McBride, J. A.	Pte.	K. i. a. 27-9-18 (Cambrai)	Lennwood, Larkhall, Scot.
3314368	McBride, W. M.	Pte.	W. 27-9-18 (Cambrai) to Eng	Mrs. McBride, 1215 Clay St., Topeka, Kansas, U.S.A.
703626	McCabe, R. S.	Pte.	Tr. to 51st Bn. 2-8-16	Hagarsville, Ont.
1003421	McCabe, W. I.	Pte.	W. 31-10-17 (Passchendaele) to Eng	Ardley P.O., B.C.
1022551	McCall, H.	Pte.	W. 16-5-17 (1st Triangle)to Eng	c/o Mrs. C. R. Secord, 429 Sumach St., Toronto, Ont.
703021	McCallum, A. C.	Pte.	Dec. M.M. (Passchendaele) C.R.O. 1571; d. o. w. 27-9-18 (Cambrai)	2414 Mowett St., Victoria, B.C.
760511	McCallum, D.	Pte.	D. o. w. 6-6-17 (1st Triangle)	A. C. McCallum, Lake Hill P.O., Victoria, B.C.
252515	McCallum, J. B.	Pte.	K. i. a. 9-4-17 (Vimy)	G. McCallum, Lancaster, Ont.
703399	McCallum, W. H.	Pte.	Evac. from P.B. 8-10-17	P. McCallum, Success, Sask.
252172	McCandless, J.	Pte.	W. 9-4-17 (Vimy) to Eng	Box 781, Vancouver, B.C.
704087	McCandlish, A. L.	Pte.	Tr. to 75th Bn. 26-7-18	Swift Current, Sask.
249831	McCarten, S.	Pte.	W. 1-10-18 (Cambrai) to Eng.; tr. to 4th M.G.C. 1-5-18	210 Victoria St., Nelson, B.C.
703904	McCauley, F.	Pte.	W. 21-10-16 (Regina)	c/o T. McCarten, Keady, Mowilliam, Co. Armagh, Ire.
663655	McCleary, B.	Pte.		Seaforth, Ont.
249164	McCleery, J.	Pte.	K. i. a. 27-9-18 (Cambrai)	Oakville, Ont.
907478	McClenaghan, E. C.	Pte.	K. i. a. 9-4-17 (Vimy)	Mrs. McCleery, 48 Pembroke St., Toronto, Ont.
908231	McClure, A. N.	Pte.	Evac. sick 11-5-17 to Eng	Mrs. McClenaghan, 1341 Carnival St., Regina, Sask.
101247	McConnell, J. S.	Pte.	W. 14-5-17 (1st Triangle); w. 1-9-17 (Lens) to Eng	Tiverton, Ont.
703462	McConnell, M.	Pte.	W. 20-11-16 (Somme) to Eng.; died in Vancouver, March, 1919	744 34th Ave., South Vancouver, B.C.
907049	McCormac, T. H.	Pte.	W. 9-4-17 (Vimy) to Eng	W. McConnell, c/o Imperial Oil Ltd., Gleichen, Alta.
907863	McCormick, A. A.	Pte.	Evac. sick 3-12-16 to Eng	1252 Elphinstone St., Regina, Sask.
703771	McCracken, J.	Cpl.	N.C.O. 2nd I/c Signal Section	Surges Narrows, B.C.
1004118	McCrary, J.	Pte.	Tr. to Lbr. Pool 16-8-18	276 Johnston Ave., Winnipeg, Man.
703766	McCreery, J. L.	Pte.	Evac. sick 3-1-18 to Eng	514 Chicago St., Jackson, Mich., U.S.A.
703721	McCubbin, J. S.	Pte.	Evac. sick 20-4-17 to Eng	Glenhazel, Elk Co., Penn., U.S.A.
663185	McCulloch, T. W.	Pte.	Tr. to 4th C.M.R. 6-8-18	c/o Bank of B.N.A., Prince Rupert, B.C.
183321	McCurrach, C. J.	Cpl.	Dec. M.M. (Lens) C.R.O. 1419; w. 27-9-18 (Cambrai) to Eng	Grand Valley, Ont.
3109894	McCutcheon, W. L.	Pte.		Three Hills, Alta.
145832	McDevitt, R.	Pte.	Tr. to 77th Bn. 10-8-16	R.R. No. 1, Honeywood, Ont.
447695	McDonald, A.	Pte.	Evac. sick 21-10-16	Box 427, Renfrew, Ont.
				No address available.

145205	McDonald, D. R.	Pte.	Tr. to 77th Bn. 10-8-16	Alexandria, Ont.
703404	McDonald, E.	Pte.	W. 9-4-17 (Vimy); w. 10-6-17 (2nd Triangle) to Eng.	
703259	McDonald, G.	Cpl.	K. i. a. 27-8-16 (St. Eloi)	Kerrisdale, B.C.
703631	McDonald, G.	Pte.	K. i. a. 12-5-17 (1st Triangle)	W. McDonald, Murrayville, B.C.
706715	McDonald, H. C.	Sgt.	Dec. M.M. (Oppy) C.R.O. 1866; w. 27-7-18 (Oppy) to Eng.	Mrs. McDonald, King's Rd., N. Vancouver, B.C.
706284	McDonald, J.	Pte.	Tr. to Eng. for commission 30-1-18	Summerside, P. E. I.
706015	McDonald, J. S.	Cpl.	W. 12-6-17 (2nd Triangle) to Eng.	East Lodge, Dochfour, Inverness, Scot.
103070	McDonald, L. A.	Pte.	W. 1-9-16 (St. Eloi); k. i. a. 21-10-16 (Regina)	1340 George St., Victoria, B.C.
103523	McDonald, P.	Pte.	W. 4-9-17 (Lens); tr. to Lbr. Pool, 25-10-17	R.F.D. 58, Dolkith, Ont.
2631139	McDonald, R.	Pte.	W. 6-6-17 (2nd Triangle) to Eng.	Mrs. J. McDonald, West St., Peters, P. E. I.
907988	McDonnell, W.	Pte.		c/o Ira A. McDonald, Dayton, Ill., U.S.A.
704052	McDougall, A.	Pte.		Dundalk, Ont.
907975	McDougall, D.	Pte.	W. 9-4-17 (Vimy) to Eng.	Hazelton, B.C.
663434	McDougall, H. J.	Pte.	W. 1-10-18 (Cambrai) to Eng.	Underwood, Ont.
925463	McDougall, J. C.	Pte.	Tr. to 4th C.I. B.D. 24-3-18	R.R. No. 2, Grand Valley, Ont.
907245	McDougall, J. J.	Pte.		102 Sydney Rd., Bootle, Liverpool, Eng.
703049	McDougall, O. L.	Cpl.	Evac. sick 30-10-18 to Eng.	Suite 311, Donaghue Block, Regina, Sask.
704064	McDougall, P. A.	Pte.		Glenholm, Eskbank, Scot.
707183	McDougall, R. S.	Pte.	Evac. sick 11-8-17 to Eng.	Hazelton, B.C.
907247	McDowell, R. C.	Pte.	Evac. sick 18-1-17 to Eng.	Box 1123, Nanaimo, B.C.
663269	McEnteer, C. P.	Pte.	W. 6-11-18 (Valenciennes) to Eng.	1618 Atholl St., Regina, Sask.
225969	McEvers, E. C.	L-C.	W. 14-11-17 (Passchendaele) to Eng.	Milton Heights, Ont.
252710	McFarlane, R.	Pte.	K. i. a. 23-7-18 (Oppy)	238 Fairview Ave., Toronto, Ont.
727505	McPaul, A. N.	Pte.	W. 8-8-18 (Amiens); d. o. w. 1-10-18 (Cambrai)	Mrs. McEvers, Redmond, Wash., U.S.A.
1003863	McGahan, N. A.	Pte.	W. 17-11-17 (Passchendaele) to Eng.	T. McFarlane, Gore Bridge, Midlothian, Scot.
249536	McGarvie, D.	Pte.	W. 1-5-18 (Oppy) to Eng.	Rednersville, Prince Edward Co., Ont.
703959	McGee, J. A.	Pte.	Tr. to 51st Bn. 2-8-16	Sault Ste. Marie, Ont.
103396	McGhee, A.	Sgt.	W. 6-9-17 (Lens); evac. sick 29-11-18 to Eng	Drummillan, St. Maybole, Ayrshire, Scot.
703883	McGhie, A.	Pte.	Bn. Gas N.C.O. from 13-7-18	L.S.B., Creston, B.C.
704133	McGovern, N.	Pte.	Tr. to 51st Bn. 2-8-16	2708 Graham St., Victoria, B.C.
				c/o Mrs. J. Cairns, Eholt, B.C.
				c/o Mrs. Fitzpatrick, 106 Moreland St., San Francisco, Cal., U.S.A.
760556	McGowan, W.	Pte.	D. o. w. (acc.) 12-9-17	Mrs. A. McGowan, Perth, Ont.
703366	McGarth, F.	Sgt.	Evac. sick 21-10-16 to Eng.	c/o Mrs. A. Browning, 957 Richard St., Vancouver, B.C.
3314021	McGrath, J. H.	Pte.	W. 27-9-18 (Cambrai) to Eng.	Port Dalhousie, Ont.
2020175	McGrath, T.	Pte.	Tr. to C.C.R.C. 31-10-17	No address available.
769095	McGreel, J. A.	Pte.	Tr. to Eng. as minor 2-5-17	681 St. Clair Ave., Toronto, Ont.
907531	McGregor, D. E.	Pte.	K. i. a. 9-1-17 (Vimy)	J. McGregor, Scotsville, N.S.
200196	McGregor, F. H.	Pte.	Tr. to Eng. as minor 26-10-17	1422 Newport Ave., Victoria, B.C.
907559	McGregor, J.	Pte.	D. o. w. 29-4-17 (Vimy)	Mrs. A. McGregor, 21 Laurelwood Ave., Aberdeen, Scotland.
703015	McGregor, J. D.	L.-C.	Dec. M.M. (Lens) C.R.O. 1466; tr. to Eng. for commission 30-1-18	613 Bay St., Victoria, B.C.
761004	McGuigan, S. P.	Sgt.	W. 5-8-17 (Lens); tr. to 4th M.G.C. 18-3-18	Ocean Falls, B.C.
102604	McGuiness, G.	Pte.	Dec. M.M. (Somme) D.R.O. 316; d. o. w. 10-6-17 (2nd Triangle)	3118 Prince Edward St., Vancouver, B.C.
703807	McHugh, J. J.	Cpl.		M. McHugh, Simoon Sound, B.C.

Number	Name	Rank	Details	Address
755042	McHugh, T. A.	Pte.	K. l. a. 25-9-17 (Lens)	Mrs. R. McHugh, R.R. No. 2, Sault Ste. Marie, Ont.
136092	McIlvenny, C. H.	Pte.	Evac. sick 21-10-16 to Eng.	No address available.
184135	McIlwraith, G. E.	Pte.	Tr. to 11th M.G.C. 10-12-16	No address available.
220003	McInnes, J. C.	Cpl.	Evac. sick 30-1-17 to Eng.	Glasgow Station, Ont.
839046	McInnis, J. A.	Pte.	Dec. M.M. (2nd Arras) C.R.O. 1930; w. and missing after action 1-10-18 (Cambrai)	
703333	McIntosh, D.	Pte.	Dec. D.C.M. (Valenciennes) C.R.O. 2040	Mrs. J. McInnis, R.R. No. 4, Owen Sound.
1003044	McIntyre, E. R.	C.S.M.	Tr. 11th C.L.T.M.B. 10-7-16	Hazelton, B.C.
540026	McIntyre, F. C.	L.-C.	Evac sick 11-1-19 to Eng.	352 Albert St., Sault Ste. Marie, Ont.
2529378	McIntyre, J.	Pte.	K. l. a. 27-9-18 (Cambrai)	No address available.
3105197	McIntyre, R.	Pte.	K. l. a. 30-10-17 (Passchendaele)	542 Willington St., Hamilton, Ont.
1003078	McIntyre, R. C.	Pte.	W. to 26th Bn. 25-3-18	Mrs. McIntyre, 2220 E. Harold St., Philadelphia, Pa.
160383	McIvor, J.	Pte.	W. 22-11-16 (Somme) to Eng; dec. M.M. (Somme) D.R.O. 375	Sudbury, Ont.
703108	McKay, D.	Sgt.	K. i. a. 9-4-17 (Vimy)	8 New Valley, Stornoway, Scotland.
703620	McKay, D.	L.-S.	Evac. inj. to Eng. 20-1-17	Police Station, Vancouver, B.C.
3317318	McKay, H. K.	Pte.	W. 17-11-17 (Passchendaele) to Eng.	J. Mowat, Keiss, Caithness, Scot.
703067	McKay, W. J.	Pte.	W. 30-9-18 (Cambrai)	Hawkestone, Ont.
2020216	McKee, G. A.	Pte.	W. 7-4-17 (Vimy) to Eng.	595 Fleet St., Winnipeg, Man.
2528475	McKenna, P.	Pte.		967 Howe St., Vancouver, B.C.
183973	McKenzie, D.	Pte.		4 Albert Terrace, Liverpool, Eng. Carbon, Alta.
907512	McKenzie, D. J.	Pte.	K. l. a. 9-4-17 (Vimy)	Mrs. McKenzie, Convenor St., New Elgin, Scotland.
161273	McKenzie, H.	Pte.	Dec. M.M. (Somme) L.G. 29953	56 A Fountain Bridge, Edinburgh, Scot.
3106080	McKenzie, J.	Pte.	D. o. s. 1-11-18	Manor, Penn., U.S.A.
703743	McKenzie, S.	Pte.	D. 3-3-17 (Vimy) to Eng.	Mrs. M. Frost, Alberni, B.C.
184112	McKenzie, W.	Pte.		c/o Capt. S.F. McKenzie, 1686 Georgia St. W., Vancouver, B.C.
291738	McKeon, W.	Sgt.	W. 9-4-17 (Vimy) to Eng.	Fairville, St. Johns, N.B.
703545	McKewan, A. G.	L.-C.	W. 17-8-17 (Lens); k. l. a. 1-10-18 (Cambrai)	Mrs. K. Dawson, 3020 Washington Ave., Fresno, Cal.
704078	McKie, W. J.	Pte.	W. 11-6-17 (2nd Triangle) to Eng.	63 Princess St., North Shields, Eng.
3108978	McKinley, J. S	Pte.		No address available.
703226	McKinnel, F.	Pte.	W. l. a. 9-4-17 (Vimy)	Mrs. McKinnel, 90 47th Ave. W., Vancouver, B.C.
2254401	McKinnon, F. A.	Pte.	W. l. a. 18-11-17 (Passchendaele)	Miss E. McKinnon, 242 Wellington St., Brantford, Ont.
178129	McKinnon, J.	Pte.	Tr. to Lbr. Pool 4-11-17	29 Allestnee Rd., Fulham, London, Eng.
727881	McKinnon, J. A.	Pte.	K. l. a. 27-9-18 (Cambrai)	Mrs. S. McKinnon, Wiarton, Bruce Co., Ont.
925554	McKinnon, J. J.	L-C.	K. l. a. 9-4-17 (Vimy)	A. McKinnon, Sughampton, Ont.
334249	McKissick, J.	Pte.	Tr. to 4th M.G.C. 13-5-18	13 Ethel St., Pittsburg, U.S.A.
1003595	McKnight, W. A.	Pte.	W. 27-9-18 (Cambrai) to Eng.	Sudbury, Ont.
703227	McLaren, F. H.	Pte.	D. o. w. 24-11-16 (Somme)	Mrs. McLaren, 4017 Hastings St., Vancouver, B.C.
3107653	McLarkey, J.	Pte.	W. 9-4-17 (Vimy) to Eng.	R.R. No. 17, St. Mary's, Ont.
704059	McLarty, I. W.	Pte.	W. 3-10-16 (Somme) to Eng.	Fort George, B.C.
703496	McLarty, R.	Pte.	Evac. sick 13-3-17 to Eng.	210 Springburn Rd., Glasgow, Scot.
703282	McLauchlan, J. P	Pte.	W. sick 11-5-18 to Eng.	53 Clarence St., Glasgow, Scot.
102841	McLauchlan, F.	Pte.	W. 1-10-18 (Cambrai) to Eng.	22 Crescent St., Greenock, Scot.
2254492	McLauchlan, R.	Pte.	Missing after action 11-6-17 (2nd Triangle)	59 Constitution Rd., Dundee, Scot.
760012	McLaughlan, J.	Pte.		Mrs. McLaughlen, Bushtown, Macosquin, Coleraine, Co. Derry, Ire.
2529359	McLaughlin, L. A.	Pte.	W. 27-9-18 (Cambrai) to Eng.	5309 Wadnea St., Duluth, Minn, U.S.A.

102528	McLaughlin, W. A.	Pte.	Evac. sick 26-1-19	St. Stephen's, N.B.
704105	McLaurin, W. R.	Pte.	Evac. sick 7-12-16 to Eng.	207 2nd Ave. N.E., Calgary, Alta.
761169	McLean, J.	Pte.	W. 5-6-17 (2nd Triangle) to Eng.	654 Broadway West, Vancouver, B.C.
907698	McLean, J. B.	Pte.	W. 9-4-17 (Vimy); w. 1-11-17 (Passchendaele) to Eng.	33 Hunt Hill Rd., High Blantyre, Scot.
270277	McLean, J. W.	Pte.	W. 6-11-18 (Valenciennes) to Eng.	c/o Box 195, Paris, Ont.
226399	McLean, L.	Pte.	W. 23-9-17 (Lens) to Eng.	5 South St., Niagara Falls, Ont.
703380	McLellan, W. H.	Cpl.	D. o. s. 16-2-17.	A. McLean, Box 57, Nanaimo, B.C.
761088	McLennan, A.	Pte.	W. 9-4-17 (Vimy) to Eng.	2466 21st Ave. E, Vancouver, B.C.
703167	McLennan, C.	Pte.	W. 12-5-17 (1st Triangle); tr. to Lbr. Pool 11-3-18.	
252688	McLennan, J. R.	Pte.	W. 13-5-17 (1st Triangle); w. 7-6-17 (2nd Triangle); k. i. a. 2-9-18 (2nd Arras).	c/o Bank of Commerce, Courtenay, B.C.
703385	McLeod, A.	Pte.	Tr. to 51st Bn. 2-8-16.	Mrs. M. McLennan, Cadillac, Sask.
1075242	McLeod, D. A.	Pte.	Evac. sick 7-7-17 to Eng.	4463 13th Ave. W., Point Grey, Vancouver, B.C.
104440	McLeod, J.	Sgt.	Dec. M.M. (Vimy) C.R.O. 1236; d. o. w. 17-5-17 (1st Triangle).	1213 96th St., Edmonton, Alta.
908092	McLeod, J.	Pte.	Tr to 16th M.G.C. 1-1-17.	Mrs. M. McCloct, 1929 St. John St., Regina, Sask.
1075105	McLeod, J. j.	Pte.	W. 27-9-18 (Cambrai) to Eng.	No address available.
703255	McLeod, M. D.	Pte.	Tr. to C.C.R.C. 31-10-17.	Breadalbane, P. E. I.
703414	McLeod, N.	Pte.	W. 21-10-16 (Regina) to Eng.	c/o D. J. McLeod, Fort Langley, B.C.
703054	McLeod, R.	Pte.	K. i. a. 22-10-16 (Regina).	12 Arnold St., Stornoway, Scot.
				Miss C. McLeod, 3 Broom Hill Drive, Partic, Glasgow, Scotland.
908209	McLeod, T. H.	Pte.	Evac. sick 27-5-17 to Eng.	Grenfell, Sask.
3314135	McLeod, W.	Pte.	Evac. sick 29-8-18 to Eng.	No address available.
240404	McLoughlin, F. P.	Pte.	W. 27-9-18 (Cambrai); tr. to Eng. demob. duty 8-1-19.	Dundas, Ont.
225403	McLucas, J. McK.	Pte.	W. 27-9-18 (Cambrai).	14 Whitfield Ave., Hamilton, Ont.
226950	McMaster, J.	L.-C.	W. 8-8-18 (Amiens); tr. to Eng. duty 20-3-19.	2948 Yonge St., Toronto, Ont.
706806	McMillan, C. B.	Pte.	W. 9-4-17 (Vimy) to Eng.	c/o Miss E. C. Irish, Coquitlam, B.C.
253020	McMillan, J. M.	Pte.	Att. to 28th Co. C.F.C.	52 Bradford St., Walsall, Staffs, Eng.
102550	McMillan, L.	Pte.	Tr. to 8th Can. Area Emp Co. 27-9-17.	1 Galloway St., Paisley, Scot.
126116	McMillen, C. E.	Pte.	K. i. a. 8-9-16 (St. Eloi).	Mrs. McMillen, Brussels, Ont.
709327	McMullon, B. F.	Pte.	Evac. sick 14-8-18 to Eng.	St. Andrew's, N.B.
253074	McMurdo, T. G. B.	Pte.	W. 8-8-18 (Amiens) to Eng.	Windsouer, Auldgirth, Dumfrieshire, Scot.
703885	McMynn, G. G. B.	Pte.	Tr. to 51st Bn. 2-8-16.	Box 64, Midway, B.C.
833846	McNab, A. D.	Pte.	W. 13-11-17 (Passchendaele) to Eng.	R.R. No. 1, Bognor, Ont.
3108989	McNally, H. G.	Pte.		R.R. No. 3, Hanover, Ont.
703663	McNally, J. E.	L.-C.	Missing after action 13-6-17 (2nd Triangle)	J. W. McNally, Saanichton, B.C.
907996	McNaught, H. L.	Pte.	W. 11-5-17 (1st Triangle).	Moncton, Ont.
703646	McNaught, J.	Pte.	Missing 11-11-16 (Somme).	W. McNaught, Cranberry Station, Ayrshire, Scot.
703995	McNell, A.	Pte.	W. 21-10-16 (Regina) to Eng.	Mallgant Cove, Antigonish, N.S.
103309	McNicholl, W. H.	L.-C.	W. 12-6-17 (2nd Triangle); d. o. w. 5-9-18 (2nd Arras).	
907534	McNie, J. D.	Pte.	Evac. sick 29-9-17 to Eng.	Mrs. J. White, 17 Ailsa Bldgs., Girvan, Ayr, Scot.
703382	McNiven, W.	Pte.	W. 21-10-16 (Somme) to Eng.	Elliott Bl., 7th Ave, Regina, Sask.
648621	McNutt, G.	Pte.	W. 23-1-18 (Merlcourt) to Eng.	Munson, Alta.
145791	McPhail, W.	Pte.	Tr. to 77th Bn. 10-8-16.	Sturgeon Falls, Ont.
				Box 103, Cummings Bridges, Ont.

703843	McPhee, A.	Pte.	Evac. sick 3-11-16 to Eng.	No address available.
704050	McPhee, D.	Pte.	W. 22-10-16 (Regina) to Eng.	c/o Stanley Hotel, Vancouver, B.C.
703583	McPhee, D. A.	Cpl.	K. l. a. 21-10-16 (Regina)	Cranbrook, B.C.
703599	McPherson, J.	Cpl.	W. 1-11-17 (Passchendaele) to Eng.	J. McPherson, 58-60 Norfolk St., Glasgow, Scot.
225771	McPherson, J.	Pte.	Tr. to C.C.R.C. 12-2-19.	284 Salem Ave., Toronto, Ont.
3109826	McPherson, S. B.	Pte.		No address available.
3314005	McQuade, D.	Pte.	Tr. to 77th Bn. 10-8-16	Stamford, Ont.
145557	McQuattie, J. L.	Pte.	K. l. a. 9-4-17 (Vimy)	12 Simcoe St., Ottawa, Ont.
925126	McQuoid, A. F.	Pte.	Tr.to Lbr. Pool 19-2-18.	W. McQuiod, 715 Taylor St., Ft. Wayne, Ind., U.S.A.
102250	McQuoid, R.	Pte.	W. 5-8-17 (Lens) to Eng.	c/o T. McQuoid, 5 Brisbane St., Greenock, Scot.
907539	McRae, C. F. S.	Pte.		Aylesbury, Sask.
227187	McSavaney, H.	Pte.		Old Bridgeport, Cape Breton, N.S.
102338	McSween, N.	Pte.	W. 27-7-17 (Lens); w. 17-11-17 (Passchendaele) to Eng.	
441121	McVeigh, W. H.	Sgt.	Tr. to 78th Bn. 16-12-17.	Rong Dunragen, Skye, Scot.
826414	Nagle, T.	Pte.	Evac. sick 25-10-17 to Eng.	274 Redwood Ave., Winnipeg, Man.
760903	Nairne, W. D.	Pte.	W. 9-4-17 (Vimy) to Eng.	No address available.
223370	Naish, A. E.	Sgt.		4395 Fraser St., South Vancouver, B.C.
703760	Naylor, P.	Pte.	Tr. to Corps Sigs. 27-7-17	145 Epworth Circle, Niagara Falls, Ont.
225392	Neado, J.	Pte.	Evac. sick 8-1-19.	Old House, Kirkheaton, Huddersfield, Eng.
703058	Neal, A.	Pte.	W. 28-9-18 (Cambrai) to Eng.	New Liskeard, Ont.
703789	Neal, W. E.	Pte.	W. 27-9-18 (Cambrai) to Eng.	c/o Mrs. T. Bell, Quathlaski Cove, B.C.
3314376	Near, F.	Pte.	K. l. a. 27-9-18 (Cambrai).	Marpole P.O., B.C.
3314148	Near, H.	Pte.	W. 9-4-17 (Vimy) to Eng.	211 Bridge St., Niagara Falls, Ont.
761059	Nedeau, G.	Pte.	W. 6-11-16 (Somme); tr. to Lbr Pool 30-10-17	Mrs. Near, Ridgway P.O., Ont.
703357	Needham, H.	Pte.	W. 3-9-18 (2nd Arras) to Eng.	Powell River, B.C.
1003966	Needs, G.	Pte.	Tr. to Lbr. Pool 15-3-18	Lee-on-Solent, Hants, Eng.
126235	Neeley, W. G.	Pte.	Evac. sick 1-9-16 to Eng.	174 Clinton St., Toronto, Ont.
703907	Negus, T. H.	Sgt.	W. 9-4-17 (Vimy) to Eng.	R.R. No. 2, Burgessville, Ont.
907676	Nelsen, N.	Pte.		Crescent Valley, B.C.
3105864	Nelson, D.	Pte.	W. 7-4-18 (Oppy) to Eng.	Carberry Plain, Man.
760721	Nelson, D. J.	Cpl.	Evac. sick 22-5-17 to Eng.	10 Russell Place, Kirkcaldy, Scot.
703281	Nelson, E.	Pte.	W. 9-4-17 (Vimy) to Eng.	Ladner, B.C.
703607	Nelson, F. H.	Pte.	W. (acc.) 25-9-17 to Eng.	Odeholt, Sac, Iowa, U.S.A.
629081	Nelson, H. C.	Pte.	Tr. to P.B. Eng. Unit 26-2-18.	Prince Rupert, B.C.
703332	Nelson, J.	Pte.		c/o Mrs. F. Kemper, Box 1435, St. Louis, Mo., U.S.A.
703739	Nelson, J.	L.-C.	K. l. a. 1-10-18 (Cambrai).	Coppull, nr. Chorley, Lancs, Eng.
3109006	Nelson, J. V.	Pte.	Evac. sick 10-10-17 to Eng.	Mrs. P. Johnson, Box 325, Chisholm, B.C.
103361	Nelson, L. J.	Pte.	W. 27-9-18 (Cambrai) to Eng.	R.R. No. 1, Calster Centre, Ont.
2529455	Nelson, S. G.	Pte.	Fvac. sick 17-11-17 to Eng.	728 New City Rd., Glasgow, Scot.
528587	Nelson, W.	Pte.	Tr. to 54th Co. C.F.C. 26-3-18.	R.R. No. 5, Hagarsville, Ont.
1003268	Nepper, H.	Pte.	W. 23-11-16 (Somme) to Eng.	c/o Mrs. E. Wilson, 95 Catherine St., Hamilton, Ont.
474245	Ness, A.	Pte.	W. 1-10-18 (Cambrai) to Eng.	No address available.
931825	Netherly, O.	Pte.	W. 9-8-17 (Lens); w. 15-3-18 (Lens); tr. to 31st Bn.	Ranenna, Texas, U.S.A.
907616	Nevard, H. W.	Pte.		c/o F. E. Marshall, Ranenna, Texas, U.S.A.
249901	Neville, E. J.	L.-C.	K. l. a. 30-9-18 (Cambrai). 12-8-18	36th St., Road Texler, Colchester, Eng. Mrs. Neville, 70 Turner Rd., Walthamstow, Essex, England.

Reg. No.	Name	Rank	Details	Address
3110220	Newman, A.	Pte.	W. 2-9-18 (2nd Arras) to Eng.	5421 Odell Ave., St. Louis, U.S.A.
210406	Newman, F.	Pte.	W. 9-1-17 (Vimy); tr. to Eng. on demob.	115 Lloyd Ave., Hamilton, Ont.
135815	Newman, M. A.	Pte.	duty 14-3-19	c/o Mrs. H. Melville, 401 Euclid Ave., Toronto, Ont.
907351	Newth, W. R.	Pte.	K. i. a. 3-9-17 (Vimy)	L. Newth, Lipton, Sask.
1004057	Newton, A.	Pte.	Evac. sick 20-11-18 to Eng.	497 Lisgar St., Ottawa, Ont.
240647	Newton, H.	Pte.	Evac. sick 15-11-18 to Eng.	153 Ferrie St., Hamilton, Ont.
703534	Newton, W.	Pte.	Missing 11-11-16 (Somme)	Mrs. Newton, 21 Golden Hill, Horfield, Bristol, Eng.
3109002	Ney, M. W.	Pte.	K. i. a. 2-11-18 (2nd Arras)	W. Ney, R.R. No. 1, Midland, Ont.
2528384	Nichols, S.	Pte.	K. i. a. 6-11-18 (Valenciennes)	Mrs. E. Nicholls, 1833 Quebec St., Regina, Sask.
3317083	Nicholson, E. R.	Pte.		61 Clinton St., Toronto, Ont.
760667	Nicholson, L. B.	Pte.	D. o. w. 15-4-17 (Vimy)	Mrs. J. E. Nicholson, Collingwood East, B.C.
1003563	Nicholson, R. G. S.	Pte.	W. 1-11-17 (Passchendaele) to Eng.	182 Cathcart St., Steelton, Ont.
1090013	Nicholson, W. B.	Pte.	W. 27-9-18 (Cambrai) to Eng.	83 Victoria St., Kingston, Ont.
760546	Nicol, W.	Pte.	Evac. sick 2-8-17 to Eng.	Collingwood East, B.C.
3105896	Nicoll, J. P.	Pte.	W. 23-7-18 (Oppy)	29 Shawsheen Rd., Andover, Mass., U.S.A.
2528442	Nicoletti, J. P.	Pte.	W. 17-11-17 (Passchendaele) to Eng.	136 Edward St., Toronto, Ont.
703604	Nielsen, T. B.	Pte.	W. 22-12-17 (Mericourt) to Eng.	Prince Rupert, B.C.
1003132	Nigh, J.	Pte.	Tr. to 2nd Can. Lbr. Bn. 16-8-17.	Trout Creek P.O., Ont.
703779	Nightwine, F.	Pte.	Dec. M.M. (2nd Arras) C.R.O. 1930; evac.	c/o Miss E. Frank, Terrace, B.C.
103317	Niven, J.	L.-S.	sick 17-1-19	
703377	Nixon, A. F.	L.-C.	Tr. to Eng. for commission 19-12-17	3 John St., Mary Hill, Glasgow, Scot.
703844	Nixon, C. J.	Pte.	Bn. Gas N.C.O. 20-5-17 to 13-7-18; d. o. w. 2-9-18 (2nd Arras)	1831 Trafalgar Rd., Vancouver, B.C.
249141	Nixon, F. C.	Pte.	W. 8-8-18 (Amiens) to Eng.	Mrs. M. Nixon, 209 10½ St. N.W., Calgary, Alta.
103032	Nixon, J. D.	Pte.	W. 17-8-17 (Lens) to Eng.	987 Gerrard St. E., Toronto, Ont.
226873	Nixon, W. J.	Cpl.	Dec. M.M. (2nd Arras) C.R.O. 1930.	28 Lindum Ave., Lincoln, Eng.
931836	Noble, A. J.	Pte.	Tr. to Lbr. Pool 14-10-18	274 Cannon St. E., Hamilton, Ont.
249606	Noble, L.	Pte.	K. i. a. 27-9-18 (Cambrai)	c/o Mrs. L. Binns, Kamloops, B.C.
703972	Noble, T.	Pte.	W. 9-8-17 (Lens) to Eng.	Mrs. Noble, 25 Oxford St., Toronto, Ont.
226907	Noblet, L. J.	Pte.	K. i. a. 8-8-18 (Amiens)	Fairview P.O., Penticton, B.C.
703964	Noel, U. J.	Pte.	Evac. sick 8-10-18 to Eng.	F. Noel, 109 Collingwood St., Sarnia, Ont.
760920	Nolan, D.	Pte.	W. 30-9-18 (Cambrai)	852 Thurlow St., Vancouver, B.C.
704170	Norregaard, E.	Pte.	K. i. a. 21-10-16 (Regina)	Cranbrook, B.C.
3109001	Norris, J. W.	Pte.		No address available.
703324	North, S. S.	Pte.	W. 21-10-16 (Regina); tr. to C.C.R.C. 22-2-18	1750 5th Ave. W., Vancouver, B.C.
907416	Northup, F. L.	Pte.	K. i. a. 9-4-17 (Vimy)	Mrs. S. Bible, Montpelier, Ohio, U.S.A.
225620	Norton, G. E.	Pte.	W. 4-9-18 (2nd Arras) to Eng.	20 Central Ave., Toronto, Ont.
409401	Norton, T. R.	L.-C.	W. 27-9-18 (Cambrai) to Eng.	668 4th Ave. E., Owen Sound, Ont.
760288	Notman, W.	Pte.	Evac. sick 15-5-18 to Eng.	1249 Albert St., Vancouver, B.C.
703605	Nygaard, J. L.	C.S.M.	Tr. to Eng. for commission 23-8-18	Bella Coola, B.C.
703992	Nyland, J. I.	Pte.	D. o. w. 20-4-18 (Oppy)	J. Nyland, 3346 Oxford St., Vancouver, B.C.
761255	Oates, H. M.	Pte.	W. 9-4-17 (Vimy) to Eng.	c/o Mrs. B. Allen, 7 Station Rd., West Croydon, Eng.
171667	Oatley, H. F.	Pte.		125 Epworth Circle, Niagara Falls, Ont.
1003252	O'Brien, D.	Pte.	Evac. sick 30-6-18 to Eng.	c/o Mrs. J. Sampson, Haileybury, Ont.
703117	O'Brien, J.	Pte.	W. 25-7-18 (Oppy) to Eng.	Churchfield, Clarina, Limerick, Ire.
226815	O'Brien, R. J.	Pte.	W. 23-12-17 (Mericourt)	22 Markland Rd., Kingston, Ont.

Number	Name	Rank	Movement	Address
249075	O'Callaghan, M. P.	Pte.	W. 24-3-18 (Lens) to Eng.	679 Ontario St., Toronto, Ont.
703473	O'Dell, W. H.	Pte.	Evac. sick 22-10-16 to Eng.	c/o Bank of B.N.A., Prince George, B.C.
1003243	O'Flaherty, B. A.	L.-C.	W. 3-10-17 (Passchendaele)	201 Providence St., Hamilton, Ont.
2499410	O'Gorman, J. J.	Pte.		Georgia St., Mitchelstown, Cork, Ire.
907785	Ohearn, J.	Pte.	W. 9-4-17 (Vimy) to Eng.	Gananoque, Ont.
240723	Oldland, W. H.	Pte.	Dec. M.M. (Valenciennes) C.R.O. 2028	209 James St. North, Hamilton, Ont.
908116	Oleynik, P.	Pte.	Tr. to 71st Co. C.F.C. 9-4-18	No address available.
703949	Oliphant, A.	Pte.	W. 27-9-18 (Cambrai) to Eng.	Hillhead, Phulgast, Fraserburgh, Aberdeen, Scot.
540353	Oliver, F. C.	Cpl.	D. o. w. 20-11-16 (Somme)	No address available.
727327	Oliver, J. O.	Sgt.		Ayr, Waterloo Co., Ont.
225348	Ollen-Bittle, W. A.	Pte.	Dec. M.M. (Valenciennes) C.R.O. 2028; tr. to Eng. demob. duty 14-3-19	
703359	Olliff, F.	Pte.	Tr. to 67th Bn. 8-7-16	c/o J. W. Woodley, Fullarton, Ont.
226976	Olsen, W.	Pte.	K. i. a. 8-8-18 (Amiens)	14 Precis Ave., Margate, Kent, Eng.
907717	Olson, L. J.	Pte.	W. 12-6-17 (2nd Triangle)	T. Maine, 306 Albert St., Oshawa, Ont.
925686	Olson, O. J.	Cpl.	W. 9-8-17 (Amiens); evac. sick in Eng. 29-12-17	c/o Mrs. Julen, Box 47, Cushing, Wis., U.S.A.
219237	O'Malley, G.	Pte.	Evac. sick 21-10-16 to Eng. from C.L.T.M.B.	Brooking, Sask.
907191	O'May, R.	Pte.	K. i. a. 9-4-17 (Vimy)	No address available.
703231	O'Neill, E. M.	Pte.	W. 22-10-16 (Regina); acc. inj. 16-11-17	Mrs. G. Johnson, National Park, N.J., U.S.A.
249114	O'Neill, E. M.	Pte.	W. 8-8-18 (Amiens) to Eng.	75 Josephine Ave., Windsor, Ont.
703301	Onions, H.	Cpl.	Evac. sick 26-8-16 to Eng.	140 Broadway Ave. E., Vancouver, B.C.
703267	Oransky, P.	Pte.	Evac. sick 21-10-16 to Eng.	2103 Columbia St., Vancouver, B.C.
102380	Ord, H.	Pte.	W. 7-6-17 (2nd Triangle) to Eng.	c/o Mrs. I. Easton, 2565 Prior St., Victoria, B.C.
838151	Orford, A.	Pte.	W. 8-8-18 (Amiens) to Eng.	38½ 7th St. E., Owen Sound, Ont.
1001002	Orgnacco, G.	Pte.		No address available.
3031146	O'Reilly, F.	Pte.		10½ Park Place, Saranac, New York, U.S.A.
760358	Orr, H. G.	Sgt.		High St., Killyleigh, Co. Down, Ire.
103181	Orr, R. G.	Pte.	W. 9-4-17 (Vimy) to Eng.	2343 Yew St., Vancouver, B.C.
103240	Orr, W. S.	Cpl.	W. 27-9-18 (Cambrai); evac. sick 11-2-19	c/o Mrs. A. Jamieson, 20 Elizabeth St., Throx, Glasgow, Scot.
184097	Orrick, J. R.	Pte.	W. 9-4-17 (Vimy) to Eng.	c/o Mrs. Burgess, Youngstown, Alta.
925559	Osborne, B. J. A.	Pte.	K. i. a. 9-4-17 (Vimy)	H. Osborne, Kisbey, Sask.
760483	Osborne, G. M.	Pte.	W. 9-4-17 (Vimy) to Eng.	Joyce P.O., Collingwood, B.C.
907669	Osborne, G. M.	Pte.	W. 9-6-17 (2nd Triangle); w. 2-9-18 (2nd Arras) to Eng.	4 Kildeyers Terrace, Rochdale, Lancs., Eng.
704031	Osmond, W.	Pte.		
703529	Oster, E. V.	Pte.	Evac. sick 21-11-16 to Eng.	c/o Italian-American Bank, San Francisco, U.S.A.
3107578	Ottaway, R.	Pte.		West Toronto Junction, Toronto, Ont.
704373	Ovesen, A. J.	Pte.	Dec. M.M. (Somme) D.R.O. 316; evac. sick 17-11-18 to Eng.	c/o Mrs. Rinker, Lowbanks, Ont.
704074	Owen, B. R.	Pte.	W. 21-10-16 (Regina) to Eng.	Hagensburg, B.C.
102475	Owen, T. R.	Pte.	Evac. sick 17-7-17 to Eng.	3 Price St., Vernon, B.C.
225346	Owings, S. F.	Pte.	D. o. w. 29-9-18 (Cambrai)	31 New St., Pwllheli, North Wales.
908081	Pabert, S.	Pte.	K. i. a. 10-6-17 (2nd Triangle)	G. Owings, Holliday Cove, West Virginia, U.S.A.
703593	Paeper, H. J.	Pte.	W. 11-5-17 (1st Triangle) to Eng.	No address available.
850711	Page, C. J.	Pte.	W. 2-9-18 (2nd Arras) to Eng.	c/o Mrs. Mills, 814 Hornby St., Vancouver, B.C.
3311157	Page, W. A.	Pte.	W. 1-10-18 (Cambrai) to Eng.	194 Lake St., St. Catherines, Ont. Lowbanks, Ont.

Number	Name	Rank	Notes	Address
226840	Pain, J.	Pte.	W. (acc.) 19-8-16; w. 2-11-18 to Eng.	6 Brighton St., City Rd, Bristol, Eng.
704083	Paisley, C.	L.-C.		712 Richards St., Vancouver, B.C.
135821	Pakenham, G. E.	Pte.	K. i. a. 9-4-17 (Vimy)	85 Crawford St., Toronto, Ont.
908185	Pallett, W. D.	Pte.		No address available.
3106939	Palmer, A. E.	Pte.		Hunter P.O., New Ontario.
763089	Palmer, C. K. A.	Pte.	W. 7-5-18 (Oppy); tr. to Eng. for disch. 14-3-19	Fern Glen P.O., Ont
1003618	Palmer, C. J.	Pte.	W. 31-10-17 (Passchendaele); W. 2-9-18 (2nd Arras) to Eng.	
704084	Palmer, G.	Pte.	W. 21-10-18 (Passchendaele) to Eng.	Blickling, Aylsham, Norfolk, Eng.
704116	Palmer, P. I.	Pte.		James Rd. P.O., South Vancouver, B.C.
249716	Palmer, W. G.	Pte.	W. 8-8-18 (Amiens); w. 6-11-18 (Valenciennes)	Prince Rupert, B.C.
703133	Pannell, E. E.	Pte.	Tr. to 51st Bn 16-7-16.	84 Trinity St, Toronto, Ont.
225249	Papasidero, A.	Pte.	W. 4-9-18 (2nd Arras)	Cowichan Station, B.C.
1003024	Paquette, J.	Pte.	K. i. a. 31-10-17 (Passchendaele)	No address available.
1004128	Paquette, J.	Pte.	W. 4-9-18 (2nd Arras)	P. Paquette, Korah Road, Korah Twnp., Ont.
925737	Parer, A.	Pte.	Tr. to Eng. from P.B. 8-10-17.	c/o Mrs. Pommier, River Desert, Que.
328950	Parfitt, G.	Pte.	K. i. a. 11-5-17 (1st Triangle)	171 Boulevard, Langelier, Co. St. Sourerar, Que.
				Mrs. F. Hastings, Heathmere, Wood St., Ashvale, Surrey, Eng.
1004053	Parise, H.	Pte.	W. 2-9-18 (2nd Arras) to Eng.	Paquetteville, Gloucester Co., N.B.
703812	Parker, H.	Pte.	Evac. sick 21-11-16 to Eng.	Box 67, Slocan City, B.C.
3030278	Parker, H.	Pte.		Altona, Iowa, U.S.A.
760702	Parkes, W. H. M.	Pte.	W. 9-6-17 (2nd Triangle) to Eng	29 Louder St., Old Kent Rd., London, Eng.
160780	Parks, A.	Pte.	W. 21-10-16 (Regina)	48 Ottawa St. (off Counlin Rd.), Belfast, Ire.
704047	Parks, J.	Pte.	D. o. w. 11-11-16 (Somme)	c/o Bank of Montreal, Prince Rupert, B.C.
540049	Parmitter, C.	Pte.	D. o. s. 27-10-18.	No address available.
703928	Parr, J.	Pte.	D. o. w. (acc.) 23-9-16.	Mrs. Parr, Cranbrook, B.C.
703189	Parsons, E. H.	L.-S.	W. 20-11-16 (Somme); dec. M.M. (Somme)	G. C. Parsons, 376 6th Ave. E., Vancouver, B.C.
703138	Parsons, J. A.	C.S.M.	D.R.O. 375	
			W. 9-4-17 (Vimy) to Eng.	376 6th Ave. E., Vancouver, B.C.
907621	Partridge, C. M.	Pte.	W. 19-4-17 (Vimy); tr. to 26th Bn. 26-3-18.	Saltcoats, Sask.
907655	Pask, A.	Pte.	Pay Sergeant in the Field; tr. to C.A.P.C. 3-5-19	Zenita, Sask.
102673	Paterson, W.	Pte.	K. i. a. 12-9-16 (St. Eloi)	1226 North Park St., Victoria, B.C.
703268	Paterson, W.	Sgt.	D. o. w. 1-9-16 (St. Eloi)	1237 19th Ave. E., Vancouver, B.C.
703412	Paton, W. R. H.	C.S.M.	Evac. sick 20-6-17 to Eng	J. Paton, 79 Lothian Rd., Edinburgh, Scot.
540027	Patten, E. H.	Cpl.	W. 25-8-17 (Lens); tr. to Lbr. Pool 31-10-17	No address available.
709362	Pattenden, S.	Pte.	W. 9-4-17 (Vimy) to Eng.	Cor. 42nd St. and East Boulevard, Kerrisdale, B.C.
703887	Patterson, A.	Pte.	W. 11-5-17 (1st Triangle); w. 9-8-17 (Lens) to Eng.	2608 Olympia Ave., Victoria, B.C.
252570	Patterson, H. P.	Pte.		Glen Ewen, Sask.
261227	Patterson, J.	Pte.	W. 15-3-18 (Lens) to Eng.	Ferney Beds, Morpeth, Widderington, Eng.
285072	Patterson, J. A.	Pte.	Tr. to Lbr. Pool 19-2-18.	107 Mutual St., Toronto, Ont.
219115	Patterson, W. A.	Pte.	W. 5-9-17 (Lens); d. o. s. 25-10-18.	Carleton Place, Ont.
102777	Pattison, W. J.	Pte.	Evac. sick 16-11-17 to Eng.	Mrs. S. Patterson, 546 Hillside Ave., Victoria, B.C.
126848	Pattison, E. A.	Pte.	Evac. sick 9-12-18 to Eng.	Clinton, Ont.
2529453	Patton, G.	Pte.	Evac. sick 1-5-17 to Eng.	c/o B. of N. S., King & Sherman Sts., Hamilton, Ont.
760390	Patton, M.	Pte.	Evac. sick 2-11-17 to Eng.	1741 34th Ave. E., Vancouver, B.C.
907590	Paul, W. A.	Pte.		Strassburg, Sask.

Number	Name	Rank	Service	Address
703428	Paulne, C. W.	Pte.	Tr. to 51st Bn. 2-8-16	3112 Glasgow Ave., Victoria, B.C.
703882	Paulsen, F. J.	Pte.	W. 12-3-18 (Lens) to Eng.	No address available.
1015604	Pavlichavich, J.	Pte.	W. 22-10-17 (Passchendaele) to Eng.	No address available.
703750	Pavluchuk, G.	Pte.	W. 17-8-16 (St. Eloi); k. l. a. 8-9-16 (St. Eloi)	No address available.
907011	Payne, A.	Pte.		3519 Henderson Terrace, 5th Ave., Regina, Sask.
706535	Payne, H. J.	Pte.	K. l. a. 8-8-18 (Amiens)	H. J. Payne, Duncan, B.C.
1003841	Payne, J.	Pte.	8-8-18 (Amiens) to Eng.	No address available.
703498	Paynter, I. P. G.	Pte.	Tr. to 2nd Co. C.F.C. 24-5-18	Gen. Del., Victoria, B.C.
200092	Peachey, G. W.	Cpl.		5 Egerton Rd., New Ferry, Birkenhead, Eng.
1003016	Peachey, R. E.	Pte.	K. l. a. 30-10-17 (Passchendaele)	Thessalon, Ont. (Mr. W. Peachey).
127685	Peacock, A. J.	Pte.	W. 30-9-18 (Cambrai)	c/o B. McDonald, 473 Drew St., Woodstock, Ont.
703167	Peacock, S.	Pte.	W. 20-1-16 (Somme); W. 8-6-17 (2nd Triangle)); tr. to 31st Bn. 12-8-18	
184252	Peacocke, T. C.	Sgt.	W. 1-11-17 (Passchendaele)	45 Tytherton Rd., Tufrell Park, London, Eng.
200070	Pearce, E. S.	Pte.	Evac. sick 5-10-17 to Eng.	Okotoks, Alta.
200172	Pearsall, L. W.	Sgt.	W. 1-9-17 (Lens); dec. M.M. (Amiens) C.R.O. 1899; w. 27-9-18 (Cambrai) to Eng.	No address available.
102254	Pearson, A.	Pte.	Tr to Lbr. Pool 4-11-17	Oro Station, Ont.
3105663	Pearson, C. H.	Pte.		Cumberland, B. C.
760686	Peck, E. W.	Pte.	Tr. to lbr. Pool 25-10-17	23 Osborne St., Barrow-on-Furness, Lancs., Eng.
703247	Peck, T. G.	Pte.	Evac. sick 14-12-18 to Eng.	2732 10th Ave. W., Vancouver, B.C.
926004	Peddle, J. W.	Cpl.	W. 11-6-17 (2nd Triangle); w. 27-9-18 (Cambrai) to Eng.	Paxton Valley, B.C.
102674	Pellow, J.	Pte.	Tr. to 75th Bn. 13-2-18	16 St. Peter's Place, Edinburgh, Scot.
441051	Peltier, A.	Pte.	Acc. w. 28-4-17 to Eng.	3163 Gamma St., Victoria, B.C.
3036681	Pendleton, C. E.	Pte.		Cooticook, Que.
2528858	Pennington, F. J.	Pte.	W. 1-10-18 (Cambrai) to Eng.	59 Hendrick St., Central Falls, R.I., U.S.A.
103437	Pentecost, J. R.	Sgt.	W. 23-7-18 (Oppy); k. l. a. 3-9-18 (2nd Arras)	1703 Park Ave., Montreal, Que.
703916	Peppard, A. L.	Pte.	Tr. to Can. Div. Emp. Co. 24-6-17	P. C. Pentecost, R.F.D., Winder, Georgia, U.S.A.
219877	Perault, A. G.	Pte.	W. 21-10-16 (Regina) to Eng.	c/o W. M. Peppard, 1013 13th Ave. W., Calgary, Alta.
126934	Perkins, A. L.	Pte.	Att. to 11th C.I.B. H-Q.	No address available.
703689	Perkins, J.	Pte.		Campbell River, B.C.
1015607	Perovich, Y.	Pte.	Evac. sick 20-11-17 to Eng.	No address available.
472322	Perrett, J. A.	Pte.	W. 9-4-17 (Vimy) to Eng.	Duck Lake, Sask.
703076	Perron, F.	Pte.	Evac. sick 15-3-17 to Eng.	c/o Rev. Father L. Rivet. O.M.I., Prince George, B.C.
200094	Petch, C. A.	Pte.	W. 2-9-18 (2nd Arras) to Eng.	Royal Oak, Conway, North Wales.
703375	Petch, F. E.	Pte.	Bn. Post Orderly Att. to 4th Div. Concert Party from May, 1917	Postoffice Staff, Victoria, B.C.
103417	Petch, R. A.	Pte.	Tr. to 2nd Tramway Co. 28-3-18	Turgoose P.O., Saanich, B.C.
129882	Peters, A. W.	Cpl.	K. l. a. 1-11-17 (Passchendaele)	Mrs. A. M. Peters, 3672 15th Ave. W., Vancouver, B.C.
703915	Peters, D. A.	Pte.	Dec. M.M. (Passchendaele) C.R.O. 1671; w. 6-11-18 (Valenciennes) to Eng.	
907532	Peters, J.	Pte.	W. and missing after action 19-5-17 (1st Triangle)	Box 129, Nelson, B.C.
102642	Peters, R.	Pte.	Tr. to Lbr. Pool 19-12-17	Mrs. A: Peters, Fort Qu-Appelle, B.C.
703378	Peterson, E. H.	Pte.	Tr. to Corps Sigs. 3-3-17	Cumberland, B.C.
703911	Peterson, L.	Pte.		Courtenay, B.C.
703610	Peterson, M.	Pte.	Tr. to Lbr. Pool 24-2-18	No address available. Albi, South Dakota, U.S.A.

No.	Name	Rank	Details	Address
706678	Peterson, O. C.	Pte.	W. 9-4-17 (Vimy) to Eng.	Bella Coola, B.C.
707152	Petre, J.	Pte.	K. i. a. 11-5-17 (1st Triangle)	Mrs. Petre, Chase River P.O., B.C.
252635	Petro, J.	Pte.	K. i. a. 8-8-18 (Amiens)	A. Petro, Coulee, Sask.
1003646	Petuchk, Y.	Pte.	Tr. to 54th Co. C.F.C. 26-3-18	No address available.
2529418	Pezzuto, L.	Pte.	K i. a. 2-9-18 (2nd Arras)	No address available.
703288	Phair, H. L.	Pte.	W. 3-9-18 (2nd Arras)	Lillooet, B.C.
2529302	Phelps, H. D.	Pte.	W. 8-8-18 (Amiens) to Eng.	c/o Mrs. N. Clark, 282 Keewatin Ave., Toronto, Ont.
2529409	Phelps, V. R.	Pte.	D. o. w. 1-10-18 (2nd Arras) to Eng.	N. Phelps, North Bay, Ont.
1015608	Phillipovich, C.	Pte.	W. 1-10-18 (Cambrai)	No address available.
706053	Phillips, D.	Pte.	K. i. a. 9-4-17 (Vimy)	W. O. Sweatman, Metchosin P.O., Victoria, B.C.
226362	Phillips, J.	Pte.	K. i. a. 30-10-17 (Passchendaele)	F. Phillips, 131 Elgar Rd., Reading, Eng.
703182	Phillips, R. M.	Cpl.	W. 2-9-18 (2nd Arras)	Orillia, Ont.
703711	Phipps, F.	Pte.	W. 9-4-17 (Vimy) to Eng.	Penticton, B.C.
1003532	Pickard, T.	Pte.	D. o. w. 31-10-17 (Passchendaele)	Mrs. T. Pickard, Athabasca Landing, Sask.
200207	Pierce, S. C.	Pte.	W. 22-4-18 (Oppy) to Eng. 21-10-16 (Regina)	Livingston, Mont., U.S.A.
703647	Piercy, M. F.	Pte.	W. 8-9-18 (St. Eloi); w. 21-10-16 (Regina); missing after action 5-8-17 (Lens); reported as prisoner of war 6-11-17	
663500	Pilgrim, W.	Pte.	Tr. to 4th M.G.C. 13-5-18	Sandwick, Vancouver Island, B.C.
102263	Pimlott, M.	Pte.	W. 19-5-17 (1st Triangle); w. 16-8-17 (Lens) to Eng.	12½ Woodlawn Apts., Fort Rouge, Winnipeg, Man.
225497	Pinkham, C. A.	Pte.	W. 28-9-18 (Cambrai) to Eng.	1 Glenrose Terrace, Upper Arton Rd. Burkdale, Eng. Scotstown, Que.
703318	Pinkerton, E.	Pte.	Att. to 11th C.L.T.M.B.	c/o Mrs. J. Thompson, R.M.D. No. 1, Royal Oak, Vancouver Island, B.C.
3030682	Pinkerton, W.	Pte.	W. 27-9-18 (Cambrai) to Eng.	75 Earle St., Central Falls, R.I., U.S.A.
102425	Pinks, B.	Pte.	Att. to 11th C.I.B. Sigs.	King Edward Hotel, Victoria, B.C.
225428	Plank, T. F.	Cpl.		Grimsby, Ont.
704030	Platt, H.	Pte.	Tr. to 11th C.I.B. 4-5-17	Comox, B.C.
249442	Plaxton, E.	Pte.	Tr. to 4th M.G.C. 1-5-18	641 Lansdowne Ave., Toronto, Ont.
704077	Player, T.	Pte.	Evac. sick 8-1-18 to Eng.	Deeside, Upton Rd., Broadstairs, Eng.
703258	Playfair, J. L.	L.-C.	Tr. to Eng. demob. duty 14-1-19.	Langley Prairie, B.C.
183702	Pocha, W. W.	Pte.	W. 17-8-17 (Lens); w. 1-10-18 (Cambrai) to Eng.	
704079	Polglase, J.	Pte.	Tr. to Lbr. Pool 19-2-18.	Nugent, Alta.
703386	Pollock, J. C.	Pte.	W. 30-12-16 (Vimy); k. i. a. 9-4-17 (Vimy)	1933 42nd Ave. E., Vancouver, B.C.
907345	Pollock, L. D.	Pte.	Tr. to 16th M.G.C. 1-1-17	A. S. Pollock, 1054 11th Ave. E., Vancouver, B.C.
467301	Pollock, S.	L.-C.	W. 9-4-17 (Vimy) to Eng.	No address available.
760613	Pollock, W.	Pte.	K. i. a. 12-6-17 (2nd Triangle)	Chesley, Ont.
907759	Pollock, W. J.	L.-C.	K. i. a. 9-4-17 (Vimy)	A. Pollock, Agassiz, B.C.
707192	Pondsford, F.	Pte.	W. 12-5-17 (1st Triangle) to Eng.	S. H. Pollock, Canora, Sask.
1066079	Poole, G. A.	Pte.	W. 2-9-18 (2nd Arras) to Eng.	Dawlish, Eng.
1045964	Poole, H.	Pte.	W. 27-9-18 (Cambrai) to Eng.	Hanover, Ont.
663398	Pope, E. A.	Pte.	W. 2-9-18 (2nd Arras) to Eng.	63 Toryglen St., South Side, Glasgow, Scot.
907792	Popowycz, J.	Pte.	Dec. Cross of St. George Cl. IV. L.G. 30476; w. 9-4-17 (Vimy) to Eng.	Oakville, Ont.
135209	Porter, H. E. D.	Pte.	D. o. w. 16-4-17 (Vimy)	No address available.
3314390	Porter, J.	Pte.	W. 30-9-18 (Cambrai) to Eng.	Mrs. M. I. Flanelle, Box 162 Owen Sound, Ont.
925796	Portsmouth, H.	Pte.	W. 27-9-18 (Cambrai) to Eng.	c/o Mrs. L. Diamond, Thorold, Ont. Devon Lodge, Churchfield Ave. N., Finchley, London. Eng.

663551	Post, H. T.	Pte.	W. 8-8-18 (Amiens) to Eng.	Trafalgar P.O., Ont.
761316	Poteet, W. J.	Pte.	Tr. to Eng. as minor 14-4-17	424 East Pine St., Portland, Ore., U.S.A.
703171	Potts, M. C.	L.-C.	W. 10-11-16 (Somme) to Eng.	Alert Bay, B.C.
703111	Potts, W. R.	Pte.	Tr. to 54th Bn. 24-3-18.	2128 Arbutus St., Vancouver, B.C.
2527334	Powell, A. G.	Pte.		122 West 90th St., New York, U.S.A.
3317091	Powell, C.	Pte.		Sebright, Ont.
249930	Powell, E. F.	Pte.	Evac. sick 7-5-17 to Eng.	28 Boon Ave., Toronto, Ont.
540384	Powell, H. P.	Cpl.	Evac. sick 24-10-18 to Eng.	590 Balmoral St., Winnipeg, Man.
703694	Powell, R.	Pte.		Lumby, B.C.
264801	Powell, T. D.	Pte.	W. 1-11-17 (Passchendaele); tr. to 4th M.G.C. 1-5-18.	Bear Lake, Mich., U.S.A.
703262	Powers, C.	Pte.	W. 21-10-16 (Regina) to Eng.	1015 Mears St., Victoria, B.C.
703310	Powers, W. R.	Pte.	Evac. sick 24-12-16 to Eng.	c/o Mrs. L. E. Bishop, White Bluffs, Burton Co., Wash., U.S.A.
925651	Pozternak, K.	Pte.	W. 16-11-17 (Passchendaele) to Eng.	No address available.
703295	Prance, P.	Pte.	K. i. a. 15-9-16 (St. Eloi).	Mrs. S. Prance, 10 Richmond Rd., Appledore, North Devon, Eng.
3317093	Pratt, E. G.	Pte.	W. 27-9-18 (Cambrai) to Eng.	Westmoreland Ave., Oshawa, Ont.
703826	Pratt, F. W.	Pte.	W. 9-6-17 (2nd Triangle) to Eng.	Thrums, B.C.
703341	Pratt, G. A.	Pte.	Evac. sick 8-7-17 to Eng.	Cockfosters, New Barnet, London, N., Eng.
3308832	Pratt, G. A.	Pte.	W. 21-10-16 (Regina) to Eng.	Thrums, B.C.
226758	Pratt, H.	Pte.	W. 20-9-17 (Lens) to Eng.	154 Colborne St., Kingston, Ont.
703110	Pratt, R. B.	Pte.	Tr. to 51st Bn. 2-8-16.	7th Ave., West Point Grey, Vancouver, B.C.
703953	Preston, W.	Cpl.	Tr. to Eng. for commission 28-3-17.	c/o Miss M L. Donnelly, 1229 Fulton St., Brooklyn, New York, U.S.A.
704106	Price, P.	Pte.	W. 17-9-16 (St. Eloi); evac. sick 31-7-18 to Eng.	29 Shop Row, Blaina, South Wales.
246530	Price, T. H.	C.Q.M.S.	Tr. to 4th M.G.C. 13-5-18.	219 Laurie Ave., Ottawa, Ont.
103293	Pringle, J.	Pte.	Dec. M.S.M. L.G. d-1-1-19.	1004 Queen's Ave., Victoria, B.C.
931832	Pritchard, E. A.	Pte.	Evac. inj. (acc.) to Eng. 16-6-18.	108 Lermere St., Elmira, N.Y., U.S.A.
102392	Pritchard, S.	Pte.	Tr. to C.C.R.C. 15-10-18.	93 Franklin St., Shrewsbury, Eng.
103163	Proctor, C.	Pte.	D o. w. 10-8-17 (Lens).	Mrs. F. Proctor, 7 Leighton Mansions, Queen's Club Gardens, Kensington, London, W., Eng.
703126	Prowse, A. W.	Pte.	W. 18-8-16 (St. Eloi); evac. sick 25-9-18 to Eng.	36 High St., Sandgate, Kent, Eng.
908144	Pugh, E. W.	Pte.		Drummondville, Que.
763154	Pulfer, H. T.	L.-C.	W. 9-4-17 (Vimy) to Eng.	Gravenhurst, Ont.
908046	Pullen, C. L.	Pte.	Dec. M.M. (Lens) C.R.O. 1419; w. 1-11-17 (Passchendaele); w. 23-7-18 (Oppy) to Eng.	Higham-on-the-Hill, Leicestershire, Eng.
1009858	Pullman, S.	Pte.	Missing after action 11-11-16 (Somme).	c/o Mrs. F. Hauson, Mitchell, Ont.
3314498	Purdy, O. J.	Pte.	Dec. M.M. (2nd Arras) C.R.O. 1930.	Lake Ave., St. Catherines, Ont.
703970	Purdy, W. M.	Pte.	Evac. sick 27-1-19 to Eng.	Mrs. J. Stevens, Boney River, Charlotte Co., N.B.
703530	Purvis, A. F.	Sgt.	Evac. sick 5-4-18 to Eng.	c/o Mrs. M. J. Price, Telkwa, B.C.
160372	Putman, J.	Pte.	W. 3-9-18 (Cambrai) C.R.O. 1899; tr. to Eng. for commission 31-10-18.	1402 First St. W., Calgary, Alta.
850919	Pye, P.	Pte.		c/o Mrs. K. Smith, Marshortle, Ont.
200238	Pyke, F.	Pte.		529 Burrard St., Vancouver, B.C.
103367	Pyman, S.	L.-C.		"The Hutte," St. Augusta Rd., Penarth, S. Wales.

Number	Name	Rank	Notes	Address
252386	Pyne, J. W. P.	L.-C.	W. 12-6-17 (2nd Triangle); dec. M.M. (Cambrai) C.R.O. 1989; tr. to Eng. for disch. 7-3-19	Sanford Dene, Sask.
102133	Quarmby, H.	Pte.	W. 12-6-17 (2nd Triangle) to Eng.	P.O. Box 1031, Victoria, B.C.
240564	Quibell, B. G.	Pte.	W. 1-10-18 (Cambrai) to Eng.	180 Ashville Rd., Leytonstone, London, Eng.
164171	Quigley, P.	Pte.	W. 9-4-17 (Vimy) to Eng.	221 Dayling St., Brantford, Ont.
703244	Quilty, T. E.	Pte.	Dec. M.M. (Passchendaele) C.R.O. 1606; tr. to Lbr. Pool 10-4-18.	
249859	Quin, A. F.	Pte.	W. 2-9-18 (2nd Arras) to Eng.	South Shore, Rocky Point, P.E.I.
703808	Quinn, A.	Pte.	Tr. to Eng. from P.B. 17-6-18.	498 Dufferin St., Toronto, Ont.
703105	Quinn, F.	L.-C.	Dec. D.C.M. (Lens) C.R.O. 1478; w. 1-10-18 (Cambrai)	560 16th Ave. W., Vancouver, B.C.
160988	Raby, C. J.	L.-S.	Tr. to 4th M.G.C. 1-5-18.	Courtenay, B.C.
101094	Raby, J.	Pte.	Tr. to 3rd Can. Div. Emp. Co. 5-7-17	Cochrane, Alta.
249953	Rachell, W.	Pte.	K. l. a. 8-8-18 (Amiens)	Cochrane, Alta.
				Mrs. E. Tuckford, 67 Balaam St., Canning Town, London, Eng.
225739	Radcliffe, H. M.	L.-C.	W. 8-8-18 (Amiens); dec. M.M. Valenciennes C.R.O. 2028	8 Cove Rd., London, Ont.
1003326	Radkiewill, W.	Pte.	Tr. to 71st Co. C.F.C. 9-4-18	No address available.
833879	Rae, C. B.	Pte.	Tr. to 4th Div. T.M.B. 27-10-17	Balaclava, Ont.
1003477	Ramesbottom, A. W.	Pte.	W. 4-9-18 (2nd Arras) to Eng.	Little Current, Ont.
703016	Rait, H. W.	Cpl.	Evac. sick 21-10-18 to Eng.	c/o Miss E. Rait, Little Kingshill, Great Missenden, Bucks, Eng.
910174	Ramsay, E. C.	Sgt.	K. l. a. 22-3-17 (Vimy)	W. I. Ramsay, Bladsworth, Sask.
704117	Randall, R.	Sgt.	W. 1-11-17 (Passchendaele) to Eng.	Okanagan Landing, B.C.
703092	Rankin, S. S.	Pte.	K. l. a. 21-10-16 (Regina)	Mrs. M. Rankin, 11 Oakley Rd., Harrow, Eng.
908041	Ransom, H. G.	Pte.	W. 21-3-17 (Vimy); k. l. a. 1-11-17 (Passchendaele)	Mrs. E. Marks, 7 Park Lane, Harefield, Middlesex, Eng.
1015617	Raspopovitch, S.	Pte.	D. o. w. 3-11-17 (Passchendaele)	W. Raspopovitch, Dawson, Y.T.
252186	Rathbone, L.	Pte.	W. 10-6-17 (2nd Triangle); w. 2-9-18 (2nd Arras) to Eng.	44 West Clowes St., Salford, Manchester, Eng.
703692	Rauffenbart, W. E.	Sgt.	W. 21-10-16 (Regina); w. 4-6-17 (2nd Triangle); w. 8-8-17 (Lens) to Eng.; d. o. s. in Eng.	J. H. Rauffenbart, 700 West End Trust Bldg., Philadelphia, U.S.A.
250109	Rausseau, J.	Pte.	Evac. sick 17-2-19	St. Madeline, Que.
703722	Raven, J. G.	Pte.	Tr. to 67th Bn. 8-7-16	27 Loring Rd., Isleworth, Eng.
127491	Ray, D. S.	Pte.	W. 10-11-16 (Somme); tr. to 11th C.L.T.M.B. 1-10-17	
2528383	Rayfield, W. S.	Pte.	W. 9-4-17 (Vimy) to Eng.	52 Oliver St., Guelph, Ont.
760374	Raymond, F.	Pte.	N.C.O. l.c. 11th C.I.R. Trnnp-Line; dec. M.M. (Somme), D.R.O. 386; tr. to Lbr. Pool 22-11-17; men. in des. L.G. of 8-7-19	128 St. Andre's St., Galt, Ont.
703966	Raymond, L.	Sgt.		c/o Mrs. H. Ostler, 54 Michael's Rd., Yeovil, Eng.
252187	Raymond, W. E.	Pte.	W. 9-4-17 (Vimy) to Eng.	Mrs. T. Des Jardin, Pembroke, Ont.
761111	Rayner, E.	Cpl.	W. 1-11-17 (Passchendaele) to Eng.	Box 136, Swift Current, Sask.
258486	Rayner, R. W.	Sgt.	Dec. M.M. (Cambrai) C.R.O. 1989.	No address available.
				1472 Quebec St., Vancouver, B.C.

Number	Name	Rank	Service	Address
706628	Read, R. A.	Cpl.	Tr. to Lbr. Pool 5-3-18	314 Michigan St., Victoria, B.C.
2528489	Reaume, A.	Pte.	K. i. a. 4-9-18 (2nd Arras)	Mrs. A. Carron, Archeaon P.O., Mile 41, A.C.Q., Ont.
102261	Redgrave, S. H.	Cpl.	W. 5-8-17 (Lens) to Eng.	1049 Hulton St., Oak Bay, Victoria, B.C.
704014	Redhouse, S.	Pte.	Evac. sick 4-3-17 to Eng.	201 Nevells Rd., Letchworth, Herts, Eng.
663400	Redshaw, A. E.	Pte.		Oakville, Ont.
102381	Reed, A. J.	Pte.	W. 11-5-17 (1st Triangle) to Eng.	Wood Heatler Cottage, Kernal Rd., Chiselhurn, Kent, Eng.
703109	Reed, H.	Pte.	W. 20-10-16 (Regina) to Eng.	2587 Napier St., Vancouver, B.C.
443390	Reed, S.	Pte.	K. i. a. 11-11-16 (Somme)	No address available.
1004072	Reed, W. J.	Pte.	Tr. to 31st Bn. 12-8-18	c/o W. Knight, Brighton, Mass., U.S.A.
249189	Reeks, F. E.	Sgt.	Dec. M.M. (Cambrai) C.R.O. 1989	78 Peterborough Ave., Toronto, Ont.
489727	Reeves, C. E.	Pte.	Acc. w. 13-5-17 to Eng.	c/o C. E. Reeves, c/o Purcell Rowe, Monadoroch Bldg., San Francisco, Cal., U.S.A.
183044	Regan, W. E.	Pte.	W. 9-4-17 (Vimy); w. 31-10-17 (Passchendaele) to Eng.	Oyen, Alta.
105634	Reid, C. E.	Pte.	Tr. to 4th M.G.C. 1-5-18	Box 40, Kelowna, B.C.
703127	Reid, C. J.	Pte.	Tr. to 4th Div. Emp. Co. 12-1-18	c/o Royal Bank, East End Branch, Vancouver, B.C.
3109317	Reid, D. T.	Pte.		R.R. No. 1, Marshville, Ont.
3109318	Reid, H.	Pte.		No address available.
703923	Reid, I. H.	Pte.	K. i. a. 28-8-16 (St. Eloi)	Mrs. J. L. Roger, De Burt Vil., Colchester Co., N.S.
836009	Reid, J.	Pte.	2-9-18 (2nd Arras) to Eng.	26 Polwarth Terrace, Holme Lodge, Edinburgh, Scot.
907337	Reid, R.	Pte.	Tr. to 16th M.G.C. 1-1-17	No address available.
704127	Reid, W.	Pte.	Evac. sick 21-10-16 to Eng.	c/o Mrs. Morland, 504 12th Ave. E., Vancouver, B.C.
925767	Relst, E.	Pte.	W. 9-4-17 (Vimy) to Eng.	920 11th St., Racine, Wis., U.S.A.
314031	Rennie, D.	Pte.		Elgin St., Port Dalhousie, Ont.
703532	Renouf, C.	Pte.	Tr. to 51st Bn. 2-8-16	2010 Stanley Ave., Victoria, Ont.
240541	Revell, A. E. M.	Pte.	K. i. a. 27-9-18 (Cambrai)	Mrs. A. Revell, 158 Hunter St. E., Hamilton, Ont.
2527345	Reynolds, G. M.	Pte.	K. i. a. 2-9-18 (2nd Arras)	J. Reynolds, Beeton, Ont.
3310372	Reynolds, R. A.	Sgt.		Dundas, Ont.
225217	Reynolds, W. C.	Pte.	Missing, believed k. i. a. 27-9-18 (Cambrai)	W. J. Reynolds, 24 Silver Ave., Toronto, Ont.
2529374	Rlach, G.	Pte.	K. i. a. 27-9-18 (Cambrai)	G. Rlach, 183 Ontario St. W., Montreal, Que.
704023	Richardson, J.	Pte.	Tr. to 51st Bn. 2-8-16	Lavant Station, Ont.
102280	Riddell, J. D.	Pte.	W. 10-6-17 (2nd Triangle) to Eng.	143 Simcoe St., Victoria, B.C.
252784	Riddick, F. A. B.	Cpl.	K. i. a. 27-9-18 (Cambrai)	T. Riddick, Farnham, Que.
907202	Ridge, F.	C.S.M.	Dec. M.M. (Amiens) C.R.O. 1899; w. 2-9-18 (2nd Arras) to Eng.	
703920	Ridgway, J.	Pte.	K. i. a. 9-4-17 (Vimy)	I P.O. Bylds, Bargoed, South Wales. Miss M. Brickhill, 9 Amsdale St., W. Galton, Manchester, Eng.
706363	Riley, A.	Pte.	Tr. to 6th Field Co. Engrs.	1009 18th Ave. E., Calgary, Alta.
249150	Riley, J. A.	Pte.	K. i. a. 2-9-18 (2nd Arras)	Mrs. E. Riley, 630 Wellington St., W. Toronto, Ont.
250080	Riley, J. W.	Pte.	K. i. a. 8-8-18 (Amiens)	Mrs. Riley, 278 Lippincott St., Toronto, Ont.
252518	Rimbeaux, D.	Pte.	W. 12-5-17 (1st Triangle) to Eng.	No address available.
252188	Rimmer, H.	Pte.	W. 20-3-17 (Vimy) to Eng.	Middlewood, Aughton, Lancs., Eng.
184227	Ringrose, G. H. J.	Pte.	Tr. to 11th C.I.B.M.G.C. 10-12-16	No address available.
703212	Rintoul, W.	Pte.	W. to Eng. from P.B. Engrs. 14-9-17	901 Burdette St., Victoria, B.C.
225775	Rishea, V. J.	Sgt.		1124 A. College St., Toronto, Ont.
760099	Risley, A.	Pte.	W. 13-3-18 (Lens) to Eng.	4309 Beatrice St., South Vancouver, B.C.
252460	Ritz, R.	Pte.	W. 9-4-17 (Vimy); evac. sick 1-2-19	Camrose, Alta.

648759	Rivers, T.	Sgt.	Dec. M.M. (Amiens) C.R.O. 1899	Massey, Ont.
704071	Roach, E.	Sgt.	Evac. sick 19-10-16 to Eng.	c/o H.M. Customs, Pinhorn, Alta.
703172	Roach, J.	Pte.		Rockingham, Ont.
1003772	Robbins, A. G. E.	L.-C.	Tr to Rly. Const. Corps 25-11-16	1139 McClure St., Victoria, B.C.
704021	Roberts, F. G.	Pte.	Evac. sick 2-11-17 to Eng.	3709 Windsor St., Vancouver, B.C.
102282	Roberts, H.	Cpl.	Evac. sick 29-9-18 to Eng.	Annie St., Lutwyche Albion, Bristol, Eng.
102731	Roberts, H. E.	Pte.	Evac. sick 27-9-17 to Eng.	534 Georgia St., Vancouver, B.C.
3105024	Roberts, H. J.	Pte.	Tr. to Eng. for demob. 9-1-19	1507 Miller St., Utica, N.Y., U.S.A.
703347	Roberts, M. W.	Pte.		Ballingtrald, Delmy, Rosshire, Scot.
2015168	Roberts, T. A.	Pte.	W. 23-4-18 (Oppy) to Eng.	c/o Miss N. C. Boyd, Orphans' Home, Vancouver, B.C.
929022	Roberts, W. E.	Pte.	D. o. w. 5-10-18 (2nd Arras)	Mount Forest, Ont.
1090038	Roberts, W. F.	Pte.	Dec. M.M. (2nd Arras) C.R.O. 1930	Mrs. Roberts, 51 Rideau St., Kingston, Ont.
249143	Robertson, A. E.	Pte.	Tr. to 31st Bn. 12-8-18	269 Symington Ave., Toronto, Ont.
1066039	Robertson, A. E.	Cpl.		R.R. No. 2, Silcott, Ont.
1015524	Robertson, D. D.	Pte.	K. i. a. 9-1-17 (Vimy)	Girton, Newark-on-Trent, Notts., Eng.
907156	Robertson, H.	Pte.	Tr. to 11th C.I.B.M.G.C. 10-12-16	Mrs. J. C. Robertson, Whitewood, Sask.
174916	Robertson, H.	Pte.	Tr. to Lbr. Pool 5-3-18	No address available.
1003324	Robertson, J.	Pte.	Tr. to 4th M.G.C. 1-5-18	588 Bon Accord St., Peterboro', Ont.
103328	Robertson, J.	Pte.	W. 15-8-17 (Lens); tr. to Rly. Const. Co. 23-11-17	24 Fairlight Rd., Ore., Hastings, Eng.
703947	Robertson, J.	Pte.		
3110134	Robertson, J. W.	Pte.	W. 17-8-17 (Lens); w. 28-9-18 (Cambrai) to Eng.	c/o Mrs. J. Robertson, Medicine Hat, Alta.
102257	Robertson, R.	Pte.		13½ Haynes Ave., St. Catherines, Ont
703770	Robertson, R.	Pte.	W. 21-10-16 (Regina); w. 9-4-17 (Vimy) to Eng.	843 Johnson St., Victoria, B.C.
706960	Robertson, R. A.	Pte.	Evac. sick 26-10-17 to Eng.	Cumberland, B.C.
703809	Robertson, W. A.	Pte.		24 Simcoe St., Victoria, B.C.
754785	Robinson, B. C.	Pte.	Tr. to 4th M.G.C. 1-5-18	40 Guildford Rd., South Lambert, London, S.W., Eng.
200054	Robinson, C. S.	Pte.	K. i. a. 9-8-17 (Lens)	Plummer P.O., Ont.
703112	Robinson, H. A.	Pte.	Evac. sick 11-6-17 to Eng.	Mrs. E. Robinson, 70 Peach St., Liverpool, Eng.
931249	Robinson, J. W.	Pte.	K. i. a. 19-8-16 (St. Eloi)	Marine Heights, Vancouver, B.C.
252809	Robinson, S.	Pte.	W. 15-8-17 (Lens); k. i. a. 1-10-18 (Cambrai)	Mrs. M. Barker, 4 Thornton Ave., Newstead St., Hull, Eng.
160735	Robinson, T.	Pte.	W. 17-8-17 (Lens); tr. to Lbr. Pool 9-6-18	E. Robinson, Pense, Sask.
703330	Robinson, T. C.	Pte.	Tr. to 4th Div. Emp. Co. 10-6-18	29 Lower Culbert St., Gateshead-on-Tyne, Eng.
703123	Robitaille, J. A.	Pte.		644 Moss St., Victoria, B.C.
850123	Robson, G.	L.-C.	K. i. a. 5-8-17 (Lens)	623 7th St. E., Medicine Hat, Alta.
703499	Robson, T. H.	Pte.	W. 18-3-18 (Lens); w. 3-9-18 (2nd Arras) to Eng.	544 Downie St., Peterboro', Ont.
931593	Rocheleau, W.	Pte.		T. Jones, Smithers, B.C.
761051	Rock, T. H.	Pte.	W. 21-3-17 (Vimy) to Eng.	c/o Mrs. E. Vermetta, St. Norbert, Man.
135830	Rodden, V. W.	Cpl.	Dec. M.M. (Cambrai) C.R.O. 1989; evac. sick 4-2-19 to Eng.	748 63rd Ave. E. South Vancouver, B.C.
225289	Rodgers, K. W.	Pte.	Evac. sick 7-11-18 to Eng.	96 Mutual St., Toronto, Ont.
135835	Roger, F. A.	Pte.	D. o. w. 11-4-17 (Vimy)	231 Oglethorpe Ave., Atlanta, Ga., U.S.A.
3108717	Roger, J.	Pte.	W. 6-11-18 (Valenciennes); tr. to Eng. for demob. 9-1-19	Mrs. F. E. Roger, 239 Parliament St., Toronto, Ont.
				c/o Mrs. M. Grant, St. George, Ont,

250117	Rogers, B. D.	Pte.		Canning, King Co., N.S.
102706	Rogers, G.	Cpl.	Tr. to 51st Bn. 2-8-16	234 36th Ave. E., South Vancouver, B.C.
541080	Rogers, W. L.	Pte.	K. i. a. 2-9-18 (2nd Arras)	No address available.
850131	Rogerson, E.	Pte.	W. 31-7-18 (Oppy)	Mrs. E. A. Rogerson, R.R. No. 1, Thorold, Ont.
103217	Roils, H.	Pte.	K. i. a. 8-8-18 (Amiens)	Box 549, Everett, Wash., U.S.A.
505997	Rolling, A. C.	Pte.	Dec. M.S.M. L.G. d-1-1-19	G. Rolling, 30 Woodward Ave., St. Thomas, Ont.
703368	Rolph, N.	C.Q.M.S.	Evac. sick 6-1-19 to Eng.	510 Sylvia Court, Vancouver, B.C.
3108829	Ronald, C. N.	Pte.		Lyden, Ont.
3310275	Ronald, G. E.	Pte.	W. 24-9-17 (Lens) to Eng.	Branchton, Ont.
464511	Rorison, R. T.	L.-C.	D. o. w. 1-11-17 (Passchendaele)	Eburne, B.C.
252599	Rosa, E. E.	L.-C.	K. i. a. 9-4-17 (Vimy)	Mrs. A. Rosa, Gravelbourg, Sask.
252889	Rosa, E. G.	Pte.	K. i. a 1-11-17 (Passchendaele)	Mrs. Rosa, Kincaid, Sask.
1003530	Roscoe, J.	Pte.	Tr. to 4th M.G.C. 1-5-18	J. Roscoe, Wahnapitae, Ont.
249435	Rose, C. A.	Pte.	K. i. a. 3-9-18 (2nd Arras)	23 Gladstone Ave., Toronto, Ont.
1007041	Rose, F.	Pte.	K. i. a. 27-9-18 (Cambrai)	Mrs. Rose, Cove Rd., St. John's, Newfoundland.
225254	Rose, H. R.	Pte.	W. 21-10-16 (Regina) to Eng.	J. G. Rose, Madoc, Ont.
100897	Rosenberg, A. E.	Pte.	W. 11-5-17 (1st Triangle) to Eng.	No address available.
127419	Ross, D.	Pte.	W. 13-4-18 (Oppy)	c/o Mrs. Merch. Kokoma, Ont.
703360	Ross, G.	Pte.		1216 Styles St., Victoria, B.C.
704107	Ross, H.	Pte.		Rosemarke, Rosshire, Scot.
3311549	Ross, H. L.	Pte.	W. 8-8-18 (Amiens) to Eng.	93 Bertmount Ave., Toronto, Ont.
225402	Ross, J.	Pte.		78 Mayflower Ave., Hamilton, Ont.
240630	Ross, W.	Pte.		1356 Cannon St. E., Hamilton, Ont.
704005	Ross, W.	Pte.	Evac. sick 14-4-17 to Eng.	Wellington, B.C.
908188	Rostalski, M.	Pte.	W. 13-5-17 (1st Triangle); tr. to 46th Co. C.F.C. 2-5-18	No address available.
1093408	Roth, F. E.	Pte.	W. 4-9-18 (2nd Arras) to Eng.	Allen Town, Penn., U.S.A.
135840	Rowe, A.	Pte.	W. 19-8-16 (St. Eloi) to Eng.	No address available.
443713	Rowe, J.	Sgt.	Evac. from P.B. to Eng. 15-3-17	c/o R. McMillan, Tete Jaune Cache, B.C.
703438	Rowley, J. M.	Pte.	W. 21-10-16 (Somme) to Eng.	District Depot XI, Hastings Park, Vancouver, B.C.
704058	Russell, G. A.	Pte.	Tr. to C.A.M.C. for commission 2-8-16	Burns Lake, B.C.
703738	Russell, H. C.	Pte.	Bn. Post Orderly to March 1918; evac. sick 22-10-18 to Eng.	
703453	Russell, J.	C.S.M.	Dec. D.C.M. (Vimy) C.R.O. 1277; w. 9-4-17 (Vimy) to Eng.	2240 5th Ave. W., Vancouver, B.C.
907094	Russell, R.	Pte.	Tr. to 16th M.G.C. 1-1-17	Returned Soldiers' Club, Vancouver, B.C.
931815	Russell, T.	Pte.	W. 17-8-17 (Lens) to Eng.	No address available.
907704	Rutherford, W. D.	Pte.	W. 13-3-18 (Lens) to Eng.	Trenton, Ont.
3109852	Rutherford, J. N. S.	Pte.		Melville, Sask.
219672	Ryan, G. C.	L.-C.	W. 21-10-16 (Regina); evac. sick 14-8-17 to Eng.	R.R. No. 4, Mansfield, Ont.
226539	Ryckman, J. H.	Pte.	W. 1-10-18 (Cambrai) to Eng.	c/o Miss Smith, 202 State St., Albany, N.Y.
931250	Ryden, F.	Pte.	W. 19-10-16 (Somme); evac. sick 5-5-17 to Eng.	39 Cedar Ave., Hamilton, Ont.
703131	Rye, R. M. S.	C.Q.M.S.	Men. in despatches L.G. d-8-7-19	c/o F. Parkson, Queen's Hotel, Cranbrook, B.C.
249440	Sadler, W.	Pte.	W. 27-9-18 (Cambrai) to Eng.	2345 Cadboro Bay Rd., Victoria, B.C.
907836	Sallans, E.	Pte.	K. i. a. 9-4-17 (Vimy)	Box 79, Holland Landing, Ont.
907697	Salley, L. H.	Pte.	K. i. a. 9-4-17 (Vimy)	J. Sallans, Huronville, Sask.
907400	Salt, C.	L.-C.	W. 26-1-17 (Vimy) to Eng.	J. E. Salley, Bouchgrove, Que. Regina, Sask.

Regt. No.	Name	Rank	Service	Address
703046	Salway, G. I.	Sgt.	N.C.O. 1-c Signals to 19-10-17; dec. M.M. (Somme) D.R.O. 316; evac. sick 19-10-17 to Eng.	210 Menzies St., Victoria, B.C.
907431	Sample, W.	Pte.	W. 9-4-17 (Vimy) to Eng.	Kerrobert, Sask.
2304314	Sample, W. S.	Pte.	W. 6-11-18 (Valenciennes) to Eng.	6 Temple St., Smith Shields, Durham, Eng.
225436	Sams, A. D.	Pte.	K. i. a. 4-9-18 (2nd Arras)	Burbridge, Macleod, Alta.
703454	Sanders, W. J.	Pte.	W. 21-10-16 (Regina); w. 9-4-17 (Vimy) to Eng.	G.P.O., Vancouver, B.C.
3105740	Sandy, F. G.	Pte.	K. i. a. 30-9-18 (Cambrai)	Mrs. I. Sandy, 2000 N. 14th St., Kansas City, U.S.A.
102538	Sanford, H. J.	Pte.	W. 11-5-17 (1st Triangle); w. 24-3-18 (Lens) to Eng.	c/o Mrs. J. Cameron, Moccan, Cumberland Co., N.S.
225499	Sanger, F. J.	Pte.	K. i. a. 27-9-18 (Cambrai)	Mrs. R. Sanger, Box 902, Collingwood, Ont.
252789	Sanger, D. L.	Pte.	W. 9-4-17 (Vimy) to Eng.	Cadillac, Sask.
207102	Sangster, W. A.	L-C.	D. o. w. 14-9-18 (2nd Arras)	J. A. Sangster, Conjuring Creek, Alta.
908150	Sapridla, P.	Pte.	Tr. to 43rd Co. C.F.C. 1-8-18	1900 Wallace St., Regina, Sask.
703354	Sarensen, S.	Sgt.	W. 30-10-16 (Somme); dec. D.C.M. (Lens) C.R.O. 1134; evac. sick in Eng. 2-1-19	c/o 2716 Fourth Ave. E., Vancouver, B.C.
704029	Sargeant, G.	Sgt.	W 20-10-16 (Regina), evac. sick 14-4-17 to Eng.	55 Clacton Rd., Walthamstow, Essex, Eng.
252603	Sauberan, G.	Pte.	Evac. sick 19-4-17 to Eng.; dec. M.M. (Vimy) C.R.O.	52 East Ave., Tonawanda, U.S.A.
703015	Saugstad, R.	Sgt.	W. 9-4-17 (Vimy); w. 13-5-17 (1st Triangle) to Eng. 1236; w. 13-5-17 (1st Triangle) to Eng.	Hagensburg, Bella Coola, B.C.
931428	Saunders, W. J.	Pte.	Dec. M.M. (Passchendaele) C.R.O. 1571; k. i. a. 16-11-17 (Passchendaele)	Mrs. L. Boyce, 76 Tilson Rd., Peckham, London, S.E., Eng.
1004127	Sauve, A.	Pte.	K. i. a. 24-9-17 (Lens)	Mrs. M. Sauve, 124 Church Ave., Verdun, Que.
1004038	Sawchuk, F.	Pte.	Tr. to 54th Co. C.F.C. 26-3-18	No address available.
907194	Sawyer, H.	Pte.	D. o. w. 15-4-17 (Vimy)	No address available.
2529451	Sayers, C. E.	Pte.	Tr. to C.C.R.C. 12-2-19	841 Camble St. W., Vancouver, B.C.
704108	Scales, H.	Pte.	W. 5-6-17 (1st Triangle); tr. to 2nd Lbr. Bn. 16-8-17	
1090268	Scarbeau, T.	Pte.	W. 5-9-18 (2nd Arras) to Eng.	c/o W. Beard, Comox, B.C.
253113	Scarlett, H.	Pte.	K. i. a. 9-4-17 (Vimy)	Moose Creek, Ont.
760194	Schofield, W.	Pte.	W. 9-4-17 (Vimy) to Eng; tr. to 7th Bn.; k. i. a. 12-10-18 (Cambrai)	Mrs. M. J. Scarlett, Box 477 Swift Current, Sask.
703392	Schooling, A.	Pte.	K. i. a. 23-11-16 (Somme)	Mrs. Schofield, 2264 45th Ave. E., S. Vancouver, B.C.
703508	Schubert, D.	Pte.	W. 19-8-16 (St. Eloi) to Eng.	O. B. Schooling, Harbuckle, Coluse Co., U.S.A.
703621	Schubert, J.	Pte.	Tr. to Eng. as minor 14-4-17	Vernon, B.C.
126319	Schultz, O. F.	Sgt.	W. 25-3-17 (Vimy); w. 16-11-17 (Passchendaele); w. 30-9-18 (Cambrai)	Vernon, B.C.
3108875	Scoble, W. J.	Pte.	K. i. a. 11-5-17 (1st Triangle)	31 Stratford St., Stratford, Ont.
161084	Scotland, D. H.	L-C.	W. 9-6-17 (2nd Triangle); w. 8-8-18 (Amiens) to Eng.	337 Lorilla St., Hamilton, Ont.
160368	Scott, A.	L-C.		W. Scotland, Tillicoultry, Clackmannanshire, Scot.
907972	Scott, A.	Pte.	K. i. a. 3-2-17 (Vimy)	44 Jasmine Terrace, Aberdeen, Scot.
102197	Scott, J.	Pte.	K. i. a. 16-8-17 (Lens)	Mrs. E. B. Scott, 2077 Stuart St., Regina, Sask. Mrs. W. Linklater, Medhouslgrath, Sandwick, Orkney, Scot.
760957	Scott, J. L.	Pte.	Evac. sick 27-3-17 to Eng.	1305 20th Ave. E., Vancouver, B.C.
1003399	Scott, L.	Pte.	K. i. a. 17-11-17 (Passchendaele)	J. Scott, Little Current, Manitoulin Island, Ont.
851109	Scott, L. E.	Pte.	W. 1-10-18 (Cambrai) to Eng.	Wooler, Ont.

Number	Name	Rank	Details	Address
908134	Scott, N. W.	Pte.	W. 17-11-17 (Passchendaele) to Eng; dec. M.M. (Passchendaele) C.R.O. 1571	Box 342, Collingwood, Ont.
908192	Scott, W.	Pte.	Evac. sick 8-5-17 to Eng.	Seaforth, Ont.
907744	Scott, W. C.	Pte.	Tr. to 4th M.G.C. 13-5-18	Montmartre, Ont.
160354	Scott, W. J.	Pte.	Tr. to Eng. from P.B. 3-10-16	No address available.
252397	Scott, W. W.	Pte.	Evac. sick 20-10-17 to Eng.	Vanguard, Sask.
160648	Scragg, W.	Pte.	Tr. to 31st Bn. 12-8-18	c/o Mrs. Wale, Greenshields, Alta.
703463	Scroxton, G.	Pte.	W. 28-8-16 (St. Eloi); tr. to Lbr. Pool 17-5-18.	1994 Williams St., Vancouver, B.C.
252267	Seabrook, E.	Pte.	W. 31-7-18 (Oppy) to Eng.	Box 20, Webb, Sask.
703675	Sealand, T.	Pte.	W. 20-11-16 (Somme); tr. to No. 1 Dist. H.-Q. C.F.C. 26-3-18	Emerson, Man.
249409	Searle, S. J.	Pte.		887 Queen St. E., Toronto, Ont.
220342	Seeley, J. E. A.	Pte.	Evac. sick 27-1-17 to Eng.	Campbell's Bay, Que.
703935	Seers, W.	Pte.	W. 21-10-16 (Regina); tr. to 44th Bn. 12-8-18	c/o G. A. Bredl, Melville, Sask.
760425	Seinturier, M.	Pte.	W. 9-4-17 (Vimy); k. i. a. 6-6-17 (2nd Triangle)	M. Seinturier, R.F.D. No. 43A, Inglewood, Cal., U. S. A.
703287	Selby- Hele, H.	Cpl.	Dec. M.M. (Somme) D.R.O. 375; w. 9-4-17 (Vimy) to Eng.	R. R. No. 1, Langley Prairie, B.C.
116078	Sellings, W. R.	Pte.	W. 24-10-17 (Passchendaele) to Eng.	G.P.O., Vancouver, B.C.
146859	Serson, P. A.	Pte.	Tr. to 77th Bn. 10-8-16	Pembroke, Ont
146830	Serson, T. E.	Pte.	Tr. to 77th Bn. 10-8-16	Pembroke, Ont
252771	Seward, G.	Pte.	W. 23-3-17 (Vimy) to Eng.	Westbourne, nr. Lincoln, Eng.
102998	Seward, W. E.	Cpl.	Dec. M.M. (2nd Arras) C.R.O. 1930	Lytton, B.C.
1003609	Sexsmith, O. F.	Cpl.	Tr. to R.A.F. 5-8-18	Glencoe, Ont.
3105511	Seymour, J.	Pte.	Evac sick 10-12-18 to Eng.	c/o Miss M. Vincent, Box 570, Tile Station, Zanesville, Ohio, U.S.A.
925474	Seymour, J. R.	Pte.	W. 1-10-18 (Cambrai)	Glasnevin, Sask.
2528432	Shackleton, G. B.	Pte.		171 Abbott St., Detroit, Mich., U.S.A.
907550	Shand, J.	Pte.	Tr. to Lbr. Pool 19-2-18	Huntly, Aberdeenshire, Scot.
145336	Shannon, J.	Pte.	Tr. to 4th M.G.C. 13-5-18	153 Frontenac St., Kingston, Ont.
850194	Shapton, T.	Pte.	K. i. a. 6-11-18 (Valenciennes)	Mrs. E. Shapton, 212 John St., Niagara Falls, Ont.
706508	Sharpe, J. W.	Pte.	W. 9-4-17 (Vimy) to Eng.	c/o Mrs. E. J. Bonner, Thurnan, Kent, Eng.
703566	Sharpe, H. W.	Pte.	Evac. sick 14-12-16 to Eng.	Box 808 Hazelton, B.C.
227048	Sharpe, W.	Pte.		64 East Ave. N., Hamilton, Ont.
252702	Shaw, J. S.	Pte.	W. 13-5-17 (1st Triangle); dec. M.M. Passchendaele) C.R.O. 1571; dec. Bar to M.M. (Amiens) C.R.O. 1899; k. i. a. 3-9-18 (2nd Arras)	
184172	Shaw, R. T.	Pte.	K. i. a. 19-3-17 (Vimy)	T. Shaw, 110 Stirling Ave., Ottawa, Ont.
761033	Shaw, W.	Pte.	W. 1-11-17 (Passchendaele) to Eng	R. Shaw, Navan, Russell Co., Ont.
184193	Shaw, W. G.	L.-C.	D. o. w. 1-11-17 (Passchendaele)	1316 Cotton Drive, Vancouver, B.C.
1003728	Shea, J.	Pte.	W. 8-8-18 (Amiens); evac. sick 28-10-18	W. J. Shaw, Imperial, Sask.
925128	Shears, C. E.	Pte.	D. o. w. 6-4-17 (2nd Triangle)	Warren, Ont.
145246	Sheldon, W. J.	Pte.	Tr. to 77th Bn. 10-8-16	W. Shears, Khedive, Sask.
141150	Shennon, W. J.	Pte.	Tr. to 77th Bn. 10-8-16	221 Frank St., Ottawa, Ont.
226920	Shephard, D.	Pte.	W. 27-9-18 (Cambrai); evac. sick 14,12-18 to Eng.	64 Royal Ave., Westboro', Ont.
2529304	Sheppard, J.	Pte.	W. 1-10-18 (Cambrai)	19 Lloyd St., Parkgate, Yorks, Eng. Mitchell Square, Ont.
703728	Sheppard, S.	Pte.	K. i. a. 8-9-16 (St. Eloi)	J. Sheppard, Harbour Grace, Newfoundland.

No.	Name	Rank	Details	Address
103212	Sheret, A. A.	Pte.	W. 18-5-17 (1st Triangle)	541 Hillside Ave., Victoria, B.C.
249167	Sheridan, E. J.	Pte.	W. 6-11-18 (Valenciennes) to Eng.	915 Bathurst St., Toronto, Ont.
3108631	Sherlock, T. E.	Sgt.		No address available.
540246	Sherlock, T. E.	Pte.	K. i. a. 17-11-17 (Passchendaele)	Mrs. Sherlock, 961 Gerrard St. E., Toronto, Ont.
704129	Sherrard, G. E.	Pte.	W. 23-1-17 (Mericourt); w. 23-9-17 (Lens) to Eng.	
703784	Sherwood, N.	Pte.	W. 31-8-16 (St. Eloi); tr. to Lbr. Pool 9-6-18.	171 Hillsboro' St., Charlottetown, P.E.I.
663117	Sherwood, R. A.	Pte.	Tr. to 4th M.G.C. 1-5-18.	c/o Union Bank, Prince Rupert, B.C.
236931	Shields, A. L.	Pte.	W. 1-10-18 (Cambrai) to Eng.	Milton, Ont.
703408	Shillito, A.	Pte.	Evac. sick 23-10-16 to Eng.	168 Edward St., Buffalo, N.Y., U.S.A.
232195	Shire, H.	Pte.	K. i. a. 4-4-17 (Vimy)	Cumberland, B.C.
706641	Shirras, J.	Pte.	W. 17-8-17 (Lens) to Eng.	No address available.
219799	Sholea, J.	Pte.	W. 22-10-16 (Regina) to Eng.	Box 844, Nanaimo, B.C.
703690	Shore, J.	Pte.	W. 19-11-16 (Somme) to Eng.	No address available.
703055	Shore, R.	Pte.	Evac. sick 26-10-16; d. o. s. in Eng 27-10-16.	General Delivery, Vancouver, B.C.
703447	Short, N. E.	Pte.	Att. to 4th Div. A.P.M.	W. T. Shore, Ottawa, Ont.
103018	Short, N. S.	Pte.	W. 9-6-17 (2nd Triangle)	3 Bayton Terrace, Kingsteignton, Devon, Eng.
161251	Shred, A.	Pte.	Dec. M.M. (Cambrai) C.R.O. 1989; w. 27-9-18 (Cambrai) to Eng.	c/o Mrs. W. Beveridge, 1815 Kingsway, Vancouver, B.C.
703785	Shrubsall, E.	Pte.	W. 21-10-16 (Regina) to Eng.	c/o Mrs. J. Lowden, Swansea, Ont.
703598	Shrubsall, R.	Pte.	W. 22-10-16 (Regina); w. 9-6-17 (2nd Triangle) to Eng.	Box 755, Prince Rupert, B.C.
931685	Shubrook, C.	Pte.	W. 7-9-17 (Lens) to Eng.	Danesbury House, Ramsgate Rd., Margate, Eng.
2529329	Shular, O. E.	Pte.	W. 30-9-18 (Cambrai) to Eng.	21 Hamilton Rd., Twickenham, Eng.
907821	Siberry, H.	Pte.	K. i. a. 9-4-17 (Vimy)	Southampton, Ont.
184234	Sigman, R.	L.-C.	W. 9-6-17 (2nd Triangle); w. 2-8-17 (Lens); evac. sick in Eng. 15-12-17.	Mrs. M. Siberry, Downsview, Ont.
931251	Sillander, G.	Pte.	W. 21-10-16 (Regina); w. 27-9-18 (Cambrai) to Eng.	Benton, Alta.
253064	Simison, C.	Pte.	W. 1-11-17 (Valenciennes); dec. M.M. (Valenciennes) C.R.O. 2028.	c/o Bank of Montreal, Quebec, Que.
703020	Simmers, R.	Pte.	K. i. a. 19-8-16 (St. Eloi)	Balfour Village, Shapinsay, Orkney, Scot.
704146	Simmers, R.	Pte.	D. o. w. 9-6-17 (2nd Triangle).	R. Simmers, 938 Collinson St., Victoria, B.C.
1000418	Simpson, L.	Pte.	W. 1-9-17 (Lens); tr. to Survey Sec. 7-7-18.	Mrs. A. Simpson, Ilfracombe, North Devon, Eng.
3108264	Simpson, W. A.	Sgt.		Neepawa, Man.
102671	Sims, C.	L.-S.	Tr. to Lbr. Pool 3-5-18.	20 O'Reilly St., Hamilton, Ont.
103249	Sims, F. R.	Pte.	W. 24-9-17 (Lens); w. 27-7-18 (Oppy) to Eng.	c/o A. Sims, 1158 May St., Victoria, B.C.
1000404	Sims, G. P.	Pte.		1318 Walnut St., Victoria, B.C.
703118	Sinclair, E.	Pte.	W. 5-6-17 (2nd Triangle) to Eng.	137 East St., Sault Ste. Marie, Ont.
161315	Singleton, H.	Pte.	Evac. sick 21-10-16 to Eng.	628 Lea Bridge Rd., Layton, Essex, Eng.
703669	Sintzel, F. C.	Pte.	W. 19-16 (St. Eloi); w. 21-10-16 (Regina) to Eng.	Turin, Alta.
2527330	Sintzel, F. C.	Pte.		543 Prince Edward St., Vancouver, B.C.
703725	Skellum, F.	Pte.		32 Grant St., Hamilton, Ont.
1004177	Skelton, F.	Pte.	Tr. to C.C.R.C. 22-2-18.	No address available.
240188	Skelton, W.	Pte.		Parry Sound, Ont.
3311701	Skinner, B.	Pte.		107 Tadcaster Rd., Woodseate, Sheffield, Eng.
249901	Skinner, G. G.	Pte.	Evac. sick 3-12-18 to Eng.	9 Olive Ave., Toronto, Ont.
				193 Asiidale Ave., Toronto, Ont.

Number	Name	Rank	Details	Address
102621	Skinner, J.	Pte.	W 9-8-17 (Lens)	15 Tolbooth St., Kircaldy, Scot.
703591	Skyrme, H.	Pte.	K. l. a. 15-9-16 (St. Eloi)	T. Skyrme, Mill Cottage, Thornbury, Herts, Eng.
225378	Slain, H.	L.-C.	Evac. slain 18-1-18 to Eng.	c/o Bank of B.N.A., Hamilton, Ont.
100409	Slater, C. E.	Pte.	W. 12-5-17 (1st Triangle); w. 12-6-17 (2nd Triangle) to Eng.	
249427	Slater, W.	Pte.	Tr. to 51st Bn. 2-8-16	78 Maisis Rd., Keighby, Yorks, Eng.
703374	Slaughter, A. G.	Pte.	W. 31-8-16 (St. Eloi) to Eng.	18 Allce St., Toronto, Ont.
703573	Slee, T.	Pte.	Dec. M.M. (Vimy) C.R.O. 1236; evac. sick 10-5-17 to Eng.	Wheat Sheaf Hotel, Wetherel, Carlisle, Eng.
703670	Slocomb, A. E.	Sgt.	Evac. sick 24-5-17 to Eng.	Courtenay, B.C.
908111	Smadu, P.	Pte.	Tr. to Royal Can. Dragoons, 11-4-18	2446 8th Ave. W., Vancouver, B.C.
663217	Small, D. M.	Pte.	W. 13-5-17 (1st Triangle); k. l. a. 7-4-18 (Oppy)	1821 Armour St., Regina, Sask.
703891	Smalley, O. B.	Pte.	Evac. sick 5-11-17 to Eng.	Shelbourne, Ont.
232323	Smart, A. W.	Pte.	W. 27-9-18 (Cambrai) to Eng.	J. Carstine, Cranbrook, B.C.
226380	Smedley, R H	Pte.	W. 2-9-18 (2nd Arras) to Eng.	Waldeck, Sask.
663118	Smillie, G. F.	Cpl.	W. 17-4-18 (Oppy) to Eng.	Box 303, Thamesville, Ont.
103063	Smith, A.	Cpl.		Milton, Ont.
669387	Smith, A.	Pte.	D. o. w. 21-10-16 (Regina)	2939 Cook St., Victoria, B.C.
703683	Smith, A.	Pte.	W. 21-10-16 (Regina) to Eng.	156 Markham St., Toronto, Ont.
703958	Smith, A.	Pte.	Evac. sick 4-12-18 to Eng.	J. F. Smith, Lavenston, nr. Vernon, B.C.
3107603	Smith, A. P.	Pte.		c/o Mrs. L. Williams, High River, Alta.
703892	Smith, A. R.	Pte.	Tr. to 4th M.G.C. 1-5-18	No address available.
250129	Smith, B. F.	Pte.	Tr. to Strathcona Horse 11-4-18	Norwood, Stonehaven, Scot.
252632	Smith, C. W.	L.-C.	W. 9-4-17 (Vimy); w. 24-3-18 (Lens) to Eng.	Moose Jaw, Sask.
252808	Smith, D. V.	Cpl.	Evac. sick 9-5-17 to Eng.	Woodfield, Arbroath, Scot.
907674	Smith, E. J.	Pte.	Tr. to Lbr. Pool 3-5-18	Wolseley, Sask.
703351	Smith, F.	Pte.	W. 9-4-17 (Vimy) to Eng.	54 Rose Crescent, Perth, Scot.
925069	Smith, F.	Pte.	W. 9-4-17 (Vimy)	Agassiz, B.C.
907730	Smith, F. A.	Pte.	D. o. w. 1-10-18 (Cambrai)	Dilke, Sask.
250076	Smith, F. E.	Pte.	W. 18-8-17 (Lens); dec. M.M. (2nd Arras) C.R.O. 1930; evac. sick 9-12-18 to Eng.	Mrs. F. M. Smith, 1 Surnach St., Toronto, Ont.
441344	Smith, F. E. W.	Sgt.	Tr. to 11th C.I.B. 30-4-18; dec. M.M. (Cambrai) C.R.O. 1989.	1901 McDermot Ave., Winnipeg, Man.
703218	Smith, F. H.	Sgt.	Dec. M.M. (Passchendaele) C.R.O. 1606; tr. to Eng. for commission 14-1-18.	Deep Cove, nr. Sidney, B.C.
760195	Smith, F. J.	Pte.	Evac sick 30-6-18 to Eng.	2036 10th Ave. W., Vancouver, B.C.
249816	Smith, F. R.	Pte.		1952 Davenport Rd., Toronto, Ont.
3107024	Smith, G. H.	Pte.	Dec. M.M. (2nd Arras) C.R.O. 1930; evac. sick 12-2-19.	No address available.
3109627	Smith, H. G.	Pte.	W. 9-4-17 (Vimy) to Eng.	R.R. No. 1, Troy, Ont.
2529415	Smith, H. P.	Pte.	K. l. a. 2-9-18 (2nd Arras)	304 Mornington St., Stratford, Ont.
252792	Smith, H. R.	Pte.	Tr. to 4th M.G.C. 1-5-18.	Scotsguard, Sask.
850218	Smith, I. W.	Pte.	W. 10-11-16 (Somme); evac. sick 21-1-18 to Eng.	J. Smith, 168 Ontario Ave., Niagara Falls, Ont.
1090101	Smith, J.	Pte.	Evac. sick in Eng. 23-12-18	c/o Miss D. Miller, 13 Westminster Apts., Calgary.
703601			W. 9-4-17 to Eng (Vimy).	2845 Quebec St., Mount Pleasant, Vancouver, B.C.
703125				Madoc, Ont.
252568				330 Crom Lane, West Earlestorm, Lancs, Eng.

225404	Smith, J. A.	Pte.	W. 16-11-17 (Passchendaele) to Eng.	Christie Lake, Ont.
3108007	Smith, J. C.	Pte.		R.R. No. 2, Durham, Ont.
703989	Smith, J. H.	Pte.	Tr. to 67th Bn. 8-7-16	420 Hornby St., Vancouver, B.C.
850472	Smith, J. H.	Pte.	W. 23-7-18 (Oppy)	13 Fitzgerald St., St. Catherines, Ont.
2523919	Smith, L. O.	Pte.	W. 28-9-18 (Cambrai) to Eng.	No address available.
102600	Smith, N. A.	Pte.	Evac. sick 17-8-17 to Eng.	c/o P. Quin, Alexandra, Quesnel, B.C.
760266	Smith, R. A.	Pte.	Evac. sick 10-3-18 to Eng.	1014 Howe St., Vancouver, B.C.
760148	Smith, S. C.	Pte.	K. i. a. 9-4-17 (Vimy)	Mrs. J. Smith, Port Gulchon, B.C.
2528315	Smith, S. G.	Pte.	W. 30-9-18 (Cambrai) to Eng.	Box 216, Stougville, Ont.
703448	Smith, S. W.	Pte.	Tr. to Lbr. Pool 12-7-18	12 Trafalgar St., Greenock, Scot.
703097	Smith, W. B.	Pte.	Tr. to 51st Bn. 2-8-16	2464 Saratoga Ave., Victoria, B.C.
160099	Smith, W. G.	Pte.	Tr. to 25th Bn. 7-10-16	No address available.
249902	Smith, W. H.	Pte.	K. i. a. 18-2-17 (Cambrai)	43 Copperfield Rd., Mile End, London, Eng.
226494	Smith, W. H.	Pte.	D. o. w. 13-8-18 (Amiens)	Mrs. W. Smith, R.R. No. 2, Ancaster, Ont.
703765	Smith, W. H.	Pte.	W. 14-9-16 (St. Eloi); evac. sick 5-2-17 to Eng.	Forest Branch, Court House, Vancouver, B.C.
3108477	Snagg, G. A.	Sgt.		Carriacou, Grenada, B.W.I.
291893	Snead, T.	Pte.	Evac. sick 9-4-17 to Eng.	723 McGee St., Winnipeg, Man.
105962	Snelgrove, R.	Pte.	K. i. a. 18-2-17 (Vimy)	R. Snelgrove, Sintaluta, Sask.
803210	Snelling, H. H.	Pte.	Evac. sick 27-11-18 to Eng.	364½ Grand Rapids Ave., Detroit, Mich., U.S.A.
225468	Sneyd, G. A.	Pte.		Box 1306, Welland, Ont.
1090291	Snider, G. E.	Pte.	Tr. to 4th M.G.C. 13-5-18	924 Stafford Rd., Fall River, Mass., U.S.A.
760889	Snow, J.	Pte.	K. i. a. 9-4-17 (Vimy) to Eng.	3246 Commercial Drive, South Vancouver, B.C.
703379	Sokolok, J.	Pte.	Tr. to 51st Bn. 2-8-16	Box 772, Vernon, B.C.
907940	Sokolok, J. T. E.	Pte.	D. o. w. 2-8-17 (Lens)	No address available.
706810	Somerville, T. E.	Pte.	W. 9-4-17 (Vimy) to Eng.	Bryson, Que.
183924	Songhurst, S.	Pte.	K. i. a. 9-4-17 (Vimy)	E. Songhurst, Hill End P.O., Alta.
249749	Sorensen, I.	Pte.	W. 4-9-18 (2nd Arras) to Eng.	42 Brookfield St., Toronto, Ont.
703788	South, A. L.	Cpl.	Tr. to Lbr. Pool 16-9-18	c/o Magistrate South, Vancouver, B.C.
703304	South, R. W.	Pte.	K. i. a. 9-4-17 (Vimy)	R. W. South, c/o O'Warralls' Ltd., 113 Bromsgrove St., Birmingham, Eng.
100644	Southall, R. C.	Pte.	Evac. sick 15-9-16 to Eng.	No address available.
925071	Southernwood, G. E.	Pte.	Tr. to 4th M.G.C. 3-5-18	c/o Mrs. M. Balls, Box 577, Estevan, Sask.
645657	Sowden, S. B.	Pte.	W. 4-9-18 (Vimy) to Eng.	1054 Pendrill St., Vancouver, B.C.
703893	Sparkes, E. G.	Pte.	K. i. a. 21-10-16 (Regina)	c/o Miss R. Weed, Midway, B.C.
139697	Spaul, T. H.	Pte.	W. i. a. 5-8-17 (Lens)	Mrs. Spaul, 68 Seaton St., Toronto, Ont.
703087	Spells, F.	Cpl.	W. 1-11-17 (Passchendaele) to Eng.	55 Vine St., Romford, Essex, Eng.
252988	Spence, A. B.	Pte.	W. 8-8-18 (Amiens) to Eng.	Lancer, Sask.
703339	Spencer, G.	Pte.	K. i. a. 5-9-16 (St. Eloi)	J. Spencer, Mervin, Sask.
249116	Speyer, C. H.	Pte.	K. i. a. 3-9-18 (2nd Arras)	205 Queen St., Toronto, Ont.
2527393	Springer, J. A.	Pte.	K. i. a. 4-9-18 (2nd Arras)	O. Springer, 244 Hunter St. W., Hamilton, Ont.
706479	Sprinkling, E. E.	Pte.	W. 10-6-17 (2nd Triangle); w. 9-8-17 (Lens) to Eng.	
249389	Sproule, E. V.	Pte.	Tr. to Can. Postal Corps 14-7-18	1263 Grant St., Victoria, B.C.
219149	Sprowl, J.	Pte.		25 Roxborough St. W., Toronto, Ont.
225296	Squires, F.	Pte.	W. 30-9-18 (Cambrai); d. o. w. 2-11-18	52 Moscow Ave., Toronto, Ont.
706459	Stacey, F.	Pte.	W. 9-4-17 (Vimy) to Eng.	Mrs. H. Squires, 13 Bradford St., Glen Rock, N.J.
703017	Stafford, A.	Pte.	Att. to Y.M.C.A. 24-8-16; evac. sick 11-9-16; ret. 21-9-16; evac. sick to Eng. 29-4-17	c/o Mrs. Humphreys, Pinehurst, R.M.D. 3, Victoria, B.C.
				Courtenay, B.C.

Number	Name	Rank	Details	Address
851031	Stainsby, W. J.	Pte.	Evac. sick 28-5-18 to Eng.	402 Birch St., Camden, N.J., U.S.A.
663071	Stansbury, C.	Pte.	W. 30-9-18 (Cambrai)	Oakville, Ont.
908191	Star-Blanket, E.	Pte.	W. 9-4-17 (Vimy) to Eng.	File Hills Reserve, B.C.
703609	Stark, C. D.	Pte.	W. 22-10-16 (Regina); tr. to Eng. as minor 23-2-17	
102279	Starling, K.	Pte.	W. 3-9-18 (2nd Arras)	154 8th St., Prince Albert, Sask.
1004004	Statuck, H.	Pte.	Tr. to 54th Co. C.F.C. 26-3-18	The Stead Hostel, Abbey Green, Bath, Eng.
2020166	Stauffer, D. L.	Pte.	K. i a. 17-11-17 (Passchendaele)	503 Stella St., Winnipeg, Man.
183087	Stawell, A. F.	Pte.	Tr. to 11th C.I.B.M.G.C. 10-12-16	Mrs. B. Stauffer, 10721 81st Ave., Strathcona, Alta.
908326	St. Clair, E.	Pte.	Evac. sick in Eng 4-1-18	No address available.
344002	Steacey, C. E.	Pte.	W. 2-11-18 (Valenciennes); evac. sick 5-12-18 to Eng.	c/o Mrs. L. Emerson, 2303 Alice St., Winnipeg, Man.
249101	Steele, H. A.	Pte.	W. 8-8-18 (Amiens) to Eng	c/o Mrs. C. Mallory, 21 Brock St., Belleville, Ont.
102076	Steele, H. C.	Pte.	W. 15-8-17 (Lens) to Eng	1061 Dovercourt Rd., Toronto, Ont.
703149	Steele, J.	Cpl.	K. i. a. 21-10-16 (Regina)	20 South Turner St., Victoria, B.C.
3317348	Steele, J. M.	Pte.		H. Steele, Winthurst, Sask.
925332	Steele, W. J.	Pte.	D. o. s. 30-1-17	Guildford, Ont.
1003694	Stefanuk, A.	Pte.	Tr. to 54th Co. C.F.C. 26-3-18	Mrs. Steele, Weyburn, Sask.
1009988	Stephen, J.	Pte.	D. o. w. 10-4-17 (Vimy)	No address available.
253123	Stephen, W.	Pte.	K. i. a. 9-4-17 (Vimy)	W. Atkins, Milo O Knilbridge, Aberdeen, Scot.
703696	Stephens, A. L.	Pte.		No address available.
540249	Stephens, A. O.	Pte.	Evac. sick 9-11-16 to Eng	1132 19th Ave. E., Vancouver, B.C.
703695	Stephens, F.	Pte.	Tr. to 51st Bn. 2-8-16.	6 Marshall St., Toronto, Ont.
249491	Stephens, W. L.	Cpl.		1132 19th Ave. E., Vancouver, B.C.
160536	Stephenson, J.	Pte.	D. o. w. 26-11-16 (Somme)	Aurora, Ont.
				J. Stephenson, Broughton-in-Furness, Cumberland, Eng.
760268	Sterling, F. A.	Pte.	Evac. sick 20-4-17 to Eng.	Merritt, B.C.
703387	Stevens, A. C.	Pte.		Box 27, Marine Heights, Vancouver, B.C.
249512	Stevens, C. J.	Pte.	D. o. s. 26-10-18.	Miss E. Stevens, 61 Swanwick Ave. E., Toronto, Ont.
225371	Stevens, F. J.	Pte.	W. 23-10-17 (Passchendaele) to Eng.	25 Wilton Ave., Toronto, Ont.
704051	Stevens, W. A.	Pte.	W. 4-4-17 (Vimy) to Eng.	22 Harvey Cloud Rd., Norton, Woodseats, Sheffield, Eng.
2528506	Stevenson, R.	Pte.	W. 3-9-18 (2nd Arras)	c/o D. M. Ferry Co., Windsor, Ont.
704146	Stewart, A.	Pte.	W. 23-7-18 (Oppy); tr. for demob. 26-1-19 to Eng.	Richard St., Vancouver, B.C.
1003310	Stewart, A.	Pte.		
703165	Stewart, A. N.	Pte.	Evac. sick 10-11-18	Little Current, Manitoulin Island, Ont.
761140	Stewart, J. A. D.	Pte.	Evac. sick 14-3-17 to Eng.	1863 8th Ave. W., Vancouver, B.C.
489691	Stewart, H. A.	Cpl.	W. 8-8-18 (Amiens) to Eng.	Ashton House, Easingwold, Yorks, Eng.
851011	Stewart, L.	Pte.	W. 27-9-18 (Cambrai) to Eng.	Box 215, Prince George, B.C.
225205	Stewart, M. O.	Pte.	D. o. w. 1-11-17 (Passchendaele)	526 West 7th St., Plainfield, N.J., U.S.A.
3110218	Stewart, R. L.	Pte.		Mrs. M. J. Stewart, West River St., Paris, Ont.
703457	Stewart, R. M.	Pte.		Hillsdale, Bergen Co., N.J., U.S.A.
1003540	St. George, R. G.	Pte.	Evac. sick 26-10-17 to Eng.	Comox, B.C.
703355	Stiles, E.	Pte.	W. 19-8-16 (St. Eloi) to Eng.	c/o Mrs. E. Chahquite, Champlain, Montreal, Que.
931664	Stiles, E.	Pte.		2716 Fourth Ave. E., Vancouver, B.C.
703407	Stiles, E. N.	L-C.	W. 14-10-16 (Somme); dec. M.M. (2nd Arras) C.R.O. 1930; w. 30-9-18 (Cambrai) to Eng	Rock Creek, B.C.
				2716 4th Ave. E., Vancouver, B.C.

1004139	Stiles, G. H.	Pte.	W. 23-9-17 (Lens); w. 26-9-17 (Lens); w. 16-3-18 (Lens); tr. to 4th M.G.C. 1-5-18	Fitzroy Harbour, Ont.
703406	Stiles, W. T.	Pte.	Dec. M.M. (Passchendaele) C.R.O. 1606; w. 6-4-18 (Oppy); w. 27-9-18 (Cambrai) to Eng.	716 4th Ave. E., Vancouver, B.C.
250064	Stone, C.	L.-C.	W. 18-10-18 (Valenciennes) to Eng.	c/o R. Robertson, 1 Patterson Place, Toronto.
706203	Stone-Sutton, D.	Pte.	W. 10-8-17 (Lens) to Eng.	645 Alpha St., Victoria, B.C.
1003917	Strachan, D. O.	Pte.	Tr. to C.F.C. 9-10-17.	Echo Bay, Ont.
931340	Strachan, E. K.	Pte.	Evac. sick 13-9-17 to Eng.	P.O. Box 567, Nelson, B.C.
252984	Stredwick, H.	Pte.	Tr. to 6th Can. Area Emp. Co. 22-8-17	No address available.
706273	Streeter, C.	Pte.	K. i. a. 9-4-17 (Vimy).	Mrs. M. Welman, Suite A, Mellor Apts., Broughton St., Victoria, B.C.
102299	Stronach, P.	Pte.	Tr. to 2nd Can. Lbr. Pool 16-8-17	55 Elmfield Ave., Aberdeen, Scot.
2529428	Stuart, G. B.	Pte.		98 Barnsdale Ave., Hamilton, Ont.
160360	Stuart, T. C.	Pte.	K. i. a. 4-6-17 (Oppy).	Mrs. C. Stuart, 1128 9th St. E., Calgary, Alta.
701139	Stutely, F. E. R.	Pte.	Evac. sick 4-5-17 to Eng.	66 Blythe Rd., W. Kensington Pk., London, W., Eng.
3105843	Suarez, F. M. J.	Pte.	W. 27-9-18 (Cambrai)	c/o Bank of Nova Scotia, Hamilton, Ont.
3314154	Sullivan, R. J. J.	Pte.	Evac. sick 5-12-18 to Eng.	Lock Two Hill, St. Catherines, Ont
703129	Suomina, G.	Pte.	W. 9-6-17 (2nd Triangle) to Eng	Sayward, B.C.
2528498	Sutherland, A.	Pte.	W. 30-4-18 (Oppy) to Eng.	193 Vancouver Ave., Detroit, Mich. U.S.A.
2528504	Sutherland, A.	Pte.	W. 1-5-17 (1st Triangle) to Eng	206 Trumball Ave., Detroit, Mich., U.S.A.
161108	Sutherland, C. R.	L.-C.	K. i. a. 2-9-18 (2nd Arras)	Berridale P.O., Caithness, Scot.
2528375	Sutherland, F. W.	Pte.		Mrs. E. Sutherland, 375 Edgecombe Ave., New York. U.S.A.
102456	Suttle, C. T.	Pte.	W. 9-8-17 (Lens) to Eng.	15 Arundel Ave., Toronto, Ont.
760163	Sutton, A.	Pte.	K. i. a. 9-4-17 (Vimy).	Mrs. H. Sutton, Edmonds, B.C.
249205	Sutton, F. E.	Pte.	Evac. sick 12-1-19 to Eng.	405 Clinton St., London, Ont.
200179	Sutton, L.	Pte.	W. 3-9-18 (2nd Arras) to Eng.	1608 Redfern St., Victoria, B.C.
703572	Swalwell, I.	Pte.	W. 11-11-16 (Somme) to Eng.	45 Burke St., Middleburgh, Eng.
123229	Swanson, C.	Cpl.		324 19th Ave. W., Vancouver, B.C.
703409	Swanson, R.	Cpl.	D.R.O. 375; k. i. a. 11-5-17 (1st Triangle)	
1066053	Swayze, W. B.	Pte.	W. 25-9-16 (St. Eloi); dec. M.M. (Somme)	Mrs. Swanson, 19th Ave. W., Vancouver, B.C.
226470	Sweeney, J. W.	Pte.	W. i. a. 8-8-18 (Amiens)	52 Keith St., Hamilton, Ont.
703204	Sweet, J. T.	Pte.	W. 6-6-17 (2nd Triangle) to Eng.	Mrs. R. Brockbank, 2605 Tree St., Cleveland Ohio.
703894	Symes, A. T.	Sgt.	Tr. to Base Co. 11-8-16	Commercial Hotel. Vancouver, B.C.
703037	Symonds, A. B.	Pte.	K. i. a. 9-4-17 (Vimy).	3505 Ash St. Vancouver, B.C. Miss N. B. Symonds, Whaley Range, Port Arlington Rd., Bournemouth, Eng.
703048	Symonds, M. H.	Sgt.	Tr. to Eng. for commission 21-3-17.	c/o the above.
2528499	Symons, R. E.	Pte.	D. o. w. 1-5-18 (Oppy)	Mrs A. Symons, 19 Curry Ave., Windsor, Ont.
760599	Taggart, G. D.	Pte.	W. 12-5-17 (1st Triangle) to Eng.	770 Union St., Vancouver, B.C.
760520	Taggart, J.	Pte.	W. i. a. 11-5-17 (1st Triangle)	Mrs. M. Taggart, 770 Union St., Vancouver, B.C.
225406	Talbot, R. M.	Pte.	Tr. to Eng. for tr. to A.E.F. 12-10-18.	4117 North Tripps Ave., Chicago, Ill., U.S.A.
704142	Talbot, T. W.	Pte.	W. i. a. 11-11-16 (Somme)	G. Talbot, Box 741, Rossland, B.C.
1601892	Tallett, W.	Pte.	W. 6-9-17 (Lens)	Buckland, Tilleigh, nr. High Hampton, N. Devon, Eng.
703896	Tallman, S.	Pte.	K. i. a. 22-10-16 (Regina)	G. D. Nicholas, 46 Randolph Gdns., Kilburn, London.
253325	Tanguay, L.	Pte.	K. 6-3-17 (Vimy); w. 6-4-17 (Vimy); w. 21-7-18 (Oppy); w. 1-10-18 (Cambrai) to Eng.	1158 Dorion St. Montreal, Que.
908221	Tann. F. G.	Pte.	W. 9-1-17 (Mericourt); evac. sick 20-3-17 to Eng.	Barking, Essex, Eng.

Number	Name	Rank	Service	Address
703069	Tapley, F. B.	Pte.	W. 19-8-16 (St. Eloi); evac. sick 15-3-18 to Eng.	c/o G. W. V. A., Prince George, B.C.
250089	Tapp, R. C.	Pte.	Tr. to Eng. as minor 27-3-18	20 Bolton Ave., Toronto, Ont.
240587	Tarlton, J. H.	Pte.	W. 4-9-18 (2nd Arras) to Eng.	110 East 24th St., Mount Hamilton, Ont.
907064	Tarves, H. D.	Pte.	W. 1-11-17 (Passchendaele) to Eng.	Birch Hills, Sask.
236497	Tarves, W. A.	Pte.	W. 1-10-18 (Cambrai) to Eng.	2364 East Grand Boulevard, Detroit, Mich., U.S.A.
2629358	Tate, E. R.	Pte.	W. 2-9-18 (2nd Arras)	766 Kimball St., Sault Ste. Marie, Mich., U.S.A.
2020215	Tavender, A.	Pte.	Tr. to Lbr. Pool 29-11-17	c/o Mrs. J. Marchant, Vernon, B.C.
704067	Tayler, C. W.	Pte.		c/o Mrs. T. H. Cowan, Portage la Prairie, Man.
704136	Taylor, A. E.	Pte.	W. 21-10-16 (Regina) to Eng.	55 Oldham Rd., Middleton, Lancs., Eng.
703500	Taylor, C. B.	Pte.	Tr. to 51st Bn. 16-7-16	596¼ South Vermont Ave., Los Angeles, Cal., U.S.A.
703303	Taylor, E. J.	Pte.	Evac. sick 15-3-17 to Eng.	Lillooet, B.C.
160248	Taylor, E. S.	Pte.	Tr. to Can. Corps Sal. Co. 1-6-17	251 Franciscan Rd., Tooting, London, S.W., Eng.
907667	Taylor, F. R.	Pte.	W. 7-3-17 (Vimy) to Eng.	Deepdale, Man.
3108870	Taylor, G.	Pte.	W. 30-9-18 (Cambrai) to Eng.	2316 Hournoy St., Chicago, Ill., U.S.A.
160643	Taylor, H.	Pte.	K. 1. a. 21-10-16 (Regina)	Mrs. E. Knowiden, 14 Byron Rd., Gillingham, Kent, Eng.
402518	Taylor, H. G.	Pte.	Att. to 8th Can. Area Emp. Co. 26-1-19	18 Duke St., Woodstock, Ont.
252880	Taylor, J.	Pte.	K. 1. a. 9-4-17 (Vimy)	Mrs. M. Taylor, 105 Menzies Rd., Torry, Aberdeen, Scot.
102265	Taylor, J.	Pte.	W. 16-8-17 (Lens)	31 Mount St., Aberdeen, Scot.
703632	Taylor, R. T.	Pte.		1837 6th Ave. E., Vancouver, B.C.
200212	Taylor, T. T.	Pte.	Tr. to 4th Div. Emp. Co. 10-6-18	1165 11th Ave. W., Vancouver, B.C.
760690	Taylor, W. A.	Pte.	W. 12-6-17 (2nd Triangle) to Eng.	2116 Horley St., South Vancouver, B.C.
102685	Taylor, W. D.	Cpl.	W. 17-11-17 (Passchendaele)	4 Langdale Rd., West Kirby, Cheshire, Eng.
703161	Teen, J.	Pte.	Tr. to 51st Bn. 16-7-16	c/o H. Armstrong, Bolder Hotel, Cordova St., Vancouver, B.C.
119040	Teesdale, J. W.	Pte.	Tr. to 11th C.I.T.M.B. 19-7-16	No address available.
1066371	Teeter, A. R.	Pte.	Tr. to Eng. as minor 15-10-18	c/o Merchants Bank of Canada, Markdale, Ont.
1066025	Teeter, W. J.	Pte.	Tr. to Can. Lbr. Pool 14-10-18	Markdale, Ont.
249635	Telfer, E. H.	Sgt.		c/o Woods & Forest Bch., Parliament Bldgs., Toronto.
3108022	Tempeny, M.	Pte.		Wilson's Corners, Que.
3109687	Tennant, E.	Pte.	Tr. to Eng. for R.A.F. 16-7-16	Box 663 Parry Sound, Ont.
200187	Terpening, G. C.	Pte.	Tr. to 11th C.I.T.M.B. 19-7-16	New Rockford, North Dakota, U.S.A.
136115	Terry, A.	Pte.	W. 27-9-18 (Cambrai) to Eng.	No address available.
663073	Terzian, J. G.	Pte.	W. 25-3-18 (Lens) to Eng.	c/o Miss N. Stonsbury, Oakville, Ont.
3105233	Tessier, X.	Pte.	W. 27-9-18 (Cambrai) to Eng.	2608 Mission St., San Francisco, Cal., U.S.A.
703410	Thacker, G. W.	Sgt.	K. 1. a. 9-4-17 (Vimy)	13 Ridge St., Arlington, R.I. U.S.A.
426356	Thibault, T.	Cpl.	Dec. M.M. (Lens) C.R.O. 1419; w. 16-8-17 (Lens); w. 1-11-17 (Passchendaele) to Eng.	Mrs. G. W. Thacker, Indian Head, Sask.
226895	Thibert, J.	Pte.	W. 8-8-18 (Amiens) to Eng.	Montmagny, Que.
704132	Thibideau, E.	Pte.	W. 15-9-16 (St. Eloi); w. 12-5-17 (1st Triangle) to Eng.	33 Klah St., Ogdenburgh, Ont.
220381	Thom, J. N.	L.-C.	W. 1-11-17 (Passchendaele)	503 Quebec Ave. W., Toronto, Ont.
907460	Thom, R.	L.-C.	W. 11-5-17 (1st Triangle) to Eng.	15-25 Garnet St., Regina, Sask.
707215	Thomas, C.	Sgt.	W. 2-9-18 (2nd Arras), tr. to Eng. for duty with R.N.W.M.P. 27-1-19	c/o Mrs. Carding, 27 Clark Rd., Wolverhampton, Eng.
				94 Cadbury St., Garston, Liverpool, Eng.

102199	Thomas, G.	Pte.	Evac. sick 1-5-17 to Eng.	30 Aubrey Rd. Walthamstow, London, Eng.
703482	Thomas, H. J.	Pte.	W. 7-4-17 (Vimy); k. l. a. 11-5-17 (1st Triangle)	E. Thomas, 2423 Cambridge St., Vancouver, B.C.
703924	Thomas, R. R.	Pte.	W. 21-10-16 (Regina) to Eng.	c/o Miss C. Roberts, 24 Caerphill Rd., Caerphill, Wales.
3109875	Thomas, W. E.	Pte.	W. 5-11-18 (2nd Arras); evac. sick 14-12-18 to Eng.	Bronte, Ont.
727050	Thompson, A. J.	Pte.	W. 8-8-18 (Amiens)	c/o W. Thistle, R.R. No. 3, Stratford, Ont.
103316	Thompson, C. S.	Pte.	Evac. sick 6-12-18 to Eng.	742 Lampson St., Esquimalt, B.C.
703641	Thompson, F.	Pte.	Att. from C.A.M.C. to Water Detail.	c/o P.O. Staff, Gen. Postoffice, Vancouver, B.C.
703022	Thompson, G. B.	Sgt.	Provost-Sgt. to 13-1-17; evac. sick 13-1-17 to Eng.	1633 Pinewood St., Victoria, B.C.
703988	Thompson, G. P.	Pte.	Tr. to Lbr. Pool 13-2-18.	107 Caron Ave., Windsor, Ont.
703113	Thompson, H. G.	Pte.	W. 12-5-17 (1st Triangle) to Eng.	Royston Rd., Cumberland, B.C.
440608	Thompson, H. G.	Pte.		Henribourg, Prince Albert, Sask
160595	Thompson, H. H.	Pte.	W. 30-9-18 (Cambrai); evac. sick in Eng. 31-12-18	47 Enfield St., Woodvale Rd., Belfast, Ire.
703501	Thompson, J.	Pte.	Acc. w. to Eng. 14-12-16	Riverhead Harbour, Grace, Newfoundland.
704049	Thompson, J. H.	Pte.	Tr. to Lbr. Pool 17-5-18.	c/o Miss A. Thompson, 100 Yorkville Ave., Toronto
703744	Thompson, J. P.	Pte.	Tr. to Base Co. 11-8-16.	Riverhead Harbour, Grace, Newfoundland.
3107390	Thompson, R.	Pte.		374 Front St. E., Toronto, Ont.
102143	Thompson, S. G.	Pte.		c/o W. Thompson, Sampson St., Esquimalt, B.C.
102598	Thompson, W. A.	Pte.	W. 30-10-17 (Passchendaele) to Eng.	Alberni, B.C.
624238	Thomson, C. R.	Pte.	W. 1-10-18 (Cambrai) to Eng.	6329 106th St., Edmonton S., Alta.
703546	Thomson, H. E.	Pte.	W. 9-4-17 (Vimy) to Eng.	1926 11th Ave. W. Vancouver, B.C.
703537	Thomson, J. B.	L.-C.	W. 12-6-17 (2nd Triangle) to Eng.	925 East 39th St., Portland, Ore.
467251	Thomson, W. F.	Pte.	Evac. sick 16-1-19.	76 Neilston Rd., Paisley, Scot.
1003689	Thomson, W. J.	L.-C.	D. o. s. 6-3-17.	Kagawong, Manitoulin Island, Ont.
135890	Thornally, H.	L.-C.	W. 19-3-18 (Lens) to Eng.	A. Thornally, Buckyard, Bingley Marsh, Lincs., Eng
70645	Thorne, W. R.	Pte.	K. l. a. 30-10-17 (Passchendaele)	c/o New England Hotel, Vancouver, B.C.
103117	Thrasher, A.	Pte.		Mrs. J. Thrasher, Forester's Falls, Ont.
760116	Thrower, E. G.	Pte.	W. 14-5-17 (1st Triangle); k. l. a. 18-6-17 (2nd Triangle)	Mrs. Thrower, 1067 Homer St., Vancouver, B.C.
2328349	Thrush, M.	Pte.	W. 4-9-18 (2nd Arras); w. 2-11-18 (Valenciennes) to Eng.	c/o Mrs. Preston, 382 Marguereta St., Toronto, Ont
240503	Thurlow, H.	Pte.	K. l. a. 8-8-18 (Amiens)	Mrs. L. Thurlow, "Hamildean," Gouldwell Ave., Ipswich, Eng.
2528333	Thurlow, W.	Pte.	Dec. M.M. (Cambrai) C.R.O. 1989; tr. to Eng. for duty 4-1-19.	c/o Mrs. Knaggs, 11 Down St., Dreffield, Yorks, Eng.
161088	Thurston, A. J.	Pte.	Tr. to 25th Bn. 7-10-16.	No address available.
703825	Thurston, R.	Pte.	Evac. sick 9-1-18 to Eng.	Creston, B.C.
761097	Tibb, R.	Pte.		1557 Parker St., Vancouver, B.C.
252423	Tilley, F. W.	Pte.	W. 2-9-18 (2nd Arras) to Eng.	179 Dougall Ave., Windsor, Ont.
226923	Thwaites, J.	Pte.	W. 8-8-18 (Amiens) to Eng.	No address available.
252308	Timoney, J. F.	Pte.	K. l. a. 21-3-17 (Vimy)	J. Timoney, Church St., Magherafelt, Co. Derry, Ire.
3314432	Titmus, J. A.	Pte.	W. 28-9-18 (Cambrai) to Eng.	Hanover, Ont.
160241	Titterington, R.	Pte.	K. l. a. 19-2-17 (Vimy)	Mrs. Titterington, Ogden P.O., Calgary, Alta.

Number	Name	Rank	Notes	Address
703834	Todd, C. F.	Sgt.	O.R.S. in the Field 14-9-17 to 27-9-17; men. in des. L.G. 30448; dec. Croix de Guerre, Belgian, (Passchendaele) C.R.O. 1635; tr. to Eng. for commission 27-9-18.	9 Mill Lane, York, Yorks, Eng.
250123	Todd, C. H.	Pte.	W. 10-4-18 (Oppy); tr. to Eng. for demob. duty 9-2-19.	13 Emerson Ave., Toronto, Ont.
907309	Todd, H.	Pte.	K. l. a. 12-5-17 (1st Triangle).	Mrs. H. Todd, c/o Mrs. Daymock, 2 Cowley Cottages, New Brent St., Hendon, Eng.
102200	Todd, N. S.	Sgt.	Dec. M.M. (Passchendaele) C.R.O. 1606; dec. Bar. to M.M. (2nd Arras) C.R.O. 1930.	c/o Mrs. Buckingham, Brambledene, Belaugh, Norwich, Eng.
907701	Todd, R. W.	Pte.	K. l. a. 9-4-17 (Vimy).	Mrs. K. Todd, Regina, Sask.
931253	Tolfree, B. W.	Cpl.	W. 21-10-16 (Regina); w. 8-8-17 (Lens); tr. to C.C.R.C. 16-11-18.	
703968	Tolfrey, A. F.	Pte.	K. l. a. 11-11-16 (Somme).	Chilcomb Rectory, nr. Winchester, Hants, Eng.
648892	Tolmie, R. S.	Sgt.	Dec. M.M. (Amiens) C.R.O. 1899.	C. F. Tolfrey, 66 Olenda St., Portsmouth, Eng.
3310366	Toman, J.	Pte.		Woodville, Ont.
703824	Tompkins, F. J.	Cpl.	W. 8-9-16 (St. Eloi); k. l. a. 22-11-16 (Somme)	56 Munroe Ave., Hamilton, Ont.
				W. Tompkins, 2, Freeman's Cottages, Red Lion Hill, London, N.E., Eng.
1003217	Tooke, L.	L.-C.	Dec. M.M. (Cambrai) C.R.O. 1989.	Thessalon, Ont.
3317707	Tooley, R. R.	Pte.	W. 30-9-18 (Cambrai) to Eng.	Courtice, Ont.
703183	Toombs, A. E.	Pte.	W. 19-8-16 (St. Eloi) to Eng.	Box 576, Nanaimo, B.C.
760725	Tootell, A.	Pte.	W. 16-8-17 (Lens) to Eng.	1140 Pender St. W., Vancouver, B.C.
252879	Topham, I. S.	Pte.	W. 6-3-17 (Vimy); w. 9-4-17 (Vimy) to Eng.	250 William St., London, Ont.
833149	Torrie, A. W.	Pte.	Evac. sick 27-4-18.	Chatsworth, Ont.
850921	Tough, J. W.	Pte.	Tr. to 4th C.M.G.C. 13-6-18.	29 Arbutus St., Rochester, N.Y., U.S.A.
663121	Tough, W. A.	Pte.		Milton, Ont.
3314645	Towers, R. C.	Pte.	W. 11-9-16 (St. Eloi) to Eng.	Bridgeburg, Ont.
703850	Towgood, C. E.	Pte.	W. 17-4-17 (Oppy) to Eng.	1433 22nd Ave., South Vancouver, B.C.
703849	Towgood, E. J.	Pte.	Evac. sick 5-2-18 to Eng.	1433 22nd Ave., South Vancouver, B.C.
703124	Towler, E. H.	Pte.	W. 8-8-18 (Amiens) to Eng.	Sayward Salmon River, B.C.
751915	Towler, W. S.	Pte.		c/o Mrs. G. Harding, 2395 Hamilton Boulevard, Highland Park, Detroit, Mich., U.S.A.
701096	Townsend, P. A.	Pte.	W. 10-11-16 (Somme); tr. to Lbr. Pool 25-10-17	c/o Mrs. J. Carr, Harveyclough Rd., Woodseats, Sheffield, Eng.
445598	Townshend, J. L.	Pte.	W. 21-10-16 (Regina) to Eng.	No address available.
3108491	Tracey, W. J.	Pte.		36 Haines St., St. Catherines, Ont.
540252	Train, G. M.	L.-S.	W. 21-10-16 (Regina); w. 17-11-17 (Passchendaele); tr. to Eng. for commission 31-10-18.	
907154	Treadwell, S. O.	Pte.	W. 11-8-17 (Lens) to Eng.	359 Pacific Ave., West Toronto, Ont.
3317355	Tregenza, D. O.	Pte.	Evac. sick 15-2-19 to Eng.	Regina, Sask.
1000322	Trembley, E. O.	Pte.	W. 8-8-18 (Amiens) to Eng.	R.R. No. 2, Orrilla, Ont.
207636	Tribe, G.	Pte.	W. 6-6-17 (2nd Triangle) to Eng.	Chapleau, Ont.
101177	Tronnes, P.	Pte.	W. 1-11-16 (Somme); w. 27-9-18 (Cambrai) to Eng.	Holstein, Ont.
703603	Tronson, O.	Pte.	Evac. sick 21-11-16 to Eng.	Camrose, Alta.
				Grand Prairie, Alta.

202020	Trousdale, E.	Pte.	W. 1-11-17 (Passchendaele); evac sick in Eng. 2-4-18	"Wybourne," St. George's Rd., Cheltenham, Eng.
126459	Truckel, W. J.	Pte.	Evac. sick 20-10-16 to Eng.	No address available.
225248	Trudel, O. L.	Pte.	K. i. a. 2-9-18 (2nd Arras)	U. Trudel, Sheppegan, N.B.
3314053	Tufford, T. L.	Pte.	W. 27-9-18 (Cambrai) to Eng.	94½ Queen St., St. Catharines, Ont.
3314431	Tulloch, R. A.	Pte.	W. 1-10-18 (Cambrai) to Eng.	Lake Thomas P.O., N.S.
760259	Turnbull, G.	Pte.	W. 9-4-17 (Vimy) to Eng.	1944 Kitchener St., Vancouver, B.C.
703596	Turner, F. J.	Pte.	Tr. to 7th Can. Lbr. Bn. 16-8-17	20 Bective Rd., Putney, London, Eng.
249136	Turner, J. A.	Pte.	Tr. to 4th C.M.G.C. 18-3-18	c/o Miss N. Verrall, 26 Ashburnham Rd., Toronto, Ont.
703786	Turner, T.	Pte.	W. 21-10-16 (Regina); k. i. a. 15-8-17 (Lens)	Mrs. E. Turner, 421 Glen Drive, Vancouver, B.C.
1003236	Twadukium, P.	Pte.	Acc. w. to Eng. 4-1-18	No address available.
1045759	Twell, G. N.	Pte.	Dec. M.M. (Oppy) C.R.O. 1866; w. 4-9-18 (2nd Arras) to Eng.	
707016	Twigg, P.	Pte.	K. i. a. 9-4-17 (Vimy)	15 Trinity Rd., Bridlington, Yorks, Eng.
145195	Tyo, J. F.	Pte.	W. 27-9-18 (Cambrai) to Eng.	Mrs. F. M. Proctor, 157 Wellington Ave., Victoria, B.C.
931448	Ukovitch, S.	Pte.	Detained in England	Cornwall, Ont.
1004224	Underdown, W.	Pte.	W. 8-8-18 (Amiens) to Eng.	No address available.
703823	Unicume, H. J.	Pte.	W. 14-5-17 (1st Triangle) to Eng.	77 Stowe Rd., Shepherds Bush, London, Eng.
225704	Upper, R. E.	Pte.	Tr. to 87th Bn. 26-6-18	459 Lansdowne Ave., Westmount, Montreal, Que.
103187	Urquhart, W.	Pte.	Evac. sick 27-6-17 to Eng.	18 Catherine St., St. Catherines, Ont.
703503	Urseth, I.	Pte.	W. 6-9-16 (St. Eloi); dec. M.M. (2nd Arras) C.R.O. 1913; tr. for demob. duty to Eng. 4-1-19	60 East Crawford St., Glasgow, Scot.
703093	Utley, W. H.	Pte.	W. 20-10-16 (Regina) to Eng.	c/o Mrs. Fougner, Bella Coola, B.C.
225293	Vachon, J.	Pte.	W. 4-9-18 (2nd Arras) to Eng.	Port Essington, B.C.
270120	Vair, J.	Pte.	W. 2-9-18 (2nd Arras) to Eng.	Sabattons Rd., Lewiston, Me., U.S.A.
2529417	Valve, M. T.	Pte.	Evac. sick 21-8-16 to Eng.	156 Eagle Ave., Brantford, Ont.
704056	Valile, C. C.	Pte.	W. 17-5-17 (1st Triangle); w. 2-8-17 (Lens)	Gatineau Point, Que.
103238	Valpy, H. H.	Pte.	w. 2-9-18 (2nd Arras) to Eng.	Hudson Hotel, Vancouver, B.C.
252343	Van Koughnett, S.	Pte.	W. 12-5-17 (1st Triangle); w. 30-9-18 (Cambrai)	Northern Hotel, Victoria, B.C.
3317912	Van Norman, R. B.	Pte.	Evac. sick 13-3-19	Morse, Sask.
687353	Van Verenbergh, T.	Pte.	W. 10-8-17 (Lens); k. i. a. 17-11-17 (Passchendaele)	Longford Mills, Ont.
225281	Vanzile, E. D.	Pte.	Acc. w. 22-8-18; dec. D.C.M. (Valenciennes) C.R.O. 2040	Mr. Van Verenbergh, Chase, B.C.
515160	Varley, J.	Pte.	Tr. to Lbr. Pool 16-9-18	49 Church Rd., Cheriton, Kent, Eng.
703300	Varrick, F.	Pte.	W. 22-10-16 (Regina) to Eng.	310 Ottawa St., Hamilton, Ont.
907178	Varty, G. B.	Pte.	Evac. sick 31-5-17 to Eng.	c/o G.W.V.A., Vancouver, B.C.
703292	Vatcher, H. W.	Pte.	K. i. a. 22-10-16 (Regina)	Tugaski, Sask.
1015641	Vaukalre, G.	Pte.	Evac. sick 14-10-17 to Eng.	R. Vatcher, Burgeo, Newfoundland.
136155	Veal, F. J.	Pte.	Tr. to 4th Div. Emp. Co. 24-10-17	No address available.
2591326	Vedder, A. R.	Pte.	W. 1-11-17 (Passchendaele) to Eng.	12 Theford Place, Toronto, Ont.
103426	Veitch, F.	Pte.	Tr. to 16th M.G.C. 1-1-17	71 Mary St., Hamilton, Ont.
908078	Vemel, G.	Pte.	Tr. to Eng. from P.B. 17-6-18	9 Burghley Rd., Highgate, London, N., Eng.
703326	Veness, C.	Pte.	Tr. to 16th M.G.C. 1-1-17	No address available.
219374	Viau, R.	Pte.	W. 23-4-18 (Oppy) to Eng.	Colwood, B.C.
227196	Vickers, C. E.	Pte.		131 Cathcart St., Sault Ste. Marie, Ont.
				R.R. No. 1, Grimsby, Ont.

931254	Visnoski, W.	Pte.	Evac. sick 13-9-17 (Lens)	P.O. Box 65, Sheridan, Wyoming, U.S.A.
703035	Vogel, F. B.	Sgt.	W. 22-3-17 (Vimy); k. l. a. 9-4-17 (Vimy)	Miss M. Vogel, Lazo P.O., Comox, B.C.
703896	Vogel, J. E.	L.-C.	W. 1-9-16 (St. Eloi) to Eng.	Miss M. Vogel, Lazo P.O., Comox, B.C.
931730	Vona, R.	Pte.	Detained in Eng.	No address available.
1015548	Vucinich, S.	Pte.	W. 1-11-17 (Passchendaele); w. 8-8-18 (Amiens); w. 1-10-18 (Valenciennes)	
1015647	Vukovitch, B.	Pte.	W. 1-11-17 (Passchendaele); w. 8-8-18 (Amiens)	Dominion Hotel, Yates Street, Victoria, B.C.
202010	Waddell, G. W.	Pte.	K. i. a. 17-11-17 (Passchendaele)	Dominion Hotel, Yates Street, Victoria, B.C.
225843	Wagstaff, G. W.	Pte.	W. 16-8-18 (Amiens)	T. Waddell, North Lonsdale P.O., B.C.
704075	Walstell, G. W.	Sgt.	W. 20-10-16 (Regina) to Eng.	No address available.
663603	Waldron, W. J.	Pte.		Dominion Express Co., Calgary, Alta.
703089	Walford, W. G.	Pte.	W. 18-11-16 (Somme) to Eng.	134 Canada St., Hamilton, Ont.
703335	Walker, A. G.	Sgt.	Tr. to 51st Bn. 2-8-16	Englefield Green, Surrey, Eng.
703455	Walker, C.	Arm-Cpl.	W. 1-9-16 (St. Eloi); w. 4-9-18 (2nd Arras) to Eng.	Terrace, B.C.
541170	Walker, D. L.	Pte.	Att. from 11th C.L.T.M.B. for instruction; k. i. a. 15-9-16 (St. Eloi)	2133 First St., Long Beach, Cal. U.S.A.
704072	Walker, H. K.	L.-C.	D. o. w. 25-10-16 (St. Eloi)	No address available. H. W. Walker, National Provincial Bank of England, Bishopsgate, London, Eng.
3311707	Walker, M. W.	Pte.	W. 8-8-18 (Amiens) to Eng.	40 Alfred St., Brantford, Ont.
1003001	Walker, R.	Pte.	W. 9-4-17 (Vimy) to Eng.	18 Isabella St., Toronto, Ont.
706499	Walker, W.	Cpl.	W. 9-4-17 (Vimy) to Eng.	339 Simcoe St., Victoria, B.C.
925151	Wall, H. E.	Pte.		4600 South Paulina St., Chicago, Ill., U.S.A.
523749	Wall, W. H. P.	Pte.	Att. from C.A.M.C. to Water Detail; w. 28-9-18 (Cambrai)	
103310	Wallace, C.	Pte.	W. 17-5-17 (1st Triangle) to Eng.	15 York Rd., Maidenhead, Berks, Eng.
1003272	Wallace, G.	Pte.	W. 27-9-18 (Cambrai)	24 Rivine Grove, Plumstead, London, S.E., Eng.
102666	Wallace, J.	Pte.	Evac. sick 20-11-17 to Eng.	Kewstoke, Eng.
2020186	Wallace, J. W. A.	Pte.	Tr. to Eng. as minor 29-10-17	General Delivery, Victoria, B.C.
703768	Walrath, L. E.	Pte.	W. 16-8-17 (Lens)	General Delivery, Vancouver, B.C.
703576	Walsh, A. V.	Pte.	K. l. a. 19-10-16 (Somme)	Union Bay, B.C.
				Mrs. M. A. Seymour, 2262 Cambridge St., Vancouver, B.C.
3108592	Walsh, J.	Pte.	W. 11-6-17 (2nd Triangle) to Eng.	Mrs. C. Bonnet, 44 Bell St., North Shields, Eng.
1027722	Walsh, T.	Pte.	W. 27-9-18 (Cambrai) to Eng.	25 Richmond Hill, Rathmines, Dublin, Ire.
2507320	Walsh, W. C.	L.-C.	Dec. M.M. (Cambrai) C.R.O. 1989	10 Horse St., Dowlais, South Wales.
200208	Walton, W. C.	Pte.	Evac. sick 3-1-17 to Eng.	3125 Emma St., Victoria, B.C.
703897	Warburton, J.	Pte.	W. 21-10-16 (Regina); k. l. a. 24-1-17 (Passchendaele)	c/o J. R. Jackson, Midway, B.C.
160429	Ward, C.	Pte.	Tr. to 11th C.L.T.M.B. 19-7-16	
14546	Ward, G.	Pte.	Evac. sick 23-10-16 to Eng.	Mrs. R. Ward, 636 18th Ave. N.W., Calgary, Alta.
703810	Ward, M.	Pte.	Evac. sick 8-5-17 to Eng.	No address available.
703731	Ward, R.	L.-C.	W. 2-9-18 (2nd Arras) to Eng.	Alert Bay, B.C.
227144	Warmington, C. L.	Pte.	W. 9-4-17 (Vimy) to Eng.	Lumby, B.C.
252690	Warner, C. A.	Pte.	W. 15-5-17 (1st Triangle); dec. D.C.M. (Cambrai) G.R.O. 418	164 Western Ave., Toronto, Ont.
907181	Warner, J. T.	Sgt.		Shaunavon, Sask.
135908	Warner, W. J.	Pte.	K. l. a. 1-10-18 (Cambrai)	General Delivery, Regina, Sask.
100937	Warren, G. F.	Pte.	K. i. a. 22-10-16 (Regina)	Mrs. A. Warner, 233 Wilton Ave., Toronto, Ont. G. Warren, 7 Enlanger Rd., New Cross Gate, London.

Number	Name	Rank	Details	Address
703668	Warren, L. A.	Pte.	Tr. to Lbr. Pool 15-5-18	c/o Bank of Comemrce, Prince George, B.C.
702747	Wate, J. P.	Pte.	Tr. to 54th Bn. 13-7-17	2612 Western Ave., North Vancouver, B.C.
126592	Waterhouse, H.	Pte.	W. 2-8-17 (Lens) to Eng.	89 York Rd., Guelph, Ont.
704032	Waterhouse, S. H.	Pte.		38 Ashwell Rd., Heaton, Bradford, Eng.
703509	Waters, J.	Sgt.	W. 20-11-16 (Somme); evac. sick 27-8-17 to Eng.	Oyama, B.C.
707017	Waters, W. S.	Pte.	K. i. a. 9-4-17 (Vimy)	No address available.
703460	Watkins, W.	Pte.	W. 28-9-18 (Cambrai) to Eng.	General Delivery, Vancouver, B.C.
760617	Watson, A.	Pte.	Evac. sick 20-6-17 to Eng.	c/o Mrs. C. Spink, No. 1 Hollin St., Claremont, Halifax, Yorks, Eng.
317014	Watson, C. S.	Sgt.	Tr. to Base Co. 11-8-16	No address available.
703274	Watson, F.	Pte.		5097 Chester St., South Vancouver, B.C.
761221	Watson, R.	Pte.	K. l. a. 9-4-17 (Vimy)	Mrs. G. Booth, 42 Howard St., East Hartpool, Durham, Eng.
703769	Watson, S.	Pte.	Missing after action 11-11-16	Mrs. M. Watson, Cumberland, B.C.
703388	Watt, F. R.	Pte.	Evac. sick 13-5-18 to Eng.; w. 4-9-18 (2nd Arras)	1161 Howe St., Vancouver, B.C.
102714	Watts, A.	Cpl.	W. 11-5-17 (1st Triangle); dec. M.M. (Valenciennes) C.R.O. 2028	
760319	Watts, E. T.	Pte.	W. 9-4-17 (Vimy) to Eng.	Box 791, Nanaimo, B.C.
704119	Waughn, J. N.	Pte.	W. 15-8-17 (Lens); w. 8-8-18 (Amiens) to Eng.	c/o Mrs. G. Shobridge, 939 Queen St. W. Toronto, Ont.
703180	Weatherspoon, A. J.	Pte.	W. 2-9-18 (2nd Arras) to Eng.	200 Cumberland St., Charlottetown, P.E.I.
226776	Weatherston, W.	Pte.	W. 2-9-18 (2nd Arras)	437 Main St. St. John's, N.B.
226285	Weaver, B. C.	Cpl.	Evac. sick 4-3-19	95 John St., Brockville, Ont.
703436	Weaver, T. H.	Sgt.	W. 21-10-16 (Regina); w. 9-4-17 (Vimy); evac. sick 27-12-17 to Eng.	c/o E. H. Baxter, 2982 Paxton Rd., Cincinnati, U.S.A.
703434	Webb, C.	L.-C.	W. 9-4-17 (Vimy) to Eng.	c/o Miss Fussel, 112 Water St., Vancouver, B.C.
252435	Webb, G. F.	Pte.	Tr. to Lbr. Pool 25-10-17	12 Moore Lane, Witton, Birmingham, Eng.
127497	Webb, J. H.	Pte.	W. 4-9-18 (2nd Arras); d. o. w. 2-11-18 (Valenciennes)	Alcaster, Warwickshire, Eng.
3105605	Webb, J.	Pte.		Hornton, Banbury, Oxfordshire, Eng.
704066	Webb, S. R.	Pte.	Tr. to Can. Postal Corps 16-8-18	J. A. Webb, Weston, Ont.
703577	Webb, T. W. S.	Pte.	Evac. sick 21-10-16 to Eng.; dec. M.M. (Amiens)	413 Vancouver St., Victoria, B.C.
907548	Webb, W. H.	Cpl.	W. 23-1-17 (Mericourt); dec. M.M. 1-10-18 (Cambrai) C.R.O. 1899: k. i. a. 1-10-18 (Cambrai)	Arden, Bexley, Kent, Eng.
703697	Weber, G.	Pte.	W. 21-10-16 (Regina)	A. Webb, Browning, Sask.
174958	Webster, H. S.	Pte.	D. o. w. 5-2-17 (Vimy)	1719 Yew St., Vancouver, B.C.
908220	Webster, J. E.	Pte.	W. 9-4-17 (Vimy) to Eng.	Mrs. Webster, 83 Oak Ave., Hamilton, Ont.
760749	Wedderburn, L. McL.	Pte.	W. 9-4-17 (Vimy) to Eng.	Dilke, Sask.
1090193	Weegar, C. H.	Pte.	W. 8-8-18 (Amiens) to Eng.	Kerrisdale, B.C.
704172	Weeks, J.	Pte.	W. 15-5-17 (1st Triangle); evac. sick 30-6-18	Morrisburgh, Ont.
703166	Weeks, T.	Pte.	Tr. to 4th Div. Emp. Co. 11-5-17	c/o Bank of Commerce, Vancouver, B.C.
252804	Weightman, G. W.	Pte.	W. 13-5-17 (1st Triangle); tr. to 1st Lbr. Bn. 16-7-17	21 Norcopp Rd. Stoke Newington, London, Eng.
907828	Weir, E. R.	L.-C.	Evac. sick 30-3-17 to Eng.	c/o Mrs. E. Tibbles, Hythe, Kent, Eng.
3108497	Weir, G. A.	Pte.		Kerrobert, Sask.
703709	Weir, F. F.	S.-S.	Tr. to 51st Bn. 2-8-16	Livingston Creek, Ont. U.S.A.
440052	Welch, E.	Pte.	Att. to 4th Can. Div. H.-Q. with C.A.P.C. 16-9-17	Elkin, North Carolina, U.S.A. 1557 11th Ave., Vancouver, B.C.
925134	Wells, G. L.	Pte.	W. 17-8-17 (Lens) to Eng.	575 William Ave., Winnipeg, Man.

Number	Name	Rank	Notes	Address
703062	Welsh, E. J.	Cpl.	K. l. a. 22-10-16 (Regina)	M. Welsh, 21 Wellgate, Greatland, Eng.
464380	Welsh, E. J.	Sgt.	W. 30-9-18 (Cambrai) to Eng.; granted commission in R.A.F.	
703426	Welsh, W. H.	Pte.	W. 21-10-16 (Regina) to Eng.; granted commission in R.A.F.	1557 11th Ave. W., Vancouver, B.C.
102442	Wensley, A.	Pte.	Tr. to 4th Div. Emp. Co. 11-5-17	1557 11th Ave. W., Vancouver, B.C.
1004032	Werefey, J.	Pte.	Tr. to H.-Q. 1st Bde. C.E. 10-7-18	Mark, nr. Highbridge, Somerset, Eng.
102268	West, J. D.	Cpl.	Evac. sick 9-5-17 to Eng.	128 Candler Ave., Highland Park, Detroit, Mich., U.S.A
703456	Westcott, E.	S.-S.	Armourer Sergeant	Fernie, B.C.
81943	Westwood, W.	C.S.M.	Tr. to Lbr. Pool 25-10-17	428 East White Oak, Monrovia, Cal., U.S.A.
317015	Whale, H. R.	Pte.	W. 21-10-16 (Regina) to Eng.	c/o Mrs Butcher, 67 Ashley Ave., Cheriton, Kent, Eng.
249861	Whalen, P.	Pte.	W. 27-9-18 (Cambrai) to Eng.	No address available.
648952	Wharram, F. I.	Pte.	Tr. to Lbr. Pool 26-12-17	49 Wellington.St. E., Toronto, Ont.
704044	Wharton, S. O. E.	Pte.	Tr. to Audit Office, London 16-7-16	93 Burton Ave., Allendale, Ont.
101677	Wheatley, G.	Pte.	K. l. a. 16-1-17 (Vimy)	G.T.P. Ticket Office, 527 Seymour St., Vancouver, B.C.
853310	Wheeler, C.	Pte.	Tr. to 4th M.G.C. 18-3-18	T. C. Wheatley, R.R. No. 3, Sarnia, Ont.
225459	Wheeler, F. E.	Pte.	K. l. a. 21-8-18 (Amiens)	Lindsay, Ont.
703343	Whelan, E. E.	Pte.	D. o. w. 23-11-16 (Somme)	B. Marriage, R.R. No. 1, Port Robson, Ont.
703649	Whelan, G. K.	Pte.	W. 22-10-16 (Somme) to Eng.	Mrs. Whelan, Lazo, nr. Comox, B.C.
925180	Wheler, F. J.	Pte.	W. 9-4-17 (Vimy); w. 17-5-17 (1st Triangle); d. o. w. 13-11-17 (Passchendaele)	Lazo, Comox, B.C.
703783	Whettel, E.	L.-C.	D. o. w. 29-10-16 (Regina)	H. Wheler, Box 395, Weyburn, Sask. Mrs. Jones, Longwood Cottage, Treglaston, nr. Welshpool, Wales.
252798	Whibley, A.	Pte.	W. 9-4-17 (Vimy) to Eng.	c/o Mrs. Young, Hazlemere, Surrey, Eng.
703898	Whipler, W. J.	Pte.	Evac. sick 25-2-17 to Eng.	c/o H. Ross, 1052 14th Ave. E., Vancouver, B.C.
252351	White, C.	Pte.	K. l. a. 9-4-17 (Vimy)	Mrs. White, Swift Current, Sask.
703217	White, F.	Sgt.	Sergeant Shoemaker	1311 Blanchard St., Victoria, B.C.
761158	White, H.	Cpl.	Dec. M.M. (Passchendaele) C.R.O. 1606; k. l. a. 16-11-17 (Passchendaele)	
225359	White, J. H.	Pte.	W. 6-8-17 (Lens) to Eng.	Mrs. M. M. White, 12 Jericho St., Oxford, Eng.
658054	White, R. H.	Pte.	To P.B. 23-3-17; tr. to Eng. P.B. Unit 26-2-18.	99 River Rd. Niagara Falls, Ont.
703132	White-Fraser, G.	C.S.M.		309 Yorkshire L. Bldg., Seymour St., Vancouver, B.C
663623	Whitehead, C.	Pte.		c/o O. Crane, Milton, Ont.
160336	Whitehead, F. C.	Pte.	W. 20-11-16 (Somme); tr. to 75th Bn. 19-2-17.	"The Shaws," Uppevinici, nr. Oldham, Eng.
138254	Whitehouse, F. G.	Pte.	W. 27-9-18 (Cambrai) to Eng.	No address available.
663319	Whiteman, E. K.	Pte.	K. l. a. 9-4-17 (Vimy)	Marysville, Ont.
907376	Whitham, J.	Pte.	Tr. to 4th M.G.C. 18-3-18.	Mrs. J. Whitham, Wood Cottage, Skipton, Yorks, Eng.
250028	Whitla, W.	Pte.	Evac. sick 27-3-17 to Eng.	40 Haddington St., Galt, Ont.
703549	Whitlock, J.	Pte.	W. 9-4-17 (Vimy); k. l. a. 6-6-17 (2nd Triangle)	2145 10th Ave. W., Vancouver, B.C.
907042	Whitman, R. A.	Pte.		
703633	Whitney, B. MacD.	Sgt.	D. o. w. 24-11-16 (Somme)	Mrs. A. Whitman, c/o Arlington House, Regina, Sask.
136169	Whitney, H. E.	Pte.	Tr. to 11th M.G.C. 28-6-17.	Mrs. L. Whitney, 1750 Nelson St., Vancouver, B.C.
270494	Whittington, J. G.	Pte.	W. 24-3-17 (Lens) to Eng.	23 Tintern St., Brixton, London, Eng.
3105981	Whylie, F.	Pte.	W. 27-9-18 (Cambrai) to Eng.	11 Meredith St., Clerkenwell, London, Eng.
703617	Whyte, W.	Pte.	Dec. M.M. (Vimy) C.R.O. 1236.	No address available. Suite 4, Lakewood Apts., 406 Lakewood Drive, Vancouver, B.C.
703909	Whyter, A.	Pte.	K. l. a. 20-10-16 (Regina)	Mrs. Forman, Reston, Man.
704086	Wicklund, W.	Pte.	Tr. to Eng. on demob. duty 13-1-19.	112 Esplanade, North Vancouver, B.C.

1066260	Widmeyer, L. H.	Pte.	W. 30-9-18 (Cambrai)	Ayton, Ont.
663722	Wiffen, H. E.	Cpl.		8 Colne Rd., Halstead, Essex, Eng.
219804	Wight, W. T.	Pte.	K. i. a. 9-4-17 (Vimy)	Mrs. E. Wight, c/o Box 623, Renfrew, Ont.
252318	Wightman, T.	Pte.	K. i. a. 9-4-17 (Vimy)	Mrs. Wightman, Nesbit, Man.
226368	Wilkie, F. H.	L.-C.	W. 4-9-18 (2nd Arras)	20 Oliver St., Guelph, Ont.
1003313	Wilkin, A. R.	Pte.	K. i. a. 27-9-18 (Cambrai)	W. Wilkin, Little Current, Ont.
908020	Wilkins, A. P.	Pte.	K. i. a. 9-1-17 (Vimy)	Mrs. Wilkins, Ross St., North Regina Village, Sask.
136170	Wilkinson, A. C.	Pte.	K. i. a. 24-10-17 (Passchendaele)	c/o Mrs. E. Smale, 119 Russet Ave., Toronto, Ont.
703657	Wilkinson, E.	L.-C.	K. i. a. 21-10-16 (Regina)	Miss A. E. Wilkinson, 210 Virginia St., Vallejo, U.S.A.
663728	Wilkinson, F. S.	Pte.	W. 23-7-18 (Oppy) to Eng.	Bronte, Ont.
907090	Wilkinson, J. F.	Sgt.	Dec. M.M. (Vimy) C.R.O. 1236; w. 9-6-17 (2nd Triangle) to Eng.	Eaglescliffe, Durham, Eng.
226459	Wilkinson, R. W.	Cpl.	W. 17-3-18 (Lens); w. 16-8-18 (Amiens)	Soldiers' Colony, Kapuskasing, Ont.
252563	Willdey, J. R.	Pte.	W. 13-4-17 (Vimy)	442 Frederick St., Brandon, Man.
1003958	Willette, J.	Pte.	D. o. s. 15-5-18	Mrs. M. Willette, Blind River, Ont.
240716	Williams, A. B.	Pte.	Tr. to Canada as Instructor 2-8-18	21 Robart St., Anfield, Liverpool, Eng.
703774	Williams, A. B. B.	Cpl.	Evac. sick 15-9-18 to Eng.	1382 St. Patrick's St., Oak Bay, Victoria, B.C.
703538	Williams, B.	Pte.		Stratford Hotel, cor. Gore and Keefer Sts., Vancouver, B.C.
3030634	Williams, C. R.	Pte.	K. i. a. 27-9-18 (Cambrai)	Mrs. J. Williams, 8 Fairfield St., Worcester, Mass.
772297	Williams, G. A.	L.-C.		34 Ana St., Orneau Rd., Belfast, Ire.
703400	Williams, G. C.	Cpl.	D. o. w. 23-9-16 (St. Eloi)	H. Williams, 801 8th St., Sacramento, Cal., U.S.A.
226445	Williams, J.	Pte.		938 St. Clair Ave., Detroit, Mich., U.S.A.
703650	Williams, J.	Pte.	Tr. to 6th Can. Area Emp. Co. 22-3-17	c/o J. S. Harvey, 157 3rd St. W., N. Vancouver, B.C.
225673	Williams, L. E.	Pte.	Evac. sick 10-11-17 to Eng.	226 Brock St., Brantford, Ont.
226416	Williams, R. A.	Pte.		Station Hotel, Haselden, Durham, Eng.
240214	Williams, T. E.	Pte.	Evac. sick 4-10-18 to Eng.	96 Birch Ave., Hamilton, Ont.
102336	Williams, W. J.	Pte.	W. 23-1-18 (Mericourt) to Eng.	11 Doors, Charlestown, St. Anstell, Cornwall, Eng.
704000	Williamson, A. J.	L.-C.	K. i. a. 9-4-17 (Vimy)	Mrs. S. A. W. Williamson, 1830 Comox St., Vancouver, B.C.
226418	Williamson, A. J.	Pte.	K. i. a. 22-10-17 (Passchendaele)	Mrs. E. Williamson, 21 Faint St., Edinburgh, Scot.
704149	Williamson, A. H.	Pte.	K. i. a. 9-4-17 (Vimy)	S. Williamson, Bathurst, N.B.
931256	Williamson, W.	Pte.	Evac. sick 14-10-16 to Eng.	Baynes Lake, B.C.
2528419	Willis, C.	Pte.	W. 2-9-18 (2nd Arras)	62 Lisbon Ave., Detroit, Mich., U.S.A.
1003137	Willis, J.	Pte.	Tr. to Eng. as minor 5-10-18	East End P.O., Sault Ste. Marle, Ont.
100044	Willis, P.	L.-C.	W. 11-8-17 (Lens) to Eng.	Kinsale Mills, Co. Cork, Ire.
669464	Willmot, C. R.	Pte.	W. 27-9-18 (Cambrai) to Eng.	607 Huron St., Toronto, Ont.
102701	Wilson, A.	Pte.	W. 16-5-17 (1st Triangle); w. 2-8-17 (Lens) to Eng.	465 Grafton St., Esquimalt, B.C.
252229	Wilson, C.	Pte.	W. 7-5-17 (1st Triangle) to Eng.	Fosmour, via Webb, Sask.
760559	Wilson, E. E.	Pte.		752 22nd Ave. E., Vancouver, B.C.
161146	Wilson, E. E.	Pte.	K. i. a. 10-11-16 (Somme)	W. J. Wilson, 421 11th St. N.W., Calgary, Alta.
703537	Wilson, G. C.	Pte.	Evac. sick in Eng. 18-11-18	1758 Ontario St., Vancouver, B.C.
3106982	Wilson, G. C.	Pte.	Evac. sick 21-2-19 to Eng.	2 Kirkhill, Cults, Aberdeen, Scot
252521	Wilson, H.	Pte.	W. 9-4-17 (Vimy); w. 9-6-17 (2nd Triangle) to Eng.	Cedar House, Garton, Yorks, Eng.
760560	Wilson, H.	Pte.	W. 9-4-17 (Vimy) to Eng.	752 22nd Ave. E., Vancouver, B.C.
663293	Wilson, H. W.	Pte.	W. 24-3-18 (Lens)	104 Hughson St. N., Hamilton, Ont.
703018	Wilson, J.	S.-S.	Tr. to C.A.P.C. 7-7-16	1617 Amphion St., Victoria, B.C.

Number	Name	Rank	Details	Address
3105522	Wilson, J. H.	Pte.	W. 27-9-18 (Cambrai) to Eng.	1025 Walnut St., Philadelphia, U.S.A.
102492	Wilson, J. O.	L.-C.	W. 24-3-18 (Lens) to Eng.	Prince George, B.C.
103332	Wilson, L. R.	Pte.	Tr. to 75th Bn. 6-6-17.	1 Stuart St., Banff, Scot.
926003	Wilson, L. R.	Pte.	K. i. a. 23-3-17 (Vimy).	Mrs. E. M. Snyder, Melita, Man.
103443	Wilson, R. V.	Pte.	Tr. to 75th Bn. 28-5-18.	2722 Shelbourne St., Victoria, B.C.
100656	Wilson, R. V.	L.-C.	W. 9-4-17 (Vimy) to Eng.	9217 112th Ave., Edmonton, Alta.
252393	Wilson, T. H.	Pte.	W. 9-4-17 (Vimy) to Eng.	c/o Mrs. S. E. Parker, Boulton, Lancs., Eng.
126300	Wilson, T. M.	Sgt.	Tr. to 16th M.G.C. 31-1-17.	Walkerton, Ont.
703726	Wilson, W.	Cpl.	W. 28-8-16 (St. Eloi); evac. sick 22-1-17 to Eng.	
225480	Wilson, W. W.	Pte.	D. o. w. 1-10-18 (Cambrai).	Fisheries Dept., Nanaimo, B.C.
703560	Wilton, C. A.	Pte.	W. 21-10-16 (Regina) to Eng.	L. Wilson, Port Robinson, Ont.
663225	Winchester, W. J.	Pte.	W. 2-11-18 (Valenciennes) to Eng.	138 Rursell St., South Vancouver, B.C.
703257	Windle, H.	Sgt.	Evac. sick 20-10-16 to Eng.	c/o Miss I. Tupling, Honeywood, Ont.
225676	Winship, J. A.	Pte.	W. 13-11-17 (Passchendaele) to Eng.	Castle Hotel, Vancouver, B.C.
161052	Winslade, F. C.	Pte.	K. i. a. 11-11-16 (Somme)	135 North Main St., Welland, Ont.
1006067	Windsor, G. H.	Pte.	W. 27-9-18 (Cambrai) to Eng.	G. Winslade, Lyng, Taunton, Somerset, Eng.
252579	Winter, H. J.	Pte.	Tr. to Lbr. Pool 9-6-18.	Sudbury, Ont.
1090475	Wintrup, M. J. S	Pte.		Herse St. Bradninch, nr. Cullompton, Devon, Eng.
3311727	Wiseman, D.	Pte.	D. o. w. 3-10-18 (Cambrai).	25 Ramsay Lane, Portobella, Scot.
102529	Wishart, W. J.	Sgt.	Pipe Major; tr. to Eng. 30-6-18.	J. Wiseman, Box 142, Burks Falls, Ont.
706036	Witmer, H.	Pte.	W. 7-4-17 (Vimy); d. o. w. 26-9-17 (Lens)	119 Ladysmith St., Victoria, B.C.
160469	Woledge, A. H.	Pte.	Evac. sick 13-7-17 to Eng.	A. Witmer, 931 Craigflower St., Victoria, B.C.
3107652	Wolfe, C.	Pte.	Evac. sick 9-2-19.	Crossfield, Alta.
3108849	Wolfe, F.	Pte.	Evac. sick 17-11-18 to Eng.	Humberstone, Ont.
3105382	Wolstenholme, A.	Pte.	W. 1-10-18 (Cambrai) to Eng.	Box 11, Fort Erie, Ont.
703899	Wolverson, S. G.	Pte.	W. 21-10-16 (Regina); dec. M.M. (Valenciennes) C.R.O. 2028	353 Hunt St., Central Falls, R.I., U.S.A.
703740	Wood, C. H.	Pte.	W. 9-4-17 (Vimy) to Eng.	Box 587, Marcus Hook, Penn., U.S.A.
663604	Wood, F.	Pte.	W. 8-8-18 (Amiens) to Eng.	c/o Canadian Engineers, North Vancouver, B.C.
102147	Wood, F.	Pte.	Evac. sick 20-7-17 to Eng.	31 Steven St., Hamilton, Ont.
250122	Wood, H. R.	Pte.	Tr. to 4th M.G.C. 18-3-18.	3048 Washington Ave., Victoria, B.C.
703141	Wood, J.	Pte.	Tr. to 51st Bn. 2-8-16.	22 Pauline Ave., Toronto, Ont.
103124	Wood, J. G.	Pte.	Evac. sick 22-9-18 to Eng.	Travellers' Hotel, Vancouver, B.C.
703973	Wood, J. M.	L.-S.	W. 21-10-16 (Regina) to Eng.	Blackney, Dorset, Eng.
703019	Wood, R. St. J.	Pte.	K. i. a. 21-10-16 (Regina)	66 Sarsfield Rd., Balham, London, S.W., Eng.
703413	Wood, W. H.	R.S.M.	Tr. to Can. Corps School 14-8-17; prom. R.S.M. "E" Wing Bramshott.	E. J. Wood, 5803 Yew St., Vancouver, B.C.
703170	Wood, W. H.	Sgt.	Tr. from P-B. to Lbr. Pool 4-11-17.	995 Inverness St., Victoria, B.C.
9075807	Wood, W. H.	Pte.	Tr. to 16th M.G.C. 1-1-17.	559 20th Ave. W., Vancouver, B.C.
3314437	Wood, W. L.	Pte.	W. 27-9-18 (Cambrai) to Eng.	No address available.
249622	Woodcock, W.	Pte.	Tr. to 4th M.G.C. 18-3-18.	Box 747, Thorold, Ont.
2529357	Woodruff, A. C.	Pte.	D. o. w. 10-8-18 (Amiens).	44 Uxbridge St., Toronto, Ont.
703367	Woodrow, P. B.	Pte.		J. Woodruff, Kearney, Ont.
3025002	Woods, G. H.	Pte.	Tr. to Eng. demob. 19-2-19.	Kilmalcolm, Renfrewshire, Scot.
103239	Woods, R. S.	Pte.	W. 6-9-16 (St. Eloi); w. 9-6-17 (2nd Triangle) to Eng.	c/o Mrs. Simnett, Port Credit, Ont.
703836	Woodward, H. H.	Pte.	W. 24-10-17 (Passchendaele).	Kincolith, Naas River, B.C. New Lion Hotel, Brecon, South Wales.

Number	Name	Rank	Notes	Address
1003192	Woodworth, A. H.	Pte.	W. 30-9-18 (Cambrai) to Eng.	223 Emerald St. N., Hamilton, Ont.
160842	Woodworth, J. F.	Pte.	Dec. M.M. (Vimy) C.R.O. 1236; w. 9-4-17 (Vimy) to Eng.	Banff, Alta.
703811	Woolner, W.	Pte.	W. and missing after action 22-10-16 (Regina)	Mrs. I. Woolner, 219 E. Gordova St., Vancouver, B.C.
252231	Woolsey, J. H. W.	Pte.	D. o. w. 15-8-18 (Amiens)	Mrs. Woolsey, Webb, Sask.
1263325	Woolston, A. S.	Pte.	W. 27-9-18 (Cambrai) to Eng.	2 Belmont Villas, Cowper Rd., Harpenden, Herts, Eng.
252587	Wormald, L. J.	Pte.	K. i. a. 9-4-17 (Vimy)	W. Wormald, 3 Vine Cottage, Church Rd., Totterham, London, Eng.
704120	Worthington, C. R.	Sgt.	Tr. to Eng. for commission in C.A.M.C. 27-1-17.	Comox, B.C.
760778	Wozencroft, E. G.	Pte.	Evac. sick 14-4-17 to Eng.	The Bank, nr. Kingston, Radnor, Wales.
3105631	Wragg, F.	Pte.	D. o. w. 25-8-18 (Amiens)	Mrs. Wragg, 527 Wellington St. N., Hamilton, Ont.
706384	Wren, E. E.	L.-C.	W. 23-7-18 (Oppy); dec. M.M. (Oppy) C.R.O. 1866; w. 30-9-18 (Cambrai); evac. sick 20-2-19	214 Oxford St., Montreal, Que.
787181	Wren, G. D. J.	Pte.	W. 9-4-17 (Vimy) to Eng.	c/o Mr. Murphy, St. Henri Branch, Bank of Montreal. Montreal, Que.
703086	Wren, W. E.	Sgt.	Bandmaster; tr. to Base Co. 11-8-16	c/o The White Sewing Machine Co., Seattle, Wash.
273798	Wright, A.	Pte.	Tr. to 4th M.G.C. 13-5-18	c/o Mrs. G. Perkins, 77 Howard Ave., Windsor, Ont.
1066227	Wright, A. G.	Pte.	D. o. w. 26-10-16 (Regina)	Hanover, Ont.
135609	Wright, A. G.	Pte.	Tr. to Lbr. Pool 16-9-18	No address available.
703039	Wright, C.	Pte.	W. 21-10-16 (Regina) to Eng.	c/o Miss A. Finney, Box 299, Calgary, Alta.
931255	Wright, E.	Pte.		c/o Mrs. M. G. Jones, Kuskonoak, B.C.
907445	Wright, E. S. P.	L.-C.	W. 18-11-17 (Passchendaele) to Eng.	Stoughton, Sask.
252852	Wright, F.	Pte.		Port Kells, B.C.
160785	Wright, H. H.	Pte.	W. 21-10-16 (Regina); w. 12-1-17 (Vimy); att. to 4th Div. Emp. Co. 30-9-17	223 6th Ave. E., Calgary, Alta.
226432	Wright, H. S.	Pte.	W. 1-10-18 (Cambrai) to Eng.	36 Argyle Ave., Hamilton, Ont.
703504	Wright, J.	Cpl.	W. 31-8-16 (St. Eloi); k. i. a. 17-11-17 (Passchendaele)	J. Wright, 44 Cobden St., Dalton, Lancs. Eng.
160293	Wright, J. I.	Pte.	Evac. sick 13-5-17 to Eng.	School House, Scremerston, Berwick, Eng.
839073	Wright, M. J.	Pte.		Flesherton, Ont.
926178	Wright, N.	Pte.	W. 6-4-17 (Vimy); w. 2-11-18 (2nd Arras) to Eng.	Ballantyne, Ont.
703550	Wright, T. H.	Pte.	W. 9-4-17 (Vimy) to Eng.	5 Keswick Rd., Blackpool, Lancs., Eng.
1042486	Wright, T. M.	Pte.	Tr. to 4th M.G.C. 13-5-18	9 Rhodes Ave., Toronto, Ont.
249061	Wright, W. E.	Pte.	W. 2-9-18 (2nd Arras) to Eng.	428 Roxton Rd., Toronto, Ont.
449901	Wyatt, A. E.	Sgt.	Tr. to Lbr. Pool 4-11-17	270 A. St. Leonard's Rd., Bromley-by-Bow, London.
160762	Wyatt, C. O. R.	Pte.	W. 1. a. 22-10-16 (Regina)	Mrs. J. R. Wyatt, 107 6th St. S.E., Calgary, Alta.
704062	Wylie, A.	Cpl.	Tr. to Can. Corps School 14-8-17	Campbelltown, Argyllshire, Scot.
907354	Wylie, A. S.	Cpl.	W. 11-6-17 (2nd Triangle); evac. sick 1-7-17 to Eng.	Regina, Sask.
145802	Wyman, H. A.	Pte.	Tr. to 77th Bn. 10-8-16	Cummings Bridge, Ont.
703088	Wynne, J.	Sgt.	W. 21-10-16 (Regina); evac. sick 16-11-17 to Eng.	"Rothesay," Wilbraham Rd., Alexandra Park, Manchester, Eng.
1002298	Yandon, W.	Pte.		Coppercliff, Ont.
907523	Yarnton, C. J.	Cpl.	Tr. to Eng. as minor 5-3-18.	43 Gainsborough Rd., HackneyWick, London, E.9, Eng.
3110198	Yates, G. E.	Pte.		Milton, Ont.

704178	Yeadon, S. B.	Pte.	D. o. w. 20-8-16 (St. Eloi)	Mrs. M. Yeadon, Todwick, nr. Sheffield, Eng.
249767	York, J. T.	Pte.	K. i. a. 2-9-18 (2nd Arras)	G. York, 72 Mill St., Wallsall, Staffs, Eng.
1003219	Young, G.	Pte.	k. i. a. 23-9-17 (Lens)	W. Young, Thessalon, Ont.
253027	Young, J.	Pte.	W. 9-4-17 (Vimy) to Eng.	Belanger P.O., via Barenscrag, Sask.
145762	Young, J. H.	Pte.	Tr. to 77th Bn. 10-8-16	P.O. Box 429, Renfrew, Ont.
838215	Young, R.	Cpl.	W. 10-4-18 (Oppy) to Eng.	R.R. No. 1, Owen Sound, Ont.
160806	Young, T. R.	Pte.	Evac. sick 12-12-16 to Eng.	"Bradley," 14 Avon Rd., Bournemouth, Eng.
103150	Young, W. L.	Cpl.	W. 17-11-17 (Passchendaele) to Eng.	508 East Aukeny St., Portland, Ore., U.S.A.
184150	Younger, R. W.	Pte.	W. 9-4-17 (Vimy) to Eng.	c/o J. Clarke, 5 Beamish St., West Stanley, Durham, Eng.
703780	Youngman, C. L.	Pte.	Evac. sick 20-11-16 to Eng.	1022 Sylvester Place, Seattle, Wash., U.S.A.
706491	Youngs, F.	L.-C.	W. 12-4-17 (Vimy); dec. M.M. (Amiens) C. R.O. 1899; w. 22-8-18 (Amiens)	1421 Chambers St., Victoria, B.C.
706744	Zazzarino, T.	Pte.	K. i. a. 9-4-17 (Vimy)	Mrs. E. Zazzarino, Marine View House, Steyne Rd.. Seaford, Sussex, Eng.
220275	Zeko, J.	Pte.	W. 7-6-17 (2nd Triangle) to Eng.	No address available.
703175	Zindich, N.	Pte.	W. 11-11-16 (Somme); k. i. a. 9-4-17 (Vimy)	No address available.
1003789	Zolgory, J.	Pte.	Tr. to 71st Co. C.F.C. 9-4-18	No address available.

www.ingramcontent.com/pod-product-compliance
Lightning Source LLC
Chambersburg PA
CBHW071818230426
43670CB00013B/2490